AF342414

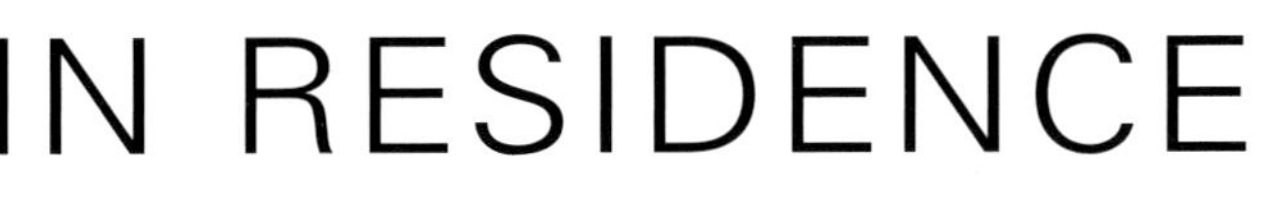

IN RESIDENCE

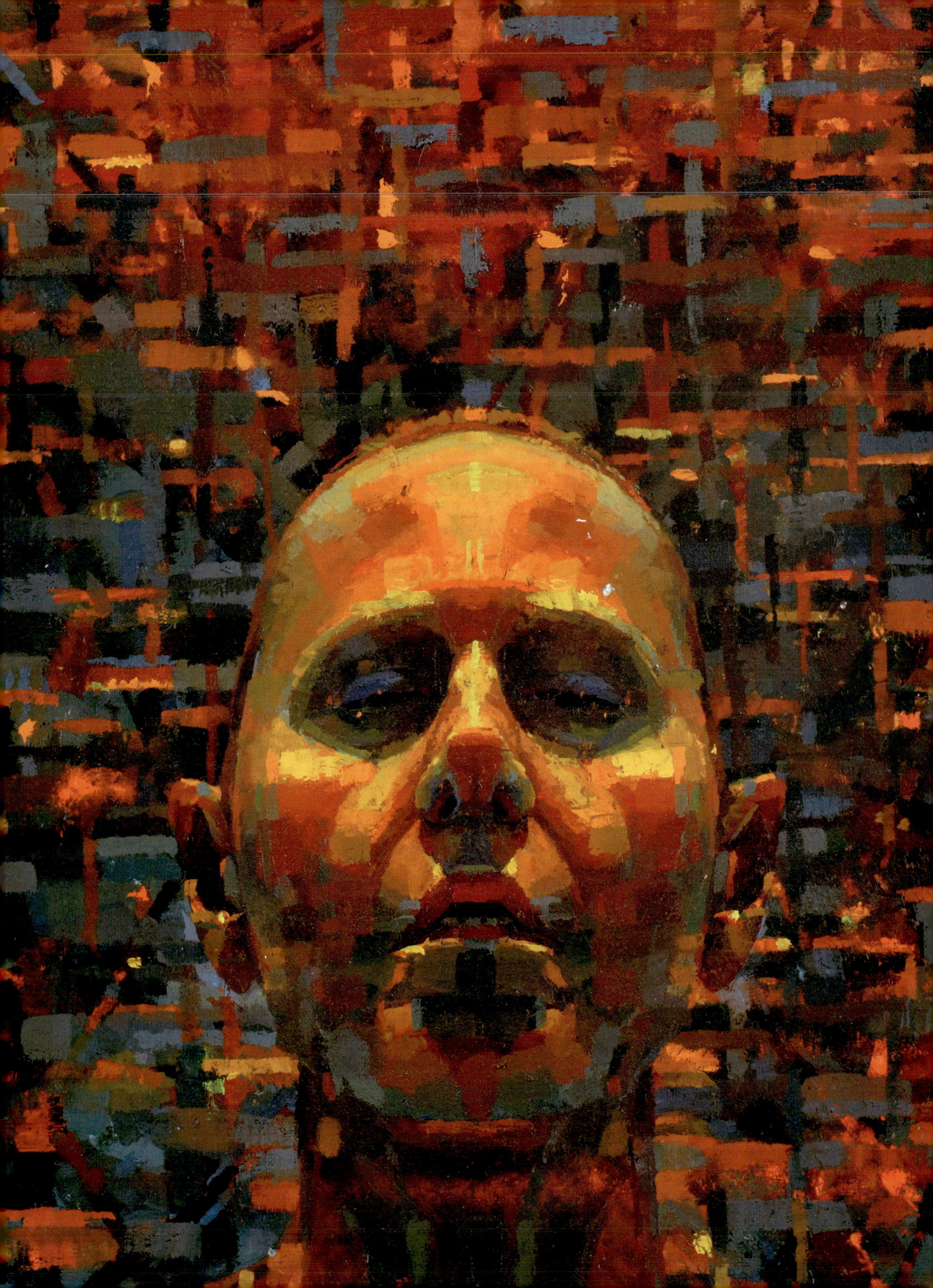

IN RESIDENCE: CONTEMPORARY ARTISTS AT DARTMOUTH

Edited by
Michael R. Taylor and Gerald Auten

Hood Museum of Art, Dartmouth College
Hanover, New Hampshire

Distributed by University Press of New England
Hanover and London

Published by
Hood Museum of Art, Dartmouth College
6 East Wheelock Street
Hanover, NH 03755
www.hoodmuseum.dartmouth.edu

Distributed by
University Press of New England
One Court Street, Lebanon, NH 03766
www.upne.com

The exhibition and catalogue titled *In Residence: Contemporary Artists at Dartmouth* were organized by the Hood Museum of Art in collaboration with the Studio Art Department. The catalogue was supported by Jonathan Dorfman and Melissa Kaish, Class of 1983, in honor of her parents, Morton and Luise Kaish, and the exhibition was made possible by Constance and Walter Burke, Class of 1944, as well as the Philip Fowler 1927 Memorial Fund and the George O. Southwick 1957 Memorial Fund.

The Artist-in-Residence Program is generously supported by the Nathan W. Pearson '32 and Sons Fund, the William B. Jaffe Memorial Fund, the Matthew Wysocki Memorial Fund, and the Arthur J. Cohen '03 Fund and Nellie Z. Cohen Fund.

Head of Publishing and Communications: Nils Nadeau

Copyeditors: Nils Nadeau and Kristin Swan

Designer: Glenn Suokko

Printer: Puritan Capital

All object photography by Jeffrey Nintzel unless otherwise indicated in the catalogue entry head matter.

Frontispiece: Susanna Coffey, *Intake*, 2008, oil on panel. Purchased through the Contemporary Fund; 2013.24. © Susanna Coffey

Printed in the United States of America

Library of Congress Cataloging-in-Publication Data

In residence : contemporary artists at Dartmouth / edited by Michael R. Taylor and Gerald Auten.
    pages cm
Includes index.
ISBN 978-0-944722-46-6
1. Art, American—New Hampshire—Hanover—20th century—Exhibitions. 2. Art, American—New Hampshire—Hanover—21st century—Exhibitions. I. Taylor, Michael R., 1966– editor of compilation. II. Taylor, Michael R., 1966- In residence. III. Hood Museum of Art.
N6535.H36I5 2014
709.04'00747423—dc23   2013036037

CONTENTS

ACKNOWLEDGMENTS

This catalogue is published on the occasion of the *In Residence: Contemporary Artists at Dartmouth* exhibition at the Hood Museum of Art. The impetus for organizing this exhibition was the recent gift to the museum of two paintings by the Guatemalan painter Carlos Sánchez, Class of 1923, who in 1931 became the first artist-in-residence at Dartmouth College. Sánchez's *Self Portrait*, which was donated by the artist's niece, Cristina Falla de Echeverría, was made while the artist was an undergraduate at Dartmouth, while *Young Man with Bird*, which was a gift from the artist's nephew Juan José Falla, was completed during the artist's residency in 1931. We are enormously grateful to Cristina and Juan José, as well as their brothers Ricardo and Ernesto Falla, for helping us to fill an important gap in the Hood's collection through the donation of these paintings by Carlos Sánchez, which allowed us to embark on an ambitious exhibition project that would celebrate the important history and legacy of the Artist-in-Residence Program. The herculean task of creating a coherent exhibition from such a large body of work made by a diverse range of artists has been both challenging and deeply rewarding. Realizing that the organization of this exhibition could not be accomplished alone, I was very fortunate to collaborate with Gerald "Jerry" Auten, Director of Exhibitions and Senior Lecturer in Studio Art, who has run the Artist-in-Residence Program at Dartmouth since 1995. Working with Jerry has been one of the greatest pleasures of my professional career and I am proud of the exhibition we put together, which showcases the work of more than eighty former artists-in-residence. In addition, we explored the history of this outstanding program through archival research that unearthed a wealth of information about the artists who have come to campus since Sánchez's residency, including letters, photographs, and posters that we are excited to document in this momentous catalogue. Thus, it is with deep gratitude that I extend my heartfelt thanks to Jerry and his colleagues in the Studio Art Department, who have all been a joy to work with: Virginia Beahan, Jennifer Caine, Brenda Garand, Louise Hamlin, Karolina Kawiaka, John Kemp Lee, Brian Miller, Soo Sunny Park, Colleen Randall, Enrico Riley, Esmé Thompson, and Jack Wilson.

This publication would not have been realized without the important contributions of the fifteen essayists who provided insightful entries on the work of the artists in the exhibition: Juliette Bianco, Emily Schubert Burke, Mary Coffey, Kristin Monahan Garcia, Stephen Gilchrist, Katherine Hart, Amelia Kahl, Brian Kennedy, Barbara Mac-Adam, Sarah Powers, Joseph Sanchez, Barbara Thompson, Abigail Weir, and Phoebe Wolfskill. Nicole Gilbert, exhibitions coordinator, assembled the first working checklist of everything in the Hood's collection by former artists-in-residence and coordinated the logistics for the exhibition and catalogue with impeccable attention to detail. Deborah T. Haynes, collections documentation manager and cataloguer, also merits special praise for creating a comprehensive and chronological list of the artists-in-residence and their exhibitions, which can be found at the back of the catalogue. Nils Nadeau, head of publishing and communications, guided the design and production of this catalogue with tremendous skill and dedication under conditions made all the more difficult by compressed deadlines. Likewise, Kristin Swan copyedited the catalogue entries with great sensitivity to ensure that they maintained the high standards of scholarly excellence that have been the hallmark of the museum's catalogues since we opened in 1985. Glenn Suokko created the handsome design of this publication, drawing upon his extensive history with the Artist-in-Residence Program, having designed so many of the artists' catalogues for their exhibitions in the Jaffe-Friede Gallery over the years. Finally, Jeff Nintzel provided a significant portion of the beautiful catalogue photography.

We also owe an enormous debt of gratitude to many of our colleagues at Dartmouth College, including President Philip J. Hanlon '77, who has shown great support of this landmark project, as well as Lindsay Whaley and Rachel Silver in the Provost's Office, who also fully understood the importance and timeliness of this undertaking. Jeff Horrell, Dean of Libraries and Librarian of the College, and Jay Satterfield of the Rauner Special Collections Library also played an essential role in the realization of this project, which relied a great deal on Dartmouth's archives and photographic records. I would particularly like to thank Photographic Records Specialist Patricia Cope, who helped us to secure historical images related to the Artist-in-Residence Program. Adrian Randolph, Leon E. Williams Professor of Art History and Associate Dean of the Arts and Humanities, also offered his steadfast support and encouragement of this project. Varujan Boghosian, Professor Emeritus of Studio Art at Dartmouth College and artist-in-residence in the summer of 1968, offered the important historical perspective of a participant during the program's early years at the Hopkins Center for the Arts. As the former George Frederick Jewett Professor of Art, Varujan interacted with many of the artists-in-residence over the decades, often exchanging works of art and acting as an important ambassador for the program. I also wish to express my profound appreciation to Jessica Womack, Class of 2014, for her superb research into the life and work of Carlos Sánchez, which informed our understanding of the artist's work in this exhibition and catalogue. I would also like to extend my sincere thanks to Jeff James, the Howard Gilman Director of the Hopkins Center, for making the Top of the Hop available for the exhibition of screenprint posters by former artists-in-residence. Beyond the Dartmouth campus, I would like to thank Adam Anuszkiewicz, whose father was artist-in-residence in the fall of 1967, for generously lending a copy of a remarkable film that was made during Richard Anuszkiewicz's time on campus. This film, which will be shown during the exhibition, captures the energy and excitement of the program, as Anuszkiewicz completes his op art paintings in front of the camera.

A project of this magnitude does not happen without the dedication of the entire Hood Museum of Art staff. I would especially like to thank Kathleen O'Malley, registrar, for her help and expertise in pulling together photography for the publication, along with Jonathan Benoit, TMS project/digital asset manager, for assisting in this process. Special thanks also go to Cynthia Gilliland, associate registrar, and Rebecca Fawcett, registrarial assistant, for handling the innumerable details involved in arranging the loans from this country and abroad.

Lesley Wellman, Hood Foundation Curator of Education, and the education team of Rebecca Karp, Adrienne Kermond, Neely McNulty, and Vivian Ladd were instrumental in developing the exciting educational programming to accompany the exhibition. Sharon Reed, programs and events coordinator, did a magnificent job in handling the exhibition programming, including a record number of faculty gallery talks. I also wish to express my profound appreciation to Patrick Dunfey, exhibition designer/preparations supervisor, for working with Jerry and me to create a dynamic exhibition design that responded to the contemporary art on display. The exhibition was prepared and installed with great skill by preparators John Reynolds and Matt Zayatz, and art handler Sue Achenbach. My gratitude likewise goes to Nancy McLain, business manager, who helped to oversee the exhibition budget, as well as Julie Ann Otis, development and membership coordinator, who, along with Carrie Pelzel and Dennis Brown in Dartmouth's advancement office, helped with the fundraising efforts. I would like to thank Lindsey Dewar, assistant to the director, who assumed numerous responsibilities in connection with the day-to-day work, such as correspondence and research, that is essential to the success of any museum exhibition. I am also immensely beholden to Kathy Hart, senior curator of collections and Barbara C. and Harvey P. Hood 1918 Curator of Academic Programming, for providing me with advice on the checklist and a sympathetic ear during the research phase of this project, and to Juliette Bianco, deputy director, who embraced this project with great enthusiasm and unflagging energy from its inception.

I am deeply thankful to Melissa Kaish Dorfman, Class of 1983, whose parents, Morton and Luise Kaish, were artists-in-residence in the summer of 1974, for generously supporting the exhibition catalogue. This five-venue exhibition has been generously funded by Constance and Walter Burke, Class of 1944, as well as the Philip Fowler 1927 Memorial Fund and the George O. Southwick 1957 Memorial Fund. The installations in the Strauss and Jaffe-Friede Galleries in the Hopkins Center, as well as the display of posters by former artists-in-residence in the Top of the Hop and the presentation of architectural projects by James Cutler, artist-in-residence at Dartmouth in the spring of 2004, in the Nearburg Gallery in the Black Family Visual Arts Center received additional support from the Arthur J. Cohen '03 and Nellie Z. Cohen Fund, the Nathan W. Pearson '32 and Sons Fund, the William B. Jaffe Memorial Fund, and the Matthew Wysocki Memorial Fund. As always, the entire Hood Board of Overseers, under the inspired leadership of board chair Jonathan L. Cohen, has been wonderfully supportive of this exhibition and its educational outreach.

No exhibition of this scale and importance can be organized without the aforementioned support and hard work of everyone involved, whose combined efforts have ensured the success of *In Residence: Contemporary Artists at Dartmouth*. The co-curator of this exhibition, Jerry Auten, joins me in recognizing the enormous contributions of the artists who have participated in the Artist-in-Residence Program throughout its history, along with the three previous directors of the program. Every artist has not only brought their artistic talents and vision to the Dartmouth campus but also worked closely with students, faculty, and various staff at the college—including those at the Hood Museum of Art, where many of their works have found a permanent home. It is our sincere hope that this exhibition not only serves as a record of the Artist-in-Residence Program but also as inspiration for the continued interest in and support of this significant program at Dartmouth College.

Michael R. Taylor, Director

IN RESIDENCE

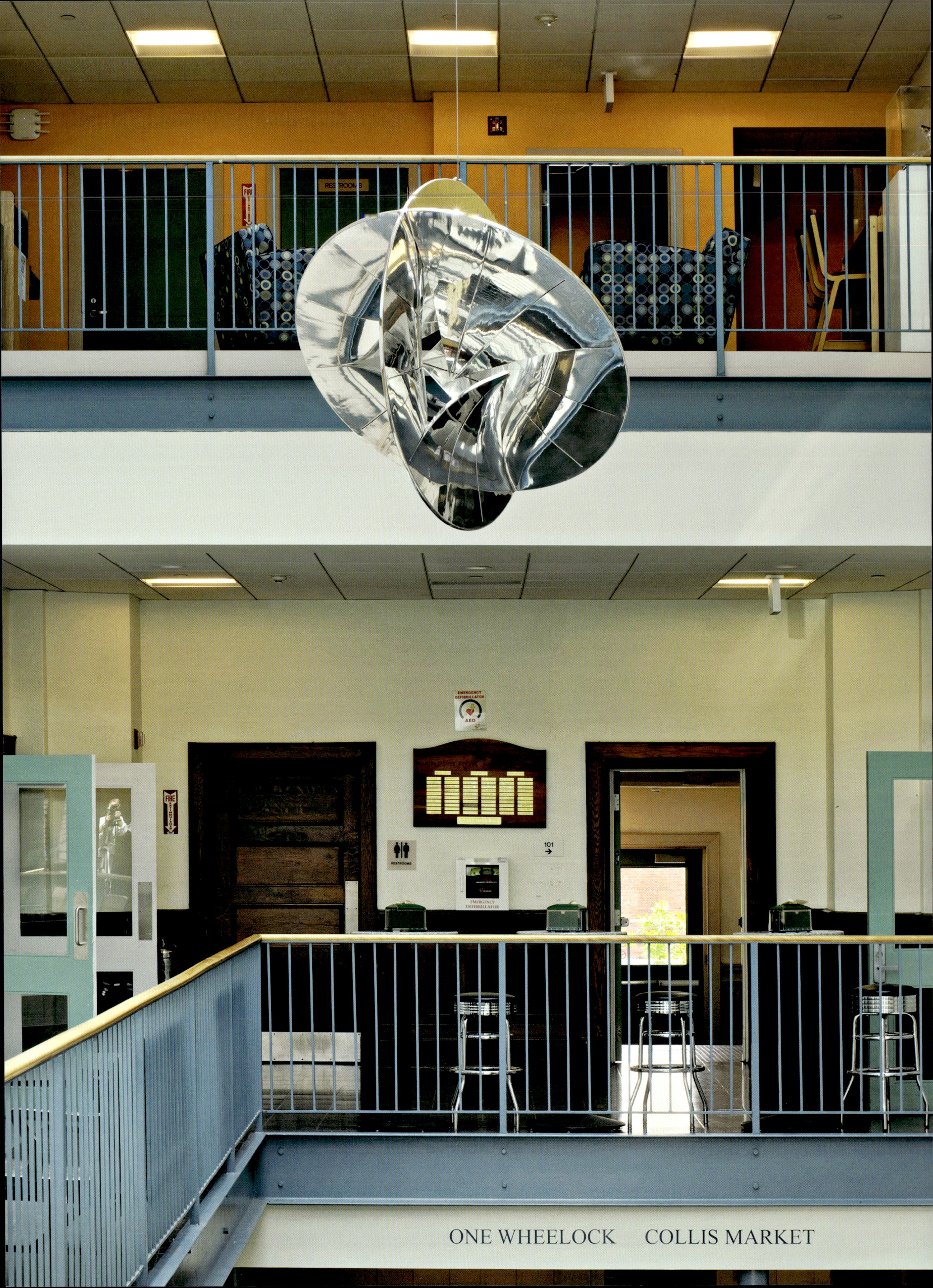
ONE WHEELOCK   COLLIS MARKET

Michael R. Taylor and Gerald Auten

IN RESIDENCE: CONTEMPORARY ARTISTS AT DARTMOUTH

The tradition of inviting practicing artists to Dartmouth College—to make works of art, to interact with students, faculty, and the local community, and to exhibit their work on campus—is a long-standing one. The artist-in-residence program at Dartmouth was established in 1931 when Churchill P. "Jerry" Lathrop received permission from President Ernest Hopkins to use a discretionary tutorial fund, generously provided by Mr. and Mrs. John D. Rockefeller Jr., to bring the Guatemalan painter Carlos Sánchez back to campus for a year-long fellowship. A member of the Dartmouth Class of 1923, Sánchez had recently spent a year in Mexico assisting Diego Rivera on two major public mural projects. As a young Dartmouth graduate whose work was beginning to receive critical acclaim in both the United States and Mexico, Sánchez was the perfect choice to be the first artist-in-residence at the College. His selection also spoke to Lathrop's aspiration to bring artists from around the world to campus, and this desire to create a program with an international reach continues to this day. Following the completion of his fellowship, during which he made paintings and engaged with students interested in the arts, Sánchez remained on campus for another two years as an assistant and translator for the second artist-in-residence, José Clemente Orozco. The Mexican muralist was invited to Hanover by Lathrop and fellow art history professor

Artemas S. Packard, with the full support of President Hopkins. Packard envisioned a series of residencies on campus for "the most competent artists available so that in the course of time we should have in this one place a sequence of original works such as no institution of our day possesses."[1]

Between 1932 and 1934, Orozco painted a remarkable fresco mural cycle titled *The Epic of American Civilization* in the College's Baker Library (figs. 1 and 2). Many of the Dartmouth students who witnessed the noted Mexican modernist creating this ambitious, brightly colored mural in the library's lower-level reserve reading room never forgot the experience, and the mural's impact is still palpable almost eighty years later. *The Epic of American Civilization* draws upon indigenous and European traditions to create a vast historical narrative devoted to pre-Hispanic and post-conquest civilizations, with recurring themes, such as human conflict, sacrifice, and regeneration, being used to suggest the cyclical nature of these events. The historical importance of Orozco's mural was recently recognized by the National Park Service and the Department of the Interior of the United States Government, which granted National Historic Landmark status to *The Epic of American Civilization* in March 2013.

Orozco was followed by the landscape painter and pioneer member of the Canadian Group of Seven Lawren Stewart Harris, whose uncle William Kilborne Stewart was a professor of comparative literature at Dartmouth. Harris was the artist-in-residence from 1934 to 1938, when he was succeeded by Paul Sample, a member of the Dartmouth

Luise Kaish's *Sphere*, 1976, in the atrium of the Collis Center for Student Involvement, Dartmouth College (see also fig. 14).

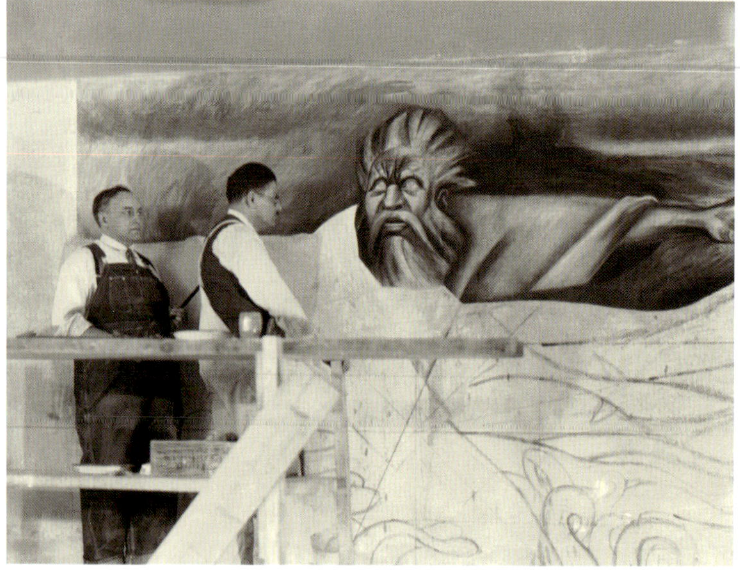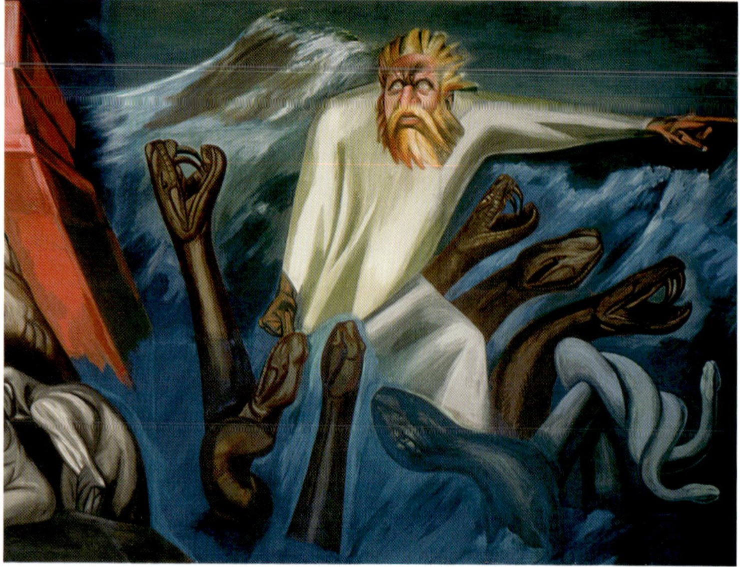

1

2

Fig. 1

José Clemente Orozco on scaffolding with Leo Katz, May 1932. Dartmouth College Library.

Fig. 2

José Clemente Orozco, *The Departure of Quetzalcoatl* (panel 7) for *The Epic of American Civilization*, 1932–34, fresco, Orozco Room, Baker Library, Dartmouth College. Commissioned by the Trustees of Dartmouth College; P.934.13.7. Photo by Eli Burakian.

Fig. 3

Paul Sample working in his studio, Carpenter Hall, April 1949. Dartmouth College Library. Photo by Adrian N. Bouchard.

Fig. 4

Richard Anuszkiewicz working in the artist-in-residence studio at the Hopkins Center, fall 1967. Dartmouth College Library. Photo by Matthew Wysocki.

Class of 1920 and a distinguished American Regionalist painter (fig. 3). Lathrop gave Sample a lifetime appointment as artist-in-residence with the rank of full professor. Over the next twenty-four years, he taught and mentored countless Dartmouth students, both through "honors work" classes, for which the students received course credit, and through private conversations in his studio on the top floor of Carpenter Hall, where students were invited to drop in and watch him paint.

The program adopted its current format of four residencies per year following the inauguration of the Hopkins Center for the Arts in the fall of 1962. Designed by the internationally acclaimed architect Wallace K. Harrison, the Hopkins Center included two new exhibition spaces—the Jaffe-Friede and Beaumont-May Galleries—and a specially designed artist-in-residence studio. Rejecting the earlier model of lengthy appointments, which in the case of Paul Sample lasted more than two decades, Dartmouth now invited artists of considerable stature and international renown to reside on campus for a ten-week term that coincided with the College's quarter system. To meet the practical needs of a visiting artist, residents were provided with comfortable living quarters and an honorarium. They were also invited to exhibit their work in one of the new gallery spaces, make art in their studio, and give a public lecture about their work and ideas; furthermore, although there was no formal teaching assignment, they were strongly encouraged to interact with students, faculty, and community members. Finally, every effort was made to provide artists with equipment to aid in their artistic production, including the new printmaking facilities in

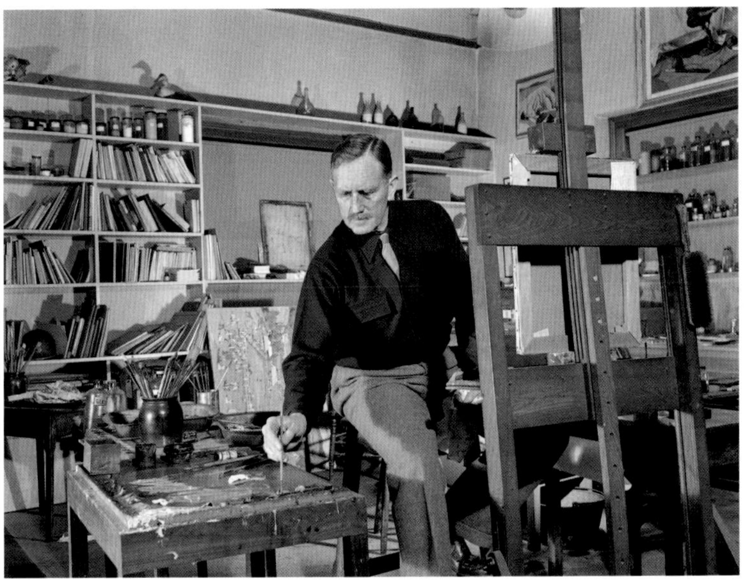

3

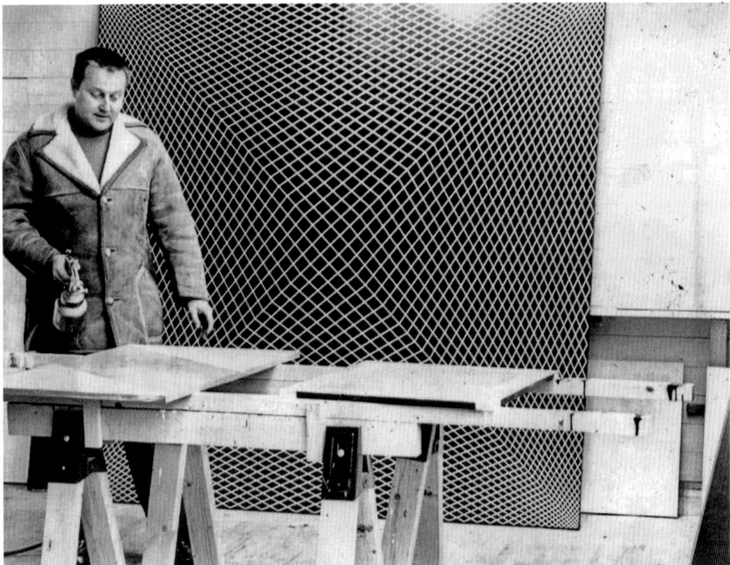

4

the Hop that allowed the post-1962 generation of artists-in-residence to create screenprint posters to promote their work and exhibitions on campus. Artists-in-residence were thus provided with a stimulating and supportive atmosphere conducive to the creative process for a period of ten weeks, which, as Jerry Lathrop later recalled, "was long enough for them to have a real change of pace in a new and pleasant environment and it was not too long a time for them to be away from their professional sources."[2]

The first artist-in-residence to work in the Hopkins Center facility was Friedel Dzubas, a German-born abstract painter whose lyrical, stained-color compositions represented a significant departure from the realism of the previous artists-in-residence. During the 1960s, the exciting modern facilities attracted a new generation of avant-garde painters and sculptors to participate in the artist-in-residence program, including Robert Rauschenberg, Frank Stella, George Rickey, Donald Judd, and Richard Anuszkiewicz (fig. 4). The program remained international in outlook as well, bringing the Mexican artist Xavier Esqueda to campus in the fall of 1965; the Canadian artists Jacques Hurtubise and Sorel Etrog in the winter and spring of 1967, respectively; and, in the fall of 1963, the South African–born British sculptor Thomas Bayliss Huxley-Jones (fig. 5), who was so popular on campus that he was invited back for a second residency in the spring of 1968.

In 1967, following Jerry Lathrop's retirement the previous year, Matthew Wysocki was appointed director of the Visual Arts Program at the Hopkins Center; he subsequently oversaw the artist-in-residence program until his own retirement in 1989. A professor of art in Dartmouth's Visual Studies Department, Wysocki was a graduate of Yale University, where he had studied with Josef Albers. As a painter and designer, he had executed several stained-glass commissions for churches in New England, but during his tenure at Dartmouth he was best known for his prodigious toy collection and his carefully composed black-and-white photographs of the earliest performances by Pilobolus, the internationally acclaimed modern American dance company that was founded by four Dartmouth students in October 1971. Wysocki brought a new vision and clarity of purpose to the Artist-in-Residence Program, which he expressed in a letter, dated April 7, 1971, to a colleague in the Department of Art at Florida State University:

> The purpose of the program is twofold: to afford students, faculty, and community the opportunity of witnessing a contemporary artist at work, exchanging ideas, opening new doors; and to offer the visitor a fresh environment in which to work—an academic environment where liberal, humanistic studies are in the forepoint at the undergraduate level, and in which creative endeavor in the arts and scholarship are encouraged. To further these ends, each artist is given an exhibition at the Center during his term of appointment. Also he has no teaching appointments.[3]

The revamped Artist-in-Residence Program offered Dartmouth students and faculty members an invaluable opportunity to see fine

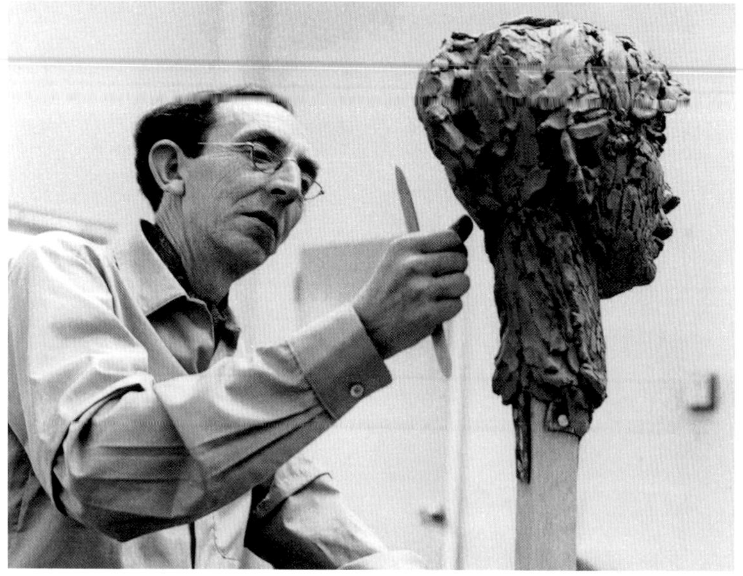

5

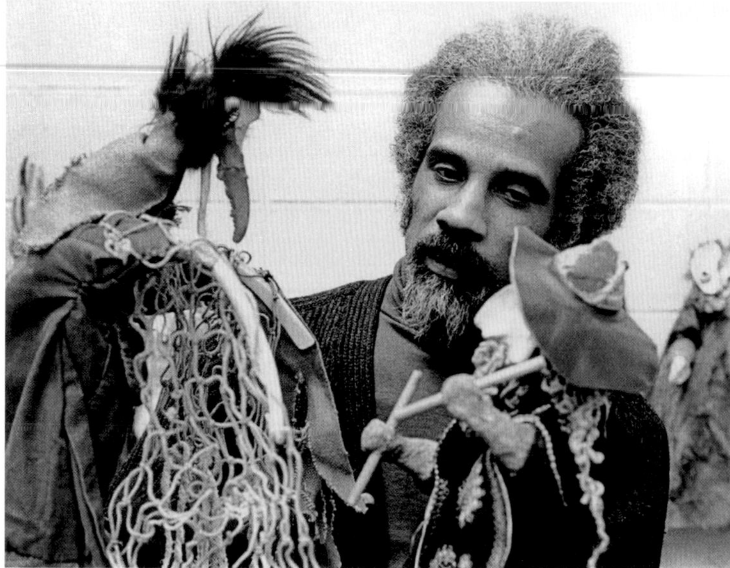

6

Fig. 5

Thomas Bayliss Huxley-Jones working in the artist-in-residence studio at the Hopkins Center, December 1963. Dartmouth College Library.

Fig. 6

Ashley Bryan with puppets, February 1974. Dartmouth College Library. Photo by Matthew Wysocki.

Fig. 7

Fritz Scholder in the artist-in-residence studio at the Hopkins Center with some of the *Dartmouth Portraits*, February 13, 1974. Dartmouth College Library. Photo by Matthew Wysocki.

Fig. 8

David Rettig, T. C. Cannon, and Varujan Boghosian in front of *Cloud Madonna*, Hopkins Center, summer 1975. Photo by Matthew Wysocki.

examples of contemporary art and to meet, work with, and observe a leading professional artist in the act of creating a new body of work whose realization often unfolded before their very eyes. As Luise Kaish later recalled of her own residency in the fall term of 1974,

> The opportunities afforded the Resident to enter into the academic life of the College, to participate and yet remain autonomous, are exceptional for the working artist. At the same time a unique opportunity for the students to observe, inquire, and perhaps even to compare is implicit in the relationship. The quality of student interest, involvement and performance was particularly impressive.[4]

Under Wysocki's leadership, the 1970s saw a number of important milestones for the program, beginning in the spring of 1971 with Alexander "A. B." Jackson, who was the first African American artist-in-residence at Dartmouth. Jackson was closely followed by another African American artist, Ashley Bryan, the children's book illustrator and painter, who came to campus in the winter of 1974 and later became a faculty member in the Visual Studies Department at Dartmouth (fig. 6). The program became a proven testing ground for future faculty members, including Varujan Boghosian, who was artist-in-residence in the summer of 1968, and Fumio Yoshimura, who came in the spring of 1981. As Boghosian recalled in 1976,

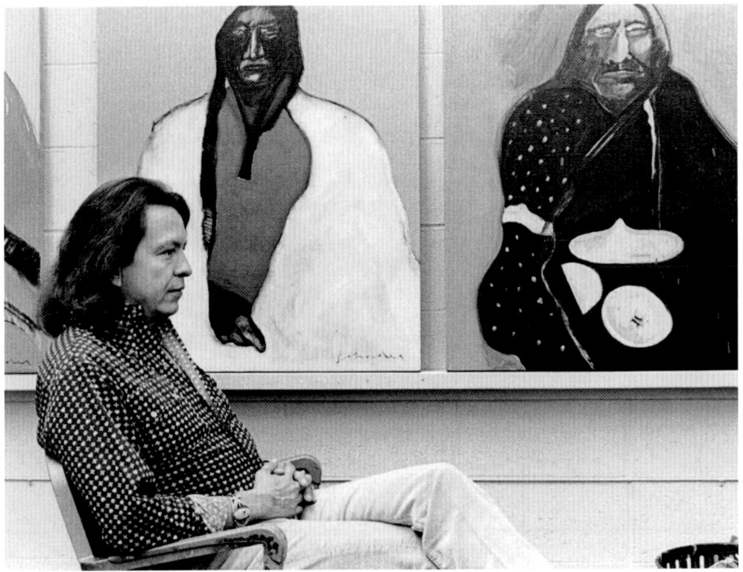

7

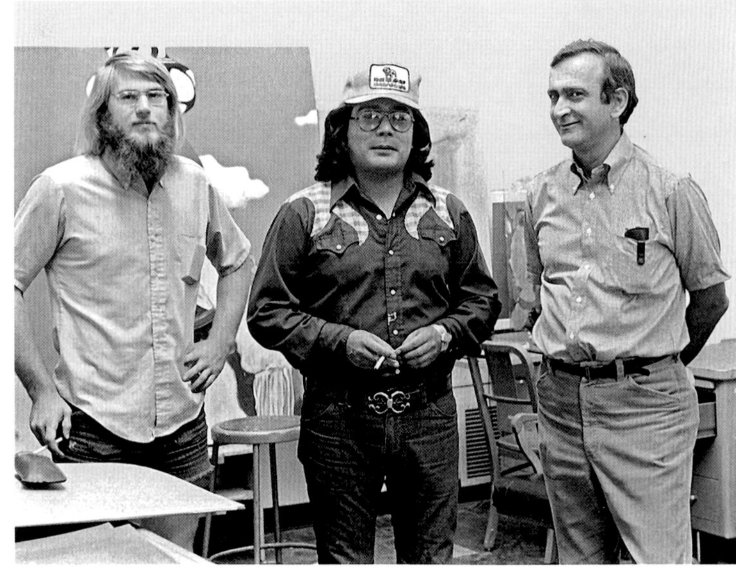

8

One of the reasons Dartmouth had great appeal for me as I considered the move from Brown University was the artist-in-residence program. All of us in the profession had heard of Paul Sample's tenure at Dartmouth as artist-in-residence and I must say that it was a point of envy with many institutions which did not have equivalent programs. . . . Its value, as I have observed during my seven years here, is far reaching. It brings to an isolated community an outstanding practicing professional who has contact with students, faculty, and community residents, as well as people in neighboring states; I find it to have immense value in faculty associations. We in the faculty find it extremely difficult during many times of the year to be able to leave Hanover. To have an artist-in-residence at hand helps us to maintain our contact with the creative world outside. In my case, time and time again it has refreshed my point of view and extended my energy.[5]

In the fall of 1973, Fritz Scholder (fig. 7) became the first Native American artist in residence at Dartmouth. His appointment was especially meaningful at a time when the College had recently reaffirmed its founding commitment to the education of Native Americans. Scholder was followed by his friend and former student T. C. Cannon, who came to Hanover in the summer of 1975 (fig. 8); the sculptor Allan C. Houser, who came in the spring of 1979; and Bob Haozous, Houser's son, who came to campus in the summer of 1989. Dartmouth's transformation to coeducation in 1972 ushered in a new era at the College and informed

Wysocki's decision to invite Laura Ziegler (fig. 9) to be the first woman artist to participate in the program in the summer of 1974. She was followed by such notable women artists as Susanna Coffey, Lois Dodd, Louise Fishman, Luise Kaish, Beryl Korot, Linda Matalon, Ruth Miller, Magdalene Odundo, Judy Pfaff, Alison Saar, and Amy Sillman. Indeed, this commitment to diversity in gender and race, as well as to Dartmouth's Native American legacy, has become one of the hallmarks and guiding principles of the Artist-in-Residence Program and the Studio Art Department, through which it is administrated.

The 1970s and 1980s saw a number of notable artists participate in the program, including Bernard Chaet, Jim Dine, Walker Evans, Wolf Kahn (fig. 10), György Kepes, R. B. Kitaj, Leroy Lamis (fig. 11), Paul Resika, Richard Stankiewicz, and Jack Tworkov, many of whom had ties to Wysocki through his connections at Yale University. Dine later thanked Wysocki for inviting him to be artist-in-residence in the fall of 1974:

It was an extremely valuable experience for me. I was able to see and communicate with bright, articulate students in surroundings which were extremely congenial. Not only did I accomplish a great deal personally but I had the satisfaction of a give-and-take situation with the students and staff. My needs, as well as those of the people I was involved with, were well thought out and efficiently dealt with. It was a fine experience for me [and] I know the students benefitted.[6]

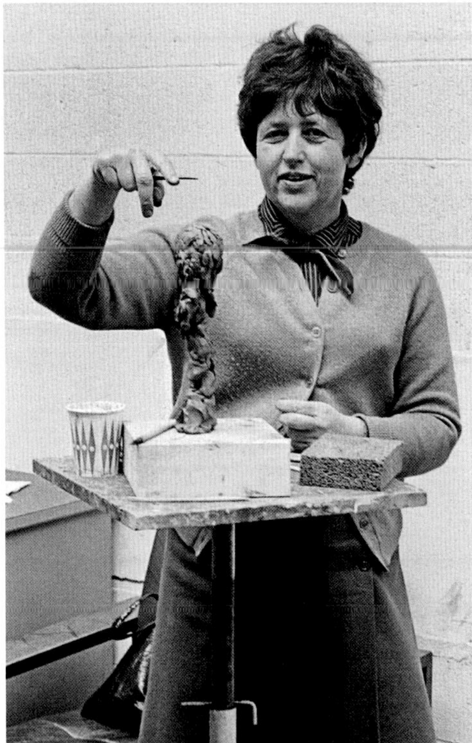

9

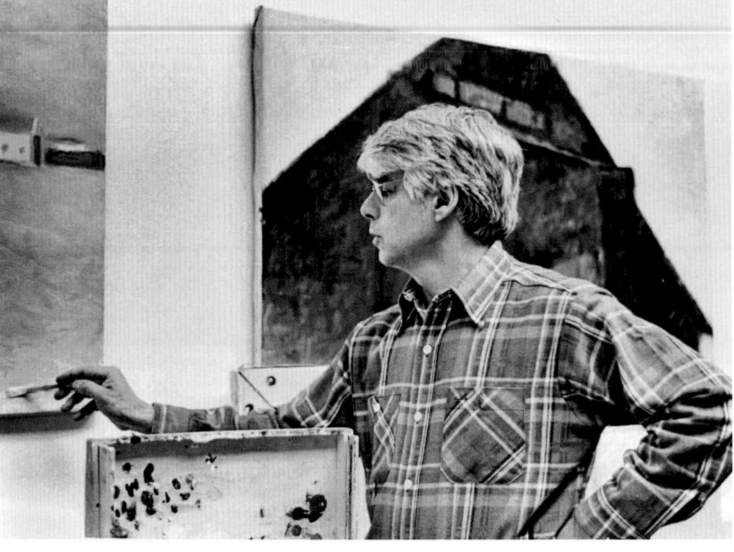

10

Fig. 9

Laura Ziegler working in the artist-in-residence studio at the Hopkins Center, May 1974. Dartmouth College Library. Photo by Matthew Wysocki.

Fig. 10

Wolf Kahn working in the artist-in-residence studio at the Hopkins Center, winter 1984. Dartmouth College Library. Photo by Nancy Wasserman.

Fig. 11

Leroy Lamis discussing his Plexiglas construction with Matthew Wysocki, October 1970. Dartmouth College Library.

Fig. 12

Charles Burwell teaching in the Hopkins Center, February 21, 1995. Dartmouth College Library.

Walker Evans was the first photographer to be invited to Dartmouth, and his residency in the fall of 1972 was followed by a number of other outstanding photographer residencies, including Maria Cosindas in the fall of 1976, Ralph Steiner in the winter of 1979, Joel Sternfeld in the fall of 1985, Olivia Parker in the winter of 1988, Pablo Delano in the winter of 1997, William Christenberry in the winter of 2003, Andrew Moore in the fall of 2006, and Subhankar Banerjee in the winter of 2009. Both Steiner and Sternfeld were Dartmouth graduates, which, as we have seen, has been an important feature of the program since its founding. In addition to Carlos Sánchez, Paul Sample, Steiner, and Sternfeld, another graduate, Daniel Heyman, was artist-in-residence in the fall of 2013. In 1989 the printmaker Joel Elgin took over the program and for the next six years continued to build upon Wysocki's legacy of bringing distinguished artists to campus, including a number of important painters, such as Rosemarie Beck in the spring of 1992, James McGarrell in the spring of 1993, Charles Burwell in the winter of 1995 (fig. 12), Louis Finkelstein in the spring of 1995, and Jack Berthot in the fall of 1995.

Today the program is directed by Gerald "Jerry" Auten, a professor in the Studio Art Department and the co-curator of this exhibition. Under Jerry's visionary leadership, the Artist-in-Residence Program has adopted a philosophy of collaboration, flexibility, openness, and innovation that ensures that each residency benefits the artist, institution, and community in a multitude of ways. Prior to Auten's

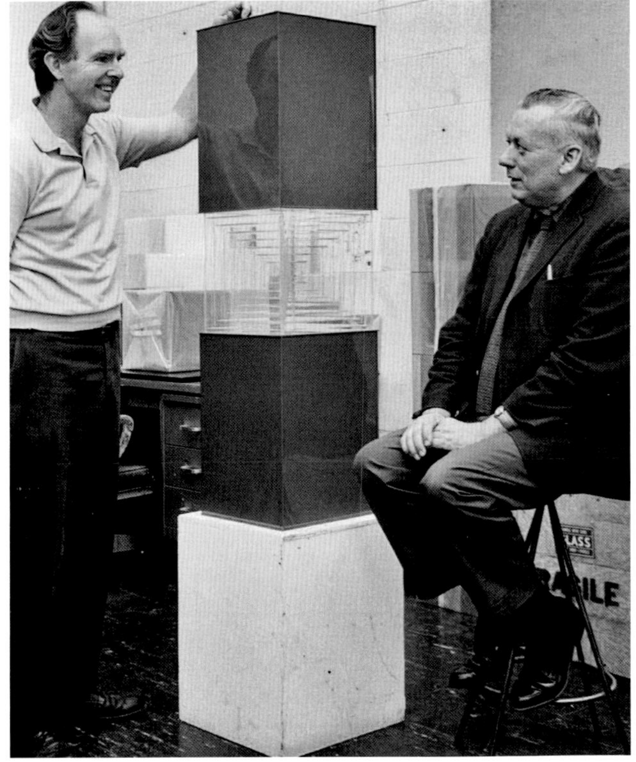

11

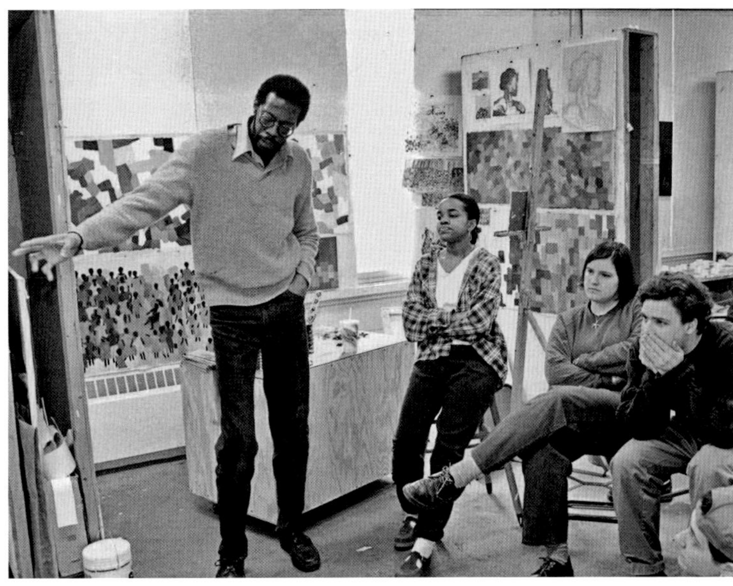

12

appointment in 1995, artists were selected by the director alone, which led to a popular misconception, especially during Wysocki's tenure, that residencies were handed out to friends and colleagues of the director rather than to the most exciting and innovative practitioners in the field. Seeking to address this perceived flaw in the program's selection process, Auten joined with the tenured and tenure-track professors in the Studio Art Department to institute a new policy whereby artists where chosen through an exhibition committee that meets in the fall, winter, and spring terms. Each member of the committee brings the names of two artists for consideration as artist-in-residence, based on the quality of their work or the relevance of their artistic practice to the department's teaching goals. Following an extensive group discussion, the committee then has a blind vote the following week. The votes are counted by the director and chair of the department, and the artist with the most votes is then invited by the director to participate in the program. The director and the faculty member who put forward the name of the artist selected then work together to curate the artist's exhibition and organize the residency.

This system has worked extremely well in bringing the widest possible range of artists to campus and addressing the need for the program to reflect and embrace new developments in contemporary artistic practice. Auten and the studio art faculty have invited artists working in film, video, and other forms of new media, as well as installation art, including multimedia environments, performance art, and sound art; they have also maintained a strong commitment to

sculpture, painting, drawing, architecture, printmaking, photography, and ceramics. The program continues to offer students an opportunity each term to observe the processes and products of individual creativity and artistic innovation firsthand, and the commitment to diverse artistic practices ensures that during their four years at Dartmouth, undergraduate students will have been exposed to the work and ideas of twelve established or emerging artists with experience in a variety of media and disciplines.

The Artist-in-Residence Program has had a significant impact on the careers of many visiting artists, whose work has been stimulated by the natural beauty and distinctive architecture of the Upper Valley, as seen in Bernard Chaet's bravura watercolor of the bridge at White River Junction, Vermont (see cat. 72), or Walker Evans's unforgettable photograph of Trinity Church in Cornish, New Hampshire (see cat. 40). Artists-in-residence often make repeat visits to Dartmouth's Baker-Berry Library and Rauner Special Collections Library for research purposes. They also find inspiration in the exhibitions and permanent installations on view at the Hood Museum of Art, which reflect that institution's teaching mission and the global reach of its collections. As Linda Matalon reminisced about her stay at Dartmouth in the fall of 2012:

> I didn't go to college, so this was the first time I experienced a campus life. I really enjoyed the studio's proximity to the library and museum. Being able to visit over and over was a special luxury.

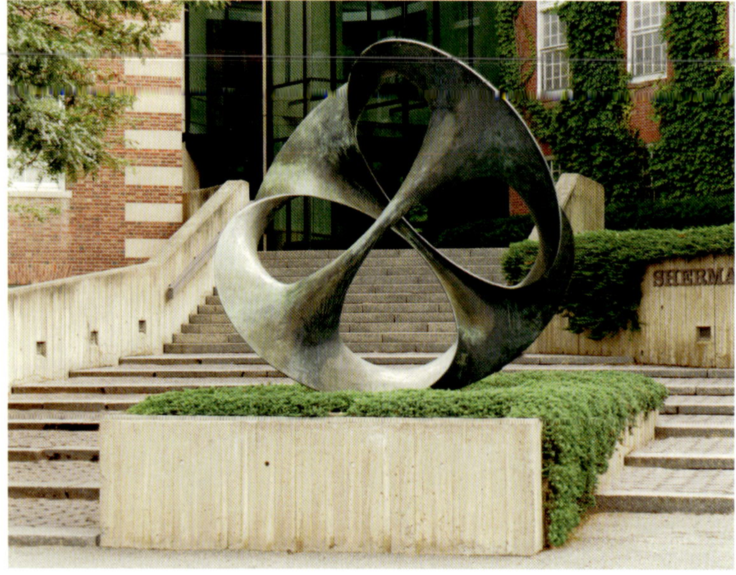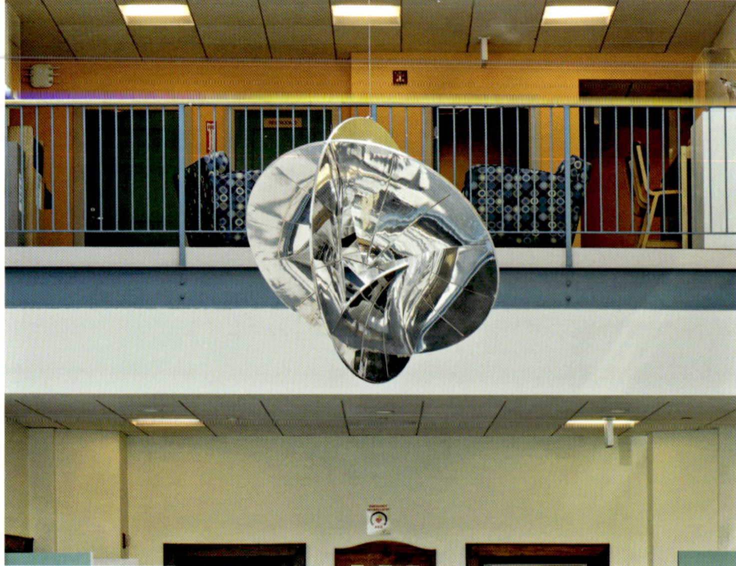

13

14

Fig. 13

Charles O. Perry, *D₂D*, 1973–75, bronze sculpture positioned in front of the Sherman Fairchild Physical Sciences Center. From this angle, Baker tower and Beverly Pepper's *Thel*, 1975–77, are visible in the background. Purchased through the Fairchild Foundation; S.975.74.

Fig. 14

Luise Kaish, *Sphere*, 1976. Polished aluminum sculpture hanging in the atrium of the Collis Center for Student Involvement. Gift of Melissa Kaish Dorfman, Class of 1983; 2012.71.

Fig. 15

Allan C. Houser, *Peaceful Serenity*, 1992, bronze-plated steel sculpture on the grounds of Sherman House. Purchased through a gift from Mary Alice Kean Raynolds and David R. W. Raynolds, Class of 1949; 2007.56.

Fig. 16

Thomas Bayliss Huxley-Jones, *Portrait of Warner Bentley*, 1968, bronze. Commissioned by the Trustees of Dartmouth College; S.969.91.

In the moment, you can't realize how these things are affecting your work, but there is a residual effect. For example, I am used to a very solitary work routine, but campus life, the camaraderie of the faculty and the way they support and nurture each other and students, led me to seek out other ways of working. I spent time in the ceramics studio and printed photographs. I actually exhibited a photograph for the first time a month after leaving Dartmouth, a print I had made there.[7]

Visiting artists have also benefitted from their engagement with Dartmouth's students and the academic community of which they become a part, forming friendships and professional relationships that have lasted well beyond their ten-week residencies on campus. In addition to their impact on Dartmouth students, faculty, and residents of the Upper Valley, artists-in-residence have also embellished the campus through works of public art, beginning with the completion of José Clemente Orozco's mural cycle *The Epic of American Civilization* in the lower-level reserve reading room of Baker Library in 1934. Other works by former artists-in-residence that grace the campus grounds include Sorel Etrog's bronze sculpture *Family Group*, 1965–67, which is installed in one of the curved bay windows of the main entrance of the Hopkins Center; Charles O. Perry's bronze sculpture *D₂D*, 1973–75 (fig. 13), which stands in front of the Sherman Fairchild Physical Sciences Center and whose title was given by a group of Dartmouth chemistry students who came up with this formula after being asked to describe

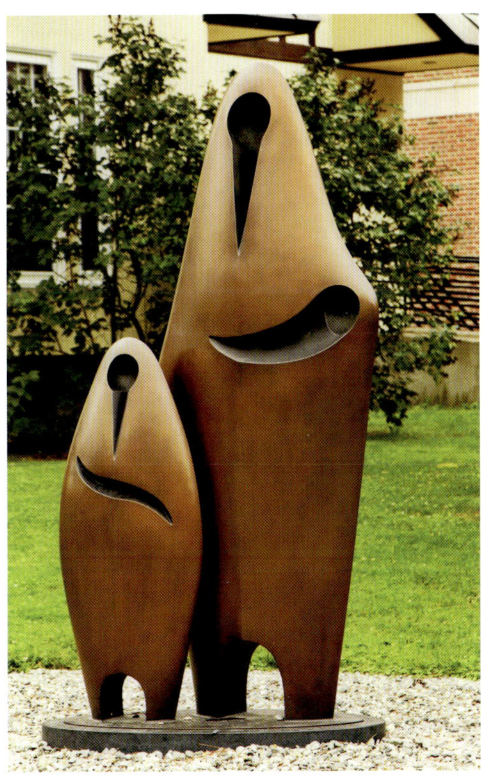

15

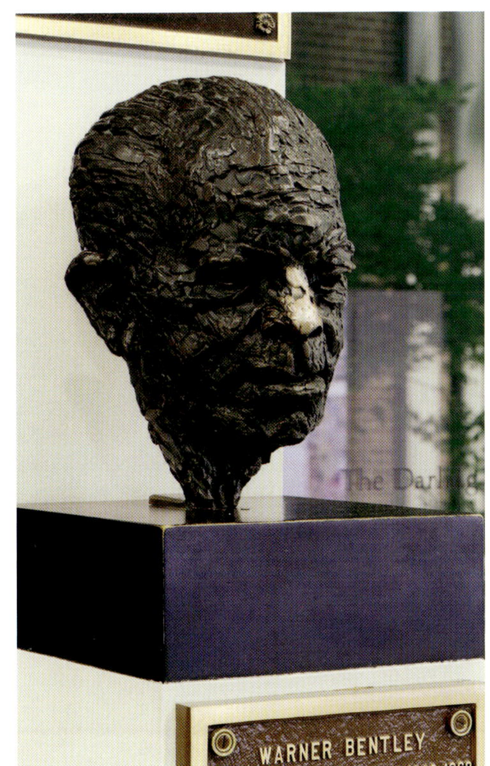

16

the sculpture's physical symmetry and topography; George Warren Rickey's kinetic stainless-steel sculpture *Two Lines Oblique Down, Variation VI*, 1976 (see fig. 17), whose gently lifting and falling metal blades delight visitors as they walk past the Darling Courtyard; Luise Kaish's polished aluminum *Sphere*, a dynamic, rotating sculpture that hangs in the atrium of the Collis Center for Student Involvement (fig. 14); and Allan C. Houser's *Peaceful Serenity*, a 1992 sculpture in bronze-plated steel installed on the grounds of Sherman House that imbues the traditional image of a Chiricahua Apache mother and child with the streamlined sensibility of abstract art (fig. 15).

Until recently, Thomas Bayliss Huxley-Jones had three works of art on display on campus, reflecting his popularity at Dartmouth during the 1960s, when he was artist-in-residence in the fall of 1963 and again in the spring of 1968. During his residency in 1963, Huxley-Jones was commissioned by representatives of the Class of 1943 to create a memorial in honor of twenty-three of their classmates, who gave their lives during World War II. The artist created *Fountain Figure*, a graceful bronze sculpture of a standing female figure clad in a diaphanous toga-like garment that was placed in a tranquil setting in the Zahm Courtyard between the Hopkins Center and the Hanover Inn. An image of quiet contemplation, reflection, and meditation, the tall figure bends at both the waist and the knees to assume a vaguely S-shaped stance as she lifts her head and eyes to the sky. In 1966 Huxley-Jones returned to campus to install *Breakthrough*, an immense fiberglass and aluminum sculpture that he had specially designed for the east façade of the new Charles Gilman Life Science Laboratory building. Mounted approximately twenty feet above ground, this sculpture consisted of two interlocking triangles, constructed from cast fiberglass-resin components stretched over an aluminum frame, which formed an abstract winged figure soaring in flight to suggest the breakthrough of human knowledge. In the fall of 2012, this sculpture was removed and placed in storage in anticipation of the impending demolition of the Gilman building, and Dartmouth's Public Art Committee is actively pursuing an alternative location for this work on campus. Finally, during his second residency in 1968, Huxley-Jones created a bronze portrait bust of Warner Bentley (fig. 16), the director of the Dartmouth Players from 1928 to 1960 and the director of the Hopkins Center from 1960 to 1969, which remains one of the best-known and most beloved works of public art on campus, as student performers about to go on stage at the Hop rub Bentley's nose for good luck. Although the glistening nose is tarnished beyond repair—staff at the Hood Museum of Art use the sculpture to explain to visitors why they should not touch works of art at the museum—the *Portrait of Warner Bentley* has become an icon of the performing arts at Dartmouth and thus remains on permanent display at the Hop.

Another memorable, if temporary, work of public art was made by Chris Martin during his residency in the winter of 2011. Martin installed a painting of a cardinal in the Darling Courtyard opposite the Jaffe-Friede Gallery (fig. 17), where his exhibition of recent work was on view that term. Surviving the harsh weather conditions for a period of

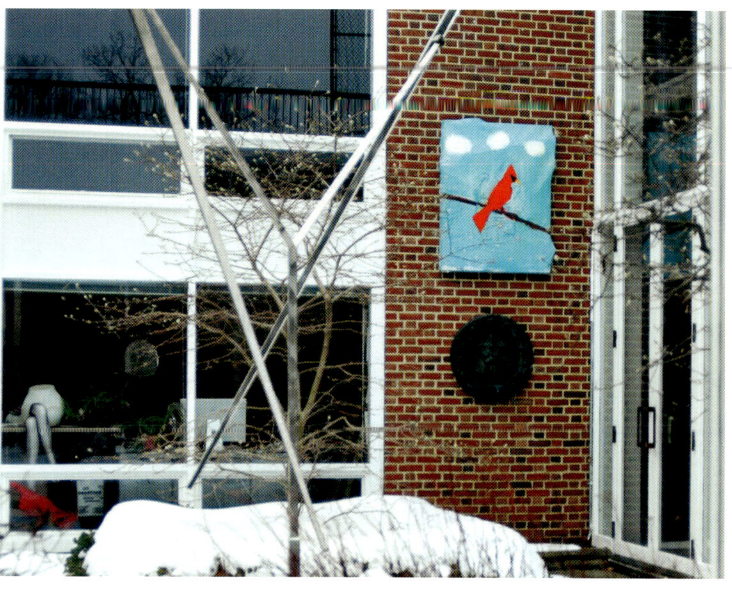

17

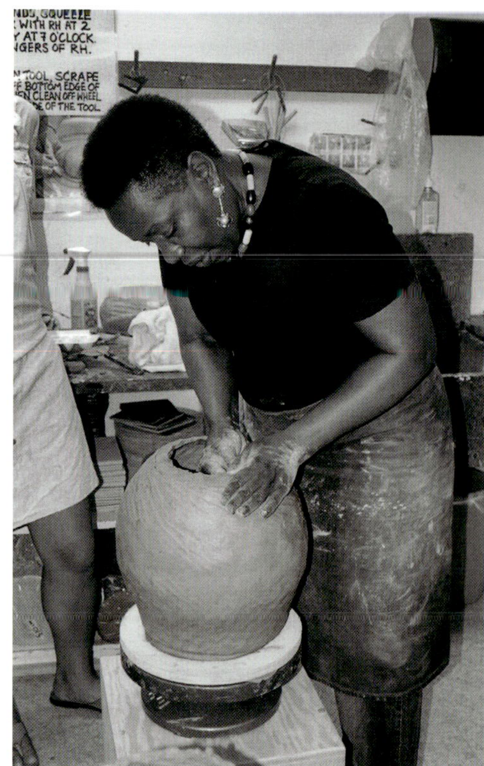

18

Fig. 17

Chris Martin, installation of a painting of a cardinal in the Darling Courtyard, winter 2011. George Warren Rickey's *Two Lines Oblique Down, Variation VI*, 1976, is in the foreground. Photo by Gerald Auten.

Fig. 18

Magdalene Odundo creating a new work in the Hopkins Center, fall 2008. Photo by Gerald Auten.

Fig. 19

Sana Musasama working in the artist-in-residence studio at the Hopkins Center, March 14, 2007. Photo by Gerald Auten.

Fig. 20

James Cutler, *Edith Green Wendell Wyatt Federal Building, Portland, Oregon, West Elevation*, 2013. Design Excellence Architect: James Cutler, FAIA, Cutler Anderson Architects; Executive Architect: Don Eggleston, AIA, SERA Architects. Photo by Nic Lehoux.

several weeks, the painted bird's bright red plumage made for a stunning juxtaposition with the snow that fell in abundance that winter, as well as the soaring tapered blades of Rickey's sculpture. Whether official commissions by the College, acquisitions by the Hood Museum of Art, or unsanctioned interventions by individual artists during their residencies, these works have all enriched the environment in which we live, work, or study, and have played a vital role in exposing Dartmouth students, faculty, and the wider community to a diverse range of public art.

The recent residencies by such noted international artists and architects as Toon Verhoef, Christopher Cozier, Magdalene Odundo (fig. 18), Subhankar Banerjee, Marjetica Potrč, and Luke Fowler reflect the same desire to expose Dartmouth students and faculty to new developments in contemporary art from around the globe as that shown by Jerry Lathrop in 1931 when he invited the Guatemalan artist Carlos Sánchez to be the first artist-in-residence at the College. Since that time, 166 artists from all over the world have shared their vision with the Dartmouth community, and their presence has undoubtedly enhanced the vitality of the arts on campus. As the program enters its eighty-third year in 2014, it has never been more dedicated to its efforts to bring extraordinary artists from around the world to Dartmouth's campus. This dynamic new chapter in the program's history is reflected by the *In Residence: Contemporary Artists at Dartmouth* exhibition at the Hood Museum of Art and four other venues on campus. The Jaffe-Friede Gallery in the Hopkins Center will present Carol Hepper's

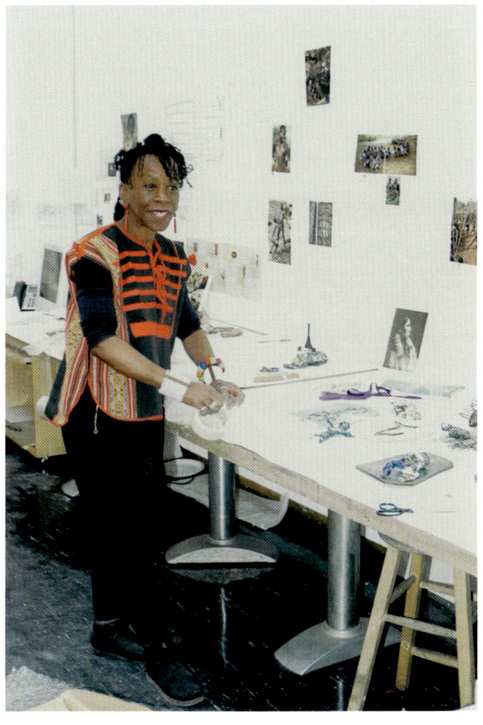

19

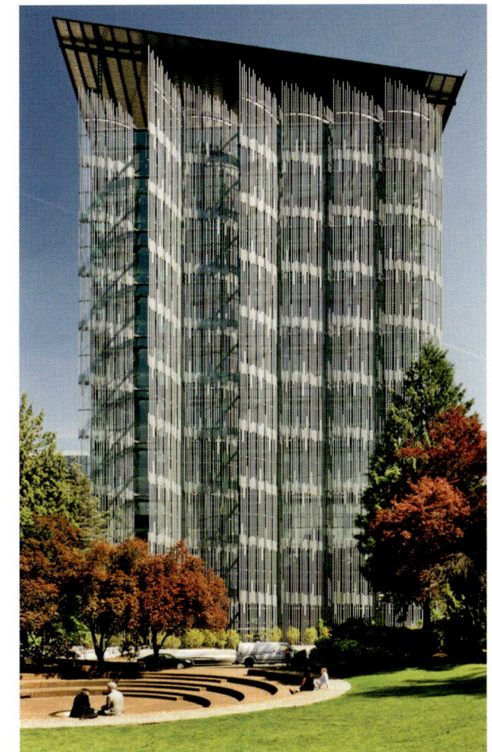

20

monumental 1987 sculpture *Tropus*, along with site-specific installations by Christopher Cozier and Sana Musasama (fig. 19). In addition, Jin Soo Kim and Won Ju Lim will be exhibiting new works in the Hopkins Center's Barrows Rotunda and Strauss Gallery, respectively, while screenprint posters by former artists-in-residence will be on display in the Top of the Hop. Finally, photography of James Cutler's recent architectural projects (fig. 20) will be shown in the Nearburg Gallery in the new Black Family Visual Arts Center, which opened on September 14, 2012. This state-of-the-art facility is home to the Studio Art and Film and Media Studies Departments and includes a spectacular new artist-in-residence studio overlooking the Maffei Arts Plaza. The exhibition's numerous venues, which, when combined, will showcase the work of more than eighty artists in a wide variety of media, speak to the important historical legacy of the Artist-in-Residence Program at Dartmouth, as well as its exciting future.

Notes

1. Artemas S. Packard, Letter to Abby Aldrich Rockefeller, August 8, 1931, in Jacqueline Baas, "Dartmouth College and *The Epic of American Civilization*," *Orozco at Dartmouth:* The Epic of American Civilization (Hanover, N.H.: Hood Museum of Art, Dartmouth College, and Dartmouth College Library, 2012), 5.
2. Churchill P. Lathrop, "Artists in Residence: A History" [June 1983], in Brian P. Kennedy and Emily Schubert Burke, eds., *Modern and Contemporary Art at Dartmouth: Highlights from the Hood Museum of Art*, exh. cat. (Hanover, N.H.: Hood Museum of Art, Dartmouth College, and University Press of New England, 2009), 219.
3. Matthew Wysocki, Letter to J. A. Draper, Acting Head, Department of Art, Florida State University, April 7, 1971 (George Warren Rickey object file, Hood Museum of Art).
4. Luise Kaish, Letter to Matthew Wysocki, May 14, 1976 (Luise Kaish, *Sphere* object file, Hood Museum of Art).
5. Varujan Boghosian, Letter to Matthew Wysocki, March 9, 1976 (Varujan Boghosian, *The Tribune* object file, Hood Museum of Art).
6. Jim Dine, Letter to Matthew Wysocki, March 8, 1976 (Jim Dine, *Dartmouth Still Life* object file, Hood Museum of Art).
7. Linda Matalon, Letter to Michael Taylor, August 3, 2013 (Linda Matalon, *Untitled, Diptych (Touching)* object file, Hood Museum of Art).

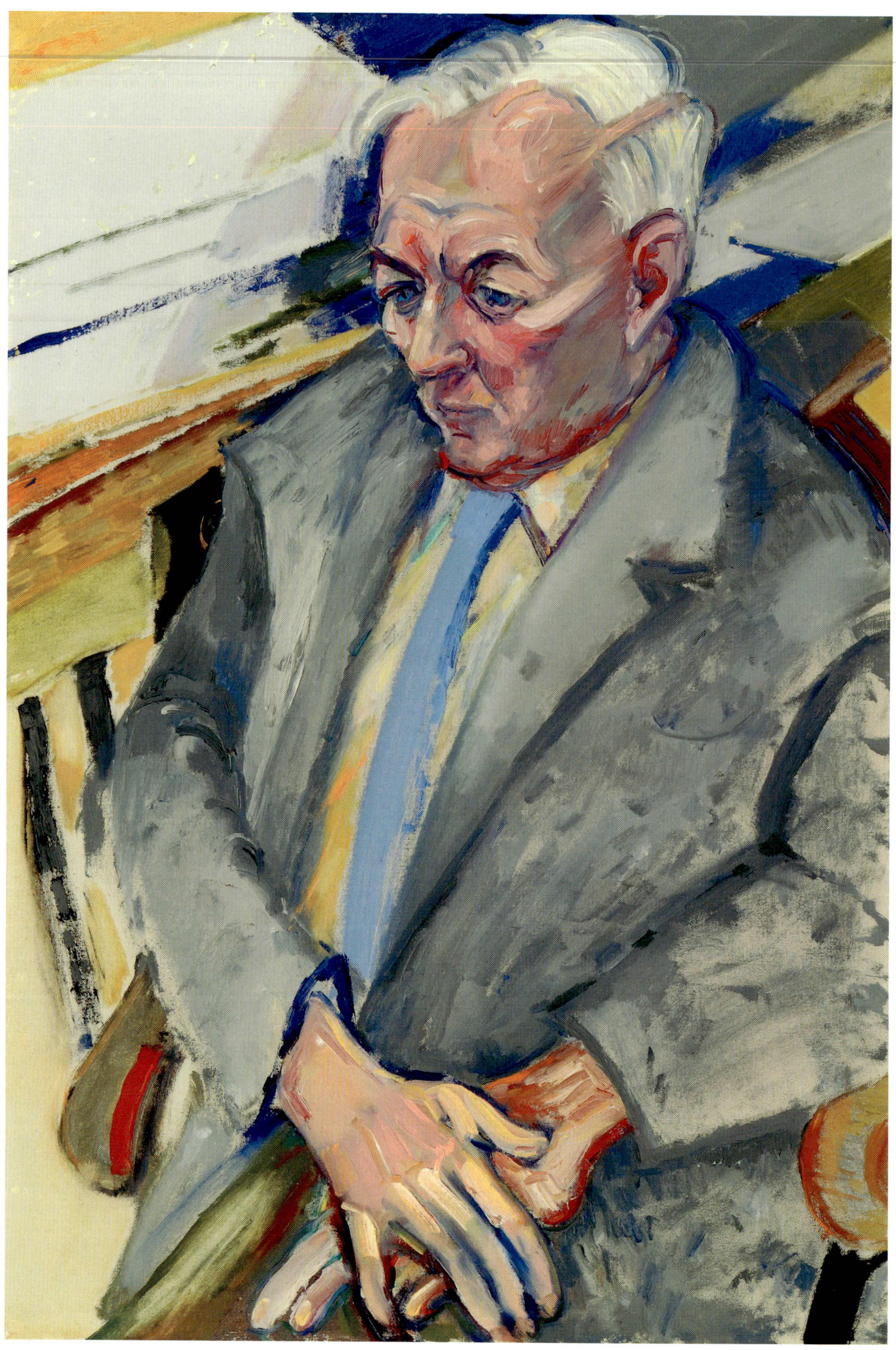

THE ARTIST-IN-RESIDENCE PROGRAM AT DARTMOUTH COLLEGE

Timothy Rub: I have one question about the Artist-in-Residence Program that confuses me sometimes. It started when? In the late 1920s?

Matthew Wysocki (opposite page): It actually had its roots in 1931, when Jerry Lathrop, who was then teaching art history, invited José Clemente Orozco to come here to do a small demonstration panel of fresco painting for his class. While Orozco was here, he walked through the Baker Library and saw some empty walls, and he said, "I would like to do a mural here" (fig. 21). So, they thought it was a great idea. It was a matter of funding the mural. They had no money; however, the president was willing to arrange some sort of deal where he would be receiving faculty pay during the two-year period of the mural painting. It was a wonderful solution, I think. It was a very small salary, but he loved doing it. He spent two years working there, and students came by every day and visited with him. They served as models for him, and many students come by and say, "You know, my father painted that gold piece in the lower-right-hand corner." It was true student involvement. The studio was not private; it was very open, and they had a chance to watch him work. So that was the first start. It was not called the Artist-in-Residence Program at that time.

Bernard Chaet, *Portrait of Matthew Wysocki,*
Chairman, Artist-in-Residence Program,
Dartmouth College, 1986, oil on canvas.
Purchased through the William S. Rubin Fund;
P.986.73.1. © Estate of Bernard Chaet

Also, during the twenty-year period, 1940–1962, Paul Sample, who was a Dartmouth grad and a competent painter, had a studio in the top of Carpenter Hall. He could paint there all day long, and students could drop in on him to watch him paint. They could receive no credit for this. The only courses for credit were the art history courses. So in a sense this was the roots or the background of the program. The program actually started in 1962. The building of the Hopkins Center made it much more formal. There were four artists invited each year, each for a ten-week period, and they were not brought here as teachers but as artists who worked in the studio.

TR: Before you go on, was there any Visual Studies Department before 1962?

MW: No. It first became a studio art program in conjunction with art history. It was called the Art Department. It got off to a rather stormy start with all sorts of problems, and that was when I was approached to organize a new program for the Hop, and I think that all the faculty at that time who were teaching student courses were out. So we then worked with the art history faculty to reorganize the program as the Visual Studies Department, which was more formal, in which students would receive credit for their work in both art history and art together.

TR: So the Artist-in-Residence Program in its current incarnation came into being at that time?

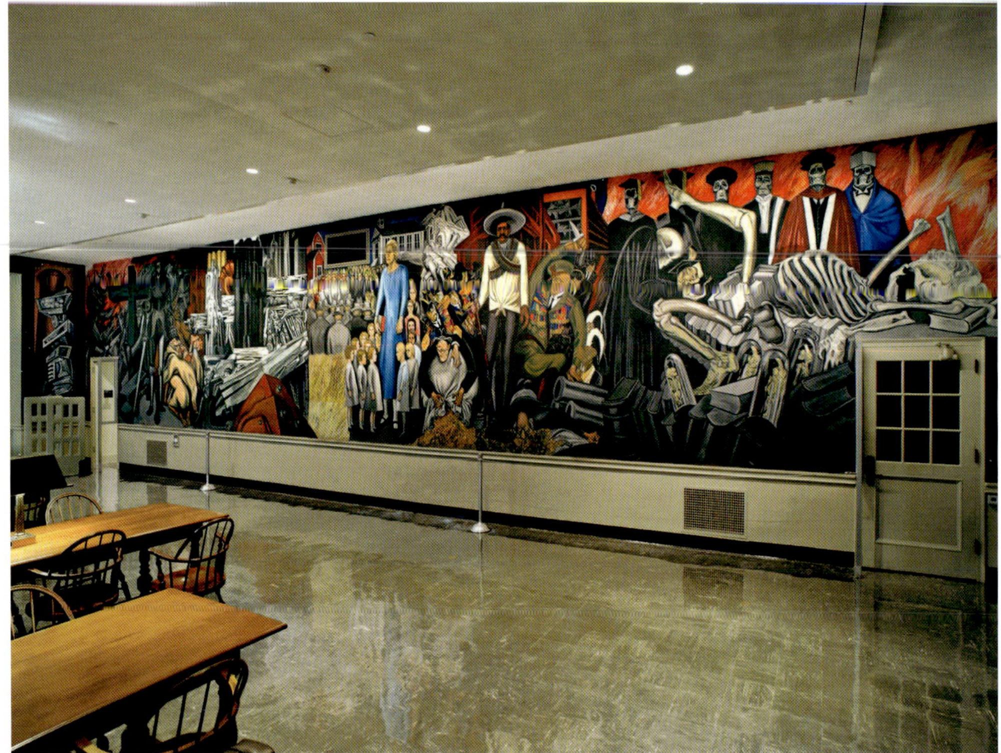

José Clemente Orozco, mural images from *The Epic of American Civilization*, 1932–34, fresco. Orozco Room, Baker Library, Dartmouth College. Commissioned by the Trustees of Dartmouth College; P.934.13.13–17.

MW: Yes. In 1962, our first artist was Friedel Dzubas, who came here and spent one term painting in his studio and students could come by for visits, critiques, and actually see him in operation. All the artists knew before they came that they'd be subject to students' visits, and they liked it. They met a lot of interesting students, and they had a great chance to work, help, and do all sorts of favors for the students which would encourage them in artistic participation. I wanted to mention the fact that this was all housed in the Hopkins Center, and the idea of the program was to get the students involved from the entire campus. It wasn't just the visual studies students who would meet the artist. We had people from the Religion Department, from other disciplines, from pre-engineering or pre-med who would come in. They were very excited, for many of them had never been in an artist's studio before. It had a dialogue.

TR: Let me ask you on that point. The Hopkins Center was a very different facility for the visual arts and the performing arts than Dartmouth had ever had before that point. How did you facilitate the teaching of the visual arts? It is the twenty-fifth anniversary of the Hopkins Center now. Obviously it began on a very different footing from 1962 on. Can you talk about that?

MW: Well, I think that many people felt very uncomfortable about the Hopkins Center being built. It was a modern building built right on the Green, in competition with the traditional buildings. So there was a certain sense of resentment. Many people did not think that a cultural center was necessary at the College. So, in the initial stages, students here were referred to [by other students] as the Hop rats, and things of that sort, which were derogatory. The only reason they came to the Hop was to get their mail, and they were isolated. But as time went on, they just found that the programs were great and they began participating in the programs. We had the Film Society and a little snack bar here. It became a way of life, and often the people who complained about the Hop began to love it.

TR: How did the building lend itself to that kind of atmosphere?

MW: The architect, [Wallace K.] Harrison, was a firm believer in having a window in every room. It was like a big shopping mall. You could go by and watch people participating in drawing, in sculpture or jewelry-making. It was a place for observers. I sort of objected to that, because drawing classes were rather private, and you can imagine what would happen when we had a nude model there. The crowds were too great, so we began creating more private areas. The concept was to make the arts visible, and that was a good start.

TR: And that ties in with the fundamental change in the artist residency program, which is perhaps the beginning of the real Artist-in-Residence Program?

MW: It was the beginning of the Artist-in-Residence Program because then you had four visitors a year for a ten-week period, and we tried to vary that with the type of person we brought in. And the type of person who would like a new environment, who would respond to the challenge of a new environment and the attitude of the College, and who had a humanistic background. All of the artists who came here loved it very much and sometimes at the end of the period they would say, "Gee, I hate to leave."

TR: Tell me, first of all, before you get into taking about the artists themselves and their experiences at Dartmouth. Why was it decided to a have a different artist-in-residence four times a year? How much work does that entail from the administrative side?

MW: Well, there is an awful lot of work to bring in an artist-in-residence. It's much easier to bring in an artist who's on the teaching faculty as a guest instructor for the year. That is easy. But then on the other hand the salary is much higher. We often can't get the biggest names, because the big names do not want to commit themselves to anyplace for one whole year. So we found out that the ten-week period was ideal for big names to come here, like George Rickey. It was great to have him up here for ten weeks. That was all the time he wanted because he had other commitments elsewhere. They could make time for us. It was just right. They also got a comparatively small fee for being here in residency, and I know that a lot of the artists from New York who I knew personally felt that it was fun to come to the country and work and meet with students.

TR: So you could stretch a small budget a long way?

MW: Exactly, and that's what we've been doing ever since. I don't think the budget has caught up drastically. That's certainly not why they come. It's the good time they have here, the friendly people, and they are allowed to do their own work.

TR: How is it trying to schedule these things?

MW: Hectic. For example, with Peter Milton, who I admire as a great printmaker, it literally took me ten years to get him to finally come here. With Olivia Parker, it took me five years. When I approached her, she said that she had two children still at school. Well, now the problem is solved. The two children are at Dartmouth, she's here, and her husband, John, comes up every weekend. It's a great family affair.

TR: So, you actually set your sights on artists and pursue them diligently?

MW: Yes. And sometimes we do have an emergency when someone is very firm about coming, but then other commitments suddenly come up. Fortunately I have enough of a backlog of people I can call and work on to see if I can get them up here.

TR: Talk about the exhibitions, because when the artists-in-residence are here working each term, they also have an exhibition of their work at that time too. Why was that particular structure set up?

MW: Well, I think that we wanted the Dartmouth community to see the great variety in art, and this gave us the chance to bring in the people who were current, who were in the running, so-called, in New York City, who had national recognition, leave New York City and show in Hanover. So the show was an event that everyone really looked forward to. The artists also had a chance to lecture to students, meet with them, and it was also a chance for students to visit the artists' studios and see what was in progress. So, it was a visual world, and that's what made it exciting. It was also exciting for the Hop to have something up visually. Remember that drama and music were very prominent, and the visual studies had never been a strong element here, so this was the first that we had.

TR: So also in a sense, it's been a way for Dartmouth to be involved in contemporary art on a very regular basis.

MW: Yes. Without having to buy it, or owning it, or forming a collection. It is all on a loan basis and many of our artists are kind enough to leave things as a gift, and sometimes we make purchases.

TR: Which form the core of the present exhibition?

MW: Yes, yes.

TR: Let me get back to the selection process, because it's quite an interesting one. Can you describe with any rhyme or reason as to how you or anyone else has gone about choosing artists? Now, I haven't even asked you who has done the choosing over the years.

MW: Well, initially, I had to take a lot of the initiative, because a lot of people just didn't know who was active in the New York scene and who was available. I have been personal friends with many of the people. But many times I would have a suggestion made by someone which is a really very good one. That person could be a faculty member, or Warner Bentley or Peter Smith. If it worked out, if it was a person who fit in to scheme of things and was available, then we did it.

TR: Do you remember any suggestions that were made?

MW: I don't specifically right now, no. But there were suggestions that were made, and Professor [Varujan] Boghosian was very valuable, and he was a New York artist, so he would often make good suggestions.

TR: That's interesting, because you've been up here for more than twenty years now. How does one keep in touch with the world outside?

MW: Well, it means I go to New York City quite frequently to see exhibits, and I have a lot of friends and meet new friends, and also I'm a member of the Century Club, which is an association for artists. So there, I'm at dinners and meetings and make many new acquaintances. It's quite easy for me. And any time I'm in Europe I'm always looking for European artists who I've heard of and know, like R. B. Kitaj, who was in London at the time of [one of my trips to London]. I was able to contact him and take him out of hiding. Once I got him here, every college in the country was calling and asking, "How did you ever get R. B. Kitaj here, how did you do it?" He was a great contributor and a great person, and he still is.

TR: When you look at the work as a whole, there is a great range of media, of styles, of approaches to the visual arts. The selection process is obviously responsible for that.

MW: Some of these artists came in because they were part of a theme year. We used to do a Japanese year. During that year, [Yu] Fujiwara, who is a famous Japanese ceramicist, came and spent a term. He was a good friend of Warner Bentley's. Another year was a Canadian year, and Sorel Etrog was here at that time. I thought theme years were particularly difficult to do, because you not only had to get artists, but the other departments also had to get people—for drama, music. There's always this tremendous effort, and it never quite clicked. It's hard enough to get one show without having to coordinate everything

else. In 1966, Donald Judd, who did constructions in steel, and was a great controversial figure in New York City, came in what was sort of a minimal year. There was difficulty in the public here accepting his steel structures, which are very beautiful. And then, in 1967, Etrog, who worked in bronze, worked on a major plaster in his studio in the Hopkins Center. When he was finished we couldn't get the thing out—the door was too small. We had to go in there with hatchets and break it up. It made the B&G men rather furious to have to go in there and clean up all that plaster. That's when I decided to change the doors, to double them, because we had people like [Richard] Anuszkiewicz who were doing enormous paintings, 10 feet x 12 feet. Everything was beginning to develop into a big size. With that we had to make changes in the architecture. Then, of course, in 1968, Jason Seley worked here with car bumpers. And that was a great experience because he always had a group of interested students who would visit the local junkyard to buy bumpers, which he would then weld together. He was an awful lot of fun. Then in 1968, Varujan Boghosian began his constructions of steel, wood, and paper collages, and he was a great contributor, and of course became a faculty member. Then in 1969, Will Carter, English, a great typographer and designer. He's the artist who did all the wonderful carved-wooden signs in the Hop, which are very beautiful.

In 1971, another good stained glass designer, Robert Sowers. It was interesting because his show was not confined to any gallery, and was spread throughout the Hopkins Center. Wherever we had a window, we put one of his glass pieces. That was very impressive. He believed in

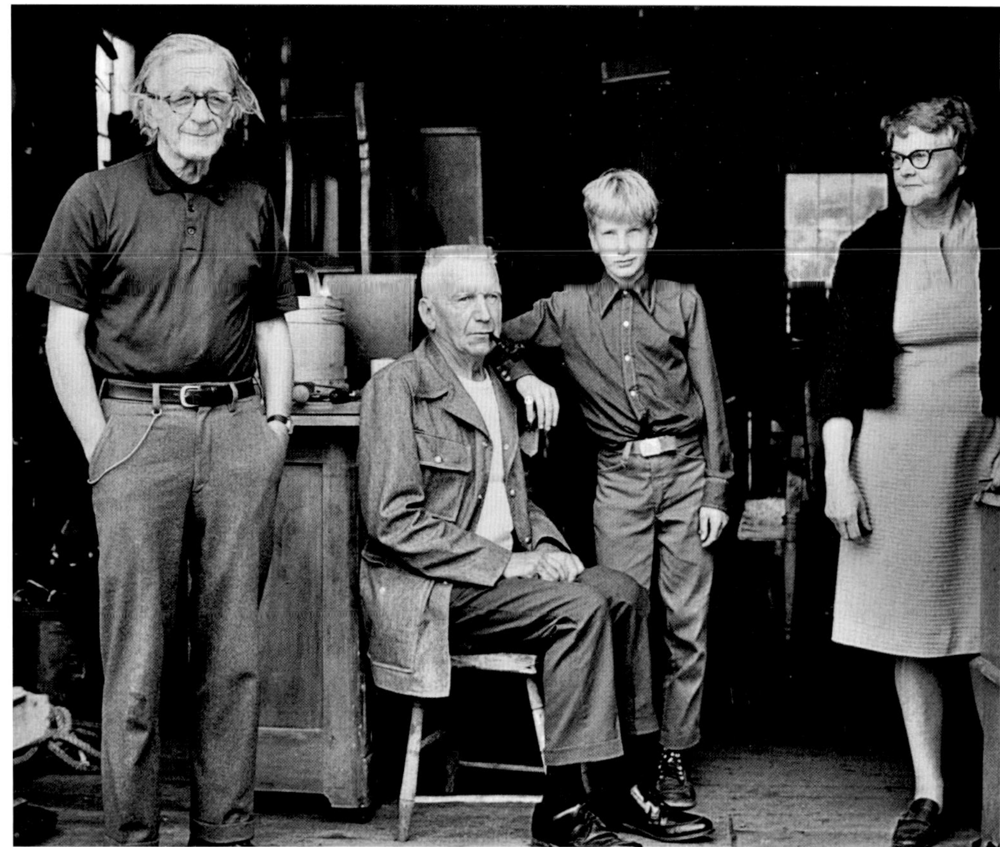

Fig. 22

Matthew Wysocki, *Walker Evans, Alfred Petersen, Raymond Collins and Martha Viola (Pierce) Petersen*, 1972, gelatin silver print. Gift of Janet Petersen Mayers, Class of 1947W; 2008.25.5.

working with natural light. And then Philip Grausman in 1972. He was here with his wife, who was a dancer, Martha Clarke. They were very active because this was the time when Pilobolus was forming. She was very much involved with that group. He did a lot of bronze sculpture, and then he worked with aluminum. He also worked with unorthodox materials. And then in 1976, Marie Cosindas, a great photographer who worked with large Polaroid prints, and then, in 1978, Costantino Nivola worked in sculpture mostly, concrete casting and sand molds. This was interesting to see. He had a class learn the process and do demonstrations, and then [in 1979] Richard Stankiewicz, who did large welding with steel. He worked in Roger's Garage, and I know that we had to get a big lift for him, and he worked with a student by the name of Ben White. Again, it was an open house. You could drop by any time and watch him work. That was a very exciting session. He was a hard worker. Then, of course, in 1981, Fumio Yoshimura came here, a wood carver, and he has stayed on with the faculty. Again in 1981, John Alcorn, a graphic designer, who was a recipient of many international awards in graphic design, and he received many art directors' awards. In 1985 we had a rebirth in interest in the Orozco murals. We had Richard Britell here, who actually did fresco murals in the Orozco tradition. This was an exciting situation. It goes on and on. I just mentioned a few of the outstanding people working in these disciplines. Many of our other people have always been painters, or printmakers, or sometimes we had wonderful drawing shows.

TR: That's a nice summary. Which of the residencies really stands out in your mind, either for the way things worked out with the community, for their successes or their outrageousness?

MW: They all had their own particular character, and their own particular strength, but I think that some of the most colorful ones, the ones that really packed in the halls were: Walker Evans, who I would travel with quite a bit in the Upper Valley, to photograph his favorite scenes, and he would always say, "Stop, Mat! That's a 1930s view!" So we'd get out and he'd do his photographing. [One time when] we happened to visit a farm out in Enfield, he was interested in the barn and the people there, and he wanted to photograph them (figs. 22 and 23), so I said, "This is my friend Walker Evans," and their reply was, "Isn't it nice that you would have a senior citizen friend, who has found a hobby in photography." He loved that.

TR: He was here in 1972, wasn't he?

MW: Yes.

TR: So there must have been lots of 1930s views still available?

MW: Oh, yes, yes. And as a matter of fact, I made a record of places that he wanted to go back to photograph. But unfortunately he became very ill and had a major operation here, and he always claimed that Dr.

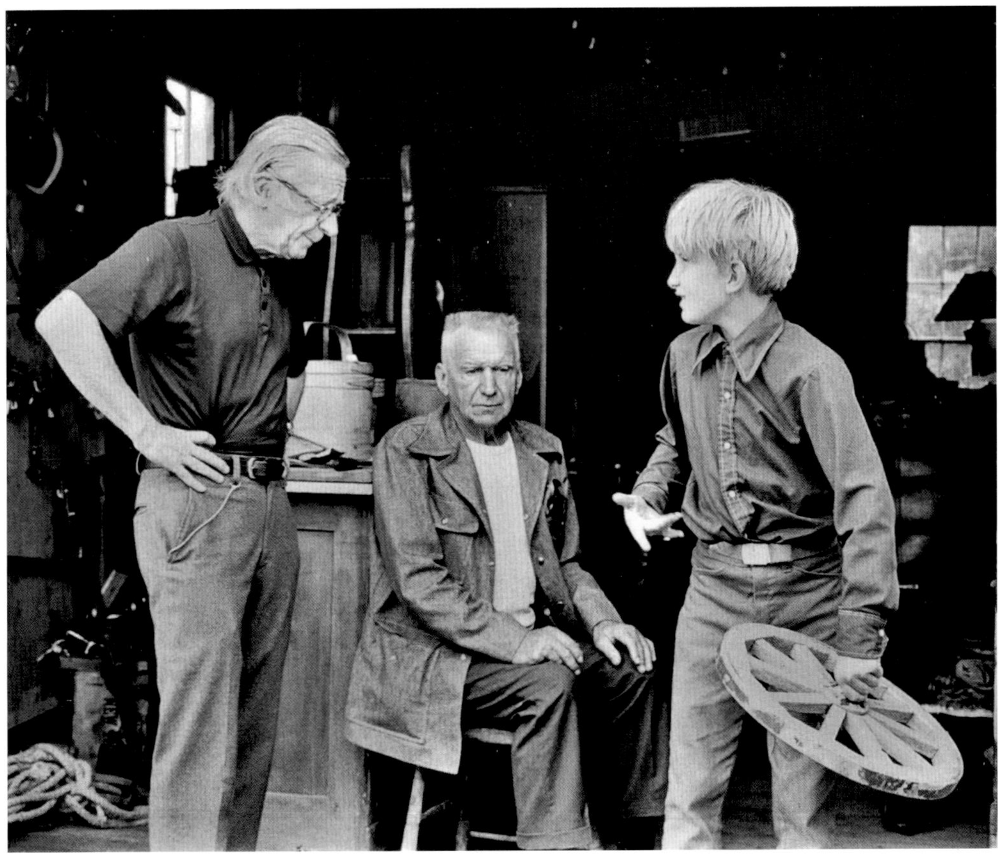

Rosenthal at Mary Hitchcock saved his life. He lived about four or five years after that. He was a wonderful person.

TR: He must have been quite a celebrity to have up here as well?

MW: He was. He decided to give a gallery talk, and it was just impossible to get in there. People were on the floor, and standing, and it was really quite something. But he was a kind person. He loved authors and writers, so he had quite a relationship with the English Department and other people who were visiting the campus at the time.

TR: You had some names here very early in their career, people who have gone on to be really central to American painting and sculpture over the last two and a half decades—people like [Robert] Rauschenberg, [Frank] Stella, [Donald] Judd, George Rickey, and so on. How did that come about? They weren't really known yet.

MW: Yes, but they really had something quite nice to offer, and it was sort of visible if you were doing interesting things, and so you really took a chance on them. Many of them have, of course, grown, and many of them have had their first start here, their first major one-man show. I know when Kitaj was here, he had already had an international reputation, but he made practically all of his paintings and prints for his next Marlborough show while at Dartmouth. There are a few other people who went on to major shows from Dartmouth. Also, Wolf Kahn, who is well known as a watercolorist and pastel landscape painter. His show opened here, and then went on to thirty museums throughout the country. This was the start of it. So we've had a nice tradition of getting exciting people, and what is very nice is that they were all good people. They were interested in what they doing. They loved communicating with the young. I hear from alumni [who graduated] twenty years ago—"Do you remember that wonderful session I had?" I remember when [Richard] Anuszkiewicz was here, he was our first optical artist. During that time he had an assistant named Don Clausing, who, I think, was majoring in English. He helped him work on the Dartmouth football, which was a football made so we could win the Cornell game that weekend (fig. 24). Unfortunately, we lost [the game], but the football has been embalmed and it is on view over at the gym. Yes, it's an Op football. There are sometimes firsts that we've had here.

TR: Why don't you talk about how that interaction between artists and various members of the Dartmouth community evolved. Obviously it really depends on the artist how that interaction works out. It must have been very interesting to watch the rapports between them over the past twenty years.

MW: Yes, I would like to just mention this past year because I think it's fresh in our mind. The people that we've had—Bernard Chaet from Yale who did that book on art drawing. That had a great appeal to our contemporaries, people who'd come by [would say that they] all used it as

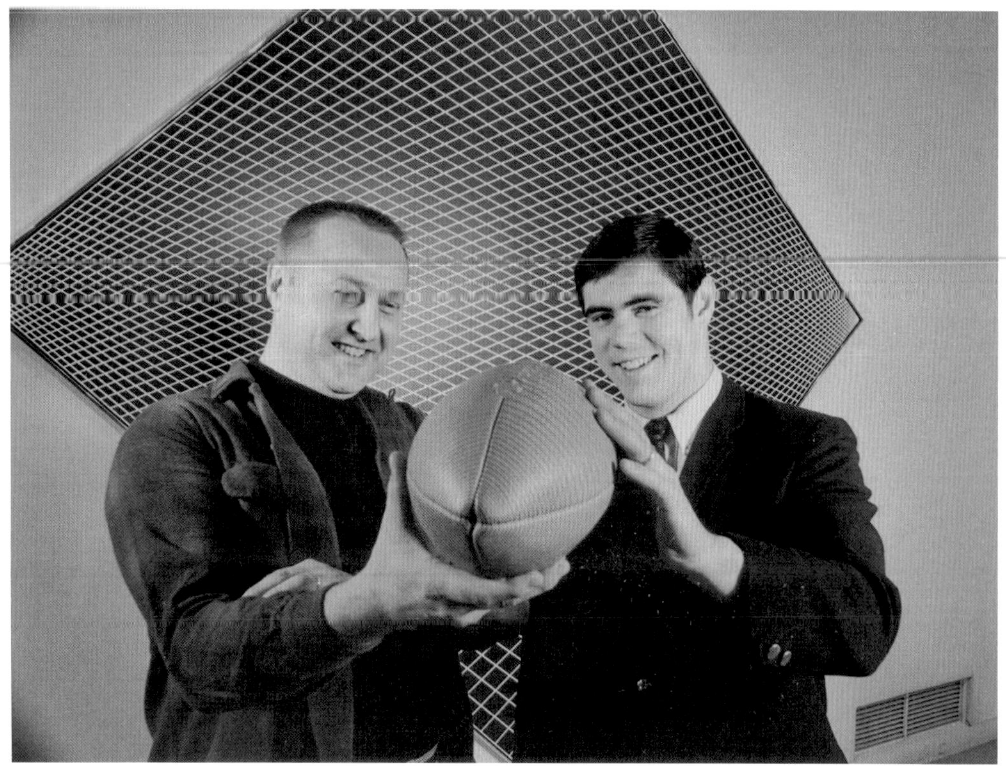

Fig. 24

Richard Anuszkiewicz presenting Steve Luxford, captain of the Dartmouth football team, with the Op football, November 1967. Dartmouth College Library. Photo by Matthew Wysocki.

a textbook and were all familiar with it. Bernard gave a lecture, but he also conducted some of the classes as a visitor, and many people visited his studio. I think Robert Vickrey, who has a very good reputation as a solid painter. He again had a following. Many people in Hanover said, "Oh, I have a painting of his," and they would introduce him to other people. Some of these names were known. Then I think Gabor Peterdi was very popular, both as a printmaker and painter, and he put on many demonstrations and many people visited him.

TR: Did he actually demonstrate printmaking techniques?

MW: Yes. And now, of course, Olivia Parker. Her show is tremendous, over ninety photographs. She gave a lecture to the public which was standing-room only. Then we have the Delta Delta Delta sorority, who wanted a meeting with her. That was a lot of fun, because she took them into the studio, and they had a chance to see her work. And then last night there was a Class of '88 [function]. They all showed up, and we served refreshments in the museum. They all had a chance to meet her and ask questions.

TR: Have all the artists been so gracious in their willingness to meet different types of people on campus, because you have people in the community, you have doctors, you have faculty, you have sorority members, as you just said, you have art students, and you have art historians like myself.

MW: Well, I think that the exchange we've had with the society of Hanover has been very great, and of course the artists always love the doctors, because the doctors may come over and want to buy a painting. They may be our greatest patrons. I think [the artists] like the mix that they've found in the Dartmouth community. And also, this is a very rich area where you'll find people who have retired, or people who have studios here, and they will come by to meet with these people. There are many wonderful people working in the hills, so you don't hear about them when they are so private, but once an artist comes, they will want to identify themselves. One of the great drawing cards was that every artist who came here, somehow I would bring up the name of Ivan Albright, and they'd say, "Is Ivan Albright here? I do want to meet him." This was that very special occasion, where they would get a visit to Ivan's studio, and he and his wife, Josephine, were very kind and gracious, and they always had a marvelous visit. And then there were return visits. They were quite amazed at the type of artistic life they could have. Some artists had been holed up in their studios, so they were not used to dealing with people, but within two or three weeks they liked it. They liked the type of exchange. The students asked them very good questions and did great favors for them, and helped them, sometimes serving as assistants.

TR: I guess for the artists-in-residence who were at work in the Hopkins Center, the center itself must have been a great resource for them, with all the cultural events there, week in and week out.

MW: Yes. Like Olivia Parker said the other day, "It's so easy for me. I can just run across the street and get hardware. I can run over to the Hood and see the Rembrandt show. I can see a production, I can see a dance group." So, the access to everything is very simple, and I think this is why the Hop has been such a popular place, and why attitudes are changing. Many graduates who were here prior to the Hop come back and say, "Boy, I wish we had this institution when I was a student." Winters were very lonely, and there's not much you can do. Now you had not only a great social gathering place, but a very nice art activity going on.

TR: Speaking of that, it would be interesting to hear you talk about trials and tribulations and the fun of putting on an exhibition on a very regular basis in the Jaffe-Friede [Gallery]. Year in and year out, it's a very hectic schedule, and there must be many memories that you have pulling exhibitions together, because it's always a different story, I'm sure.

MW: Well, it's always a trying situation. We really don't have the type of facilities for proper storage, for proper preparation, so we always try to encourage artists to bring things which are already framed or matted to make it much easier for us. Sometimes it worked and sometimes it didn't. We had problems with lighting, or with water coming through the ceiling, but somehow we did it. But the strength of the Jaffe-Friede and the Strauss galleries is the fact that they are on the main road to the center of the Hopkins Center, so everyone comes in to look at the shows. The great windows lure them in, and then we have many repeaters who come back and back and back. But then I think they continue from there to go on to the Hood, because you can enter it through that area. So you get a nice complex of facilities for the arts. The Hood has been a great addition to it.

TR: The Jaffe-Friede, to put it kindly, has got a flowing shape. It must have presented some difficulties at times, even to the enterprising exhibition installer.

MW: Well, you know there's that curved wall. You think it's solid, but I think there's about six inches between the cloth and the wall in the background, so it's always a problem to find a long enough spike to drive into the wall and get the painting up. Yes, that's a major concern. But I think it's a very valuable space.

TR: I'd like to end with two questions, asking you to look back over the last twenty-five years, and summarize where you feel the Artist-in-Residence Program has been, and what it has meant to the Hopkins Center and to the College.

MW: Well, I think that its greatest service has been that it is not a teaching appointment. The very fact that the artist came in as an independent, and he was available to many, many students. There were many students who fell in love with the work of an artist like Peter Milton, and began collecting and now have very distinguished collections. This has been an area where we could start people thinking about art and enjoying art. That is far-reaching. It affects the alumni group and I think it will have a great effect on future collectors.

TR: Okay, here's the crystal ball question: You'll be retiring in two years, after a very long, distinguished career at Dartmouth, doing many, many things—being chair of the Visual Studies Department, as well as being responsible for the Artist-in-Residence Program, directly responsible for over a generation. Where do you see things going from here with the Artist-in-Residence Program, and what would you like to see as its future?

MW: As long as there are artists painting in the world, and I think that there are always great people out there, I think that they should be brought here to Dartmouth to share their experience with the students. And I think it won't be any different. We'll get different names, different attitudes, new experimentation, new concepts, and new ideas. I think it's great that this can be brought up to Hanover where students can see the latest going-on. And sometimes it's popular, and sometimes it isn't. I think some of the work of Judd, they didn't understand the instructions, but after a while they have a better understanding and a better appreciation, so I think the role of the Artist-in-Residence Program is to instruct people culturally in what is happening in the arts, and that the scene is ever changing. It's never going to be constant,

and this is the exciting part of it. I would like to see it continue that way.

TR: I suppose at the very bottom of it all, it teaches people about the role of the artist in society. It brings it close to home, right into the Hopkins Center.

MW: Yes, and I think that as far as many students are concerned—"Can I make a living as an artist?" And here they have a chance to meet the artist who is making a living, and who is very successful, and has a way of life. I think this gives them more confidence to perhaps take the chance at becoming a painter or a sculptor.

TR: Or perhaps, as you said before, have the chance to become a collector.

MW: Yes, why not invest in art? And why only donate to sports centers? Eventually we hope that some of these great alumni donors will give their collections to Dartmouth! This is always the major plan.

TR: I knew the plug was behind this somewhere!

CATALOGUE

Please note that this section has been arranged aesthetically,
not strictly chronologically, and it is intended to be complemented
by the index of artists on page 140.

Contributors

Juliette M. Bianco (JMB)

Emily Shubert Burke (ESB)

Mary K. Coffey (MKC)

Kristin Monahan Garcia (KMG)

Stephen Gilchrist (SG)

Katherine W. Hart (KWH)

Amelia B. Kahl (ABK)

Brian P. Kennedy (BPK)

Barbara J. MacAdam (BJM)

Sarah G. Powers (SGP)

Joseph Sanchez (JS)

Michael R. Taylor (MRT)

Barbara Thompson (BT)

Abigail Weir (AW)

Phoebe Wolfskill (PW)

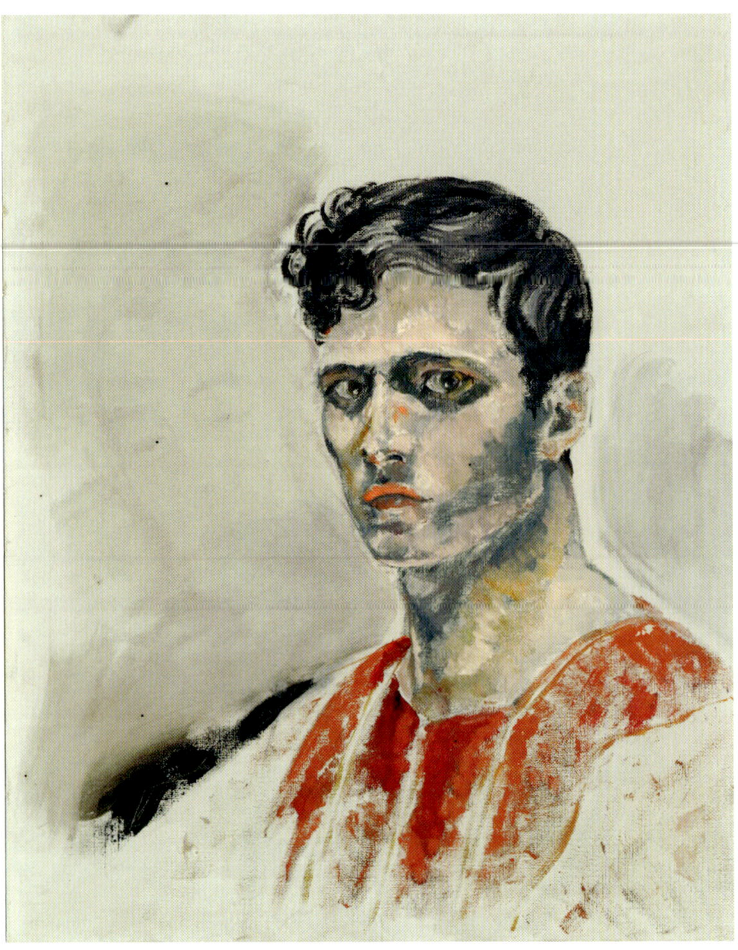

CARLOS SÁNCHEZ
American, born in Guatemala,
1898–1997
Self-Portrait, about 1923
Oil on canvas, 25¹/₂ x 20¹/₄ in.
Gift of Cristina Falla de
Echeverria; 2012.68
© Christina Falla de Echeverría

Carlos Sánchez, Dartmouth Class of 1923, was the College's first artist-in-residence and helped to found the Studio Art Department. The seventh of ten children, Sánchez was born in Guatemala City on October 31, 1898. He was fluent in English and enrolled at Dartmouth College after World War I to study engineering on a Pan American Institute scholarship. He enjoyed fraternity life as a member of Chi Phi and later recalled the inspiration and friendship of John T. Dallas, then chaplain of the College and later the Episcopal Bishop of New Hampshire. Devoutly Catholic as a teenager, Sánchez struggled with his religious beliefs at Dartmouth, where his professors questioned his foundation of faith. In a 1988 interview, Sánchez recalled that these "brilliant academicians" left religion out of their classes. "In their minds you could not be truly educated and religious at the same time."[1] This crisis of faith is expressed in the brooding, angst-ridden *Self-Portrait* that Sánchez completed as an undergraduate at Dartmouth. "I don't think I have ever suffered as much as during that struggle for my faith. That goes deep, you know. I hated God."[2] Painting became an important outlet for the artist during this period, continuing an interest in art that began when he was a young boy in Guatemala. "I loved to draw as a child. My mother told me that when I was a small boy I drew a picture of my little brother in the sand, using a stick. However, [at that time] art was not something you pursued as a career."[3] Following graduation he moved to Germany to study medicine at the University of Berlin, having been inspired by the work of medical missionaries in his homeland. However, Sánchez was also fully aware of Berlin's reputation

during the Weimar era as a hotbed of avant-garde activity and knew he could continue his art education there. "You couldn't help getting a rich, cultural education in Germany," he later reminisced.[4] In the mid-1920s Sánchez returned to New England to enroll in a master's degree program in architecture at Yale University, which he completed in 1928. Sánchez then moved to New York, working briefly as a junior draftsman for Shreve, Lamb, and Harmon architects, who were at that time designing New York's famous Empire State Building.

Although he enjoyed utilizing his significant drawing skills on these building projects, Sánchez recognized that his passion was for painting rather than architecture. In 1930 he moved to Mexico and worked as an assistant to Diego Rivera on a fresco mural on the second floor of the Palace of Cortés at Cuernavaca and another, entitled *The Epic of the Mexican People*, in the stairwell of the National Palace in Mexico City. Working as Rivera's assistant on these celebrated murals established Sánchez's reputation as a painter, and in 1931 he returned to Dartmouth College as its first artist-in-residence, known at that time as the College's "Fellow in Art" and funded by the Rockefeller family. During his yearlong residency Sánchez completed *Young Man with Bird*. This painting, which can be considered the artist's masterpiece, reflects the impact of his recent sojourn in Mexico, especially the work of Diego Rivera, Juan Soriano, and Frida Kahlo. In comparison to the sketchy and tentative *Self-Portrait*, *Young Man with Bird* exhibits the technical accomplishment and maturity that Sánchez had gained through his training and experience since graduating from Dartmouth

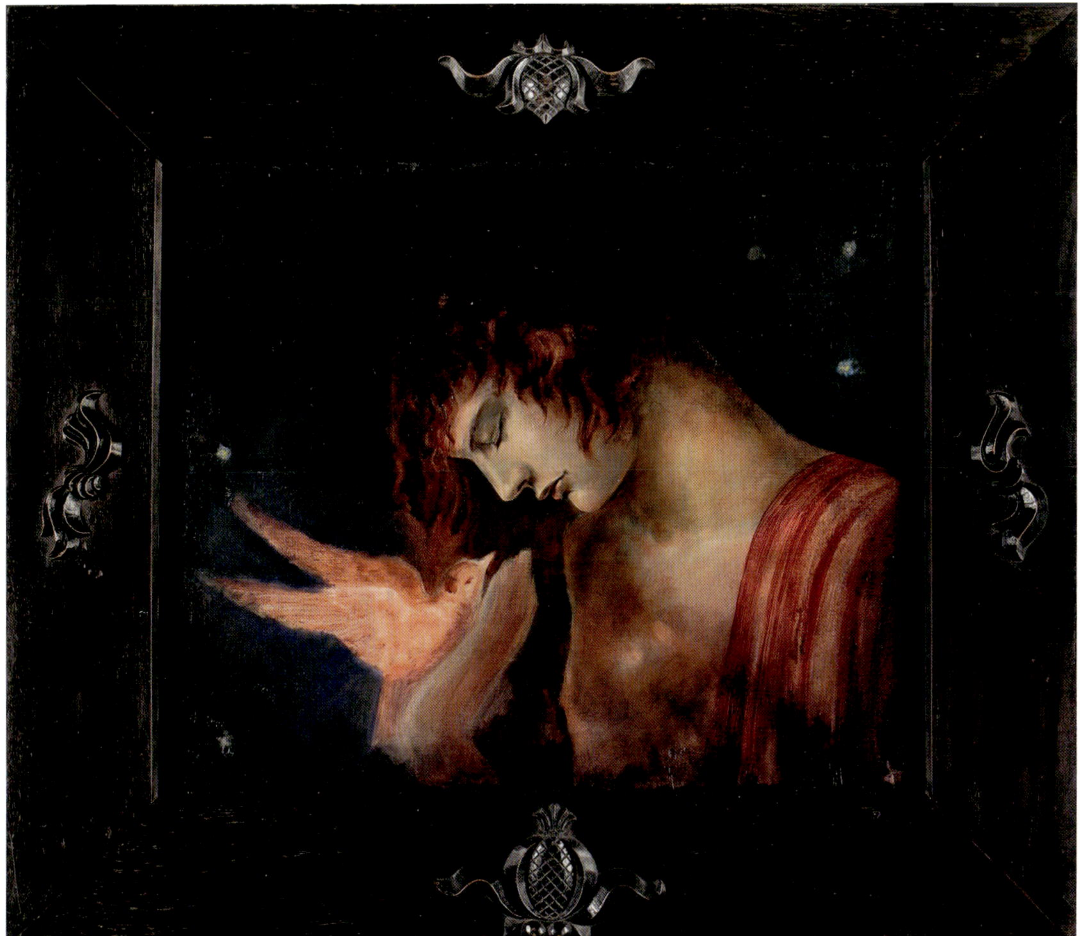

in 1923. A young, red-haired man embraces a glowing orange bird, while framed against a star-filled night sky. His closed eyes suggest a religious experience, although the ultimate meaning of the painting remains unknown. The artist designed and made his own frame for the work, again underscoring its importance in his oeuvre. After the end of his residency at Dartmouth, Sánchez remained on campus to help the second artist-in-residence, the noted Mexican muralist José Clemente Orozco, paint *The Epic of American Civilization* in the Reserve Room of the new Baker Library. His earlier experience of working as Rivera's assistant in Mexico, along with his fluency in Spanish and knowledge of Dartmouth's history and culture, must have been of great help to Orozco during his two-year period as artist-in-residence from 1932 to 1934. Although Orozco's fame as one of the leading mural painters of his generation far eclipsed that of Carlos Sánchez, the Guatemalan-born artist nonetheless left a remarkable legacy at Dartmouth as the first artist-in-residence, from 1931 to 1932, which we honor through this exhibition.

MRT

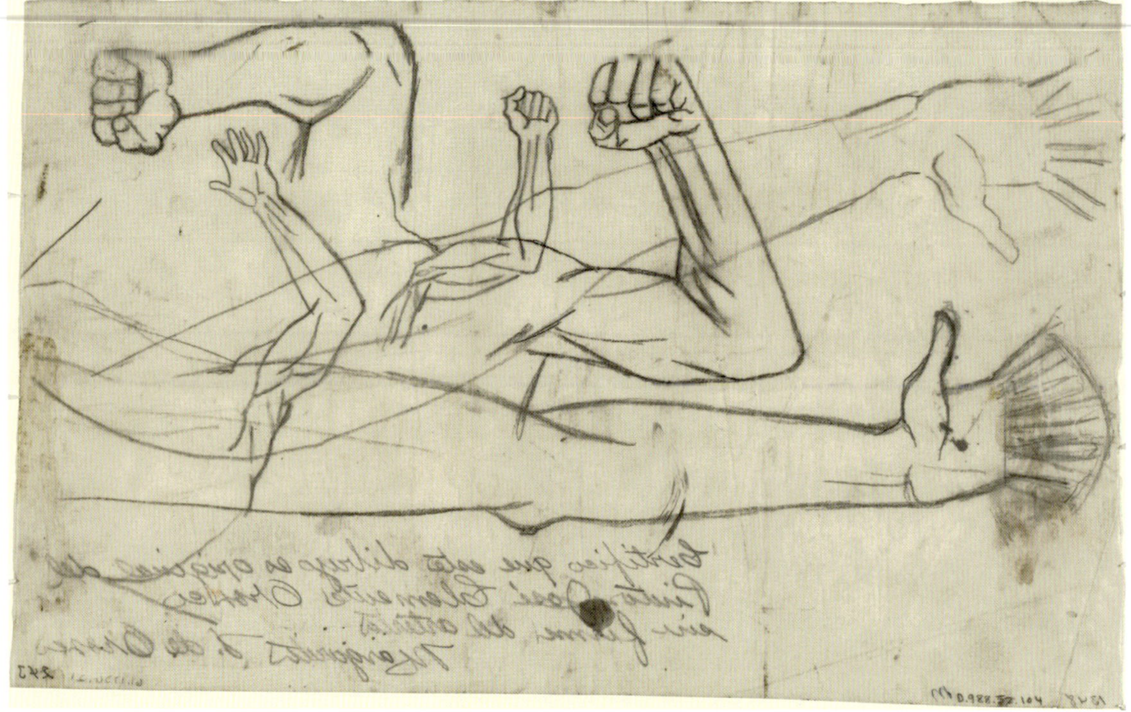

JOSÉ CLEMENTE OROZCO
Mexican, 1883–1949
*Study for The Departure of
Quetzalcoatl (Panel 7) for The
Epic of American Civilization,*
1932–34
Graphite on tracing paper,
7 x 11¼ in.
Purchased through gifts from
Kirsten and Peter Bedford, Class
of 1989P; Jane and Raphael
Bernstein; Walter Burke, Class
of 1944; Mr. and Mrs. Richard D.
Lombard, Class of 1953; Nathan
Pearson, Class of 1932; David V.
Picker, Class of 1953; Rodman C.
Rockefeller, Class of 1954;
Kenneth Roman Jr., Class of
1952; and Adolph Weil Jr.,
Class of 1935; D.988.52.104

Between 1932 and 1934, the acclaimed Mexican Muralist José Clemente Orozco resided at Dartmouth College, planning and executing the major mural cycle for Baker Library entitled *The Epic of American Civilization*. The idea for commissioning a mural by Orozco formed as early as 1929, after the completion of the new building for the art department, Carpenter Hall. Two members of the art faculty, Artemas S. Packard and Churchill P. Lathrop, began persuading the college administration to invite one of the "Big Three" Mexican muralists to campus to paint a mural for the new building. Both professors preferred Orozco over the better known Diego Rivera for this commission, so they organized several exhibitions of Orozco's prints and drawings in the galleries of Carpenter Hall in order to make his work better known in New England. They also made contact with Orozco's New York dealer, Alma Reed, who helped convince the artist of the importance of the commission.

Nelson Rockefeller, Dartmouth Class of 1930, had been a student of Lathrop, and his mother, Abby Aldrich Rockefeller, set up a tutorial fund for special educational initiatives. These funds were used to invite Orozco to campus to deliver a series of lecture-demonstrations on fresco painting. During his visit from March 18 to 20, 1932, Orozco painted a fresco in the corridor connecting Carpenter Hall to the library. The work, *Man Released from the Mechanistic to the Creative Life*, was meant to be the first panel of a possible mural cycle on the theme of the Greek mechanical genius, Daedalus. After this preliminary visit, Orozco and members of the art department set their sights on a larger and more visible location for a mural, the reserve reading room (now called the Orozco Room) on the ground floor of the library, which contained a large, empty expanse of wall. By May, Orozco had abandoned the idea of a mural based on Greek mythology, and instead planned a historical cycle specific to the Americas. A contract between the College and Orozco was signed on June 9, 1932, and the artist spent the next two years as artist-in-residence at Dartmouth. On February 13, 1934, Orozco completed, signed, and dated the mural; he left Hanover six days later.

During his tenure at Dartmouth, Orozco created more than two hundred drawings in preparation for the final mural. The Hood Museum of Art's extensive collection of these drawings provides a survey of the artist's working method, from studies of and deliberations over small details of mural, to the execution of final compositions in which entire panels are plotted out for enlargement and transfer to the plaster walls. This selection of drawings focuses on the facial expressions and dramatic gestures of Orozco's great mural cycle. The faces and hands of Orozco's subjects play important roles in his narrative as it unfolds over the cycle. The characters in the mural, like actors on a stage, were meant to be seen from below and from a reasonable distance, yet communicate clear emotional impact and intensity.

SGP

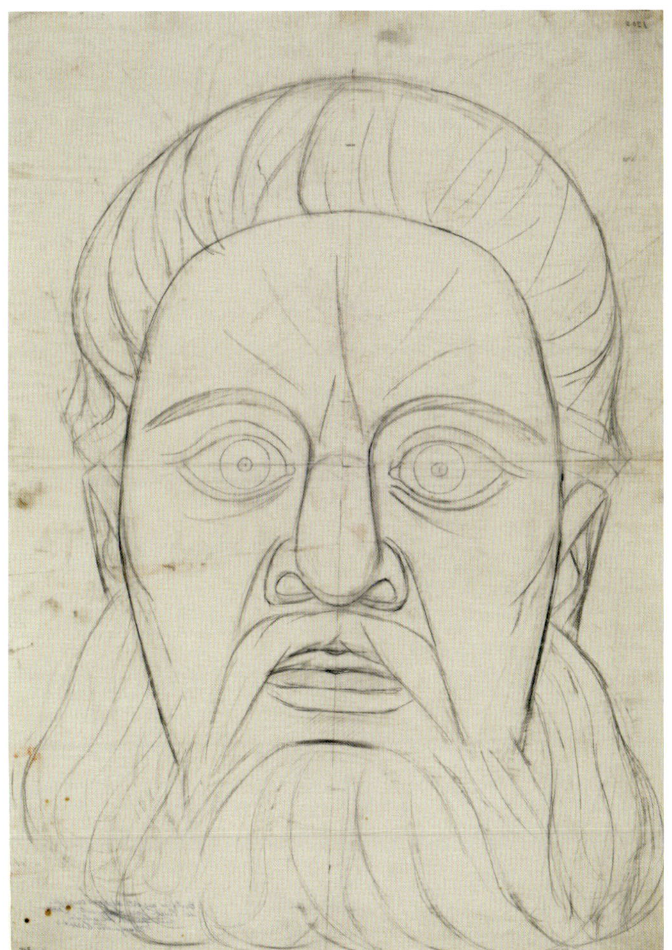

4

JOSÉ CLEMENTE OROZCO

Study of Head for The Coming of Quetzalcoatl (Panel 5) for The Epic of American Civilization, 1932–34
Graphite on tracing paper, 29³/₄ x 20¹/₂ in.
Purchased through gifts from Kirsten and Peter Bedford, Class of 1989P; Jane and Raphael Bernstein; Walter Burke, Class of 1944; Mr. and Mrs. Richard D. Lombard, Class of 1953; Nathan Pearson, Class of 1932; David V. Picker, Class of 1953; Rodman C. Rockefeller, Class of 1954; Kenneth Roman Jr., Class of 1952; and Adolph Weil Jr., Class of 1935; D.988.52.36

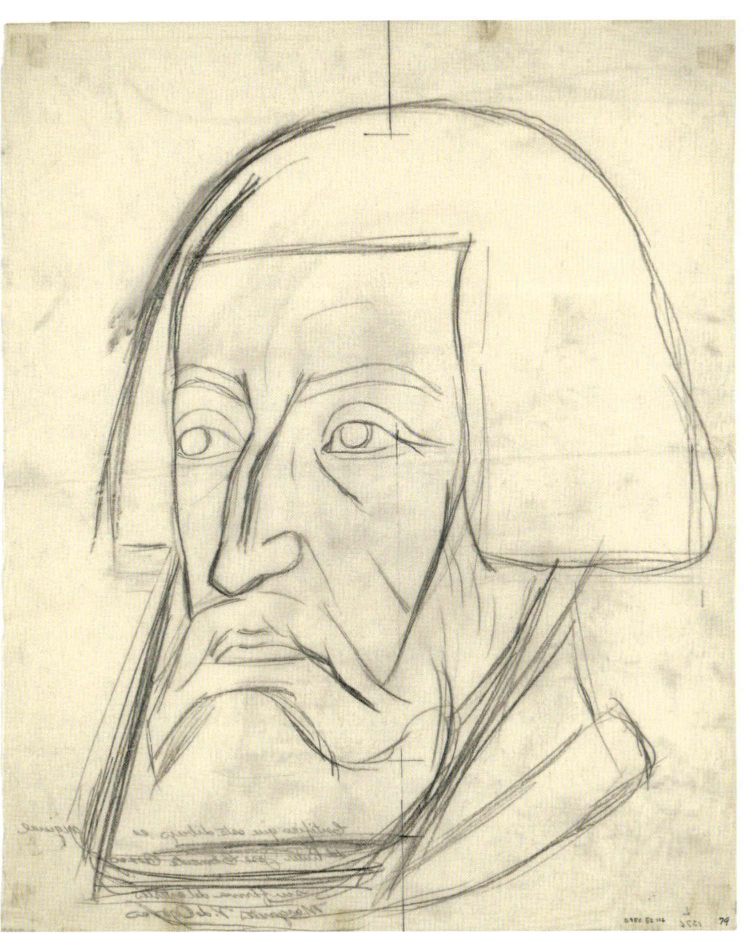

5

JOSÉ CLEMENTE OROZCO

Study for Cortez and the Cross (Panel 13) for The Epic of American Civilization, 1932–34
Graphite on tracing paper, 18³/₄ x 14¹³/₁₆ in.
Purchased through gifts from Kirsten and Peter Bedford, Class of 1989P; Jane and Raphael Bernstein; Walter Burke, Class of 1944; Mr. and Mrs. Richard D. Lombard, Class of 1953; Nathan Pearson, Class of 1932; David V. Picker, Class of 1953; Rodman C. Rockefeller, Class of 1954; Kenneth Roman Jr., Class of 1952; and Adolph Weil Jr., Class of 1935; D.988.52.116

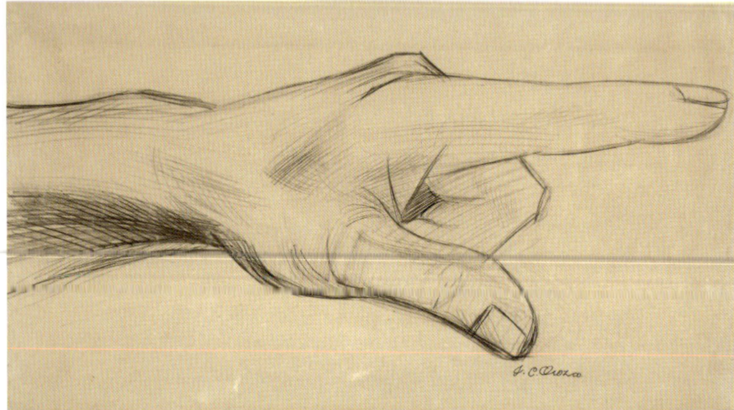

6

JOSÉ CLEMENTE OROZCO
Study for Quetzalcoatl's Hand for The Departure of Quetzalcoatl (Panel 7) for The Epic of American Civilization, 1932–34
Graphite on paper, 11^{7}/$_{8}$ x 22^{1}/$_{4}$ in.
Gift of Adolph Weil Jr., Class of 1935, and Robert S. Weil, Class of 1940, in honor of Churchill P. Lathrop; D.978.19

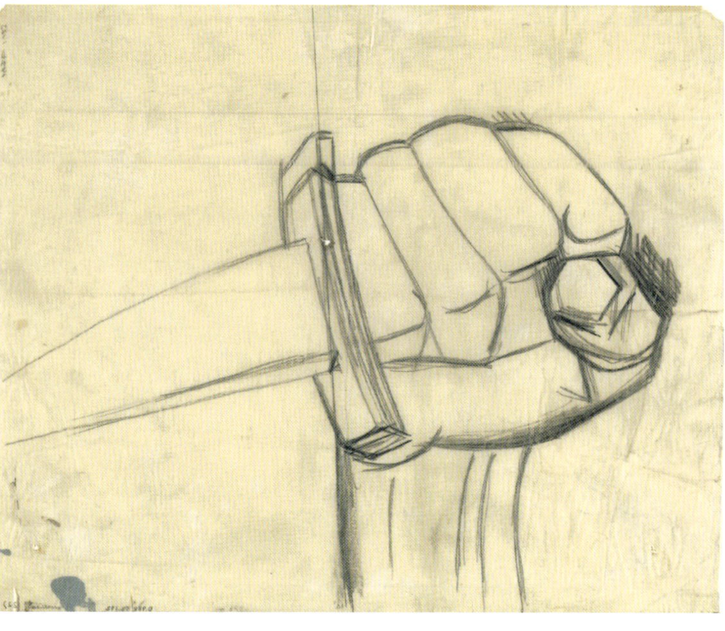

7

JOSÉ CLEMENTE OROZCO
Study of Hand for Hispano-America (Panel 16) for The Epic of American Civilization, 1932–34
Graphite on tracing paper, 16^{5}/$_{8}$ x 13^{7}/$_{8}$ in.
Purchased through gifts from Kirsten and Peter Bedford, Class of 1989P; Jane and Raphael Bernstein; Walter Burke, Class of 1944; Mr. and Mrs. Richard D. Lombard, Class of 1953; Nathan Pearson, Class of 1932; David V. Picker, Class of 1953; Rodman C. Rockefeller, Class of 1954; Kenneth Roman Jr., Class of 1952; and Adolph Weil Jr., Class of 1935; D.988.52.142

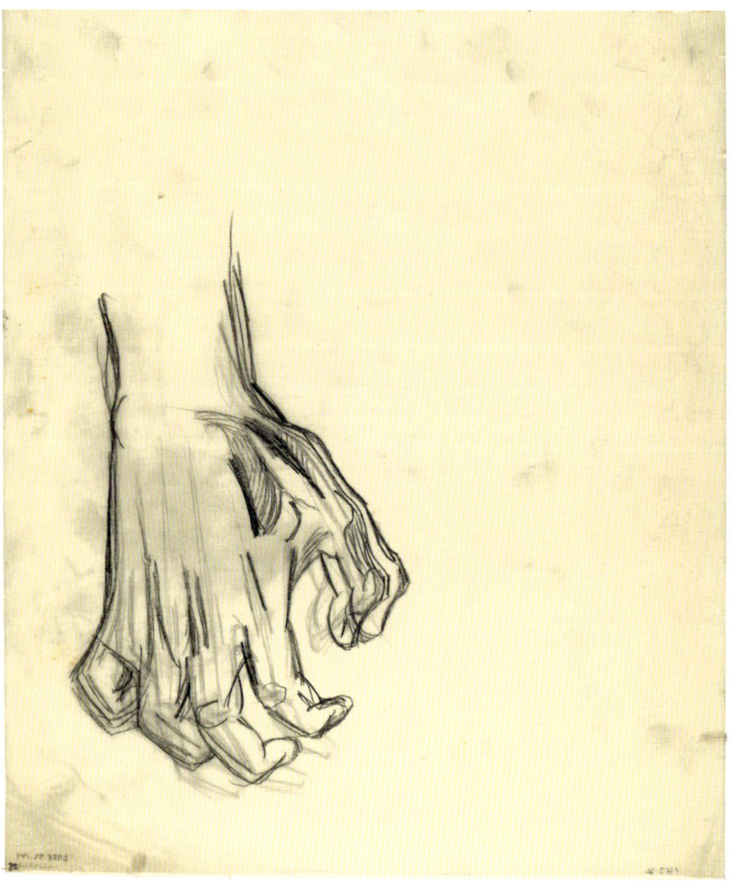

8

JOSÉ CLEMENTE OROZCO
Study of Hand for Hispano-America (Panel 16) for The Epic of American Civilization, 1932–34
Graphite on tracing paper, 16^{1}/$_{2}$ x 13^{7}/$_{8}$ in.
Purchased through gifts from Kirsten and Peter Bedford, Class of 1989P; Jane and Raphael Bernstein; Walter Burke, Class of 1944; Mr. and Mrs. Richard D. Lombard, Class of 1953; Nathan Pearson, Class of 1932; David V. Picker, Class of 1953; Rodman C. Rockefeller, Class of 1954; Kenneth Roman Jr., Class of 1952; and Adolph Weil Jr., Class of 1935; D.988.52.149

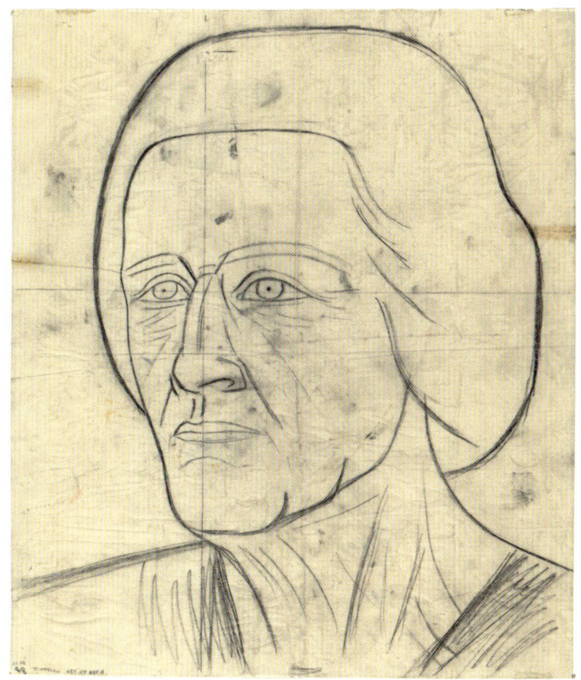

9

JOSÉ CLEMENTE OROZCO
Study of Female Head for Anglo-America (Panel 15) for The Epic of American Civilization, 1932–34
Graphite on tracing paper, sheet: 16⅝ x 14 in.
Purchased through gifts from Kirsten and Peter Bedford, Class of 1989P; Jane and Raphael Bernstein; Walter Burke, Class of 1944; Mr. and Mrs. Richard D. Lombard, Class of 1953; Nathan Pearson, Class of 1932; David V. Picker, Class of 1953; Rodman C. Rockefeller, Class of 1954; Kenneth Roman Jr., Class of 1952; and Adolph Weil Jr., Class of 1935; D.988.52.133

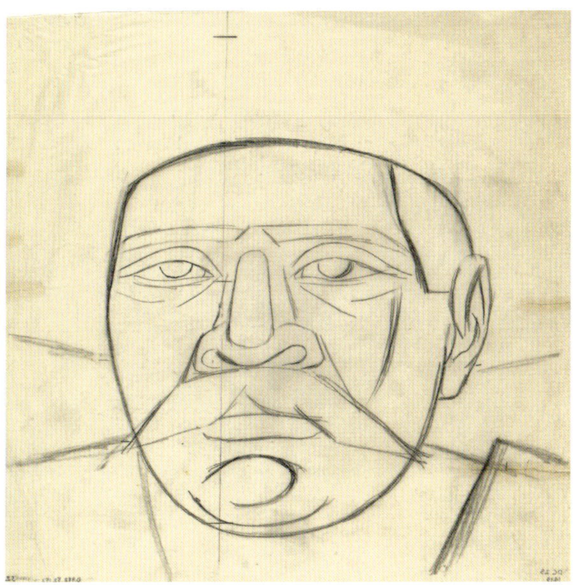

10

JOSÉ CLEMENTE OROZCO
Study of Man's Head with Mustache for Hispano-America (Panel 16) for The Epic of American Civilization, 1932–34
Graphite on tracing paper, 14 x 14 in.
Purchased through gifts from Kirsten and Peter Bedford, Class of 1989P; Jane and Raphael Bernstein; Walter Burke, Class of 1944; Mr. and Mrs. Richard D. Lombard, Class of 1953; Nathan Pearson, Class of 1932; David V. Picker, Class of 1953; Rodman C. Rockefeller, Class of 1954; Kenneth Roman Jr., Class of 1952; and Adolph Weil Jr., Class of 1935; D.988.52.153

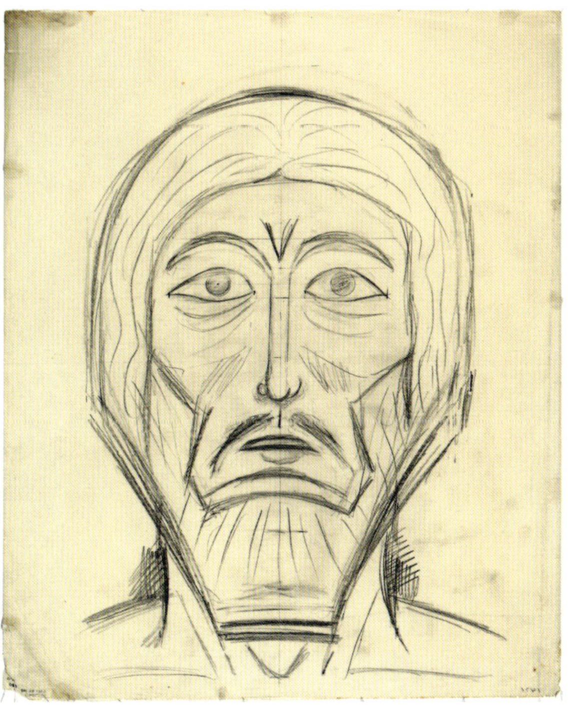

11

JOSÉ CLEMENTE OROZCO
Study of Head for Modern Migration of the Spirit (Panel 21) for The Epic of American Civilization, 1932–34
Graphite on tracing paper, 23⁷/₁₆ x 18¹¹/₁₆ in.
Purchased through gifts from Kirsten and Peter Bedford, Class of 1989P; Jane and Raphael Bernstein; Walter Burke, Class of 1944; Mr. and Mrs. Richard D. Lombard, Class of 1953; Nathan Pearson, Class of 1932; David V. Picker, Class of 1953; Rodman C. Rockefeller, Class of 1954; Kenneth Roman Jr., Class of 1952; and Adolph Weil Jr., Class of 1935; D.988.52.198

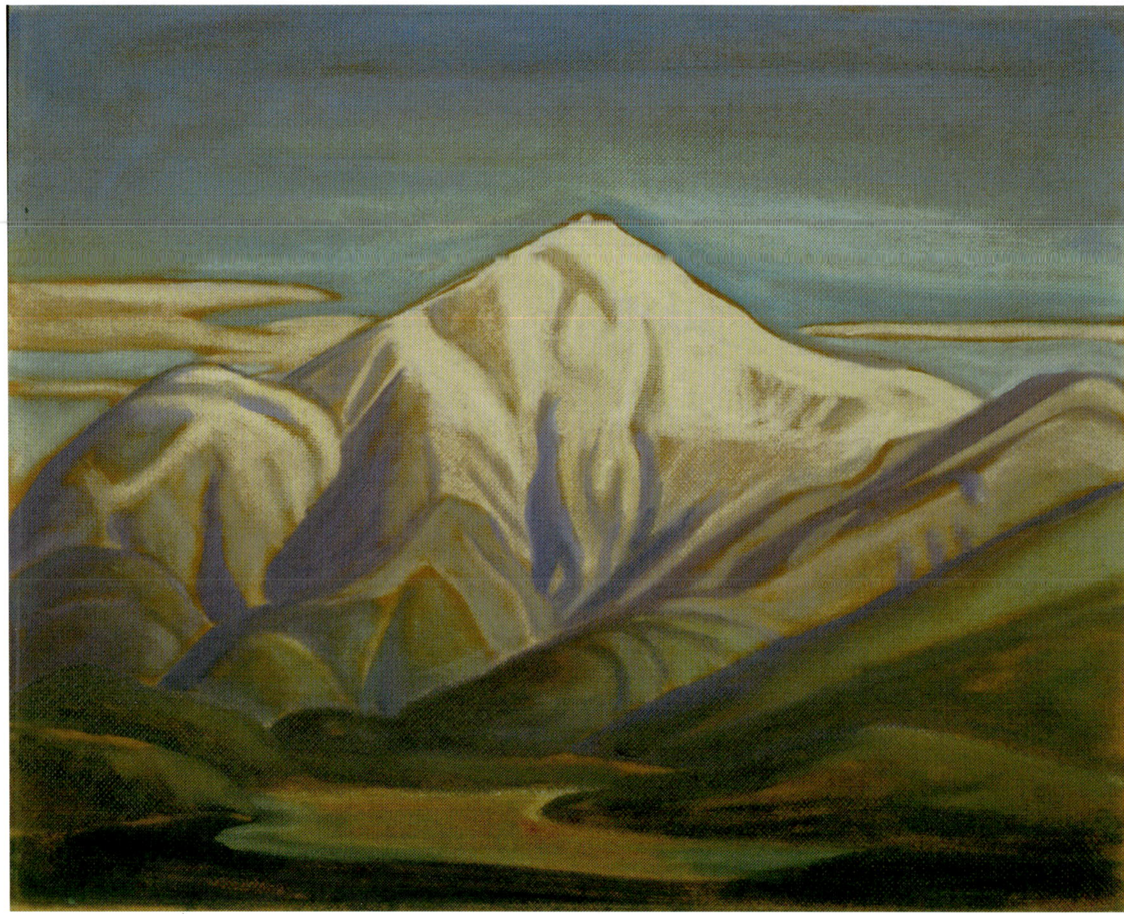

LAWREN STEWART HARRIS
Canadian, 1885–1970
Mount Washington, about 1934
Oil on Masonite, 18 x 22 in.
Gift of Ethel Scott Stewart
through the Estate of Pennington
Haile, Class of 1924; P.983.8
© Family of Lawren S. Harris

12

A scandalous divorce prompted painter Lawren Harris to abruptly leave Toronto—where he had built his reputation as Canada's most acclaimed modernist—for the United States in July 1934. He and his new wife, Bess Housser—also a painter—arrived a few months later in Hanover, New Hampshire, where Harris's uncle, William Kilborne Stewart, was a professor at Dartmouth College. The couple expected to stay in Hanover no more than a few months, but the combination of a welcoming, progressive art department, the opportunity to paint in a new studio while serving as an unpaid artist-in-residence for Dartmouth, and breathtaking mountain scenery nearby proved winning incentives to extend their stay—which they did, for four years. Shortly after his arrival Harris found release from an almost two-year artist's block and underwent a dramatic stylistic conversion, moving from a schematic, semi-abstract realism based in landscape, to a hard-edged nonrepresentational abstraction that would remain his primary focus thereafter.

Based on one of the many drawings that Harris made in December 1934, *Mount Washington* may be his first New Hampshire painting and points to the White Mountains as a powerful source of artistic and spiritual inspiration. Bess Harris shared his enthusiasm for the region and extolled its virtues to a friend in Toronto: "It is a beauty spot in winter, the whole place drenched in it—the hill tops almost Himalayan in character!"[1] Within the context of the mystical, vaguely Buddhist-inspired precepts of theosophy, in which she and Harris shared keen interest, the world's highest mountain range represented the ultimate source of spiritual knowledge. While not the Himalayas, Mount Washington would have held similar associations, since nowhere else in New Hampshire does the earth reach so deeply into the heavens. In his painted tribute to the peak, he used the rough, absorbent side of a Masonite board for his support, thereby giving the work a soft, atmospheric appearance. Rippling contours evoke the peak's muscular form and contained inner force, while the central placement of its white summit highlights the most elevated point of contact between earth and sky, the profane and the sacred. Though modest in scale and reflecting his earlier stark landscape style rather than the pure abstractions that would soon follow, *Mount Washington* marks an early expression of Harris's renewed artistic ambitions, which would find greater realization during his remaining stay in Hanover.

BJM

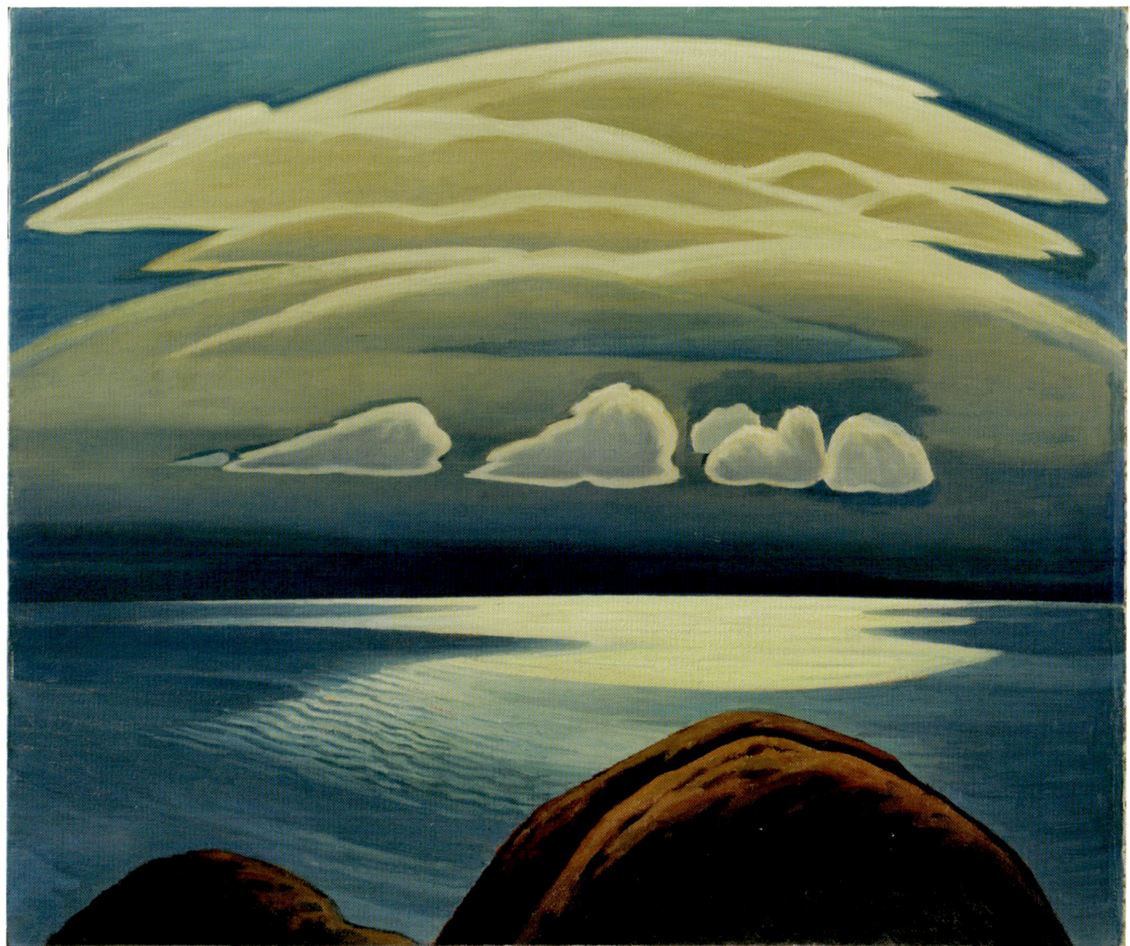

13

LAWREN STEWART HARRIS
Lake Superior, about 1948,
additions 1951
Oil on canvas, 34^{5}/$_{16}$ x 40^{1}/$_{2}$ in.
Gift of the artist, Lawren
S. Harris, in memory of his
uncle, William Kilborne
Stewart, through the Friends of
Dartmouth Library; P.951.77
© Family of Lawren S. Harris

Lake Superior represents a rare instance of Lawren Harris returning to the schematic topographic realism that won him fame in the 1920s, but which he had abandoned for pure geometric abstraction in the mid-1930s, while serving as an informal artist-in-residence at Dartmouth (see cat. 12). Harris's conversion to nonrepresentational abstraction deepened when, after leaving Hanover in 1938, he spent two years in Santa Fe, New Mexico. There, he and his wife, Bess Housser, joined the Transcendental Painting Group, whose members also found pure abstraction an ideal mode of expression for their mystical, theosophist-derived spirituality. The Harrises might have stayed in Santa Fe indefinitely were it not for wartime Canadian regulations that limited access to bank accounts from outside the country. Reliant on those funds, they returned to Canada in late 1940, settling in Vancouver, where Harris continued to paint but devoted increasing time to his leadership role in various arts organizations.

It is not known why in *Lake Superior* and a few other works from the late 1940s Harris abandoned nonrepresentational abstraction and returned to his earlier Northern landscape subjects and semi-abstracted manner. Around 1944 he retrieved from storage many early paintings that he had left in Toronto when he departed for the United States in 1934. Perhaps the experience of encountering this work anew rekindled Harris's interest and pride in his earlier achievements. Among the older canvases was his small *Lake Superior* (about 1923), which he copied almost exactly in creating this much larger composition of the same title in about 1948.[1] In 1951 he apparently did "a little work on" the painting before sending it to the College as a gift in memory of his uncle, Dartmouth professor William Kilborne Stewart.[2] This bold, magisterial composition serves as a summation of Harris's theosophist belief in the unity and order of the universe and his desire to inspire a sense of elevated spirituality in the viewer. In this and his other spare landscapes he used light as a metaphor for pure spirituality, and specific colors and shapes as indicators of emotions and states of being. Here the repeated arc-like shapes representing rocks, clouds, and reflections on water integrate the composition visually and invoke Harris's belief in the underlying harmony of the universe. The color blue, associated with faith and spirituality, predominates, while the radiant golden light suggests a transcendent presence.

BJM

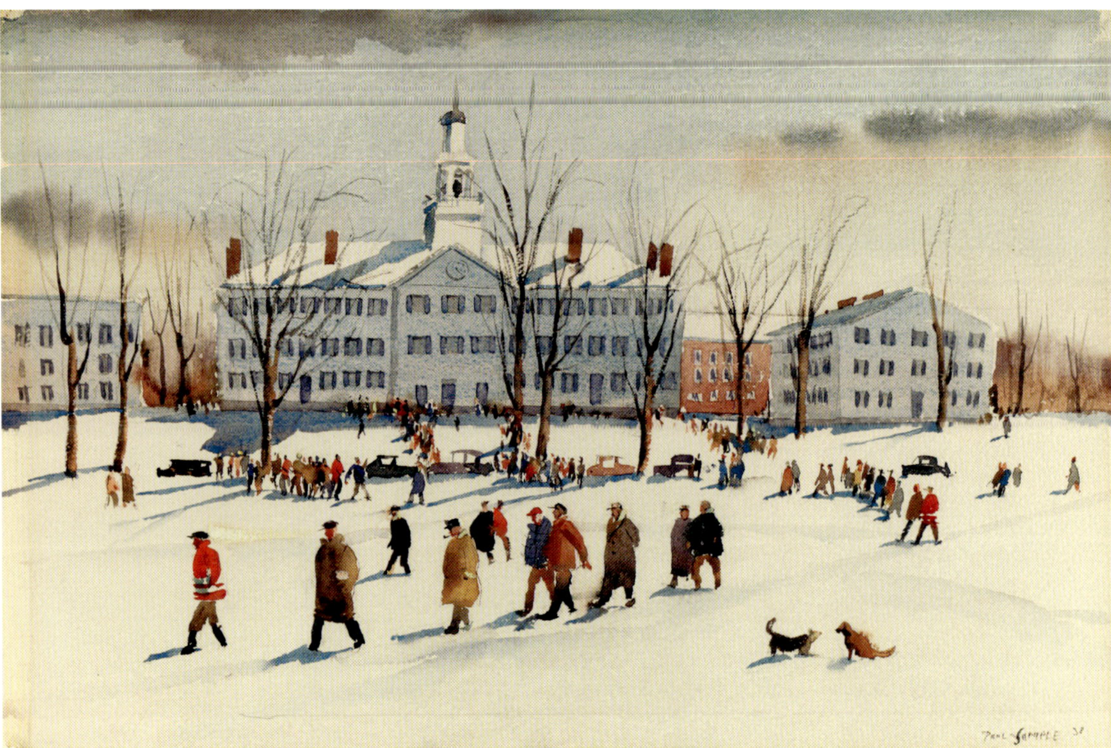

PAUL SAMPLE
American, 1896–1974
Between Classes, 1938
Watercolor on wove Arches
paper, 15⅛ x 22¾ in.
Gift of Frederick B. Whittemore,
Class of 1953, Tuck 1954; 2012.22

Paul Sample, Dartmouth Class of 1920, was by far Dartmouth's longest-serving artist-in-residence, having held the position from September 1938 until 1962. During that period he maintained a studio on campus and conducted informal art classes for students and community members. Sample's choice of profession had been late in coming. As a Dartmouth student he took greatest pride in his reputation as a heavyweight boxing champion and jazz musician, and did not take up painting until 1923, during an extended recovery from tuberculosis. Following his recuperation, he studied briefly at the Greenleaf Art School in New York and at the Otis Art Institute in Los Angeles in 1925. By the following year he had begun teaching art at the University of Southern California and by the mid-1930s had been appointed chairman of the university's art department and was exhibiting his work nationally. When Dartmouth invited Sample to return to his alma mater as artist-in-residence, the prospect appealed to him both professionally and personally. He had tired of teaching formally and in 1928 had married a Vermonter, Sylvia Howland, from Montpelier. The many summers the couple spent in the state through the 1930s had deepened his attachment to the region. Paul Sample went on to spend the rest of his life in the Upper Connecticut River Valley, where he became a celebrated painter of northern New England's land and people.

Dating to 1938, *Between Classes* is one of the earliest works Sample created as Dartmouth's artist-in-residence and an early example of the winter compositions for which he would gain particular acclaim. He had honed his talent for watercolor during his years in southern California, where he worked alongside some of the best-known "California-style" watercolorists, including Barse Miller and Millard Sheets. Once in New England, he continued his watercolor practice, but adapted his subjects and palette to the region's rugged topography, rural population, and varied seasons. In this work he captures the bustle of students and professors traversing the snow-covered college Green between classes. The arcing line of brightly colored coats enlivens the composition and leads our eye back toward the College's most revered historic buildings, Dartmouth Hall and its flanking classroom buildings Thornton and Wentworth Halls. As he often did, Sample injected into the composition an element of humor through the inclusion of animals—in this case two dogs investigating one another—that echo the behavior of their human counterparts. Through this image and at least three other watercolors that he painted of this scene in various seasons, Sample paid affectionate homage to both the social and academic aspects of collegiate life at Dartmouth.[1]

BJM

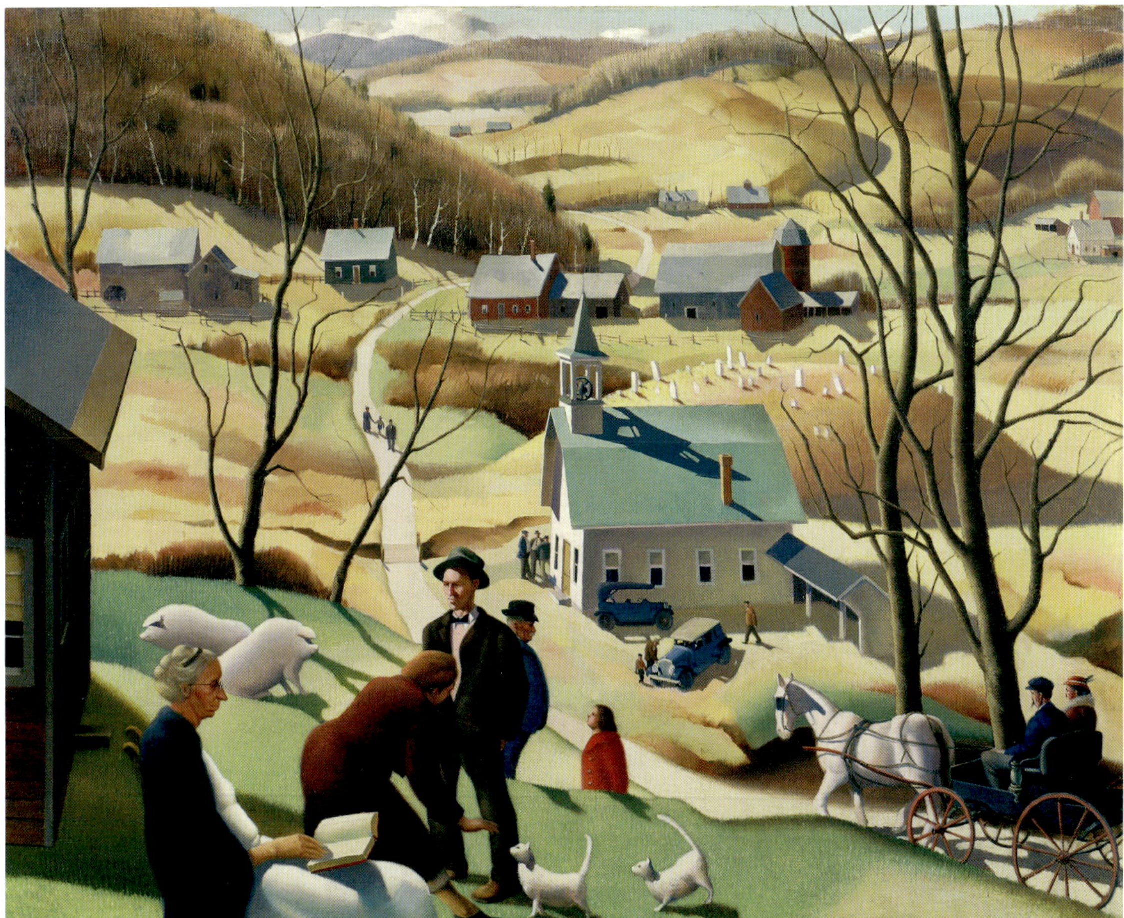

PAUL SAMPLE
Beaver Meadow, 1939
Oil on canvas, 40 x 48¼ in.
Gift of the artist, Class of 1920,
in memory of his brother,
Donald M. Sample, Class of
1921; P.943.126.1

By the time Paul Sample (see cat. 14) moved in 1938 from California to New England to assume his post as Dartmouth's artist-in-residence, a prominent critic had dubbed him an "eminently American success story" for having received such immediate "acceptance and reward."[1] Sample had built his reputation through a varied body of work that ranged from gritty urban realist scenes and precisionist industrial compositions to regionalist paintings that celebrated the distinct qualities of rural life both in arid Southern California and verdant Vermont, where he spent summers.

Sample brought his regionalist sympathies to bear in *Beaver Meadow*, the first major painting to pay homage to his new home and one of his most admired compositions. Sample later recalled Beaver Meadow as an

> almost abandoned community back in the hills about seven miles distant from my home in Vermont. . . . The people in the picture were all living there at the time the picture was painted. Old Mrs. Roberts on the left used to give me a cup of tea on chilly autumn afternoons. On several occasions she has played hymns on her small organ for me as I sat in her parlor.[2]

In this painting Sample celebrates qualities associated with a stereotypical Vermont village: the harmonious relationships between humans and nature, as reflected in the tidy fields and farm buildings nestled in the hills, and among the members of this apparently idyllic settlement, whose sense of community is strengthened through weekly worship. Its decorative composition, stripped of extraneous detail, recalls popular illustration, caricature, and American folk art traditions, reflecting the populist sentiments of 1930s America. Yet the picture also evokes an undercurrent of reserve, and even suspicion, as suggested by the rigidity of the figures in the foreground and their detachment from one another. The rather schoolmarmish Mrs. Roberts sits outdoors reading, her pose taken directly from James McNeill Whistler's famous portrait of his mother. Her male counterpart, a rather gaunt Yankee type, stands looking absently downward, while between the two a woman seems to retract her gesture of affection towards two cats. Further beyond, two rotund figures face one another along the same plane as a pair of stout white pigs.[3] Like the work of his Midwestern counterpart Grant Wood, Sample's depiction of his neighbors can be read as both admiring and mildly satirical, suggesting a more complex response to his environs than the all-out boosterism generally associated with the regionalist aesthetic.

BJM

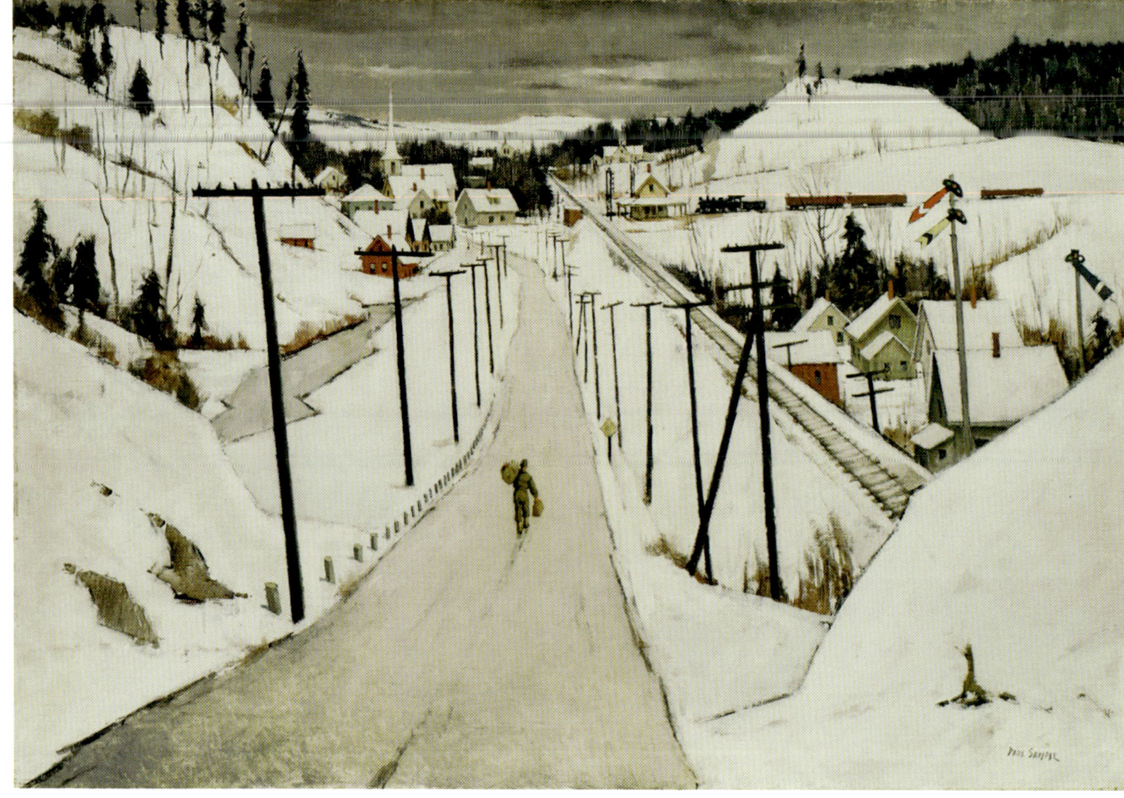

16

PAUL SAMPLE
The Return, 1946
Oil on canvas, 36 x 50 in.
Promised gift of Judith D. and
Charles H. Hood, Class of 1951;
EL.2010.55.9

Best known for his pastoral landscapes and genre scenes set in New England, Paul Sample (see cat. 14) also served as an artist-correspondent for *Life* magazine during World War II and, from the mid-1930s onward, supplied images for a host of magazines, commercial advertisers, and private businesses. Through his war coverage, for which he took several leaves of absence from his position as Dartmouth's artist-in-residence, Sample witnessed not only the daily routines of soldiers at sea but also gruesome casualties on both sides of the conflict, especially as he accompanied troops invading the island of Leyte.

Having seen firsthand the costs of war, Sample likely had special appreciation for the relief and poignancy that would surround a soldier's safe arrival at home. *The Return* was part of Maxwell House's "American Scene" collection and appeared in a magazine advertisement for their coffee, which, as the ad claimed, was also "part of the American scene." Presumably, in Sample's painting family and a welcoming cup of coffee lie at the end of the road and will mark the soldier's full return to America. The surging recession of the road, train tracks, and endless telephone poles conveys a sense of the distance he's traveled and perhaps also the uncertainties of life ahead. A preliminary sketch for the painting indicates that the setting is Wells River, about forty miles north of Sample's own home in Norwich, Vermont.[1] Such patriotic and nostalgic images by regionalist artists in the 1930s and 1940s ideally matched the reassuring messages offered by advertisers of consumer goods in the same period.[2] *The Return* received acclaim as a work of art in its own right when it was featured in a 1946 exhibition of American paintings at the Carnegie Institute in Pittsburgh.

BJM

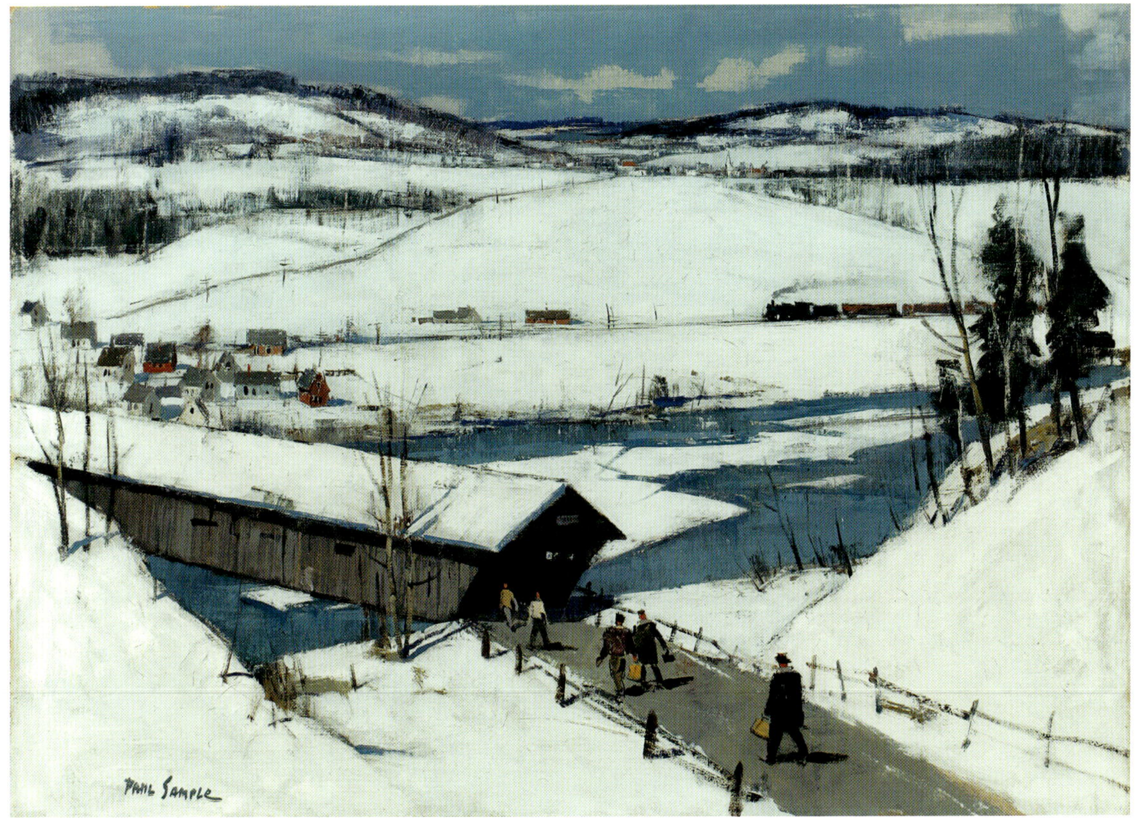

PAUL SAMPLE
Old Ledyard Bridge, 1954
Oil on canvas, 22 1/8 x 30 1/4 in.
Purchased through gifts from
Everett Parker, Class of 1952;
David J. Parker, Class of 1982;
and William Bannister-Parker,
Class of 1984; 2011.2

Paul Sample (see cat. 14), Dartmouth's longest-serving artist-in-residence, gained particular acclaim for his scenes of rural life in New Hampshire and Vermont, especially in winter. Such images have long held special significance and appeal for Dartmouth alumni and students. In fact Sample painted this work as a demonstration during a Dartmouth Alumni Association fundraising event held in Chicago in January 1954, and that spring the College reproduced the painting as part of a fundraising mailing. One recipient wrote to the College in response: "I am sure all the Alumni will be overjoyed to see the folder with the wonderful picture of the dear old Ledyard Bridge—through it we trudged on up the hill to the grandest college in all the world."[1]

In this work Sample depicts the old Ledyard Bridge as viewed from the Hanover side, with Lewiston, a former village within the township of Norwich, Vermont, seen immediately across the river. Built in 1859, the covered bridge was the fourth span on this site and was named for world traveler John Ledyard, who attended Dartmouth in 1772–73. It was removed in 1934, twenty years before Sample painted this image, and replaced by subsequent spans in 1935 and 1999. As was often his method, Sample used a degree of artistic license in the configuration of compositional elements and with the bridge itself, which had latticed sides, not the solid vertical planking seen here.

Old Ledyard Bridge no doubt held nostalgic appeal from the outset. Not only did it commemorate a beloved icon associated with Dartmouth's past, but covered bridges evoked rural New England's bygone days more broadly. The village of Lewiston also played an important role in the life of the College for decades. Its railroad depot was the point of arrival for Dartmouth students and furnished necessary campus supplies. Lewiston's low-lying farmlands were submerged after the 1950 construction of the Wilder Dam and most of the remainder of the town was destroyed in 1967 with the construction of Interstate 91 and the consequent widening of Route 10A. In *Old Ledyard Bridge*, therefore, Sample not only paid tribute to a venerated former landmark, but also unwittingly created an important document of a settlement that would soon be largely obliterated.

BJM

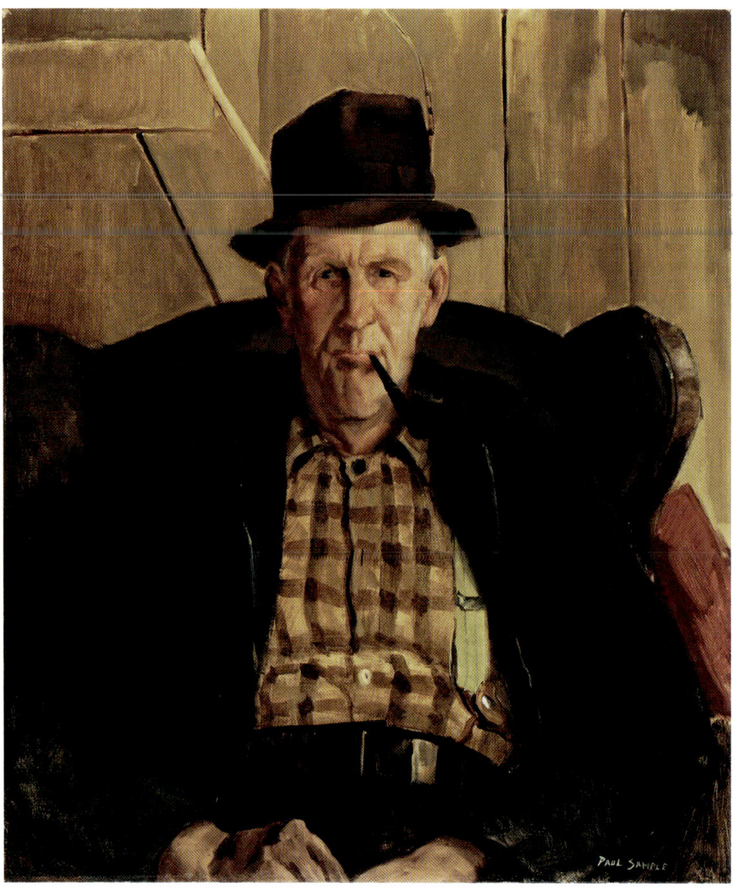

PAUL SAMPLE
Will Bond, 1940
Oil on canvas, 30 x 25 in.
Gift of the artist, Class of 1920
in memory of his brother,
Donald M. Sample, Class of
1921; P.943.126.2

In his attempt to convey what was distinctive about New England in his art and meet popular expectations regarding the region, Paul Sample (see cat. 14) focused not only on the area's pastoral beauty but also its aged farmers, whose very presence signified a bygone era and whose customs and dress best exemplified the region's "Yankee" character. Beginning with this 1940 portrait, Sample conveyed his affection for his elderly Norwich, Vermont, neighbor, Will Bond, through numerous portrayals, including several drawings, a watercolor, at least one other oil portrait, and a multifigure genre painting.[1] Most of these images depict Bond in work clothes, posed frontally with his worn, angular face and gaze directed straight at the viewer. Sample thereby accentuated the stereotypical reticence and underlying force of character associated with the native New Englander in a manner that recalls Grant Wood's almost comically severe portrayal of a Midwestern farmer in his famous 1930 canvas *American Gothic*. Sample's images of Bond, however, are more individualized and convey a deep underlying fondness and respect for the artist's friend, who boarded his beloved horses and from whom he purchased the land for his home.

In this portrait, which is believed to be Sample's first painted likeness of his neighbor, Will Bond sits in a winged upholstered armchair that is incongruously situated against a rough-hewn barn wall—a pose Sample would return to repeatedly in his portraits of Bond. A pheasant feather sprouts from the farmer's hat, its alternating blocks of tan and brown echoing those of his plaid shirt, which lacks its middle button. Whereas Bond's attire marks him as a man of work, his direct, assessing gaze meets the viewer with disarming assurance, and his clenched, pipe-gripping jaw strengthens the impression of a determined man who knows his mind. Sample's close vantage point and tight cropping accentuate Bond's imposing presence, which belies his slight features and relaxed posture. The flat, sharply-outlined barn boards behind him create an abstract, patterned backdrop that reveals Sample's gradual shift away from the rounded stylization of his work of the 1930s toward a more angular, linear manner and a growing interest in interlocking shapes. Such subtle stylistic shifts demonstrate Sample's early efforts to integrate more schematic approaches to form, which he would explore in greater depth in subsequent decades.

BJM

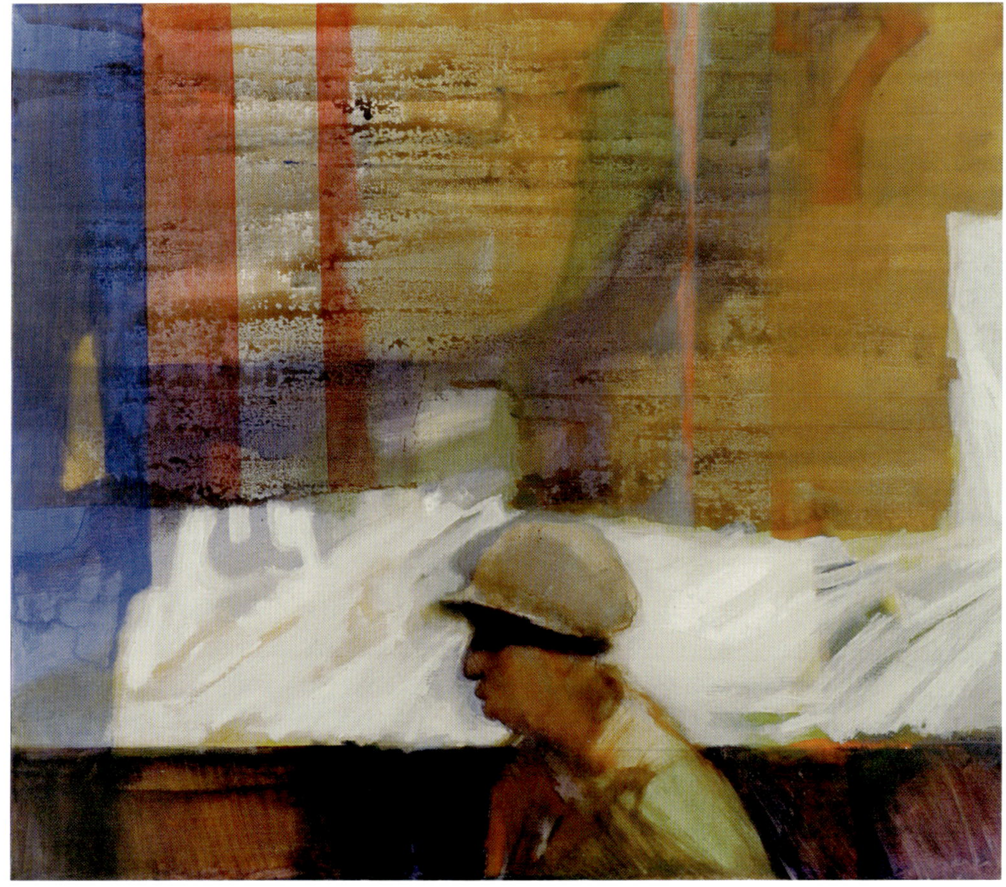

ALEXANDER BROOKS JACKSON
American, 1925–1981
Man and the Wall #7, 1968
Oil and acrylic on canvas,
39^{15}/$_{16}$ x 45 in.
Purchased through the Julia L. Whittier Fund; P.971.12

Alexander Brooks "A. B." Jackson was the first African American artist-in-residence at Dartmouth. Born in New Haven, Connecticut, to an Irish mother and an African American father, Jackson received a BFA in painting in 1953 and an MFA in graphic design in 1955 from Yale University, where he studied with the Bauhaus artist Josef Albers. In 1956 he joined the faculty of Virginia State College, Norfolk (now Norfolk State College), where he served as chairman of the Department of Fine Arts from 1960 to 1967. He then joined Old Dominion University in Norfolk, Virginia, as their first African American faculty member. Before pursuing an academic career, Jackson worked for three years in the Watson-Manning advertising agency in Stratford, Connecticut. This experience informed his teaching, which included painting and printmaking techniques with commercial art and design. In 1962 Jackson was denied entry to a public exhibition in Virginia Beach because of his race. After a four-year struggle to have his work accepted by the all-white jury, Jackson was allowed to exhibit his work in 1966, winning first prize and national acclaim for his efforts. Despite the difficulties of working as an African American artist during the Civil Rights era, he won numerous awards for his masterful draftsmanship, painting, photography, and printmaking. Jackson believed that art transcended race and worked with the National Association for the Advancement of Colored People to ensure that future African American artists would not face the racism and discrimination that he experienced in Virginia in the 1960s.

Jackson was artist-in-residence at Dartmouth during the spring of 1971. His exhibition in the Jaffe-Friede Gallery featured his critically acclaimed *Porch People* series, which established his reputation as a highly original and technically accomplished painter. These works depict the artist's neighborhood in the Ghent district of Norfolk, including his African American neighbors on porches, where they sit, chat, chew, and stare at the passersby. Jackson in turn observes them as part of a life that is fast disappearing. His concern with the interplay of figure and architecture also gives his paintings a sense of movement and vitality, as seen in *Man and the Wall #7*, which is one of the most abstract and haunting paintings in the entire series. In 1979 Jackson published *As I See Ghent: A Visual Essay*, which is composed primarily of paintings, drawings, and photographs of the neighborhood that he found so inspiring.

MRT

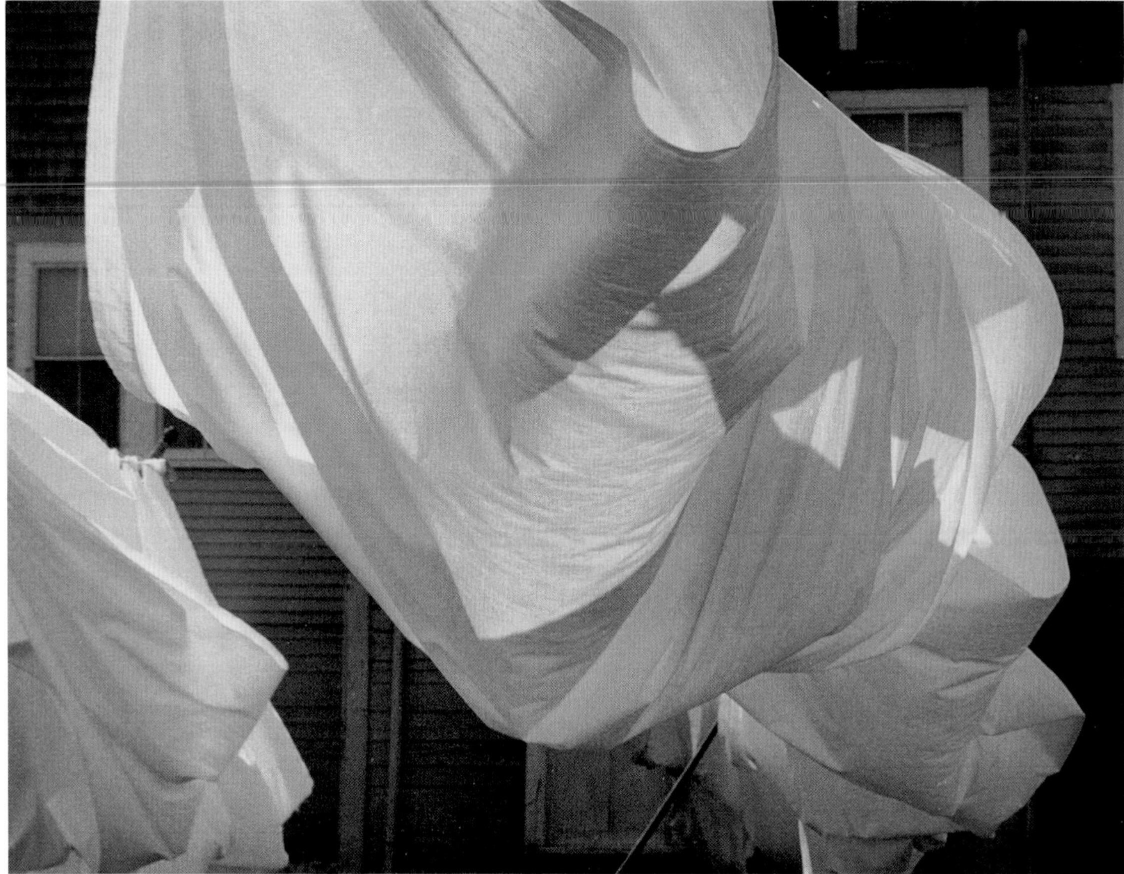

20

RALPH STEINER
American, 1899–1986
Billowing Sheets, 1960–68
Gelatin silver print,
$5^3/_{16}$ x $6^5/_8$ in.
Gift of Willard van Dyke;
PH.975.46
© Estate of Ralph Steiner

Throughout his career, photographer and filmmaker Ralph Steiner, Dartmouth Class of 1921, demonstrated a keen sense of design, profound humanism, dry wit, and contagious optimism. He purchased his first camera while still in high school and continued photographing "like a madman" at Dartmouth.[1] In 1922, twenty-four of these soft-focused campus images were published in book form. By then he was enrolled at the Clarence White School of Photography in New York, where White, a prominent pictorialist, inculcated him with compositional theories. Steiner eventually moved away from the need "to straightjacket [his subjects] into standard compositions" and developed a reputation for inventive vantage points and crisp, richly textured images.[2] A New Yorker for most of his career, he repeatedly explored the aesthetic potential of the city's looming skyscrapers, graphic advertisements, and teeming streets. He credited modernist photographer Paul Strand as a formative influence, while, in turn, Steiner's unassuming subjects and exacting compositions won the admiration of Walker Evans (cats. 40–44), to whom Steiner offered informal instruction in 1931.[3] Reliant on commercial photography for income, Steiner worked at various points for advertising firms, Hollywood film companies, and such magazines as *Fortune*. Beginning in the late 1920s, he pursued a parallel career making avant-garde and documentary films, both on his own and in collaboration with others. He is perhaps best known for having worked alongside Strand on Pare Lorentz's social documentary *The Plow that Broke the Plain* (1931). By the time of his 1979 stint as artist-in-residence at Dartmouth, Steiner had turned his lens toward subjects drawn from nature, especially after spending summers on Monhegan Island, Maine, in the 1960s and purchasing a house in Thetford, Vermont, in 1970.

Steiner shot several photographs of these sheets hanging to dry "behind a hotel" on Monhegan beginning around 1960.[4] The play of light and wind on and through the fabric creates subtle tonal transitions and a variety of forms, from limp to billowing. In *Hanging Sheets* the symmetrically configured drapery evokes ethereal evening gowns clasped by out-stretched arms in advance of a graceful turn or bow. For Steiner, the drying sheets suggested classical figures in marble. He described his related 1971 film, *A Look at Laundry*, as "sequences of washing on the line alternating with sequences of Greek sculpture and bas reliefs."[5] In referring to the sheet photographs, he expressed his characteristic humor and idealism: "For me these sheets were patrician Athenians, meeting in the cool of the evening to discuss how a man should live."[6] Steiner's firm belief in our need for affirmation in the face of hardship resulted in an exhibition he curated for the Hood Museum of Art in 1986, *In Spite of Everything, Yes!* The exhibition and catalogue featured over one hundred photographs by other artists he selected. Sadly, Steiner, who was suffering from cancer while working on the project, passed away just months before the exhibition opening.

BJM

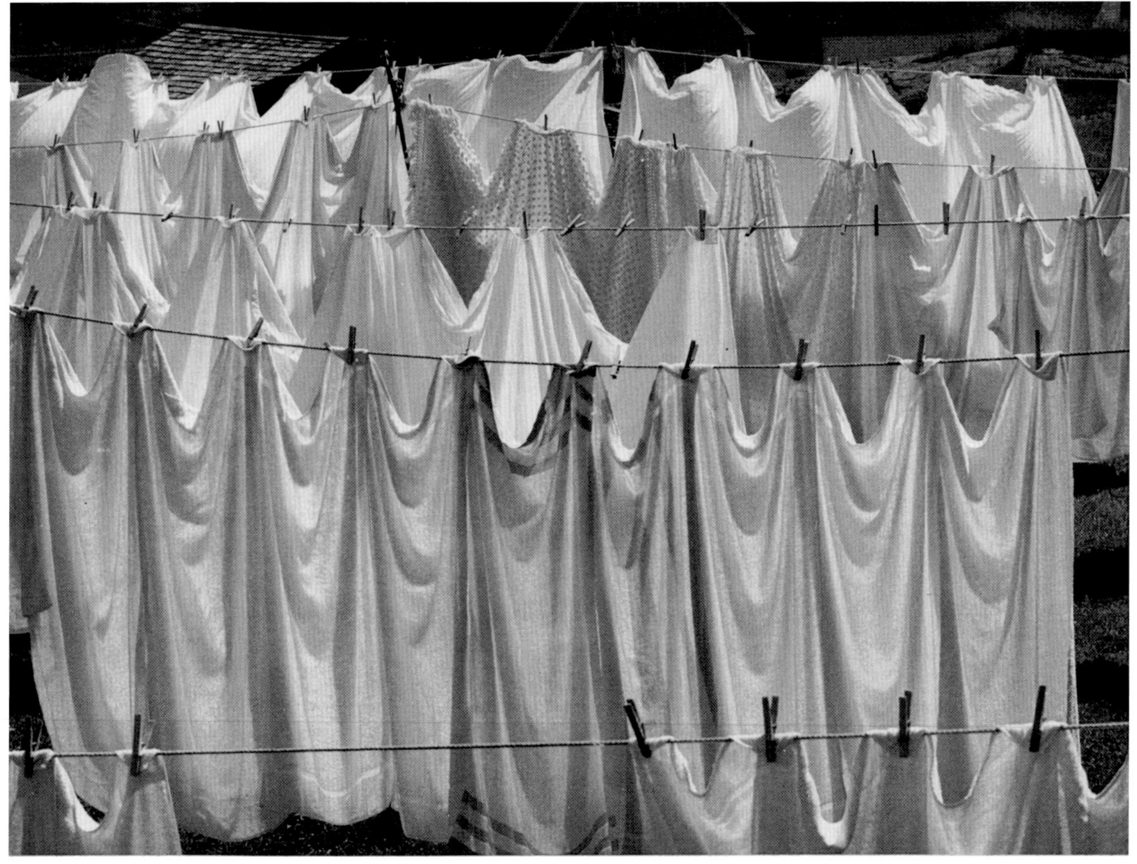

21

RALPH STEINER
Hanging Sheets, 1960–68
Gelatin silver print,
5³/₁₆ x 6¹¹/₁₆ in.
Gift of Willard van Dyke;
PH.975.47
© Estate of Ralph Steiner

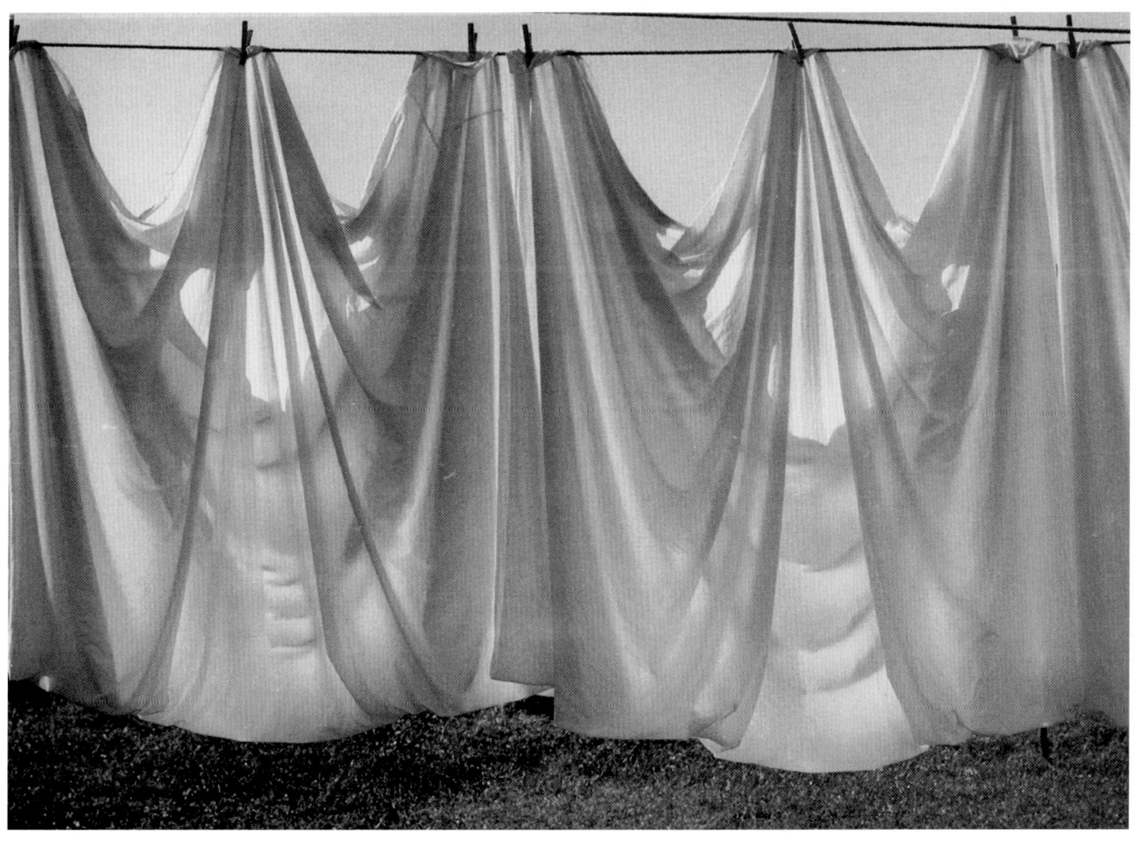

22

RALPH STEINER
Hanging Sheets, 1960–68
Gelatin silver print,
5¹/₄ x 6³/₈ in.
Gift of Willard van Dyke;
PH.975.57
© Estate of Ralph Steiner

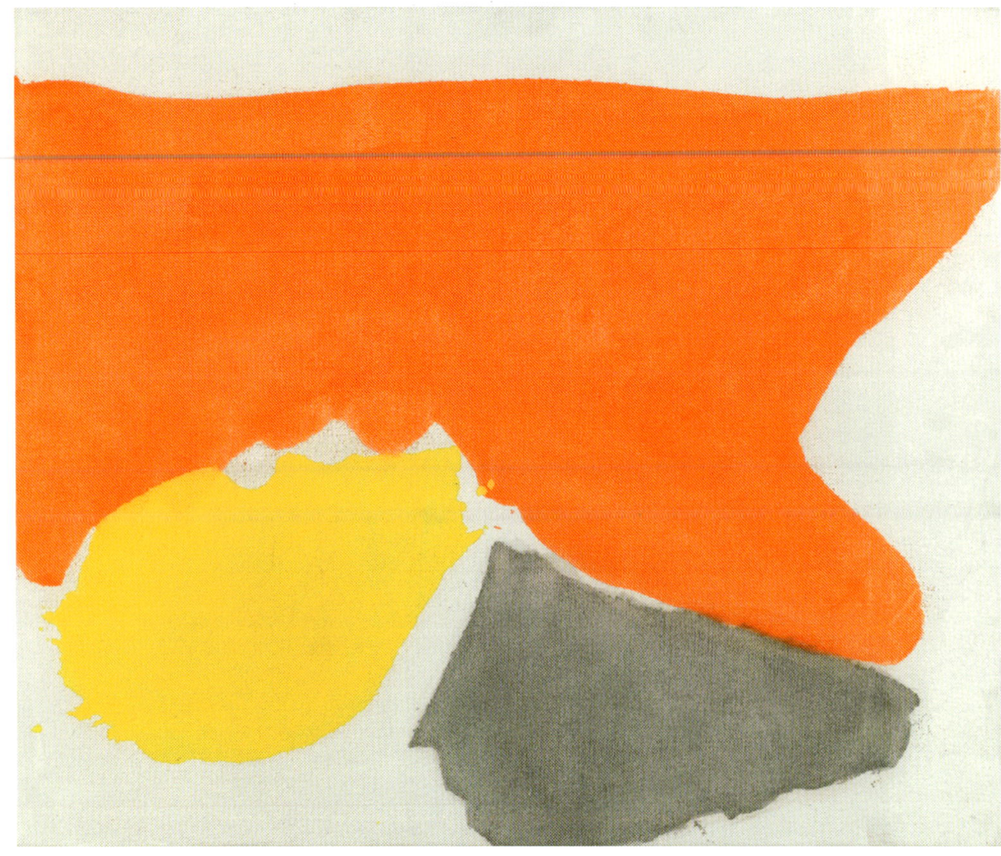

FRIEDEL DZUBAS
American, born in Germany, 1915–1994
Aegian, 1962
Oil on canvas, 20½ x 24 in.
Purchased through the Phyllis and Bertram
Geller 1937 Memorial Fund; P.963.7
© Estate of Friedel Dzubas

Friedel Dzubas lived in New York from 1949 to 1969, and his work from that time is his most famous. Born in Berlin in 1915, he immigrated to the United States in 1939, fleeing Germany on the eve of WWII. Upon his arrival, Dzubas lived in various places including New York, Chicago, and Mansfield, Ohio, and held numerous positions including delivery boy, house painter, and art director. In 1948 he participated in his first group exhibition at Weyhe Gallery in New York. That summer he met critic Clement Greenberg, who introduced him to the New York avant-garde art scene. In 1949 Dzubas became a member of the Eighth Street Club, which also included abstract expressionist painters Willem de Kooning, Franz Kline, and Ad Reinhardt. In 1952 he shared a studio with Helen Frankenthaler. Influenced by this group of artists, as well as Jackson Pollock, Dzubas's work in the fifties was highly gestural. In the early sixties this shifted to large swathes of saturated color, the kind of work Dzubas was creating at Dartmouth during his ten-week residency in the fall of 1962.

Describing this new use of color, Dzubas said, "I discovered that what I can reach emotionally and express by color is infinite. It's composed of two seemingly unrelated sources—there's a Nordic, northern European kind of grayness . . . but there's also great affinity for Mediterranean Matisse, so to speak."[1] *Aegian* is a typical example of the latter. The orange, yellow, and gray shapes float upon a white ground. Although one might expect such bright colors to feel more ethereal, their intensity and size relative to the canvas enhances their visceral presence. The colored masses feel like continents shifting and colliding. They have a quiet monumentality despite the painting's modest size. Dzubas has said that painting successful small abstractions is more difficult than painting large ones.[2]

Although the fluidity of his paintings relates to the poured and stained paintings of artists like Frankenthaler, Dzubas did not paint on bare canvas. Rather, he used a ground and allowed the colored paint to soak into it, approximating the staining technique. This gives his work a sense of deliberation despite the soft edges and amorphous shapes. Dzubas continued to explore color in the seventies and eighties, even as his shapes became less defined and his painting more gestural and expressionist. Aegian is from a brief period that lasted from 1961 to 1964. It beautifully expresses Dzubas's deftness with color and shape and underscores his connection with the leading art movements of the day.

ABK

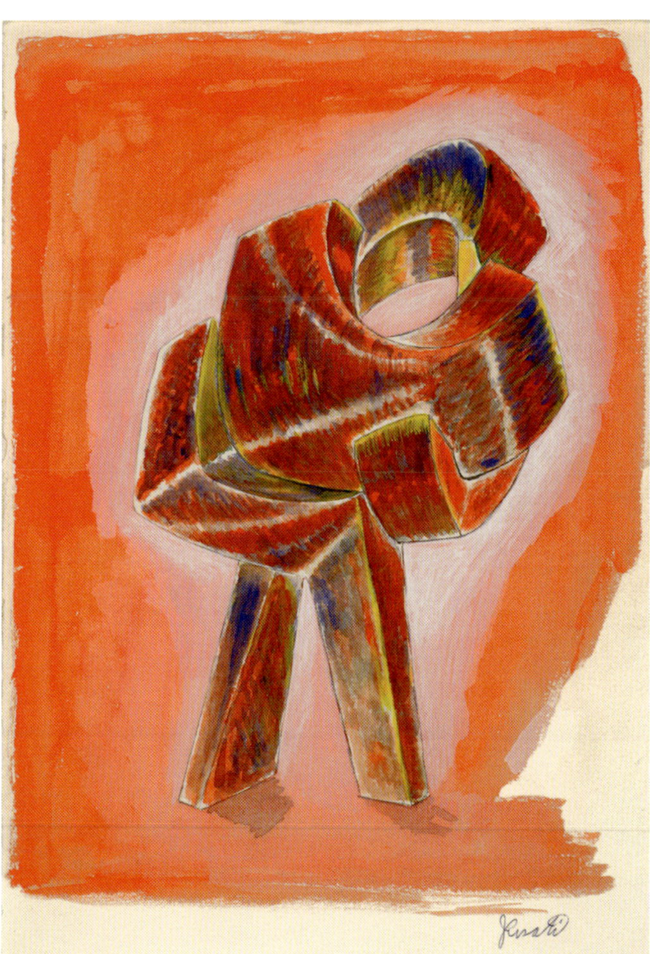

24

JAMES ROSATI
American, 1911–1988
Untitled, 1963
Wash and graphite on paper, 11 x 7½ in.
Museum purchase; D.963.99.2
© Jerald Melberg Gallery

Born in Washington, Pennsylvania, in 1911, James Rosati trained as a violinist and, as a teenager, performed with the Pittsburgh String Symphony. It was during these rehearsals and recitals that he "looked at the classical nudes in the music hall and knew [he] wanted to become a sculptor." In 1934 he dedicated himself to a sculptural practice, and from 1937 to 1941 was employed as a sculptor through the Art Project initiative of the Works Progress Administration (WPA). In the 1940s and 1950s he experimented with a variety of media including bronze, marble, limestone, wood, and stone. During this period his works made strong references to the human form, but by the 1960s they would become entirely abstract. Rosati was included in the historic *Ninth Street Art Exhibition* of 1951, which contributed to the formation of the New York School of art and announced the arrival of a radically new visual language. In the mid-1950s he taught at the Pratt Institute and Cooper Union, New York, and by the end of the decade he would become one of America's leading sculptors. In 1960 he was appointed professor of sculpture at Yale University, an influential position that he held for thirteen years. During his tenure, Rosati forged a working relationship with the pioneering Lippincott factory and began to fulfill his vision of fabricating larger-scale works in steel and aluminum that are now found in museums, gardens, and public plazas around the country.

Akin to a study, this untitled work from 1963 was created the year Rosati was a visiting critic in sculpture at Dartmouth. The drawing formally echoes his monumental outdoor constructions and reveals the artist's interest in spatial relationships, irregular volumes, and the energizing interactions of planar surfaces. Against an apricot wash, Rosati's composite creation both radiates and reflects light and demonstrates his preoccupation with the effects of light on his sculptures. For the artist, the interplay of hard edges and curvilinear forms best accentuates the differential behavior of light as it spills over and recedes into the object. While this natural phenomenon activates the work and forges a dialogue with its site, it is ultimately the physical experience of Rosati's sculptures that constitutes their richest and most consequential effect.

SG

JASON SELEY
American, 1919–1983
The Boys from Avignon, 1962–63
Chromium-plated steel, 58 x 78 x 47 in.
Purchased with a gift from Evelyn A. Jaffe
and William B. Jaffe, Class of 1964H; S.960.20

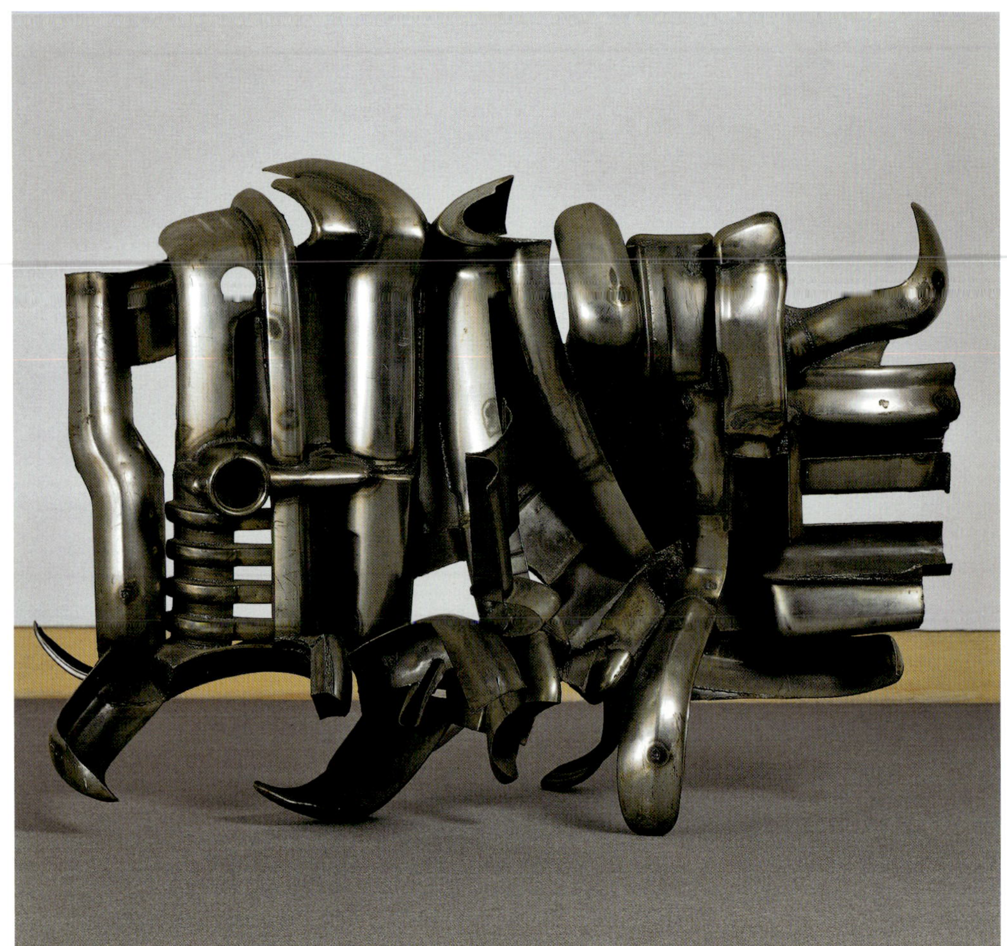

Jason Seley was born in Newark, New Jersey, and graduated in 1940 with a degree in the history of art from Cornell University, where he would later teach sculpture in the art department from 1968 until his death in 1983. Between 1943 and 1945, Seley studied at the Art Students League in New York with the cubist sculptor Ossip Zadkine. His first solo exhibition came in 1947 at the American-British Art Center in New York, and two years later, in 1949, he was awarded a Fulbright Scholarship for a year's study in Paris. The seemingly innocuous 1956 roadside discovery of a chromium-plated steel bumper from a '49 Buick greatly impacted his future artistic production. Intrigued by the smooth and stylized molded surface, Seley created the sculpture *Random Walk* using the automobile bumper as his medium in 1958. It was shown at MoMA the following year. As artist-in-residence at Dartmouth College during the winter of 1968, Seley created *Hanover I*, a sculpture also made out of chromium-plated steel, which, like *The Boys from Avignon*, resides in the Hood Museum of Art's permanent collection.

Seley's use of automobile bumpers aligns him with the work of contemporaries such as Allan D'Arcangelo, John Chamberlain, Robert Rauschenberg, and Jean Tinguely, who also worked with ready-made and found objects, including automobile parts. Seley's choice of materials clearly nods to the modern industrial processes through which they are produced. The use of the bumper serves to elevate contemporary materials to the ranks of marble or bronze and alludes to the pervasiveness of the car in popular culture. While making a departure from sculpture in traditional media, Seley references past artistic tradition and the Western canon with his title, *The Boys from Avignon,* a direct allusion to Pablo Picasso's seminal 1907 painting *Les Demoiselles d'Avignon*. Positioning himself in line with all artists working in the sculptural tradition, Seley stated:

> I work, I believe, inspired by the nature of my time and place. To me an automobile bumper is an offering of nature's abundance . . . I do not think of myself as an "automobile" or "junk" sculptor, nor an "assembler." I am a sculptor facing the challenge of the means and materials of my choice, just as my contemporaries and predecessors face, or have faced, that challenge of their own methods and media.[1]

KMG

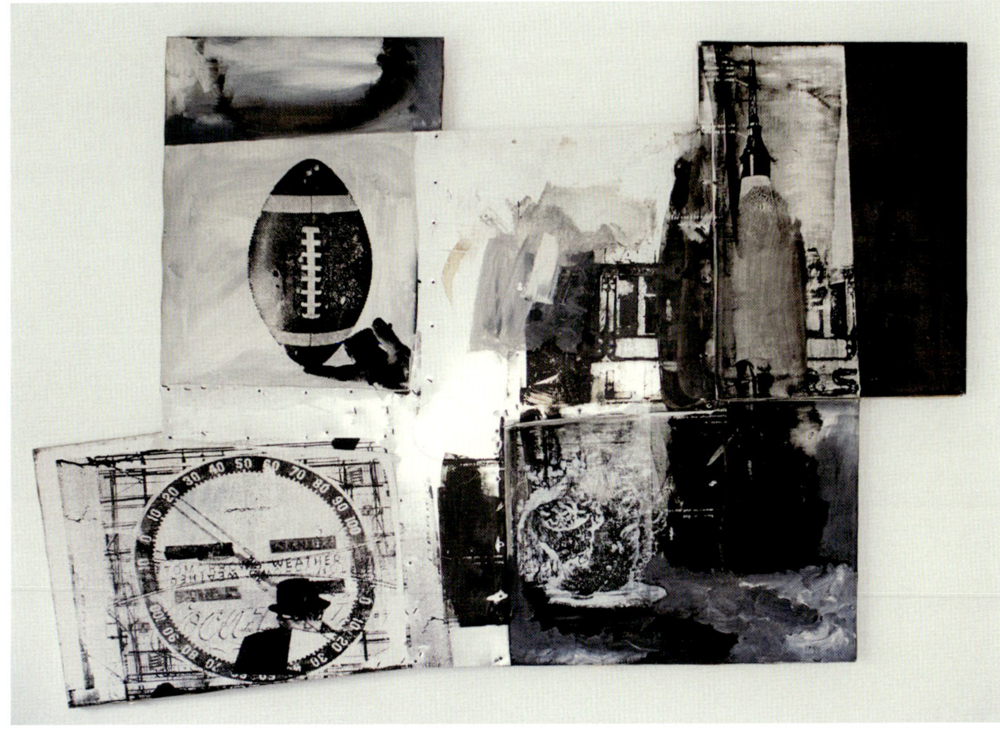

"Painting relates to both art and life," Robert Rauschenberg famously stated, "[and] I try to act in that gap between the two." Along with fellow artist Jasper Johns, whom he met in 1953 and regularly exchanged ideas with until their relationship ended in 1961, Rauschenberg attempted in the 1950s and 1960s to bridge this gap by incorporating into his art images culled from daily life. Born Milton Rauschenberg on October 22, 1925, in Port Arthur, Texas, he began to study pharmacology at the University of Texas, Austin, before being drafted into the U.S. Navy, where he served as a neuropsychiatric technician in the U.S. Navy Hospital Corps in San Diego, California. In 1947 Rauschenberg enrolled at the Kansas City Art Institute and traveled to Paris to study at the Académie Julian in the following year. In the fall of 1948, Rauschenberg returned to the United States to study under Josef Albers at Black Mountain College near Asheville, North Carolina. During his intermittent study there over the next four years he met the avant-garde composer John Cage and the dancer and choreographer Merce Cunningham, with whom he would frequently collaborate, contributing scenic, costume, and lighting designs for a large number of productions by Cunningham's dance company. In 1954 Rauschenberg began making *Combines*, a term the artist coined for his well-known three-dimensional artworks that integrated aspects of painting and sculpture and would often include such memorable artifacts as a stuffed eagle or goat, street signs, Coca-Cola bottles, and a quilt and pillow.

Rauschenberg was artist-in-residence at Dartmouth during the winter of 1963, during which he created *Junction*, whose title alludes to the local town of White River Junction, Vermont. *Junction* was one of his first paintings to use the commercial technique of the silkscreen, in which photographic images are transferred onto paper or canvas by pushing ink or paint through specially prepared fine mesh screens or wooden stretchers. Rauschenberg exploited the silkscreen process in a deliberately casual fashion, combining photographic images gleaned from newspapers and magazines with expressive brushwork to create richly textured associative paintings. Their juxtapositions are random, yet provocative enough to make the viewer speculate about the meaning of these images. The iconic football in this painting was probably intended as a deliberate reference to Dartmouth's football team, which had completed an undefeated season (9-0) to win the Ivy League championship shortly before Rauschenberg's arrival on campus.

MRT

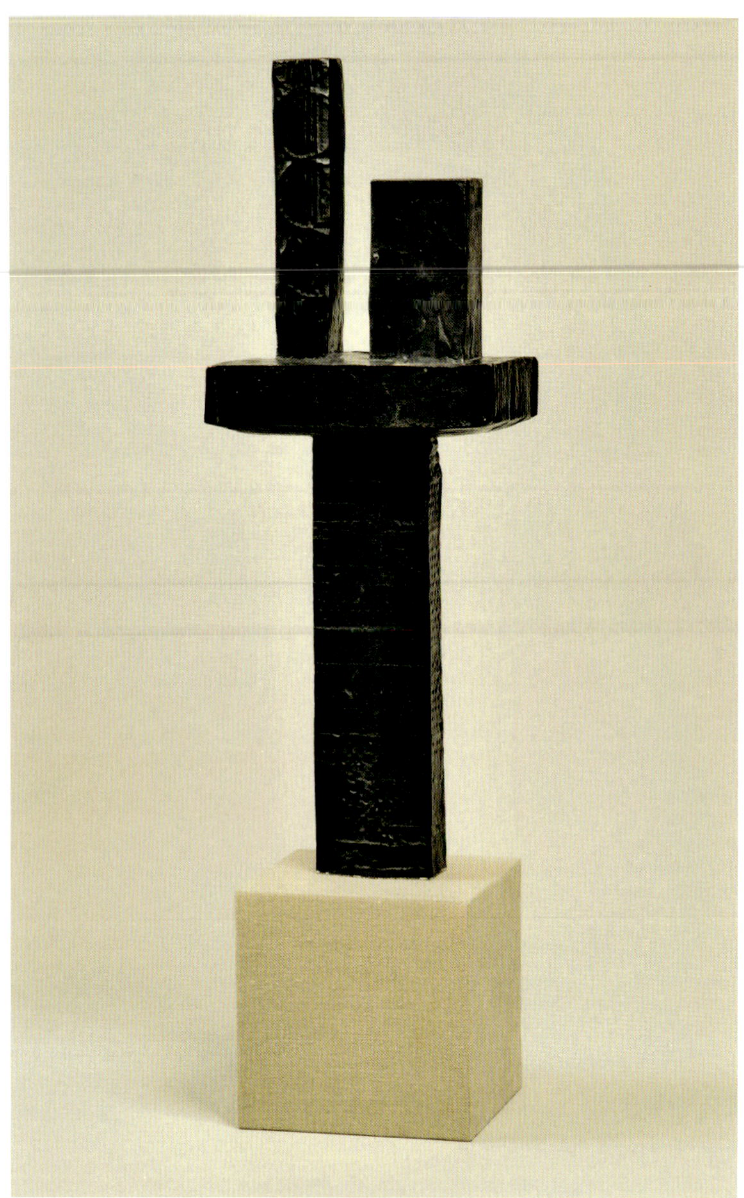

LYMAN KIPP
American, born 1929
Median II, 1963
Bronze, 31 x 11 x 7^{13}/$_{16}$ in.;
height with base 39^{7}/$_{8}$ in.
Purchased through the Julia L
Whittier Fund; S.965.37

Lyman Kipp was born in Dobbs Ferry, New York. He studied at the Pratt Institute and Cranbrook Academy of Art and later went on to teach at Bennington College, Lehman College, and Hunter College. One of his first major shows was a solo exhibition at the Betty Parsons Gallery in New York in 1954. In 1963 he was one of ten sculptors chosen to represent the United States in São Paulo, Brazil, in the seventh Biennial. Kipp's sculpture is formed of simple geometric shapes, often rectangles, in vertical and horizontal compositions. Some of his work has a uniform bronze patina; some is painted in bright primary colors that emphasize the structure of the forms. Their geometry and palette call to mind the work of the De Stijl artists such a Piet Mondrian. Kipp helped to found ConStruct, an artist-owned gallery that promoted large-scale exhibitions of sculpture across the United States.

Kipp was artist-in-residence at Dartmouth in the winter of 1965. *Median II*, made two years earlier, is made up of the strong vertical and horizontal shapes that characterize Kipp's mature work. The balanced rectangular forms have a sense of solidity and permanence. As opposed to the smooth, industrial surfaces of Donald Judd's minimalist sculpture, Kipp's irregular lines and variegated texture give his work a more organic feel. In the early sixties Kipp was using plaster casts made from corrugated cardboard, and that may be the source of the texture in *Median II*.[1] In the mid-sixties Kipp's sculpture would increase in scale, becoming more architectural. He also moved to an industrial process, rather than casting. This tabletop piece is a fine example of the blockier forms Kipp was exploring in the beginning of the decade.

ABK

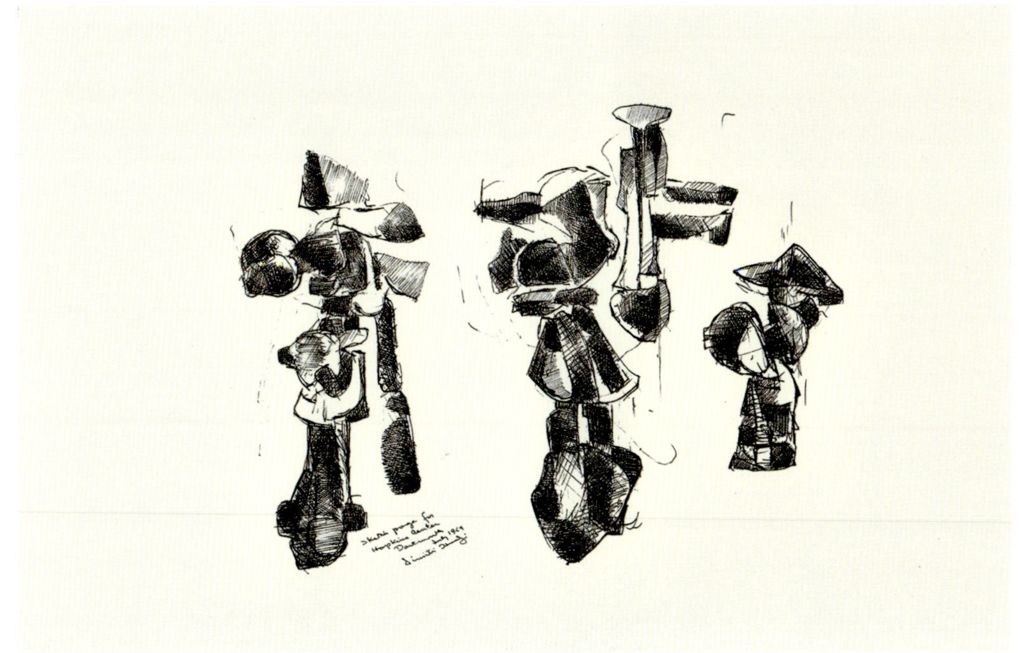

28

DIMITRI HADZI
American, 1921–2006
Sculpture Studies, 1969
Pen and ink with white gouache opaque
watercolor corrections on wove paper,
inscribed "Sketch Page for Hopkins Center
Dartmouth July 1969 Dimitri Hadzi,"
$10^{1}/_{16}$ x $14^{15}/_{16}$ in.
Gift of the artist; D.969.34
© Cynthia Hadzi

Dimitri Hadzi was a sculptor of large-scale works in bronze and stone that often were installed in public spaces. He is best known for the sixteen-foot-high bronze sculpture *Thermopylae*, commissioned by the architect Walter Gropius for the John F. Kennedy Federal Office Building in Boston. Hadzi often adopted subjects and figures from mythology and presented them in an abstract visual language drawn from modern art. His forms suggest powerful, muscular figures and his titles often refer to Greek heroes and gods, but stop short of straightforward narrative. Born to Greek parents in Greenwich Village, New York, in 1921, Hadzi saw his heritage as elective as much as genetic, and frequently drew on Greek mythology and literature for subjects of heroism and courage. After studying at Cooper Union for the Advancement of Science and Art in New York, Hadzi received a Fulbright Scholarship that allowed him to travel to Greece in 1950. He studied stone carving at the Polytechneion Athens and also closely observed the Archaic and Classical Greek sculpture that surrounded him in Greece, visiting archeological sites at Mycenae, Tiryns, and Asine. Following his time in Athens, Hadzi traveled to Rome, where he would eventually establish his first studio and continue working for much of the next twenty-five years.

As artist-in-residence at Dartmouth in the summer of 1969, Hadzi utilized his time in the studio to develop various sculptural projects, including a major commission for a set of bronze doors to be installed at the American Episcopal church in Rome, St. Paul's Within-the-Walls.

Hadzi also attended a Dartmouth course on geology to further his understanding of stone materials, which he started using more frequently in his work of the 1970s. *Sculpture Studies* was acquired from the exhibition of his work on view in the Jaffe-Friede Gallery during his stay at Dartmouth. Hadzi believed that drawing was essential to understanding sculpture, and this sketch appears to show a single sculpture from three different views. The forms in the drawing seem most closely related to *Terra III*, a sculpture cast in 1967 that Hadzi had on view in Jaffe-Friede.

SGP

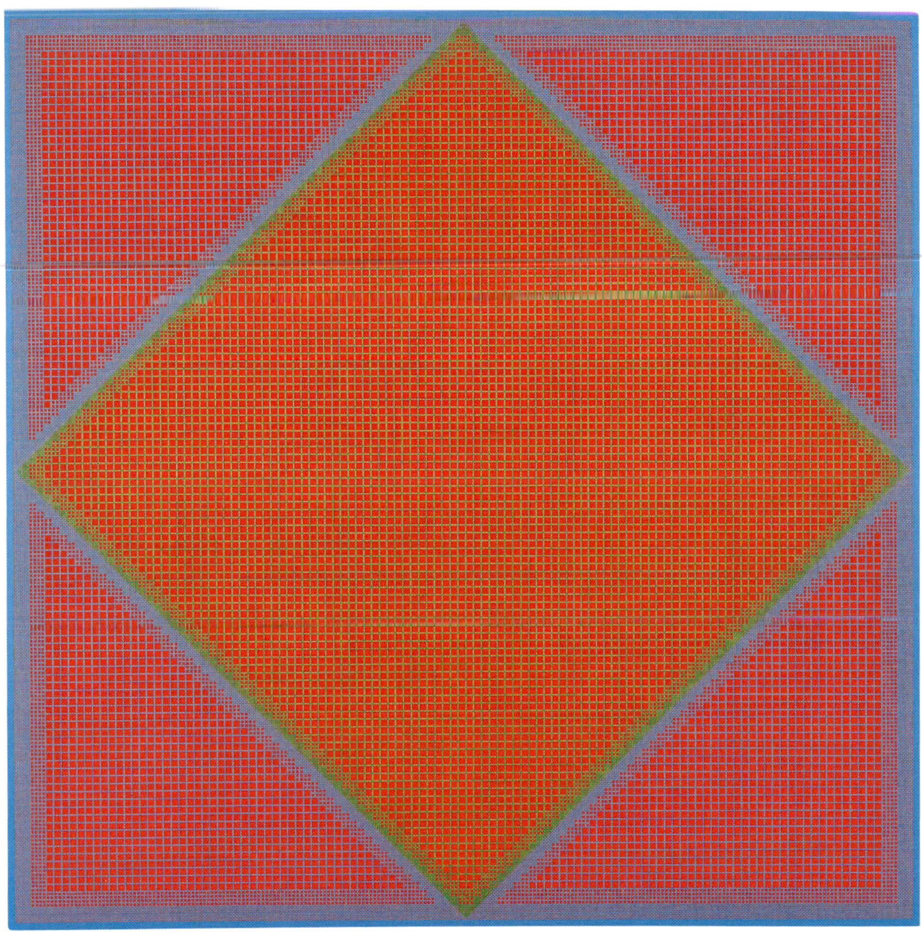

RICHARD ANUSZKIEWICZ
American, born 1930
Lunar, 1967
Liquitex on canvas, 60 x 60 in.
Purchased with a gift from Evelyn A. and
William B. Jaffe, Class of 1964H; P.007.100
Art © Richard Anuszkiewicz / Licensed by
VAGA, New York, NY

Richard Anuszkiewicz is best known for grid-based paintings that explore the optical effects of complementary colors and juxtapositions. Born in Erie, Pennsylvania, Anuszkiewicz studied at the Cleveland Institute of Art between 1948 and 1953. Following graduation he attended the Yale University School of Art, where he studied with Josef Albers, whose abstract paintings and understanding of color theory would have a lasting impact on Anuszkiewicz's future work. After receiving his master's degree from Yale in 1955, Anuszkiewicz obtained a degree in education from Kent State University and began teaching at Cooper Union in New York in 1963. His work was featured in the landmark 1965 exhibition *The Responsive Eye* at New York's Museum of Modern Art, and in the following year the Cleveland Museum of Art gave Anuszkiewicz his first retrospective exhibition. By the time he came to Dartmouth as artist-in-residence in the fall of 1967, Anuszkiewicz was at the height of his career and his large-scale geometric paintings, informed by science, mathematics, and psychological perception theory, had made him one of the leading figures in the international op art movement. His eye-catching visual illusions also had a commercial application and Anuszkiewicz designed coasters, fur coats, dresses, gift-wrapping paper, jewelry, jigsaw puzzles, rugs, and scarves. The artist would continue this interest in moving beyond the traditional boundaries of painting while at Dartmouth, where he designed an op football for Dartmouth's game with Cornell on November 18, 1967. Although the ball was intended to give the Dartmouth team a competitive advantage, Cornell ended up winning the game 24-21.

Lunar makes reference to the total lunar eclipse that took place on April 24, 1967. Using intense fluorescent colors and a grid-based geometric design, Anuszkiewicz created a highly successful optical illusion. An apparently orange diamond bordered by green and white is inscribed within a larger square that seems to be pink, while the outermost shape is outlined with blue and white squares. Despite the apparent differences in color, the diamond and the square are actually the same shade of red. The illusion is created by the interaction of the green and blue borders with the red they surround, causing the same color to be perceived in two different ways. Additionally, it also appears as if the size of the squares that make up the borders gets smaller as they approach the red they frame. In reality, all of the squares are the same shape.

MRT

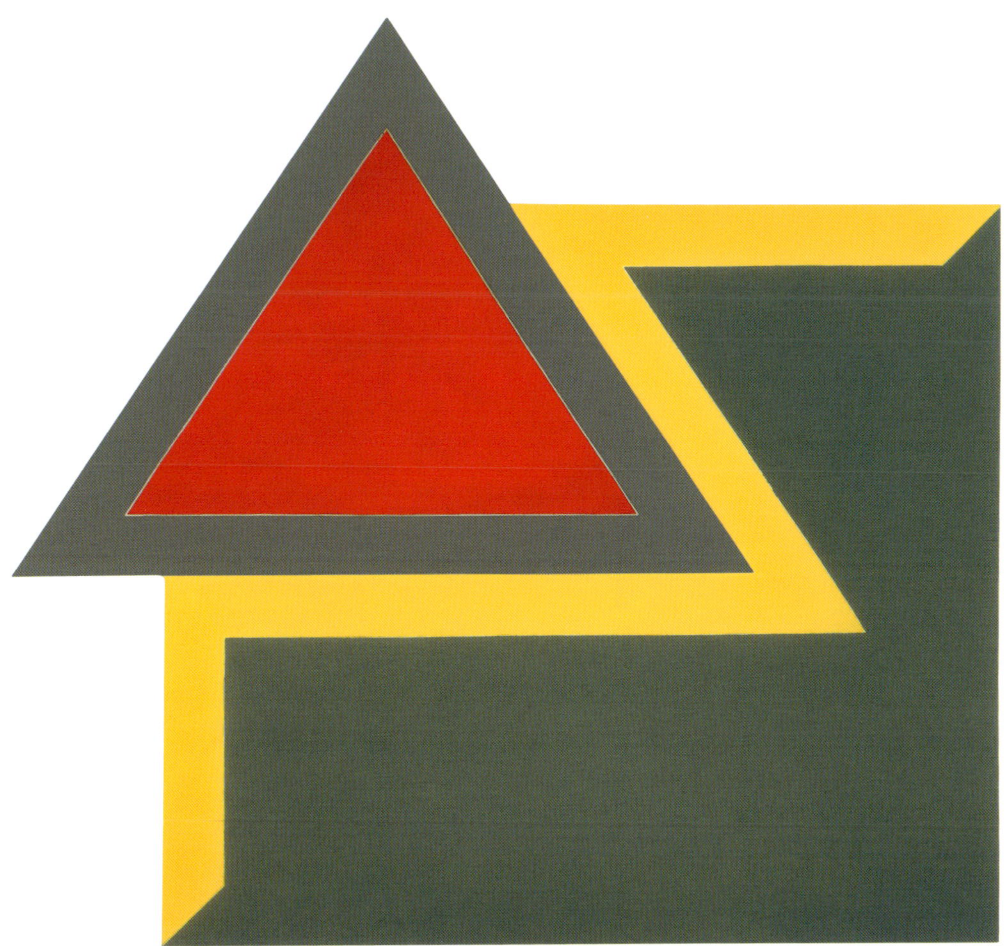

30

FRANK STELLA
American, born 1936
Chocorua IV, 1966
Fluorescent alkyd and epoxy paints on
shaped canvas, 120 x 128 x 4 in.
Purchased through the Miriam and Sidney
Stoneman Acquisition Fund, a gift from
Judson and Carol Bemis, Class of 1976, and
gifts from the Lathrop Fellows, in honor
of Brian P. Kennedy, Director of the Hood
Museum of Art, 2005–2010; 2010.50
© 2013 Frank Stella / Artists Rights Society
(ARS), New York

A consistent innovator who prefers to produce works in series, Frank Stella has had a long and prolific career at the forefront of abstract art. Stella was artist-in-residence at Dartmouth in the summer of 1963, during which he made works for the series that became known as the *Dartmouth Paintings*, each of which was named after a city in Florida that he had visited on a road trip two years before. In 1965–66, in turn, he would name each of the eleven compositions of his *Irregular Polygons* series after a small town in New Hampshire. Here the connection between art and title is more direct: during his boyhood, his father had brought him to a family camp near Ossipee for fishing trips in the lakes and rivers of the White Mountains region.

Chocorua IV is perhaps the most emphatic of Stella's *Irregular Polygon* compositions. He admits: "Some things are more immediately successful, some things work better than others. *Chocorua IV* was not so explicable but was immediately good."[1] For Museum of Modern Art curator Bill Rubin, *Chocorua IV* "states the central theme of the series in its most uncomplicated form" and has "the most primary geometrical conjunction possible in the series—namely, the interpenetration of an equilateral triangle and a square."[2] The central theme is, of course, this interpenetration and also interlocking or abutting of shapes. The illusion of depth is caused mainly by the value differentiation of the colors, because although the shapes abut or impinge on each other, in all but one painting they do not overlap. The *Irregular Polygons* are two-dimensional, as Stella explained: "There's a very shallow type of illusion going on in *Chocorua*. But once you're committed to doing this in

three-dimensions, then it really would be a pyramid inside a cube." The mitering of the lightning-like band that cushions the triangle reinforces the larger area's ability to contain the triangle, rather than appear to be seeking to eject it.

Stella associates the triangle in *Chocorua IV* with "the big mountain," Mount Chocorua in New Hampshire's White Mountains. When he began working on the *Irregular Polygons*, "they were so immediately landscape and mountainous," he decided to name them after places he had visited with his father on their fishing trips. This implies that Stella's painting titles are not always as arbitrary as he has often claimed, having personal associations with people, landscapes, and places he has visited.[3]

BPK

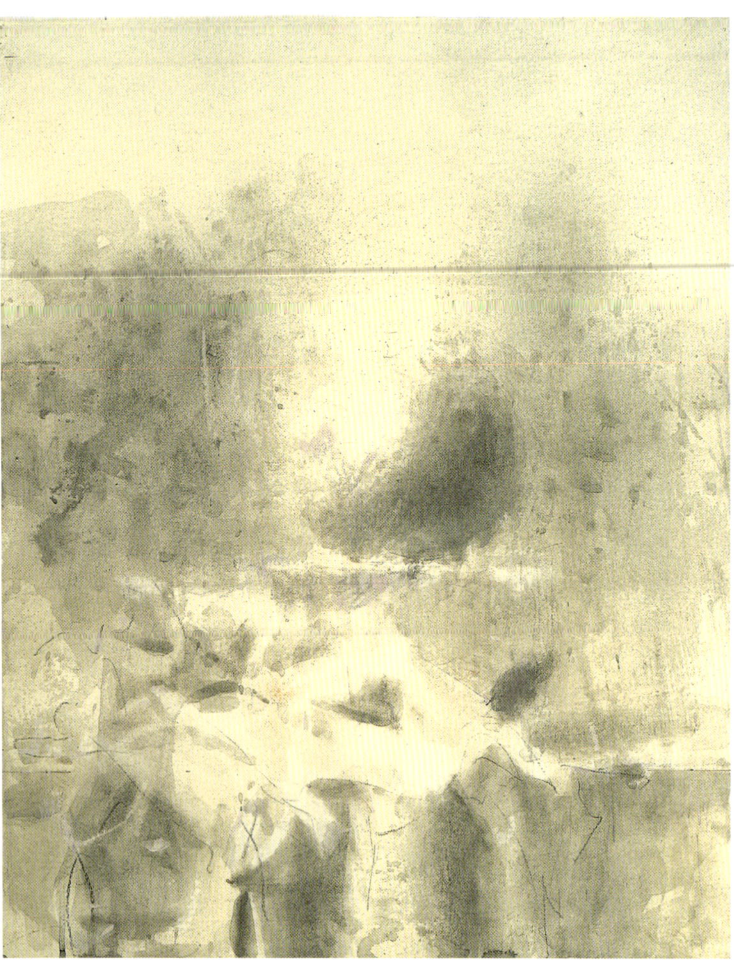

31

WALTER TANDY MURCH
American, born in Canada, 1907–1967
Study #18, 1962
Transparent and opaque watercolor and
charcoal on very thick wove paper,
23 x 17½ in
Gift of Mr. and Mrs. Thomas R. George,
Class of 1940; D.995.61

Walter Murch was artist-in-residence at Dartmouth in the fall of 1966. A Hopkins Center exhibition that celebrated the residency program featured this drawing in 1988, the year Murch's former student Ben Frank Moss was hired as the new head of the Studio Art Department, then called Visual Studies. Moss, now a professor emeritus at Dartmouth, had studied with Murch at Boston University and has a profound respect and admiration for this independent-minded mentor and artist. Moss frequently used *Study #18* to teach his own students drawing during his years at the College. In 1987 the drawing's owner, the artist and Dartmouth alumnus Thomas George, lent it to the College, where it remained until 1995, when George and his wife gave it to the Hood Museum of Art.

Throughout his artistic career, Murch created still lifes. His subjects were both human-made and natural objects—clocks, bricks, teapots, stone architectural fragments, bits of ribbon, lemons, potatoes, melons, and other quotidian inhabitants of his home and studio. In assembling the objects for this drawing, *Study #18*, Murch employed studio props—from the usual repertoire of Euclidian spheres, cylinders, pyramids, and rectangular solids, and a white cloth—that were used to train students in the fundamentals of depicting form and volume. Murch created the sphere in this drawing by a succession of small touches of wash that cohere into the rounded form. These marks are neither regular nor applied in a formulaic manner. The orb sits on a rough-edged cylinder or block, which, in turn, is mostly obscured by the cloth that is bunched around it. The light falls from above on the left and dissolves the upper-left side of the sphere as well as all but the deepest shadows in the crevices and folds of cloth. Even these seem to reflect the light, never becoming deeper than a translucent gray. In using this narrow range of tone, Murch appears to have captured on paper the air that lies between the viewer and the still life. This lends his work an otherworldly quality, a trademark of his later paintings and drawings. The forms of *Study #18* seem to exist in a Neoplatonic realm, in which the sphere takes on an authoritarian presence, equally at home in the absolutist vision of a utopian architect or the hermetic world of an artist who throughout his life sought to distill the essence of objects.

KWH

32

JULIAN STANCZAK
American, born 1928 in Poland
Consonance, 1967
Acrylic and tape on canvas, overall: 50^1/$_2$ x
43^1/$_2$ in.; frame: 52^1/$_2$ x 45^1/$_2$ in.
Purchased through the Julia L. Whittier Fund;
P.968.88
© Julian Stanczak

Julian Stanczak's abstract paintings use line, color, and tone to explore visual perception. Born in Poland in 1928, Stanczak spent two years in a Siberian labor camp during World War II. Severe maltreatment cost him the use of his right hand, and he later taught himself to be left handed. In 1942, aged 13, Stanczak escaped to join the Polish army-in-exile in Persia. After deserting, he spent his teenage years in a hut in a refugee camp in Uganda, where he received his first art lessons. He studied art in London, then immigrated to the United States in 1950. Stanczak earned a BFA from the Cleveland Institute of Art in 1954 and an MFA from Yale University in 1956. At Yale he studied with artist and color theorist Josef Albers, whose influence can be seen in Stanczak's interest in optical effects and use of abstraction. His one-man exhibition *Julian Stanczak: Optical Paintings* at the Martha Jackson Gallery in New York prompted the coining of the phrase "Op Art" in 1964. That year, he began teaching at the Cleveland Institute of Art, a position he would hold for thirty-one years.

Stanczak's work often includes vibrant color, but in the early 1960s he began experimenting with black and white.

I was watching the behavior of the rhythms of the line, you know, even the way children would play and dance, the way they would respond to my work and make noise. It was just a very primordial response to the action. So I said, well, a human response to this action is very clear, very emphatic. Let me see further what I can do. So I painted a bunch of them in black and white, instead of in different colors so much.[1]

Consonance expresses this movement, the "rhythms of the line." Stanczak first painted the canvas in shades of gray, the lighter edges and darker center creating the illusion of depth. He then drew in vertical lines in pencil. The wavy lines give the work an organic quality, a constant swaying movement. Finally he affixed rectangles of white tape, alternating them with the painted canvas. In each column the tape stripes are offset. There is no place for the eye to rest in *Consonance*; instead it moves from the lighter gray periphery, back and forth, to the darker center.

In the fall of 1968, the year after he completed *Consonance*, Stanczak was artist-in-residence at Dartmouth. His work at that time used both monochrome palettes and brilliant colors on canvases that seem to shimmer and shift before one's eyes. Stanczak continued to experiment with abstraction throughout the subsequent decades, returning to New York for a solo exhibition in 2004.

ABK

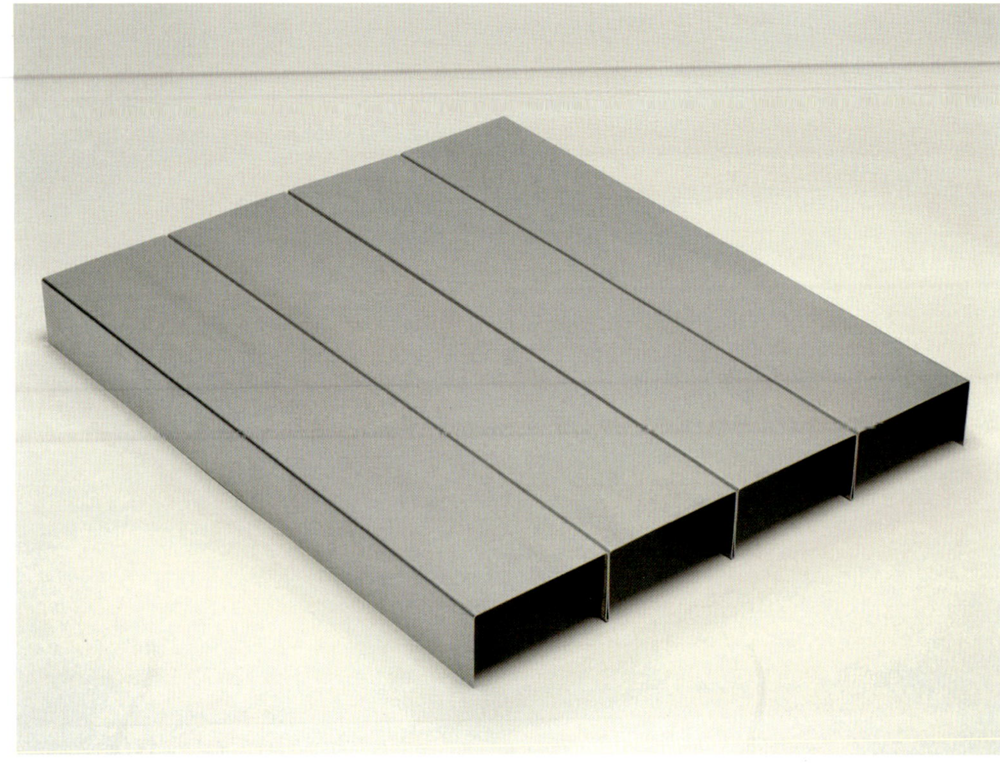

DONALD JUDD
American, 1928–1994
Table Object, 1968
Folded stainless steel, $2^5/_8$ x $20^1/_4$ x 24 in.
Lent by Trevor Fairbrother and
John T. Kirk; EL.2012.60.8
Art © Judd Foundation /
Licensed by VAGA, New York, NY

One of the most important thinkers and artists of his generation, Donald Judd was born in Excelsior Springs, Missouri. He served as an engineer in the United States Army in Korea between 1946 and 1947 before enrolling at the College of William and Mary in Williamsburg, Virginia, in 1948. He later studied in New York at the Art Students League and Columbia University, where he received a BS in philosophy, cum laude, in 1953. Judd's first solo exhibition was held in 1957 at the Panoras Gallery, New York, by which time he was also writing criticism for magazines such as *ARTnews*, *Art Magazine*, and *Art International*. Like other artists associated with minimalism, Judd began making art shortly after Jackson Pollock's death in 1956, but he wholly rejected one of the fundamental tenants of Pollock's generation—namely, the idea of a necessary connection between the inner psychology of the creator and the appearance or meaning of his art. Judd first sought to eliminate these assumptions when, in 1964, he began to have his work industrially fabricated, based on his specific instructions and drawings. This technique created taut, anonymous-looking structures characterized by unity of color, image, surface, and shape. Calling his works "specific objects," Judd emphasized his intention to create concrete physical things that did not partake of the illusionary space occupied by either painting or sculpture, categories he relegated to the past.

Judd was artist-in-residence at Dartmouth in the summer of 1966, by which time he was working entirely with fabricators. He had a number of works created by the New York–based industrial manufacturers Bernstein Brothers that summer, but the ideas and instructions for these projects may have pre-dated his time at Dartmouth. This work was made two years later in an edition of two hundred as part of the *Ten from Leo Castelli* portfolio. Published by Tanglewood Press in celebration of the tenth anniversary of the Leo Castelli Gallery in New York, which represented Judd, this edition also included works by Lee Bontecou, Jasper Johns, and Andy Warhol, as well as two former Dartmouth artists-in-residence, Robert Rauschenberg and Frank Stella. Judd created this multiple, like all of his mature works, in folded stainless steel using processes of fabrication—similar to those used to make industrial products and machinery—that allowed him to eradicate any trace of his own hand, thus revolutionizing practices and attitudes surrounding art-making in the 1960s.

MRT

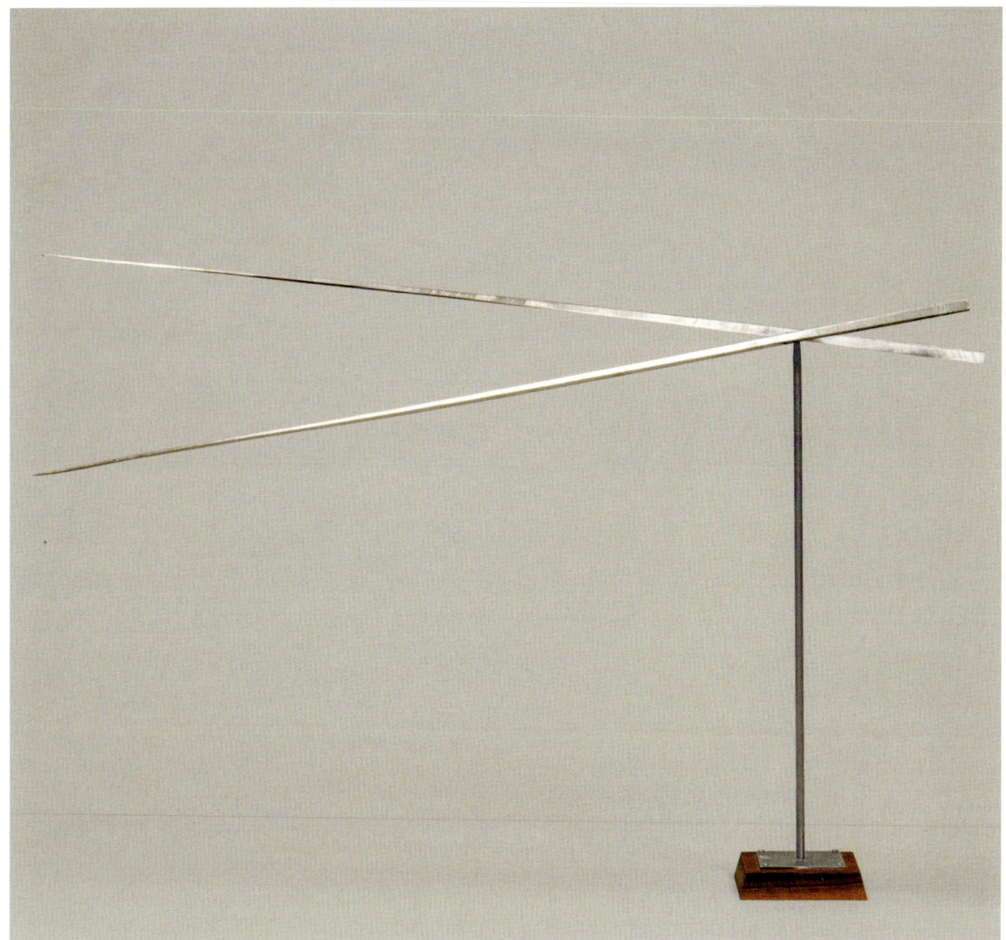

GEORGE WARREN RICKEY
American, 1907–2002
Two Horizontal Lines, 1966
Stainless steel, height: 36 in.
Gift of the artist; S.966.40
Art © Estate of George Rickey /
Licensed by VAGA, New York, NY

George Warren Rickey is best known for his large-scale stainless steel kinetic sculptures, which use wind and ambient airflow to create spontaneous, soundless movement. His work combines engineering and mechanics with abstract art and design to create soaring and graceful sculptures that move in harmony with natural elements. Born in South Bend, Indiana, Rickey was raised in Scotland and studied in Paris with André Lhote, Fernand Léger, and Amédée Ozanfant. He returned to the United States in 1934, and for the early part of his career was primarily a painter working in a social realist style. During World War II, he worked as a gunnery instructor for the Army Air Corps and had access to a machine shop. Here he created some of his first sculptures—small mobiles of plastic, copper, and wire that were influenced by the work of Alexander Calder. After discharge, Rickey studied art history at New York University's Institute of Fine Arts and design at the Chicago Institute of Design (now the Illinois Institute of Technology) under the GI Bill. While teaching at Indiana University in South Bend, he met the sculptor David Smith, who helped him further his welding techniques, and by the mid 1950s Rickey had begun using pendular motion, which would be the basis of his future kinetic work.

Rickey was artist-in-residence at Dartmouth in the winter of 1966, when he created *Two Horizontal Lines* and exhibited it in the Jaffe-Friede Gallery. After his residency, Rickey gave the sculpture to the College. Although small in scale, measuring about three feet high, it reflects the principles of his large-scale, outdoor kinetic sculptures of the same period, such as *Two Lines, Temporal I and II*, completed for the Museum of Modern Art sculpture garden in 1964. Two knife-like blades of steel pivot on a vertical fulcrum. The graduated weight of the tapered blades allows for limited random sweeping movement, in which each blade sways independently of the other, although each on the same trajectory. The result is a work that uses mechanical order to create random and rhythmic beauty.

SGP

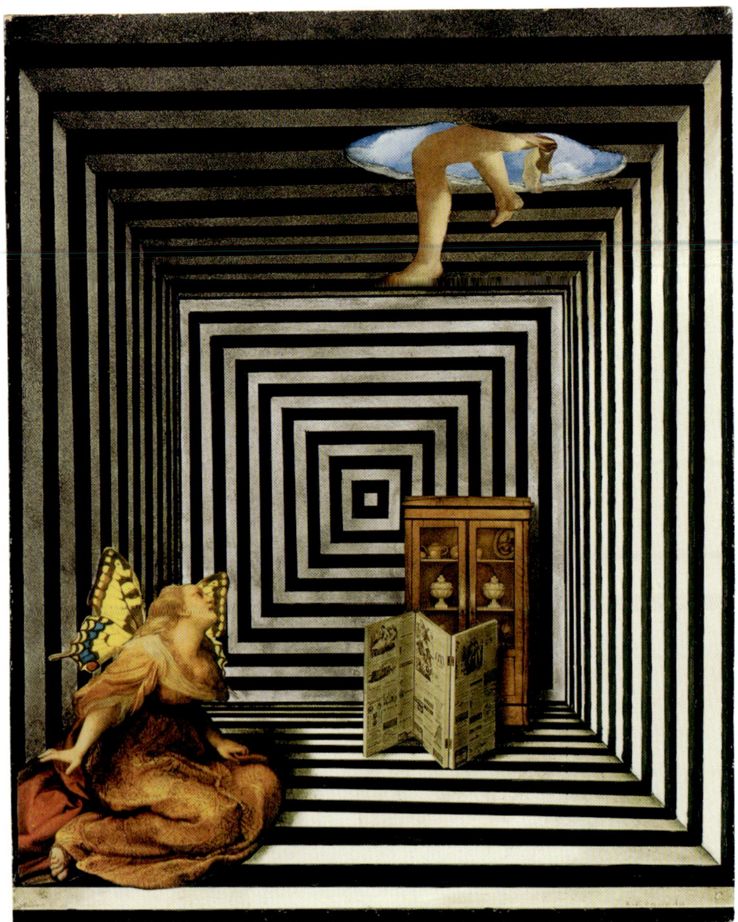

XAVIER ESQUEDA
Mexican, born 1943
The Relatives of Icarus (Los Parientes de Icaro),
about 1965
Oil and collage on composition board,
14⅞ x 11½ in.
Museum purchase; P.965.105
© Xavier Esqueda

Xavier Esqueda was only twenty-three years old when he was invited to participate in Dartmouth's Artist-in-Residence Program in 1965. Largely self-trained, Esqueda had been exhibiting his work since the age of fourteen and was already represented by the Galleria de Antonio Souza, one of the most progressive contemporary art galleries in Mexico City. *The Relatives of Icarus* reveals immediately the inscrutable fascination of Esqueda's art as well as characteristic elements of his eclectic style. Drawing on the legacy of surrealism as well as more recent movements such as op and pop art, Esqueda's work nestles playfully between the rational concerns of geometric abstraction and the deliberately irrational antics of the "panic world," the trajectory taken by postwar Mexican artists who crossed the psychedelic counterculture with esoteric religion and sexual transgression. While Esqueda's works never reach the extremes of Alejandro Jodorowsky's films or the neo-baroque complexity of Pedro Friedeberg's compositions, he shares with these colleagues an allusive exuberance that makes any single work difficult to pin down yet seemingly indebted to everything.

The *Relatives of Icarus* incorporates elements of Italian Renaissance painting with the avant-garde techniques of *papier mâché* and collage to create a virtual shadow box that evokes Joseph Cornell's miniature worlds of wonder. Esqueda invokes the myth of Icarus as the pretense for a meditation on the artist's release from the demands of any single illusionistic system. He establishes an interior space through a sequence of increasingly smaller squares. However, by placing figures and objects within this "room," Esqueda refuses this famous perceptual illusion its ability to vacillate between recession and projection. Furthermore, he cuts an oculus into the "ceiling" of his room through which a figure (Icarus?) takes flight into a blue sky. Much like the cupola in Andrea Mantegna's masterful *Camera Degli Sposi* (1465–74), Esqueda's work is filled with playful references to the art and artifice of illusionism.

MKC

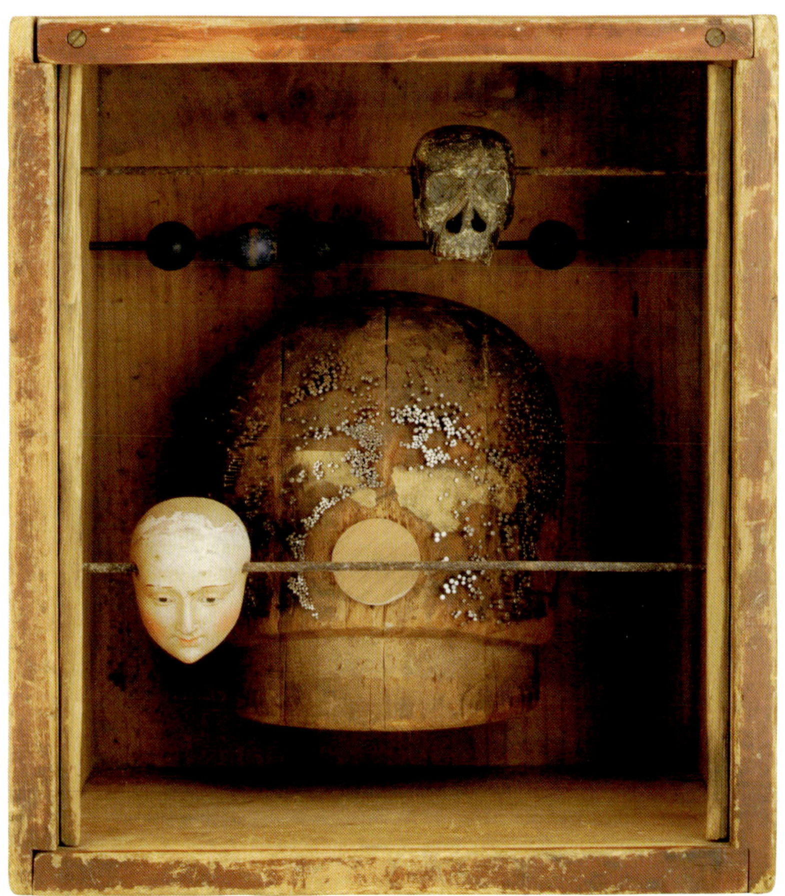

36

VARUJAN BOGHOSIAN
American, born 1926
The Tribune, 1968
Box construction with wood, steel,
and terracotta, 15 x 13 x 10 in.
Purchased through the Evelyn A. and
William B. Jaffe Fund; S.968.86
© Varujan Boghosian

Varujan Boghosian was invited to Dartmouth as an artist-in-residence in 1968 and stayed to become a professor of art in the Studio Art Department. In 1982 he was named the George Frederick Jewett Professor, a post he retired from fourteen years later. Born in New Britain, Connecticut, of Armenian heritage, Boghosian served in the Navy at the end of World War II and, like many of his generation, after his service attended college on the GI Bill. He enrolled first at Connecticut Teacher's College (1946–48) and then the Vesper School of Art in Boston (1948–50). He began to show his watercolors and woodcuts at local galleries when he was at Vespers and had his first solo exhibition in 1950. After Boghosian had traveled to Italy on a Fulbright grant, friends suggested that he meet and share his work with the ex-Bauhaus professor and master of color theory Josef Albers, who was then teaching at Yale University. Albers was impressed with the younger artist's work and admitted Boghosian to the program, where he received first his BA and then his MFA, in 1958. After Yale, he taught at the University of Florida, Cooper Union, Pratt Institute, Yale, Brown University, and then Dartmouth. He was an influential teacher during his years at the College and made a habit of befriending the artists-in-residence, often trading work with them. He continues to show his work regularly in New York and Boston.

Boghosian—like others represented in this book, such as Olivia Parker and Paul Bowen—is a collector of objects. His studio, which was for many years located in the basement of Webster Hall at Dartmouth (now Rauner Library), is filled with prints, faded advertisements, toys, mannequins, pieces of old games, and other items he has found in antique shops, estate sales, and flea markets. These objects, bearing the patina of age and use, form a corpus of material that he can draw from at will. To visit his studio is to step into world apart—one in which these remnants of the past still embody the memory of those who first owned them. Like an alchemist, Boghosian recombines and assembles to create new associations and meanings, often drawing on the intrinsic character of his materials. *Tribune* dates from the year of his residency. Framed by an old wooden box that appears to have once housed an abacus, this poetic association of objects recalls the work of Joseph Cornell, another assembler of worlds within boxes. Suspended across metal poles that have been affixed horizontally within the box are a skull and a doll's head. Another pole holds the rhyming forms of small blue wooden balls. In the center, adhered to the back of the box, is a larger wooden shape that perhaps once was used to display hats. This form looks like the back of a helmet, possibly a reference to a Roman tribune that gave the work its title. The artist has pounded many small, flat-headed nails into this form, some around a disk forming a half-halo, the nail heads polished so they shimmer as they catch the light. The grim accounting of the abacus-bead doll's head and skull in association with the Roman officer creates an enigmatic web of meaning, evoking the wielding of institutional power in matters of life and death.

KWH

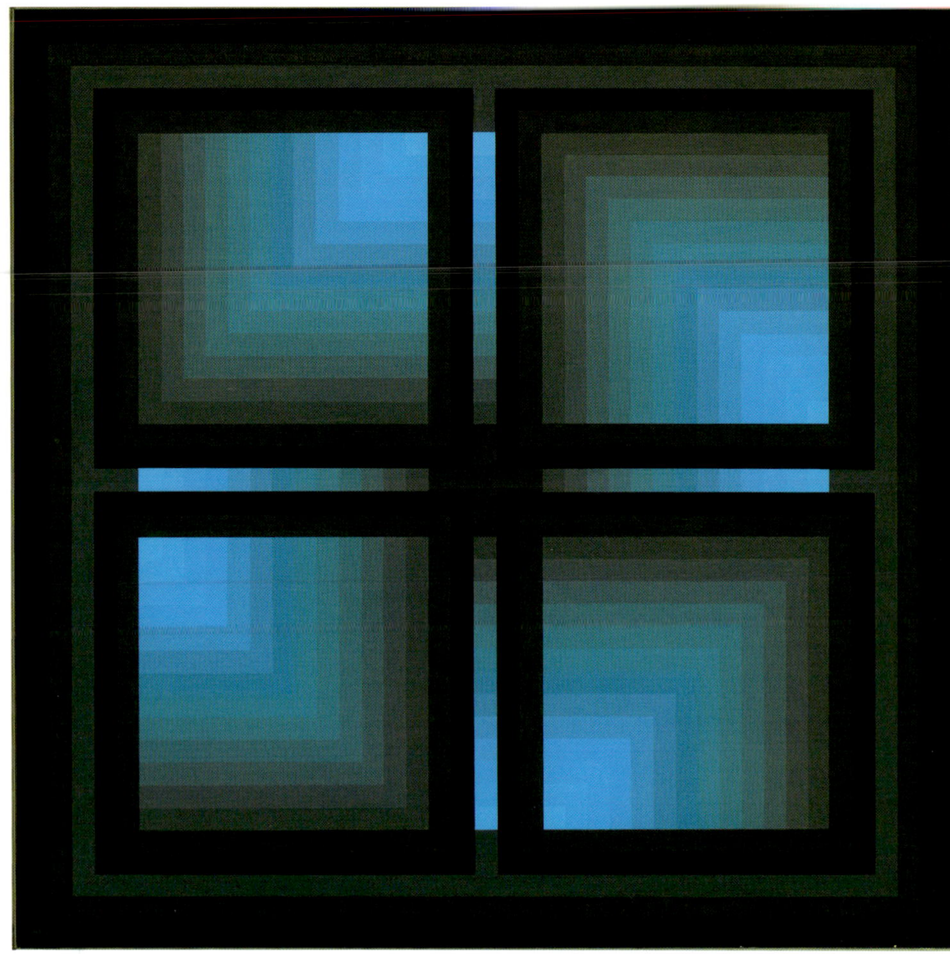

37

HANNES BECKMANN
American, born in Germany, 1909–1977
Blue Diamond, 1972
Acrylic on Masonite, 42 x 42 in.
Gift of Ann Boeckler in memory of
Erich Boeckler; 2008.81.2
© Estate of Hannes Beckmann, used
with permission

Like many German modernists of his generation, Hannes Beckmann was influenced by the country's rich artistic environment before the rise of Nazism during the 1930s. Born in Stuttgart, he studied painting and stage design at the Bauhaus, an experimental art school founded by Walter Gropius in 1919. When Beckmann enrolled there in the late 1920s, he studied with prominent twentieth-century modernists such as Joseph Albers, Paul Klee, and Wassily Kandinsky. In 1932, a year before the Nazis closed the Bauhaus, he graduated and left for Vienna, where he studied photography until 1934. Beckmann then moved to Prague to work as a press and stage photographer. During the German occupation of Czechoslovakia, he joined the resistance and was imprisoned in 1944. He immigrated to United States and became a citizen in 1948. Residing in New York, he first headed the photographic department at the Guggenheim Foundation and then taught at the Cooper Union School of Art and Architecture until 1970. That year he was first invited to be an artist-in-residence, then hired as an art professor at Dartmouth, where he remained until his retirement in 1975.

This painting, created while Beckmann was at Dartmouth, exemplifies his approach to abstraction, design, and color. In a 1977 interview, Beckmann stated, "[A] painting presents a man-made arrangement of forms and colors which may have very little resemblance to nature. We expect from a good painting that a relationship is established where all the parts are so integrated that you could not remove any one without destroying the whole."[1] His interest in the optical power of color in abstract art, which has its origins in experiments by Bauhaus artists such as Josef Albers, aligns him with the op art movement of the 1960s. *Blue Diamond* relies less on the sort of optical effects created by Bridget Riley or Richard Anuszkiewicz and more on the transmutation of color as light fades. Beckmann affixed four two-toned, black-and-gray frames to a painted Masonite sheet. In each framed quadrant, the bright blue gradually fades in segmented blocks of color that merge with the frames, much like a darkening sky after sunset.

Jan van der Marck, former director of the Dartmouth College Art Gallery, writes of Beckmann's interest in the color theories of amateur painter and Nobel prize-winning chemist Wilhelm Ostwald (1853–1932), whose color primer influenced Beckmann's Bauhaus teacher Klee, and also in the theories of David Katz, who studied color perception. Katz thought of color as having three modes: color as surface, which we look *at*; color as film, which we look *through*; and color as volume, which we look *into*. Beckman tended to work with the latter two types of color arrangements.[2] *Blue Diamond* has that transparency of color; one looks through the various shades of modulated blue to the brighter, pure color that seems to lie behind it. The bands of color recall the work of Klee, whose planes of segmented color were a hallmark of his work. However, unlike Klee's looser, painterly style, Beckmann's work features a strict, hard-edged sense of order, which he saw as a form of harmony. The rigorous structure in these paintings acts as a frame for his visual investigations into relational patterns of color.

ABK and KWH

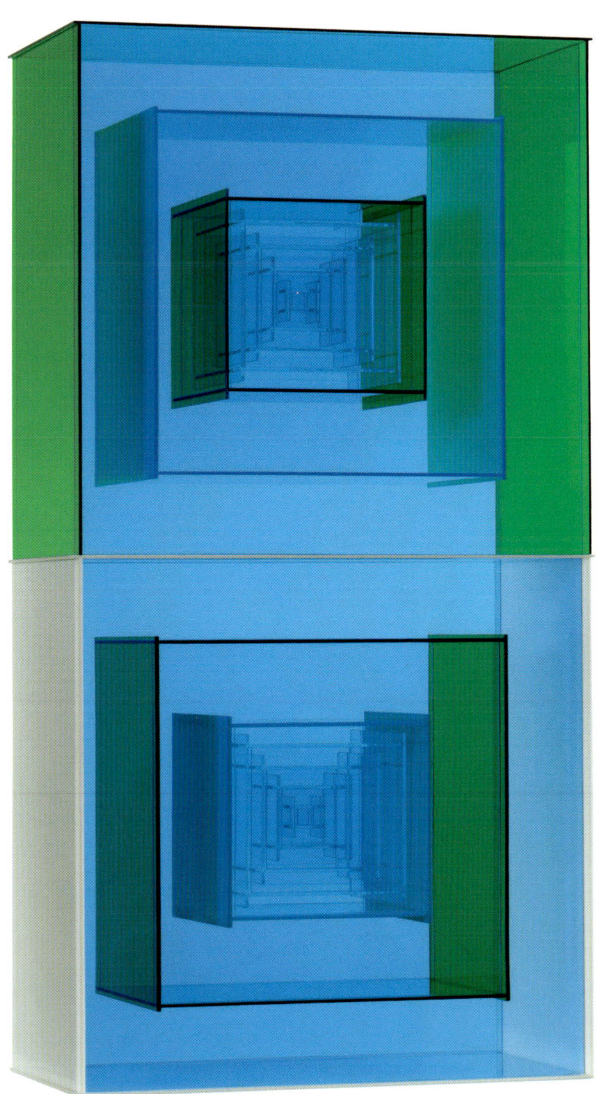

38

LEROY LAMIS
American, 1925–2010
Construction No. 194, 1970
Plexiglas, 36¹/₄ x 18¹/₂ x 10 in.
Purchased through the Virginia and
Preston T. Kelsey '58 Fund; 2012.41
© Leroy Lamis, 1970

Leroy Lamis is best known for the Plexiglas constructions he made in the 1960s and 1970s that extended the legacy of Russian Constructivism and abstract art through the use of new materials. Born in Eddyville, Iowa, in 1925, Lamis moved to California in the early 1940s and worked in the film-cutting room at MGM Studios in Hollywood, which awakened his career-long interest in light and space. Between 1943 and 1945, Lamis served in the U.S. Army Air Corps. Following his discharge, Lamis took courses in Art and Art History at UCLA and made his first sculptures out of industrial materials, including glass and metals found in local junkyards. He completed his art degree at New Mexico Highlands University in 1953 before moving to New York to enroll at Columbia University, where he completed his master's degree in 1956. He also taught art in Locust Valley, Long Island, at a high school attended by the children of the noted sculptor Richard Lippold. Through Lippold, Lamis had his first direct contact with the history and legacy of Russian Constructivism. In 1961 he began teaching art and design at Indiana State University, where he would remain until his retirement in 1982. In the spring of 1963, Lamis began showing his Plexiglas constructions at New York's Contemporaries Gallery, where he came into contact with Richard Anuszkiewicz, Harry Bertoia, George Rickey, and other leading artists of the era.

Deeply influenced by the work of Naum Gabo and Josef Albers, Lamis first worked with clear plastics in 1958 as an extension of his earlier investigation into glass and prisms. He found the limited manipulability of prisms and glass restricting and looked for a new material with which to investigate light and space, eventually finding Plexiglas to be the perfect medium to express his ideas and concepts. Between 1962 and 1978, Lamis executed 230 Plexiglas constructions, including *Construction No. 194*, which the artist completed during his residency at Dartmouth in the fall of 1970 (the work is dated November 6, 1970, on the bottom edge). This luminous composition consists of two vertically aligned boxes, built from the inside out with machine-like precision, that contain a symmetrical progression of radiating cubes in alternating shades of blue and Dartmouth green. Depending on the lighting of the work, the colors of the transparent Plexiglas subtly change and shimmer, reflecting and merging into each other.

MRT

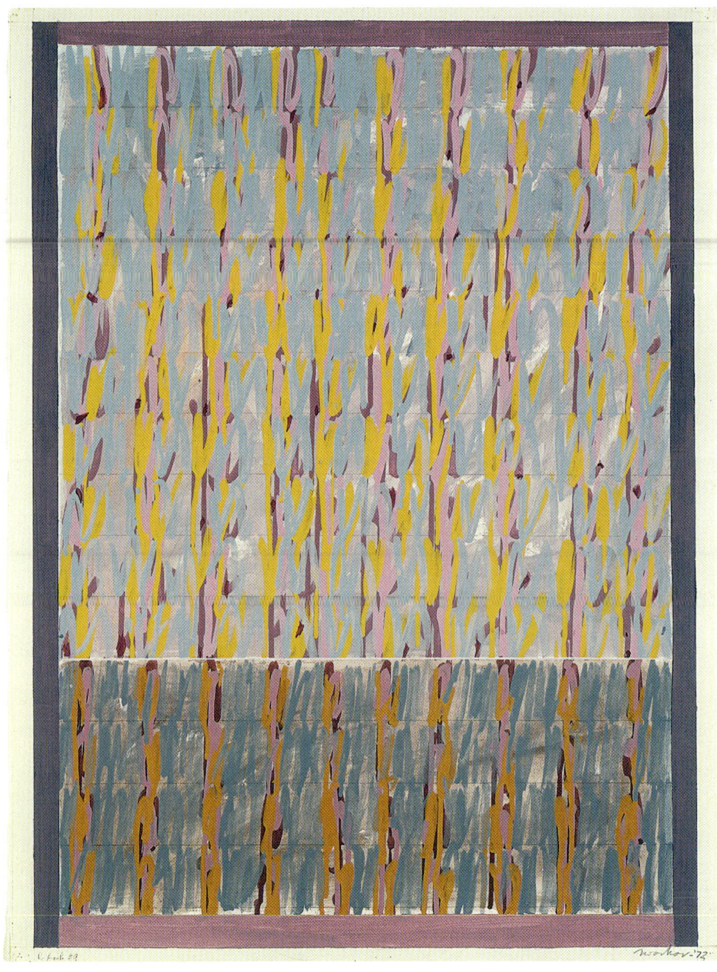

JACK TWORKOV
American, born in Poland, 1900–1982
Untitled (R. A. on P. #9), 1972
Acrylic on paper, 30⁷/₈ x 22¹/₄ in.
Purchased through the Julia L.
Whittier Fund; D.970.110
Art © Estate of Jack Tworkov /
Licensed by VAGA, New York, NY

Abstract painter Jack Tworkov, who was artist-in-residence at Dartmouth in the winter of 1973, once wrote in his journal, "I am torn between the calligraphic and the structural—between the exuberance of movement and the passion of meditation."[1] This duality, and the search for resolution, can be found throughout the artist's lengthy career. Tworkov studied English at Columbia University from 1920 to 1923, and art at the National Academy of Design from 1923 to 1925 and the Art Students League from 1925 to 1926. He suspended his artistic career during World War II to become a tool designer, but re-emerged in the mid-1940s as a major figure in the New York School of painting, also known as abstract expressionism. Citing as influences Chaïm Soutine, Paul Cézanne, and his contemporary Willem de Kooning, Tworkov created large-scale abstract canvases that were critically acclaimed for their painterly brushwork and rich surface textures. During the 1960s, however, he became disenchanted with gestural abstraction and its emotional immediacy, seeing in his work a predictability that belied the intended spontaneity of process. In order to regain the freedom to experiment, he needed "some constant I could fasten onto . . . that I could measure and repeat," transforming the remaining variables with every painting. As a result, the artist began to explore the possibilities of geometry and the structural notion of the grid.

Untitled (R. A. on P. #9) shows the result of Tworkov's stated desire to reconcile the instinctive impulse of abstract expressionism with the application of intellect and precision of form that he admired in architects' drawings. This painting also demonstrates Tworkov's masterful understanding of tone. Using blue as the background, Tworkov places orange and pink brushstrokes at regular intervals across the surface to create the rhythm of the organizational grid. The consistency of Tworkov's marks reinforces the sense of pattern. Building layer upon layer, he uses the same types of colors and lines in both the upper and lower sections of the work. However, by shifting value and hue, Tworkov achieves a powerful all-over effect. Due to his manipulation of color, the upper region of the painting seems bathed in light, while in comparison the lower third remains muted by shadow. Through this contrast Tworkov emphasizes his mastery of color and his ability to create a work in which all of the parts are equally important in the generation of the whole.

AHW

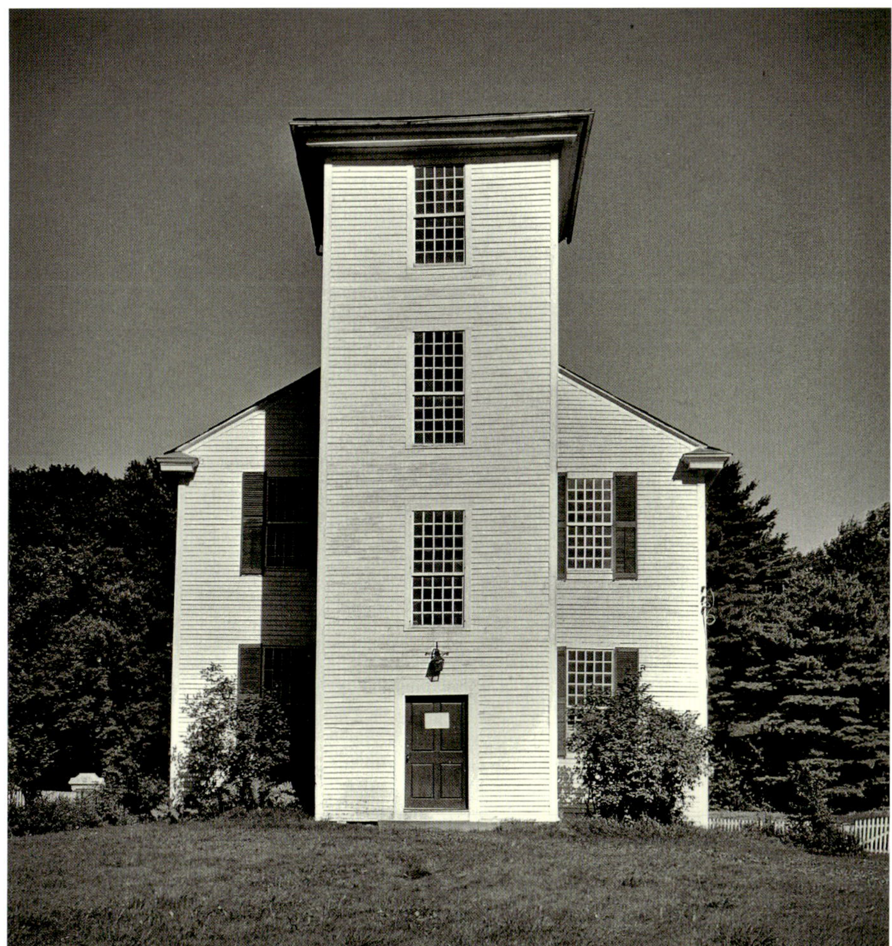

Arguably the most influential American photographer of the twentieth century, Walker Evans is celebrated for his hauntingly precise and poetic images of vernacular America, especially the rural South during the Great Depression. By the time Evans came to Hanover as Dartmouth's artist-in-residence the fall of 1972, his artistic reputation had attained a new height. He had just been honored the previous year with his second major exhibition at the Museum of Modern Art and a smaller retrospective at Yale, where he had served as a professor of photography since 1965. It was not easy to lure such a luminary to Dartmouth, but Matthew Wysocki, head of the Visual Studies Department and a devoted photographer himself, eventually succeeded.[1] Evans made a preliminary trip to Hanover in August 1972 to create work for Dartmouth's planned fall exhibition. Wysocki later recollected that when driving Evans around the Upper Valley "to photograph his favorite scenes . . . he would always say, 'Stop, Mat! That's a 1930s view!' So we'd get out and he'd do his photographing."[2] Evans readily integrated himself into the Dartmouth community, but his health deteriorated during his stay and in late December he underwent surgery for bleeding ulcers and remained hospitalized for a month before returning to Connecticut.[3]

Evans's August excursion through the Upper Valley resulted in his iconic *Trinity Church, Cornish, New Hampshire*, which represents a northern New England reprisal of a subject that had fascinated him since around 1931, empty vernacular churches. Here Evans's low, frontal vantage point accentuates the structure's stark, classical simplicity, which reads as both historic and modern. Built from 1804 to 1808 for Cornish's Trinity Episcopal Church, the structure lacks ornament, religious or secular. Strong, flat light accentuates its weathered clapboard surface and clean forms. The small-paned, capacious windows echo the building's geometric underpinnings yet relieve its severity, while the tall projecting entry pavilion is both forbidding and aspirational. One can imagine how in encountering it, Evans might have recalled an experience he shared with writer James Agee during their extended documentation of rural Alabama in 1936. Agee wrote: "It was a good enough church from the moment the curve opened and we saw it that I slowed a little and we kept our eyes on it. But as we came even with it the light so held it that it shocked us with its goodness straight through the body, so that at the same instant we said *Jesus*." [4]

BJM

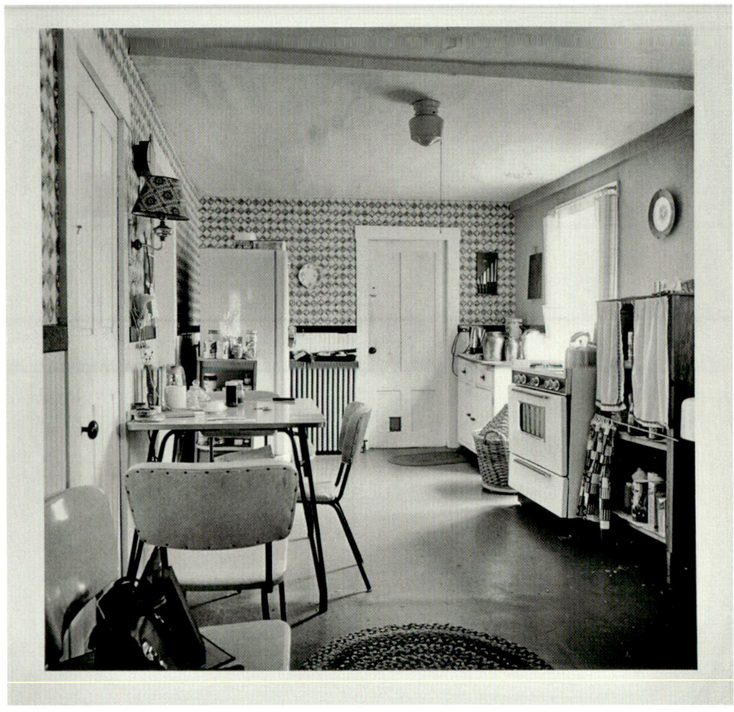 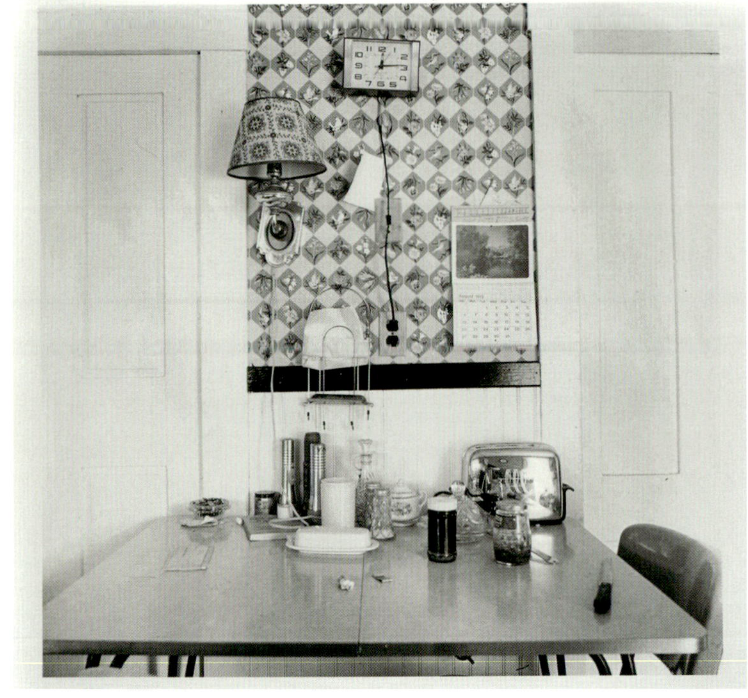

Before assuming his post as artist-in-residence at Dartmouth in the fall term of 1972, Walker Evans (see cat. 40) visited the area that August, with hopes of supplementing his forthcoming retrospective exhibition at the college with photographs of local scenes.[1] As evidenced by these farmhouse interiors, Evans enjoyed a particularly fruitful photography session at the home of Alfred Petersen in Enfield, New Hampshire, about twelve miles from Hanover. Escorting Evans on this venture was visual studies professor Matthew Wysocki, who had invited him to Dartmouth. Like Evans, Wysocki was an inveterate collector of old "stuff" and would have been well acquainted with Mr. Peterson, who sold antiques from his barn. Wysocki later remembered introducing Evans to the owners of what was likely this residence: "'This is my friend Walker Evans,' and their reply was, 'isn't it nice that you would have a senior citizen friend, who has found a hobby in photography.' He loved that."[2] The visit resulted in these spare, evocative images as well as photographs that Wysocki took of Evans and Mr. Petersen in the barn (see figs. 22 and 23).

Understated architectural interiors were a leitmotif throughout Evans's career and, as seen in these examples, he gravitated toward rooms set in modest, vernacular homes with a patina of age. Although typically devoid of people, his interiors nonetheless suggest a human presence, activated by a caressing light and intense focus on the character and placement of ordinary domestic objects. Evans achieved particular renown for his interiors of the homes of destitute sharecroppers in southern Alabama in 1936. These photographs, together with

41

WALKER EVANS
*Alfred Petersen's Kitchen, Enfield,
New Hampshire*, 1972
Gelatin silver print, 8 x 10 in.
Gift of Janet Petersen Mayers,
Class of 1947W; 2008.25.1
© Walker Evans Archive, The Metropolitan
Museum of Art

42

WALKER EVANS
*Alfred Petersen's Kitchen Table, Enfield,
New Hampshire*, 1972
Gelatin silver print, 8 x 10 in.
Gift of Janet Petersen Mayers,
Class of 1947W; 2008.25.2
© Walker Evans Archive, The Metropolitan
Museum of Art

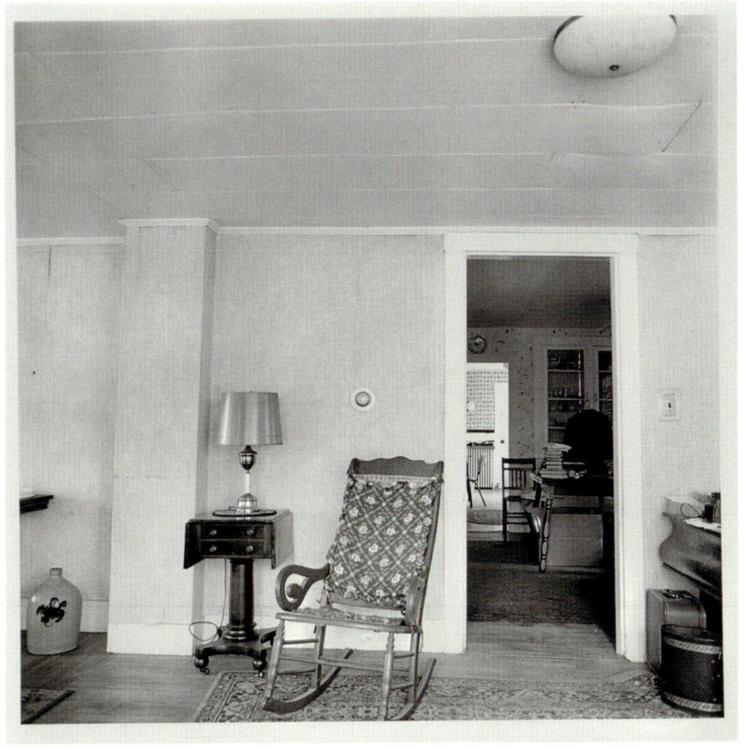

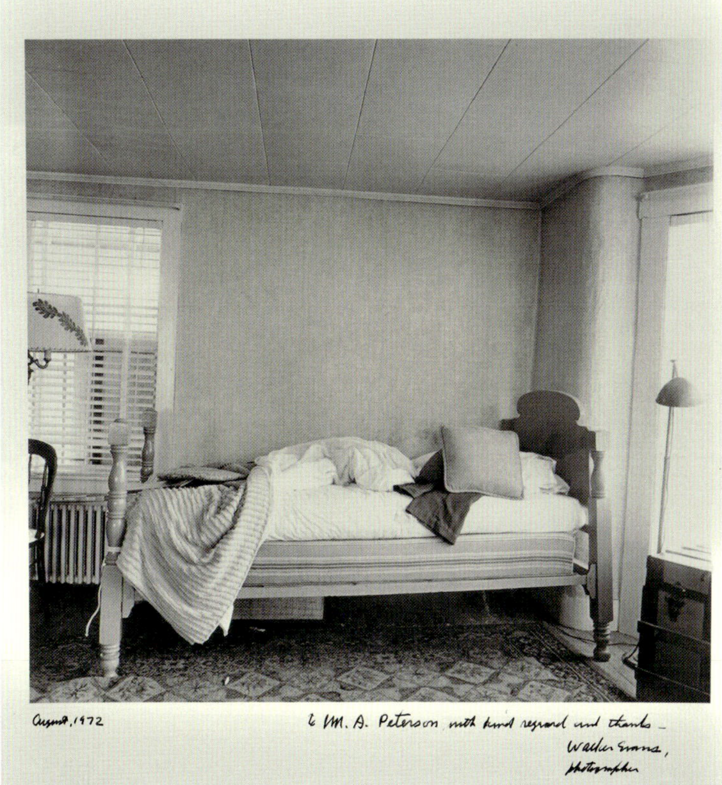

James Agee's writings, gained wide circulation when published in the landmark book *Let Us Now Praise Famous Men* (1941). The stark, frugal grace of these Depression-era images elevated them from historic documents to timeless elegies of loss, deprivation, and perseverance. Made about thirty-five years later, Evans's photographs of Mr. Petersen's New Hampshire home repeat motifs that appeared in his interiors set in Alabama and elsewhere: an empty bed (here rendered all the more intimate for its unmade state), vacant chairs, and an unpretentious, subtly artful domestic tableau, in this case centered around a kitchen table. An underlying geometry unites this New England still life, while its slightly askew components add to its unaffected air. The paper tucked behind the light switch, calendar hung on the wall, and suspended napkin holder all suggest human touch, intention, and the kind of unassuming aesthetic that Evans paid tribute to throughout his career. In doing so, he broadened inalterably our notions of both documentation and art.

DJM

43

WALKER EVANS
Alfred Petersen's Living Room, Enfield, New Hampshire, 1972
Gelatin silver print, 8 x 10 in.
Gift of Janet Petersen Mayers,
Class of 1947W; 2008.25.3
© Walker Evans Archive, The Metropolitan Museum of Art

44

WALKER EVANS
Alfred Petersen's Bedroom, Enfield, New Hampshire, 1972
Gelatin silver print, 12$^{1}/_{4}$ x 10$^{1}/_{2}$ in.
Gift of Janet Petersen Mayers,
Class of 1947W; 2008.25.4
© Walker Evans Archive, The Metropolitan Museum of Art

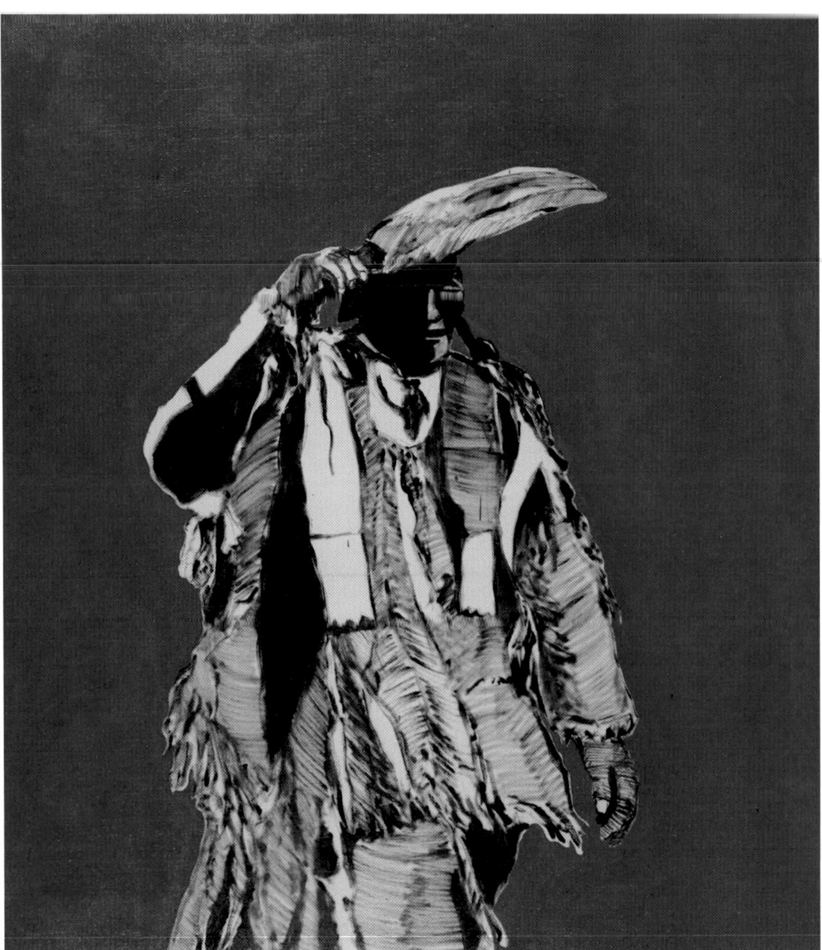

FRITZ SCHOLDER
American (Luiseño), 1937–2005
Dartmouth Portrait #17, 1973
Oil on canvas, acrylic background, 80 x 68 in.
Purchased through the William B. Jaffe and
Evelyn A. Jaffe Hall Fund; P.974.11
© Lisa Scholder

Fritz Scholder was one of the most renowned and controversial Native American artists of the twentieth century. Born in Breckenridge, Minnesota, Scholder was one-quarter Luiseño, a California Mission tribe. A prolific painter, sculptor, printmaker, and photographer, Scholder sought to deconstruct the myths and stereotypes of Native Americans, using a style and palette that owed a strong debt to pop art. Trained by the Yanktonai Sioux artist Oscar Howe from 1950 to 1954, Scholder enrolled at Wisconsin State University in 1956, but after his first year he transferred to California State University, Sacramento, where he studied with Wayne Thiebaud from 1957 to 1958. He completed his BA at Sacramento State College in 1960. Upon graduation, Scholder was granted a Rockefeller Foundation scholarship for the Southwestern Indian Art Project at the University of Arizona. After receiving his MFA in 1964 he moved to Santa Fe, New Mexico, to teach advanced painting and contemporary art history at the newly formed Institute of American Indian Arts. By the time he left in 1969 he had influenced an entire generation of Native American artists, many of whom are still working today.

In 1967 Scholder began work on a series of iconic paintings on the theme of the American Indian that would gain him national attention. These works, which depicted Native Americans drinking beer or draped in the American flag, overturned clichés and addressed the guilt of the dominant culture. In the fall of 1973, he was the first Native American to be artist-in-residence at Dartmouth College and the paintings he made on campus, known as the *Dartmouth Portraits*, were shown in an exhibition at the Cordier and Ekstrom Gallery, New York, that opened in December of that year to favorable reviews. In *Dartmouth Portrait #17*, Scholder appears to make reference to the then-current debate over Dartmouth's intercollegiate athletic teams' unofficial use of an Indian mascot. After a long protest effort by Native American faculty and students, the Trustees of Dartmouth College issued an official statement in 1974 discouraging the use of the Indian mascot on campus. This painting's predominantly green hue (Dartmouth's school color) and its depiction of a monumental and dignified figure in Native American dress offer a counterpoint to more stereotypical renderings of an Indian warrior. Instead of a bow and arrow or hatchet, for instance, Scholder's man carries an eagle-wing feather fan, a symbol of spiritual harmony and prestige.

MRT

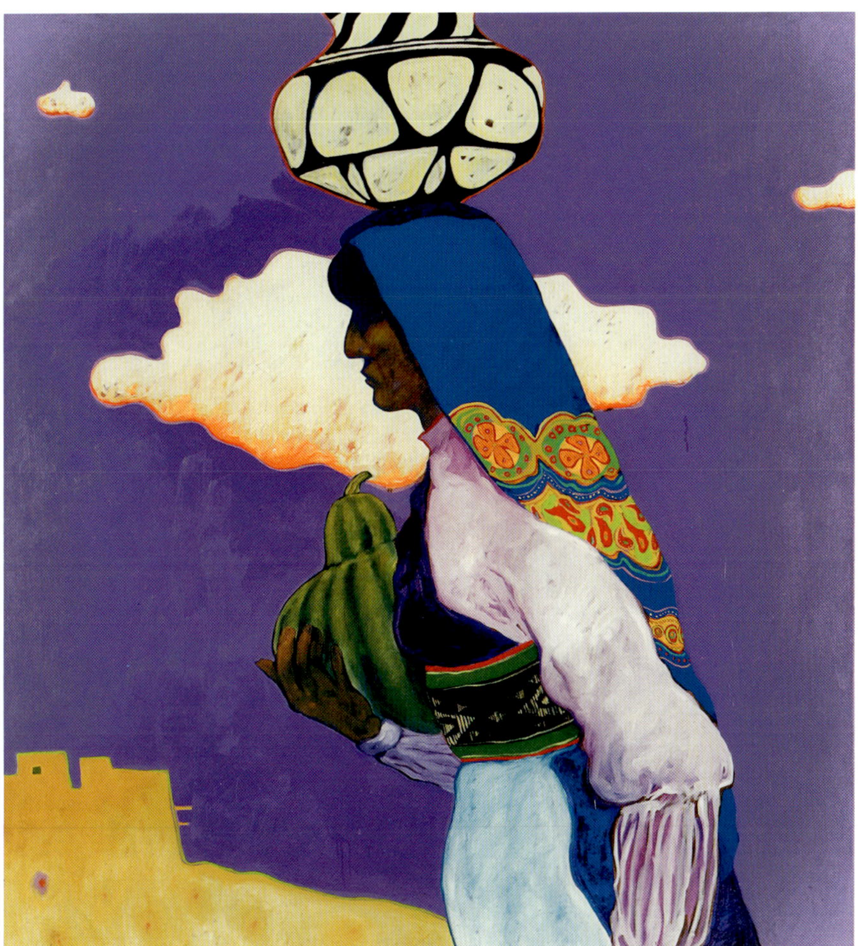

T. C. CANNON
American (Gaigwa [Kiowa]/Caddo/Choctaw),
1946–1978
Cloud Madonna, 1975
Acrylic on canvas, 59$^{15}/_{16}$ x 54 in.
Promised gift of Charles E. Nearburg,
Class of 1972; EL.2010.86
© Joyce Cannon Yi

Tommy Wayne Cannon, popularly known as T. C. Cannon, was one of the most important Native American artists of the twentieth century. An enrolled member of the Kiowa Tribe and of Caddo, French, and Choctaw descent, Cannon was born in Lawton, Oklahoma, and was raised in the Kiowa culture of his father, Walter Cannon, and the Caddo traditions of his mother, Minnie Ahdunko Cannon. From 1964 to 1966 Cannon studied at the Institute of American Indian Arts of Santa Fe, where his teachers included the noted Native American painter Fritz Scholder. After graduating from IAIA, he enrolled in the San Francisco Art Institute, but left after two months to enlist in the U.S. Army. A paratrooper in the 101st Airborne Division, Cannon was deployed to Vietnam in 1967. During the Tet Offensive, which began on January 30, 1968, Cannon earned two bronze stars for bravery. While he was stationed in Vietnam, Cannon's work was included in a major traveling exhibition of contemporary Southern Plains Indian artists, which launched his artistic career. After completing his military service, Cannon finished a BA at Central State University (now the University of Central Oklahoma) in 1972. That same year, Cannon and Scholder had a joint exhibition at the Smithsonian Institution's National Collection of Fine Arts in Washington, D.C. Following the success of the *Two American Painters* exhibition, Cannon signed a contract with the New York dealer Joaquin (Jean) Aberbach, giving Aberbach exclusive rights to all of Cannon's work. Over the next six years, Cannon produced a prodigious body of work in preparation for his first solo exhibition, which was scheduled to open at the Aberbach Gallery in New York in October

1978. Tragically, Cannon died in an automobile accident on May 8, 1978, at the age of thirty-one. The exhibition, which featured fifty works by the artist, finally opened on December 10, 1979, as *T. C. Cannon: A Memorial Exhibition*.

In the summer of 1975, Cannon was the second Native American to be invited to Dartmouth as artist-in-residence (fittingly, the first was Scholder, his great friend and mentor). Cannon's exhibition, held in the Beaumont-May Gallery from July 18 to August 31, 1975, included eight large canvases along with selected drawings and mixed-media works. While at Dartmouth, Cannon painted two of his best-known works, *Cloud Madonna* and *Collector #5*. With its gorgeous palette and formal simplicity, *Cloud Madonna* is a classic example of Cannon's unique painting style.

MRT

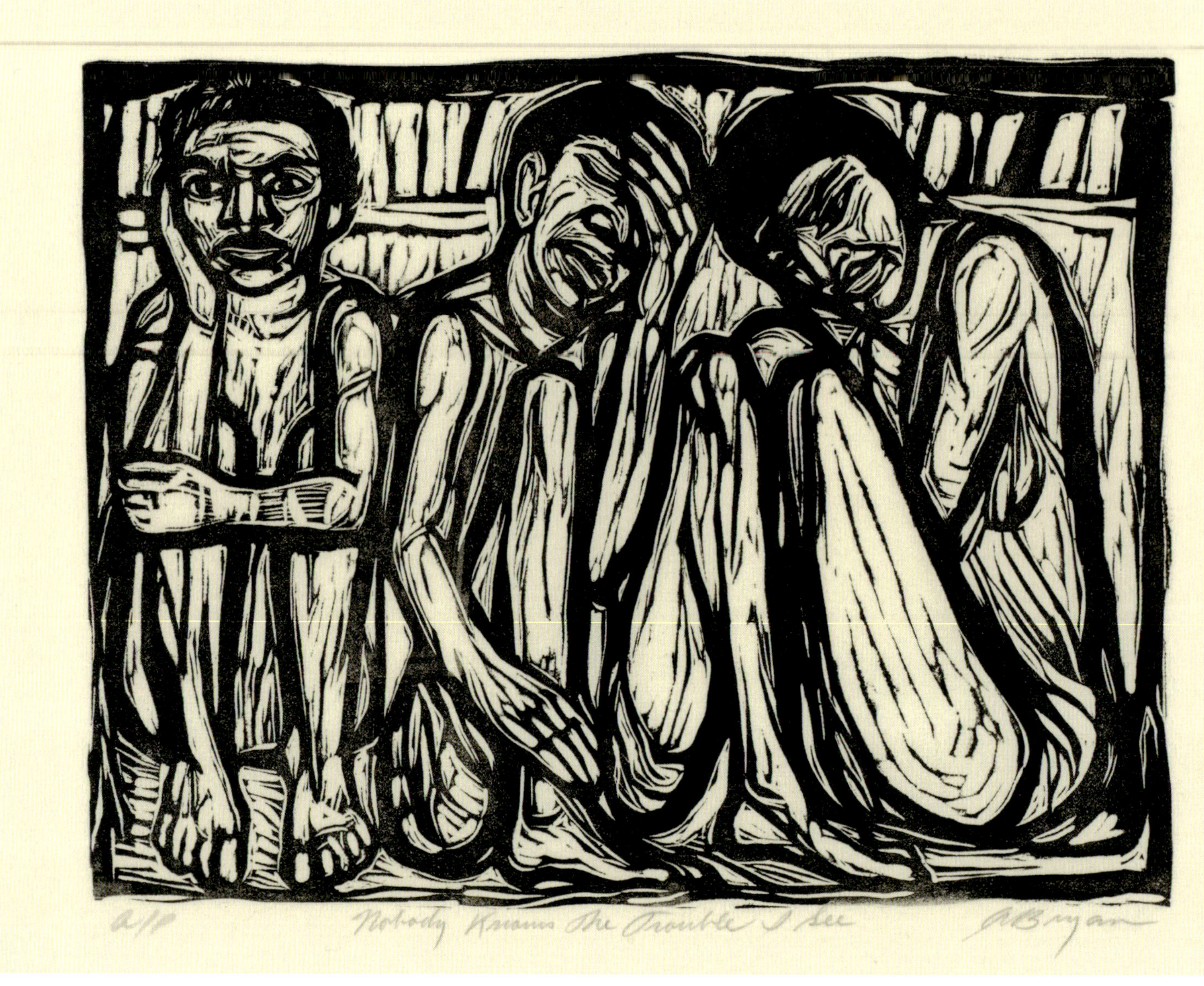

47

ASHLEY BRYAN
American, born 1923
Nobody Knows the Trouble I See, from
*Walk Together Children: Black American
Spirituals*, 1974
Linocut on wove paper, image: 8 x 10 in.;
frame: 25 x 21 in.
Purchased through the Claire and Richard P.
Morse 1953 Fund; 2013.39.1
© Ashley Bryan

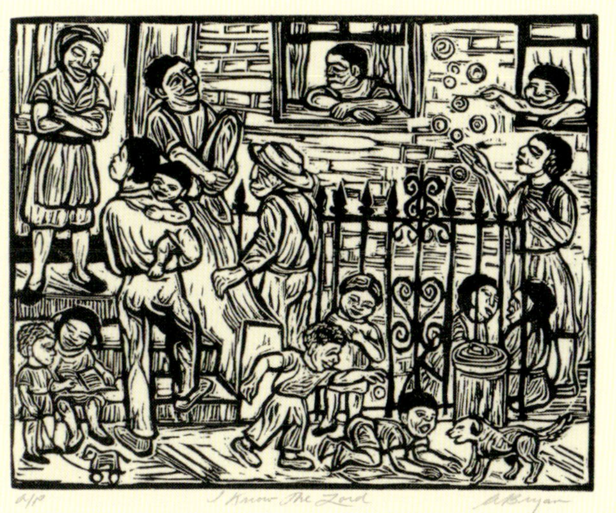

48

ASHLEY BRYAN

I Know the Lord, from *Walk Together Children:
Black American Spirituals*, 1974
Linocut on wove paper, image: 8 x 10 in.;
frame: 25 x 21 in.
Purchased through the Claire and
Richard P. Morse 1953 Fund; 2013.39.2
© Ashley Bryan

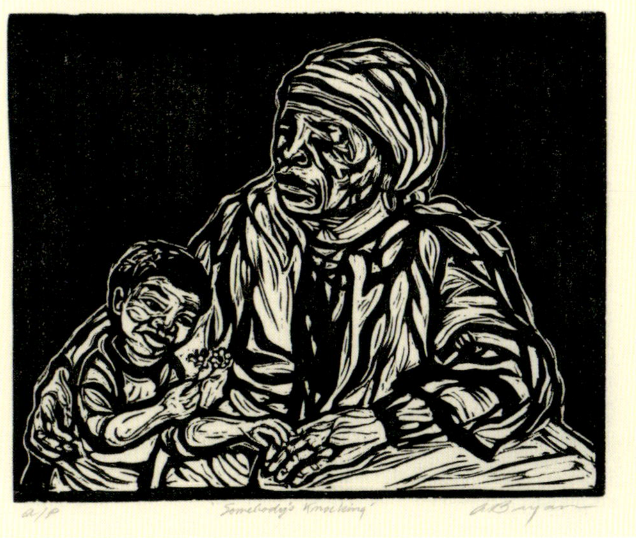

49

ASHLEY BRYAN

Somebody's Knocking at Your Door, from
*Walk Together Children: Black American
Spirituals*, 1974
Linocut on wove paper, image: 8 x 10 in.;
frame: 25 x 21 in.
Purchased through the Claire and
Richard P. Morse 1953 Fund; 2013.39.3
© Ashley Bryan

A celebrated author and illustrator of children's books, Ashley Bryan was born in Harlem and raised in the Bronx. His father worked as a printer of greeting cards, while his mother was a singer. He grew up with six brothers and sisters and three cousins in a household that also included dozens of caged birds. Bryan recalled his childhood in Depression-era New York as an idyllic time, full of art, books, and music. In kindergarten, he self-published his first book, an alphabet book, authored, illustrated, and bound by Bryan himself, which received rave reviews from teachers, family, and friends. After being rejected by several art schools on the grounds of his race, Bryan attended the Cooper Union Art School in New York and was among the first African American students to be awarded a full scholarship. At the age of nineteen, he was drafted into the U.S. Army and served in World War II, before completing his studies at Cooper Union and later at Columbia University, where he studied philosophy and also took a bookbinding course. Bryan has explored the African American experience in more than thirty publications for children, including collections of folktales, poems, and spirituals. In 2009, Bryan won the Laura Ingalls Wilder award for his contribution to American children's literature.

Bryan taught painting and visual design at Dartmouth from 1974 to 1985. He first came to the College as artist-in-residence in the winter term of 1974, during which he created handmade puppets and linocut prints related to the landmark publication *Walk Together Children: Black American Spirituals*, published later that year by Atheneum Press. Inspired by the emotional power of medieval woodblock prints, Bryan made illustrations to accompany these religious songs through a relief process known as linocut, in which the artist cuts the lines of his design into linoleum. This printmaking technique gave Bryan the kind of direct and authentic expression that he felt was needed to illustrate the musical heritage and artistry of enslaved Africans and their descendants in the United States, whose spirituals expressed the injustice, cruelties, and depravations of slavery, as well as the hope and strength they needed to persevere in the face of such challenges. His bold graphic designs provided the perfect visual complement to the joyous or sorrowful themes of these songs, which Bryan hailed as "America's most distinctive contribution to world music."[1]

MRT

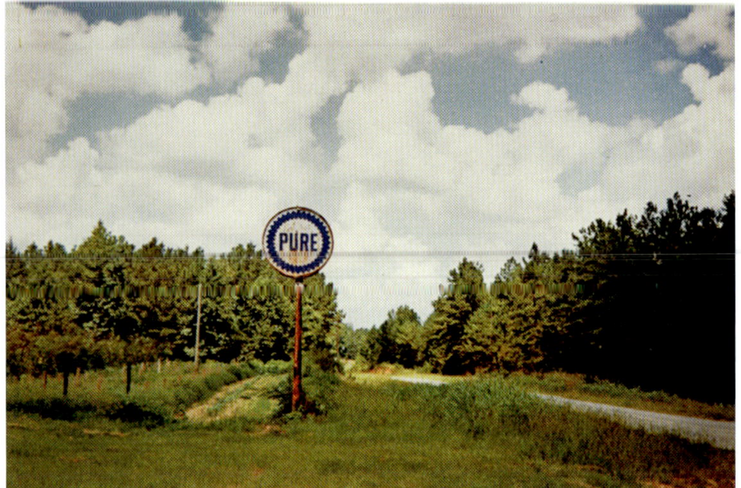

50

WILLIAM CHRISTENBERRY
American, born 1936
Pure Oil Sign in Landscape, Near Marion, Alabama, 1977
Dye transfer photograph, image:
3⁵/₁₆ x 4¹⁵/₁₆ in.; sheet: 7¹⁵/₁₆ x 10¹/₁₆ in.
Purchased through the Fund for
Contemporary Photography in honor of
Marc Efron, Class of 1965; PH.2003.35
© William Christenberry

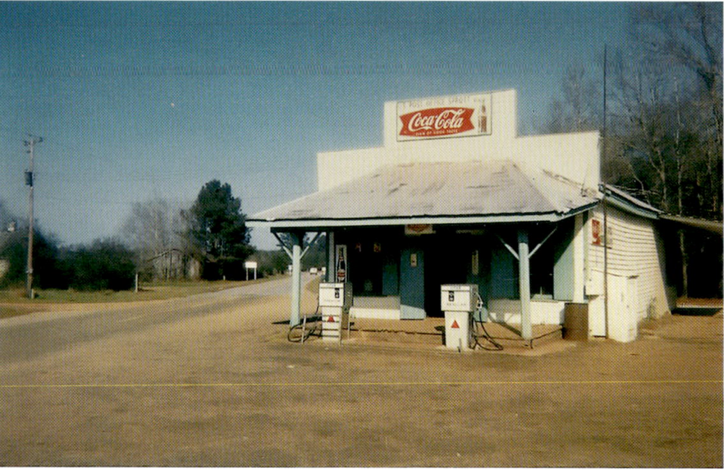

51

WILLIAM CHRISTENBERRY
Post Office, Sprott, Alabama, 1971,
1971, print 1988
Polaroid, 3¹/₈ x 4⁷/₈ in.
Gift of Marc Efron, Class of 1965, and
Barbara Bares; PH.2001.44.1
© William Christenberry

William Christenberry's life and work are inextricably linked to his childhood and family history in Alabama. Although he has resided for many years in Washington, D.C., he travels each summer to Alabama to photograph and collect objects that reflect his southern roots. For his exhibition as artist-in-residence at Dartmouth in the winter of 2003, he brought together both his sculptures and photography: images and sculptures of the vernacular architecture of Alabama as well as mixed-media and found object assemblages and photographs of the artist's puppet-like figures dressed in the regalia of the Ku Klux Klan. A formative moment in Christenberry's career was his time in the early sixties living in New York, where he moved the year after he graduated from college. He worked at various jobs to support himself and in his spare time took in the cultural life of the city. One of his part-time jobs was as a file clerk at Time-Life, where he met the photographer Walker Evans, whose Depression-era photographs of Alabama white sharecroppers from Hale County had already made a profound impression on the young artist. He later traveled with Evans to Alabama in 1973.

Christenberry began his artistic career as a painter and used a small Kodak Brownie camera to aid in his practice. He had the film processed at the drugstore and tacked the prints up as references for his expressionist paintings of vernacular architecture. Later, these photographs became a focus of his work. He relates that Evans said to him, upon seeing his photographs, that the Brownie camera was a perfect extension of his eye. Although Christenberry took his first photograph with the Brownie in 1958, he did not begin to exhibit them until the early 1970s, around the time that color photography began to be taken seriously. Their small format reflects the original three-by-five-inch size that resulted from the drugstore developing and printing.

Christenberry's image of a gas station sign, the vestige of a long-abandoned roadside business, is a classic example of his photography. When visiting his usual haunts in Alabama he would look particularly for commercial signs that had outlasted their useful life, markers of another era, which he collected both as images and also as artifacts. He would photograph the same building on successive trips, documenting changes as it was altered and weathered over time. In this way he recorded a slowly evolving way of life and the buildings to which he felt a deep personal connection. In a 2004–5 interview, he stated, "Returning to the sites allows me to record both the traces of passing time and represent how a subject is transformed by time." This is especially true of the Sprott Post Office, originally the subject of a 1936 Walker Evans photograph that would be reproduced in Evans's project with James Agee, *Let Us Now Praise Famous Men.* Christenberry's 1971 image shows the building much changed, with its false gable story significantly reduced and the building now painted white.

KWH

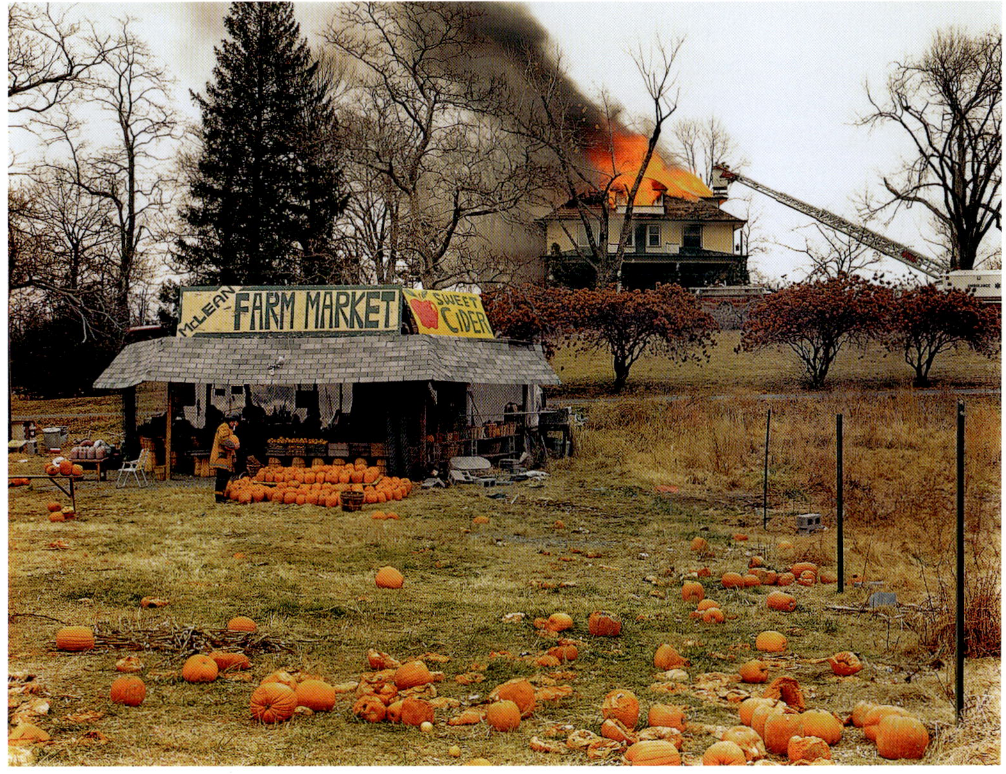

52

JOEL STERNFELD
American, born 1944
McLean, Virginia (Pumpkins), negative
December 1978, print May 1986
Dye transfer print, sheet: 15^{15}/$_{16}$ x 19^{7}/$_{8}$ in.
Gift of Joel Sternfeld, Class of 1965, and
Neil Grossman, Class of 1965, in memory
of John Pickells (1942–1972), Class of 1965;
PH.986.24
© Joel Sternfeld

Joel Sternfeld, Dartmouth Class of 1965, is among the most influential and respected photographers working today. Best known for his large-scale documentary photographs, Sternfeld—along with his contemporaries William Eggleston and Stephen Shore—was one of the first artists to establish color photography as a respected artistic medium. He began taking color photographs in the late 1960s, after reading about the color theories of Bauhaus professor Johannes Itten and his student Josef Albers, who went on to have a distinguished career as an abstract painter and teacher in the United States. Their writings encouraged Sternfeld to resist the widespread belief that color photography, due to its associations with consumer advertising and magazine illustration, could not be considered as fine art. Since the early 1970s, Sternfeld has traveled the highways and byways of the United States, from Maine to Alaska and back again, in search of compelling subject matter. Sternfeld has taught photography at Sarah Lawrence College in New York since 1985, and in the fall of that year, exactly twenty years after he graduated from Dartmouth, he returned as artist-in-residence. During his residency, he worked on his seminal book project, *American Prospects*, which was published in 1987 and has remained in print ever since.

Using a large-format, eight-by-ten-inch camera, Sternfeld has captured the American landscape and psyche in such memorable photographs as *McLean, Virginia (Pumpkins)*, which was taken in December 1978 while the artist was traveling across the United States in his Volkswagen bus. Since it was first published on the cover of *American Prospects*, this photograph has troubled and perplexed almost everyone who has seen it. At first glance, one notices the burning farmhouse in the background. The viewer's eyes are then drawn to the McLean Farm Market stand, where a fireman can be seen shopping for a pumpkin, while seemingly oblivious to the fire behind him. What is going on here? Shouldn't his attention be on the house blaze, rather than on the pumpkins for sale? Sternfeld's beguiling photograph actually depicts a controlled training exercise, and the firefighter was, in fact, purchasing a pumpkin on his break. Even without the arresting subject matter, however, the photograph is a masterpiece in terms of its composition and palette, with the pumpkins' vivid oranges matching the autumnal colors of the Virginia countryside and, ironically, the firefighter's jacket and the flames of the house fire.

MRT

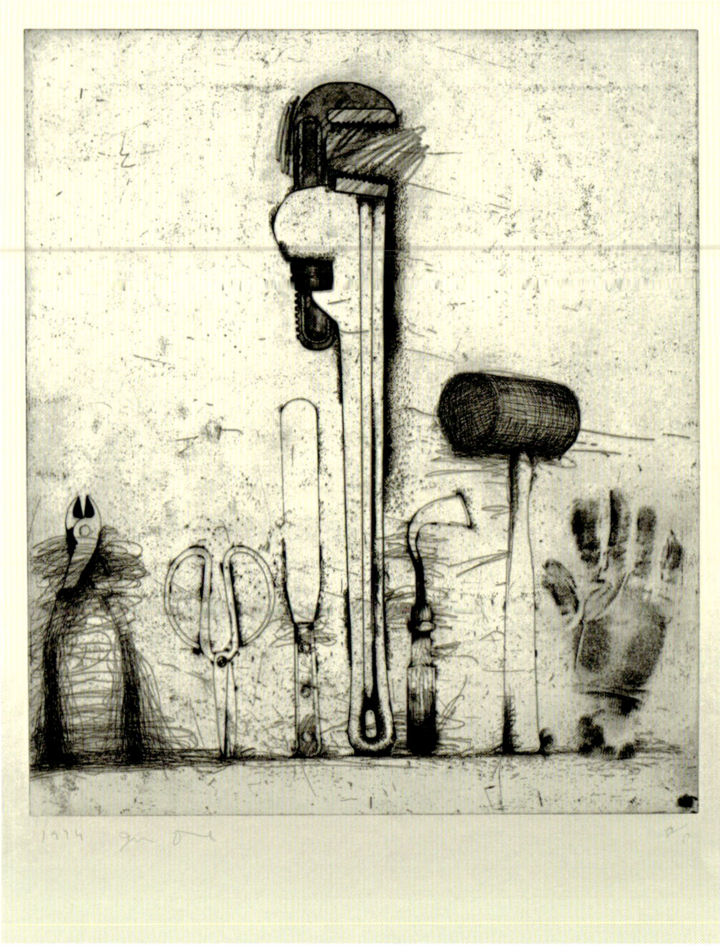

JIM DINE
American, born 1935
Dartmouth Still Life, 1974
Etching, drypoint, softground, and roulette
on paper, plate: 27⁷/₈ x 23⁵/₈ in.;
sheet: 42¹/₄ x 29¹/₂ in.
Gift of the artist in honor of Professor
Matthew Wysocki; PR.974.369
© 2013 Jim Dine / Artists Rights Society (ARS),
New York

Jim Dine is best known for pop art paintings, drawings, prints, and constructions that present mundane, everyday items with the clarity of commercial illustration. By the early 1970s, Dine began to move his art in a new direction, and his work revealed a renewed interest in drawing and the human figure. Printmaking had been a passion for Dine throughout his career, and he would often work out his ideas in various prints pulled from the same plate, which he would continually rework through successive editions. Dine owned a summer home in Putney, Vermont, less than an hour's drive south of Hanover. As Dartmouth's artist-in-residence in the fall of 1974, he worked in the printmaking studio located in the basement of the Hopkins Center for the Performing Arts. Mitchell Freidman, a recent Dartmouth graduate who had taught himself printmaking techniques, assisted Dine in the studio throughout his stay at the College and would later become Dine's master printer.

Tools were a frequent subject in both Dine's painted and printed work; they often stood as metaphors for human presence. Many of Dine's prints focus on implements of the artist, such as paintbrushes or printmaking tools, but in *Dartmouth Still Life* several of the objects are not specifically related to art-making but associated with tradesmen. They may have had a personal significance for Dine, as both his grandfather and father ran hardware stores throughout his childhood. Dine rendered each tool on the plate with absolute precision, and even pressed an actual glove into the plate surface. The glove stands out from the other objects as having a more direct tie to its maker—a strange, disembodied mark of the artist.

Dartmouth Still Life is the first of three prints in which a similar assembly of items appear. Two later prints, *Pink Chinese Scissors* (1974–76) and *Piranesi's 24 Colored Marks* (1974–76) also represent this core group of seven tools, but Dine added further marks to the plate, included new tools—such as an electric die cutter and roulette—in the group, and incorporated watercolor additions after printing. All three prints began with a copper etching plate that Dine created for an earlier etched and lithographic print, *The Wrench in Nature* (1973), in which the wrench appears on its own, hovering in a lightly shaded field.

SGP

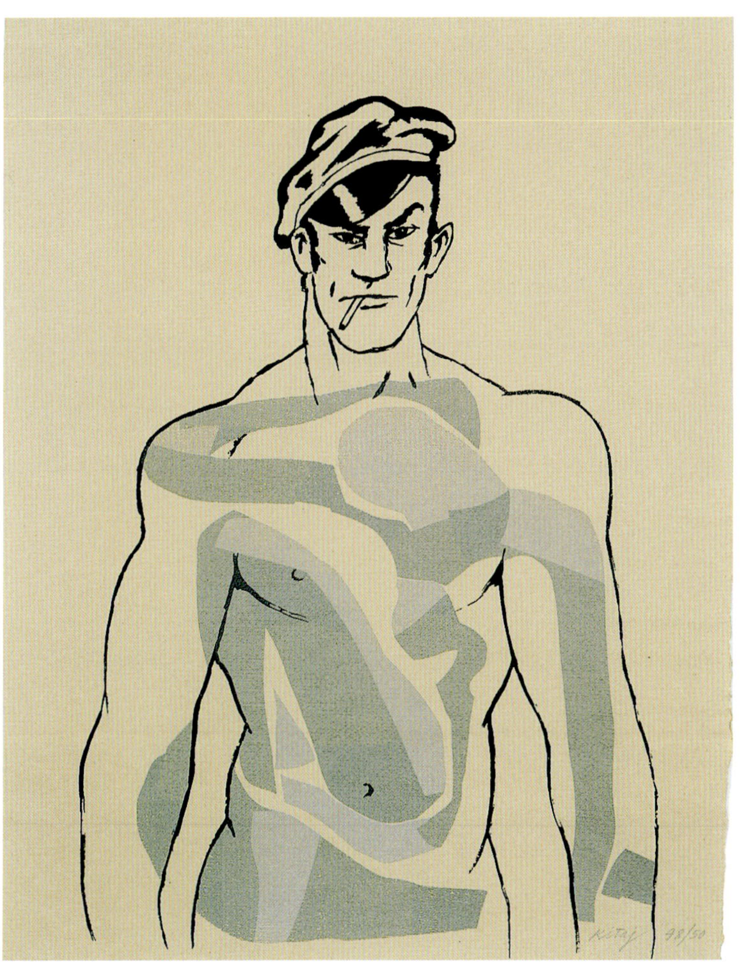

54

RONALD B. KITAJ
American, 1932–2007
Man with Matisse Tattoo, 1978
Color screenprint on buff mould-made paper,
30³/₄ x 22³/₄ in.
Purchased through the Hood Museum of Art
Acquisitions Fund; PR.978.176
© R. B. Kitaj Estate

Although R. B. Kitaj is most often associated with the British pop art movement of the 1960s, his complex and disjunctive work defies classification. Kitaj worked in a figurative style of bold colors and sharp lines, in which he frequently combined allusions to art history, literature, politics, and Jewish identity. He would invent the term "School of London" to refer to a group of artists including himself, Lucian Freud, Leon Kossoff, Michael Andrews, Reginald Grey, and eventually David Hockney. These artists, all of whom were active in London, were united by a renewed interest in the figure as a subject.

Born in Cleveland under the name Ronald Brooks, Kitaj adopted the name of his mother's second husband, Dr. Walter Kitaj, a Viennese Jew. He attended high school in Troy, New York, where his stepfather had taken a job as a research chemist. After high school, Kitaj worked as a merchant seaman for four years so that he could travel abroad. He finally settled in London, where he would work for many years until his later career, when he divided his time between the United States and Britain.

Kitaj was artist in residence at Dartmouth during the spring of 1978, and traveled to Hanover from London. The residency may have been recommended to him by his friend Jim Dine, an American artist who had worked at Dartmouth less than two years earlier, and who had a summer house in the area. While at Dartmouth, Kitaj was remarkably productive and created all of the paintings for his next exhibition at the Marlborough Gallery in London, which was a critical success. *Man with Matisse Tattoo* exemplifies Kitaj's approach to figuration in the 1970s, in which large blocks of color and unbroken lines dominate the composition. In this print, a young man in a sailor cap stares defiantly at the viewer. Here, shades of soft gray and pale blue appear to highlight the defined musculature of the man's chest, but upon closer inspection they coalesce into a tattoo in the form of a crouching woman that covers his entire torso. This particular female nude is a direct reference to a collage by Henri Matisse entitled *Blue Nude II* (1952). The quotation acts as a tribute to the famous French modern artist, while also demonstrating Kitaj's fluency in the history of art.

SGP

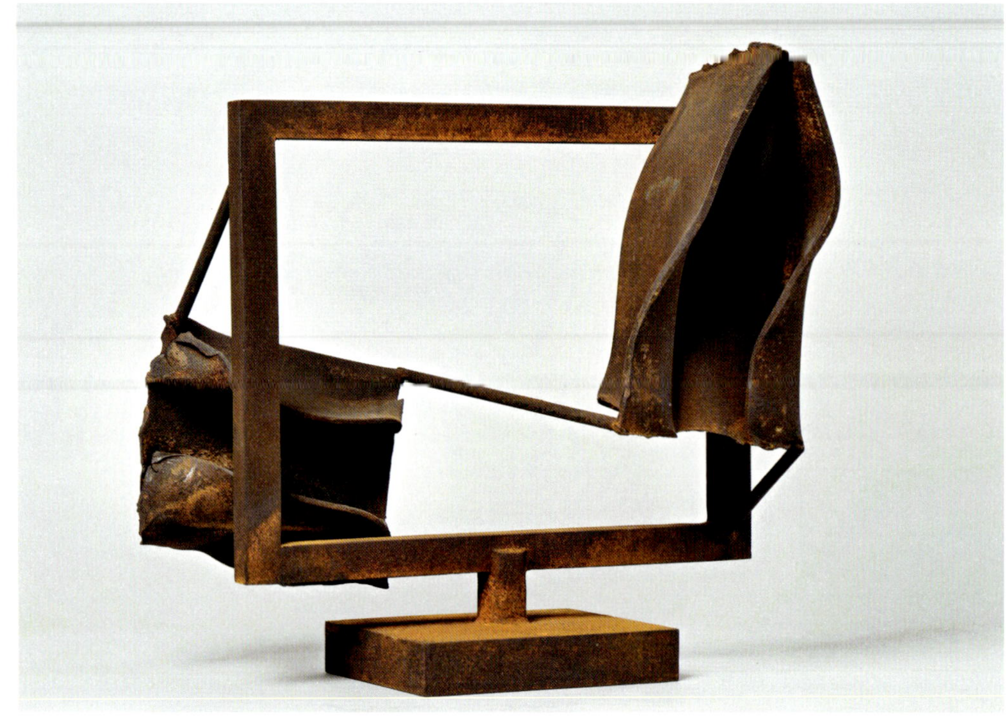

RICHARD PETER STANKIEWICZ
American, 1922–1983
Untitled, 1979
Steel, 24³/₄ x 22 x 15 in.
Gift of the artist; S.979.137
© Virginia Zabriskie

Richard Stankiewicz was best known for his so-called "junk sculptures," in which he transformed seemingly worthless industrial and mechanical metal scraps from junkyards into both figurative and abstract formal constructions. His sculptures revealed the expressive potential inherent in his materials, and inspired a generation of artists to create art that used salvaged industrial debris as its foundation. Born in Philadelphia and raised in Detroit, he began painting and sculpting while serving in the U. S. Navy. After completing military service, Stankiewicz studied with Ossip Zadkine and Fernand Léger in Paris and Hans Hofmann in New York. His early work reflected the shift from high modernist figurative and abstract sculpture to abstract expressionism. By the time Stankiewicz created the Hood sculpture, he was experienced with welding techniques and had created large-scale compositions in a steel foundry, using steel elements such as pipes, cylinders, and I-beams. Although he always exposed the essence of the raw material, by the 1970s his forms were informed by the simple geometries of minimalism.

Stankiewicz was artist-in-residence at Dartmouth in the summer of 1979. Although admired for his large-scale work, the artist focused at Dartmouth on the possibilities of smaller sculptures. He compared his smaller works to Japanese haikus, in which ideas are compressed into few syllables and demand an economy of words. This relatively small sculpture belongs to Stankiewicz's easel series of compositions incorporating rectangular frames. This format refers to his teacher Hans Hofmann and his doctrine of "push-pull," the dynamic use of brushwork to create the illusion of oscillating depth on a flat surface. Here, Stankiewicz played on the tension inherent in the act of painting on a two-dimensional surface by allowing crumpled, organic forms to break free from a rigid rectangular frame. The composition at once pays homage to the legacy of his mentor, while seeming to parody the seriousness of the abstract expressionist painting endeavor.

SGP

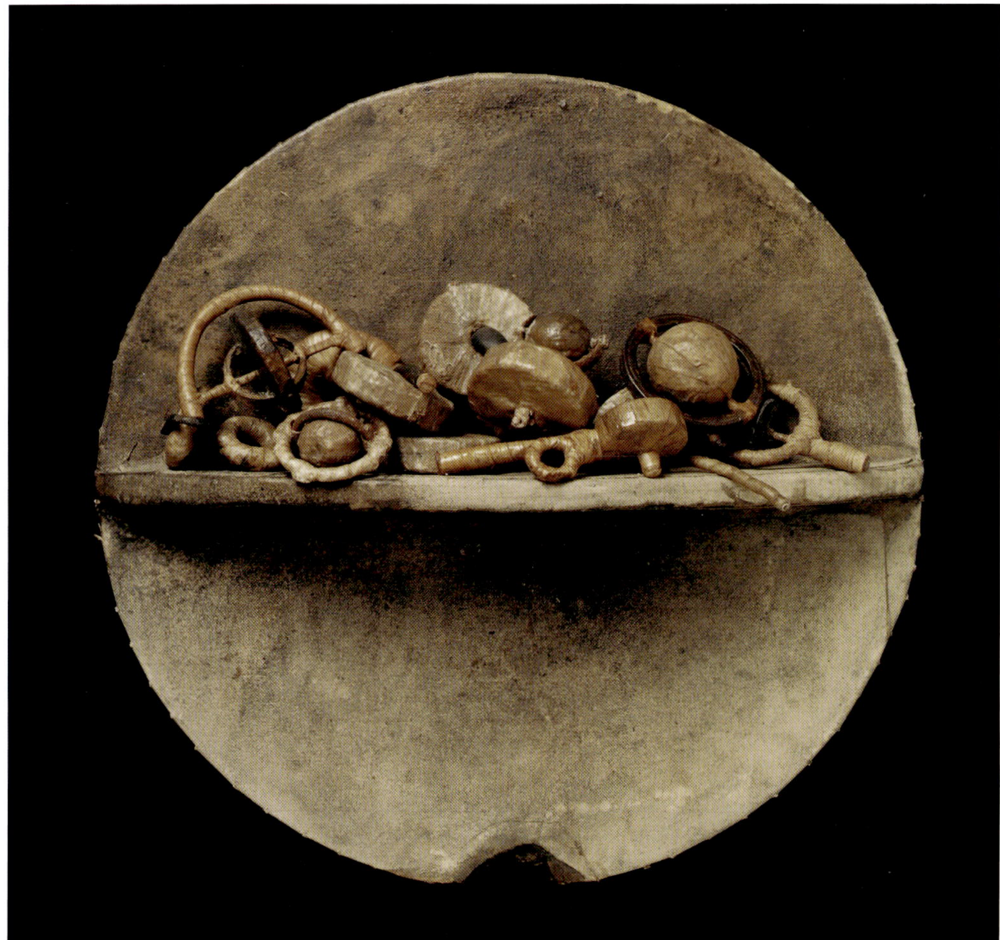

56

PAUL BOWEN
American, born 1951 in Wales
Navigator, 1980
Mixed media, overall: 28$^{7}/_{16}$ in.
Gift of the Estate of Robyn S. Watson; 2005.35
© Paul Bowen

Born in Wales, Paul Bowen was steeped in the history of his country at young age. From his hometown, Colwyn Bay in the northern part of the country, he acquired a love of the sea. As a sculptor he makes abstract objects that allude to ships, the technical equipment of seafaring, and maritime history. After graduating from an art college in Wales in 1972, he traveled to the United States to attend the Maryland College of Art in Baltimore, where he completed an MFA in 1974. A fellowship at the Fine Arts Work Center in Provincetown, Massachusetts, in 1977 had a profound impact on him. In the lively artistic environment of this beach town at the apex of the Cape Cod peninsula, Bowen met Jack Tworkov (who had been Dartmouth's artist-in-residence in 1973), Myron Stout, Jim Forsburg, Philip Malicoat, and Peter Hutchinson. He returned to Wales, but the following year was back in Provincetown to live and work. There he began to scour the beach for weathered materials for his sculpture, and what he found became a major source for his art. Bowen was Dartmouth's artist-in-residence in the winter of 2005 and has taught sculpture courses in the Studio Art Department as a visitor.

In 1980, not long after settling in Cape Cod, Bowen made *Navigator*, which introduced a new direction for his work and remains a pivotal piece for him. On a shelf affixed to a wall-mounted wooden disk, he placed various wrapped objects that reference older navigation technology, including sextants and astrolabes. Many of the forms that lie tumbled on the shelf are circular, as is the globelike background on which they are silhouetted. A small semicircle cut into the bottom of the larger disk echoes the curves of the navigators' tools. In this self-contained world, the objects point the way both literally and symbolically. These disparate smaller shapes, each enfolded in cloth, share a similar patina that joins them together visually. As in much of Bowen's work, one senses the weight of time and use in these objects—not abandoned, but obsolete. This rugged and eloquent sculpture evokes the endurance of ships at sea and their silhouetted forms against the vastness of the ocean.

KWH

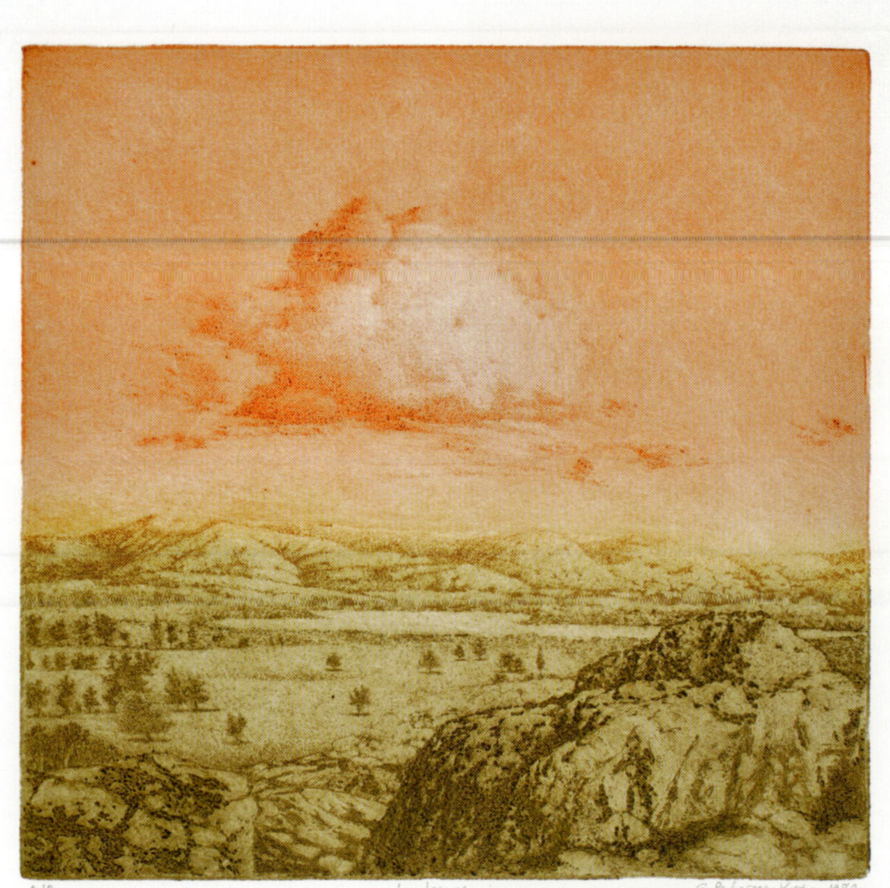

57

GILLIAN PEDERSON-KRAG
American, born 1938
Landscape (Orange Sky, Cloud, and Rock),
1980
Etching on paper, image: 10^{1}/$_{4}$ x 10^{7}/$_{16}$ in.;
sheet: 16^{7}/$_{8}$ x 15^{5}/$_{8}$ in.
Gift of Jeannot Barr; 2009.88
© Gillian Pederson-Krag

Gillian Pederson-Krag's landscapes are characterized by stillness. Representational, yet also spiritual, Pederson-Krag's aesthetic extends their meaning beyond the descriptive. Pederson-Krag grew up in New York and received her BFA in 1961 from the Rhode Island School of Design. At the end of her undergraduate studies she changed her work from abstract to figural, developing her repertoire of landscapes, seascapes, still-lifes, and interiors. She earned her MFA in 1963 from Cornell University and taught painting and drawing there from 1966 to 1979. That year she left her tenured position to devote herself full-time to making art. She was Dartmouth's artist-in-residence in the winter of 2001.

Landscape (Orange Sky, Cloud, and Rock) is typical of many of Pederson-Krag's prints with its distant horizon and defined fore-, middle-, and backgrounds. The indistinct, slightly fuzzy quality of her line creates the pervading atmosphere. The dual color is somewhat unusual in her prints; she more often creates monochromatic works, although her paintings show a rich and sophisticated use of color. Here the salmon color gives visual weight to the sky and focuses the viewer's attention on single puffy cloud. It brings the cloud into the foreground as the green landscape below recedes into distant mountains—their softly rounded forms echoing the cloud up above and the rock in the right foreground. These sloping diagonals counter the solidity of the strong horizon line, giving a sense of movement to the scene. Pederson-Krag writes:

At some point it dawned on me that I could print with oil paint, colored inks, and chin collé as a way of adding a layer of color onto the narrative and imposing a second kind of reality over the original story. This liberates the image from its role of "just reporting the facts." . . . In this situation, using color in this way dramatizes the two levels of existence.[1]

Pederson-Krag believes in essential experiences by which one is moved, and sees art as a potential vehicle for those experiences. Her paintings and prints express this philosophy. Although her landscapes often stem from observation, she brings herself to them in an attempt to create unity between representation and aesthetics, between the subject and the picture plane. She believes this "reflects a feeling that we all have a kind of nostalgia for—the notion that life is somehow meaningful and that while we are indeed separate, we continually seek out ways of discovering situations which will allow us to feel part of a larger whole."[2]

ABK

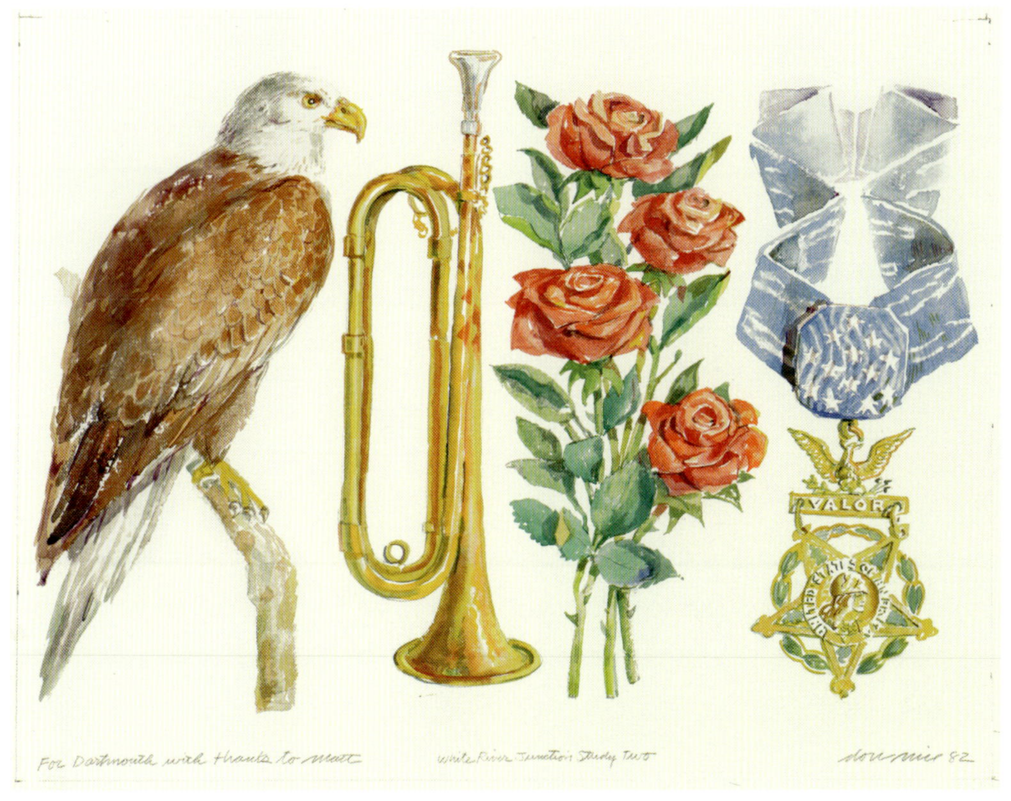

58

DON NICE
American, born 1932
White River Junction Study Two, 1982
Watercolor on wove paper, 16 x 20½ in.
Gift of the artist; W.983.14
© Don Nice

Don Nice, a contemporary American realist, grew up in California's San Joaquin Valley. During his childhood Nice worked as a cowhand, which instilled in him a love of nature. He studied art at the University of Southern California and then served in the United States Army for two years at Fort Ord in California. While there he created a twenty-four-foot mural in the mess hall. Nice went on to study painting in Rome on the GI Bill, and in Salzburg with Oskar Kokoschka. In 1962 he entered graduate school at Yale University. Over the next two years he would study with artists such as Chuck Close, Rackstraw Downes, Nancy Graves, and Alex Katz. Nice earned his MFA in 1964 and was dubbed one of the "new perceptual realists" who emerged in the 1960s.

Nice's work is typically detailed and descriptive. During the late seventies and early eighties he created his Predella works, paintings with discrete objects presented in a row on a plain ground. These included popular everyday objects like sunglasses, beer cans, and sneakers along with images of nature, particularly flowers. Each object is visually independent and together their juxtaposition creates meaning.

It was in this vein that Nice created *White River Junction Study Two*, a proposed mural design submitted to the Veterans Administration Hospital in White River Junction, Vermont, in 1982. He received the commission through the VA's Art in Architecture program, which—controversially—earmarked part of the construction budget of a new ambulatory care unit for art.[1] The first sketch Nice submitted for the project included four objects: an eagle, a bugle, a poppy flower, and a

Medal of Honor. While the poppy is a symbol of World War I stemming from John McCrae's 1915 poem "In Flanders Field," in 1982 it was also seen by VA staff members as linked to opium and, in this context, drug use during the Vietnam War. As a compromise, Nice changed the poppy to the rose seen in this version. In response to further staff objections, the VA Arts Review Committee recommended one of Nice's alternative sketches representing local culture, rather than patriotic symbols. The final mural, which Nice completed while artist-in-residence at Dartmouth in 1982, features a view of the Ottauquechee River above a band of six objects: a pair of work gloves, a sprig of red clover, a hermit thrush, a bag of Vermont apples, a can of Vermont maple syrup, a bag of popcorn, and a woodsman's hat (fig. 25). While still owned by the White River Junction VA, the mural is not currently on display.

ABK

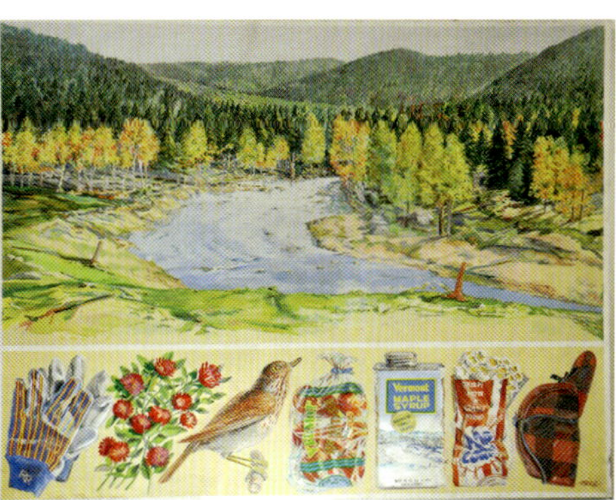

Fig. 25

White River Junction, 1982, is the mural Nice created for the VA hospital in White River Junction, Vermont, after his initial sketches were rejected.

WOLF KAHN
American, born 1927 in Germany
Barn Silhouette II, 1984
Pastel on wove paper, 22 x 30 in.
Purchased through the Hood Museum of Art
Acquisitions Fund; D.984.11
Art © Wolf Kahn / Licensed by VAGA,
New York, NY

Wolf Kahn was born in Stuttgart, Germany, in 1927 and grew up against the background of an intensifying totalitarian regime. In 1939 Kahn fled to England under the auspices of the Kindertransport rescue mission, which allowed Jewish refugee children to escape Nazi Germany, and at the age of thirteen he moved permanently to the United States. He graduated from the High School of Music and Art in New York and then served in the U.S. Navy. The Servicemen's Readjustment Act of 1944 (GI Bill) afforded Kahn the opportunity to study with the esteemed teacher, theorist, and abstract expressionist painter Hans Hofmann, whose studio assistant Kahn would eventually become. Hofmann's Push and Pull theory seems to be evident throughout the evolution of Kahn's practice, as his work is distinguished by its oppositional tensions. Kahn enrolled at the University of Chicago in 1950 and graduated the following year with a BA. He was a founding member of the Hansa Gallery, a downtown Chicago avant-garde artist collective that ran from 1952 to 1959. It was comprised of former Hofmann pupils who wanted to distance themselves from the conservative taste of the New York art establishment, and the Hansa Gallery would subsequently hold the first of Kahn's important solo exhibitions.

For many years, Kahn and his wife, artist Emily Mason, have spent the summer and autumn months on a farm in Brattleboro, Vermont, and he has absorbed the specific poetics of the place. With expressive use of color, Kahn captures the unmistakable silhouette of a New England barn, a subject that figures prominently in his oeuvre. In the fall of 1984, Kahn was artist-in-residence at Dartmouth College, where he

continued to create his unique, mood-soaked landscapes, which fuse representational elements into tonalist abstractions. But the subjects that he revisits and explores from different angles, distances, seasons, and times of the day are merely points of departure for compositions that synthesize his disciplined approach to visual dynamics with improvised color harmonies. Kahn has described pastels as the "the determining medium" of his art, and *Barn Silhouette II* revels in the medium's materiality. Intuitively rubbing and working layers of pastel pigment into and against the toothy paper grain, Kahn achieves the subtle gradations of color that give his drawings the luminous quality that has become his indelible hallmark.

SG

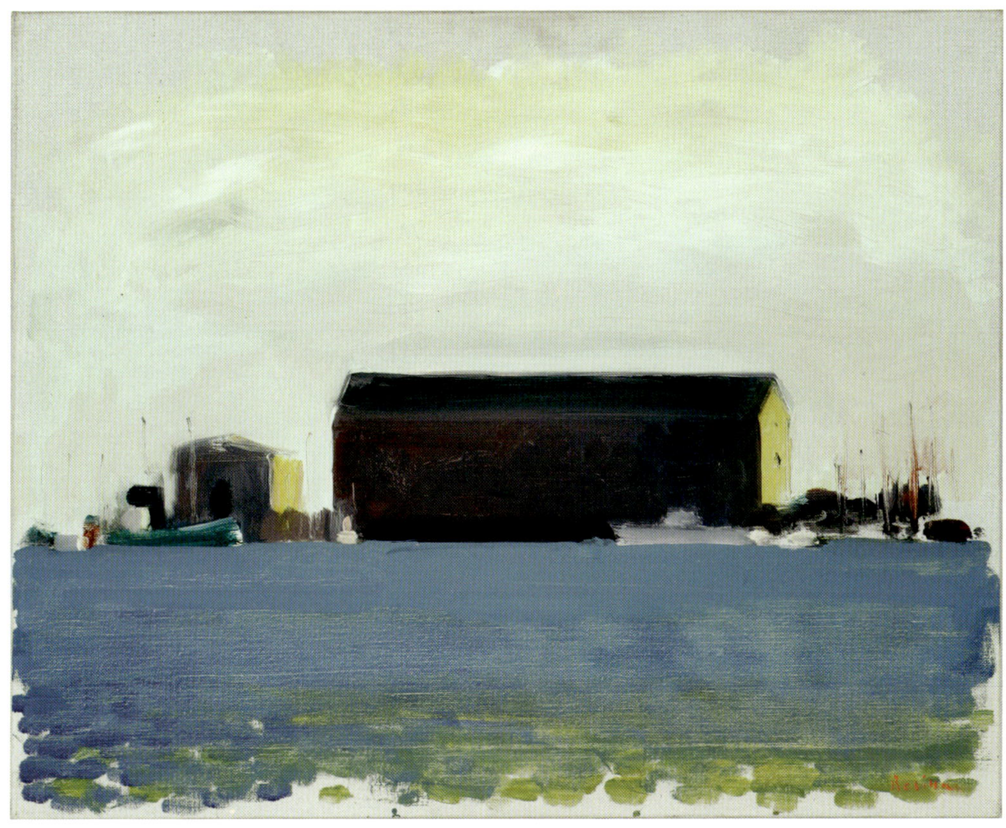

60

PAUL RESIKA
American, born 1928
Provincetown Pier: Yellow Wall, 1984
Oil on canvas, $17^{15}/_{16}$ x $21^{7}/_{8}$ in.
Gift of Varujan Boghosian; P.991.51.1
© Paul Resika

Painting in a style at the midpoint between realism and abstraction, Paul Resika works from both outdoor observation and recreated memory. To the artist, his landscapes are "never of something; rather they are something."[1] In his work, everyday forms of reality are transformed into vibrant studies of beauty and light, becoming simple yet sensuous masses meeting on the picture plane. Born in New York, Resika studied under Hans Hofmann at his school in Provincetown, Massachusetts, in the late 1940s. Resika was influenced by the work of Paul Cézanne and Henri Matisse, as well as Hofmann's emphasis on the fundamental relationship between the canonic history of art and the modern-day development of abstraction. It was during this time that Hofmann introduced Resika to the landscape that would serve as a constant in the artist's work throughout all of the decades that followed: Provincetown and the lower–Cape Cod region. Using elements of his daily life as motifs—a particular flowering tree, a grouping of sailboats in the bay—Resika explored the possibilities of color and light, both real and imagined.

In this painting, as in many others, the Provincetown pier acts as the supporting structure, allowing Resika to experiment and play. In the artist's work, color and the use of paint act as both vehicle and subject: the large blocks of color emblazoned across the canvas not only describe the scene and its physical limits but also comprise the formal elements of his particular style of painting. Recalling the heightened colors and emotional content found in the early work of Matisse and other Fauve painters, Resika—through the seemingly simple pairing of complementary colors—vigorously evokes a depth of human thought and emotion. The voluptuous broad brushstrokes that make up the water's edge in the foreground, the brilliant patch of blue water rushing back into space, and the sun-drenched buildings on the Provincetown pier combine to produce a rich understanding of the experience of the place, as well as of the artist's feelings at a particular moment in time. Resika was artist-in-residence at Dartmouth during the spring of 1972, and since then has maintained close friendships with several faculty members, including Varujan Boghosian, who donated this painting to the Hood Museum of Art in 1991.

AW

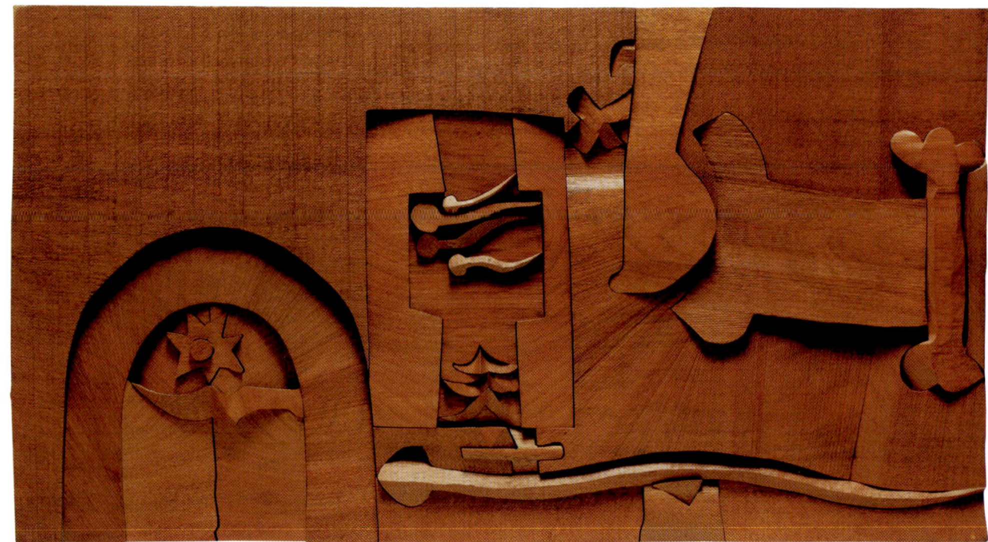

Hugh Townley's wooden sculpture is simultaneously familiar yet mysterious, approachable yet opaque. Townley began sculpting and teaching in 1952 and had a long career that lasted until his death in 2008. Born in 1923 in Lafayette, Indiana, he grew up in Madison, Wisconsin, enlisted in the U.S. Army, and served in Europe during World War II. After 1945 he enrolled in the University of Wisconsin's Fine Arts program, and subsequently studied with Ossip Zadkine in Paris. Upon his return to the United States he began a long teaching career that included positions at the Layton School of Art, Milwaukee; Beloit College; Boston University; and Harvard University. Townley's longest-held teaching position was at Brown University from 1961 until his retirement in 1989. He then moved to Vermont and continued creating sculptures and reliefs.

Townley is known for his work in wood, and his major tool was the band saw. His reliefs and sculptures are formed of discrete pieces fitted together—like a fantastical puzzle. The seams of the joined pieces give a linear quality to the work. Forms are outlined but also project outward into space, enlivening the surfaces and giving each sculpture a visual rhythm. In *Stargate* Townley uses evocative shapes to create his own visual language. The forms remind us of familiar things—a snake, a bone, a man (or is it a tree?)—but refuse to remain fixed. A definitive leftward movement in this relief guides the viewer's eyes towards an arch, presumably the eponymous stargate. The large, blank space above it acts like a visual breath. The relief suggests mythology and narrative, but none is forthcoming. Townley's many influences included poetry and his travels across the globe from Colorado to Southern India.

From the early fifties Townley made sculpture with a monochromatic, stained wooden surface. Sometimes he would use one kind of wood, sometimes a combination of different varieties—mahogany, maple, ash, walnut, cherry, obiche, and ebony. Around 1970 Townley began adding color, sometimes painting his sculptures in brilliant tones. Examples of both painted and unpainted reliefs, along with free-standing sculpture, were shown in his 1991 exhibition in the Jaffe Hall Gallery during his Dartmouth residency.

ABK

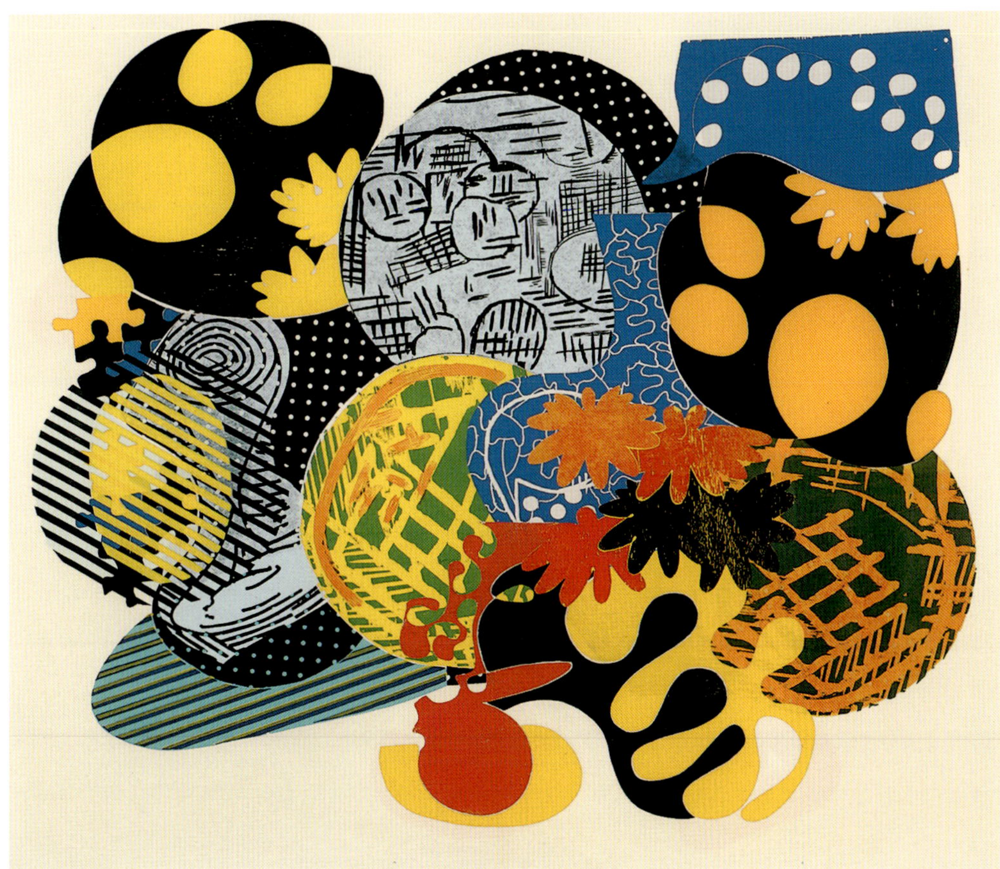

JUDY PFAFF
American, born 1946 in England
Meloné, 1987
Color woodcut and silkscreen collage,
60³/₈ x 68³/₈ in.
Gift of Susan R. Malloy in memory of her
husband, Edwin A. Malloy, Class of 1983P;
PR.2001.12.1
Art © Judy Pfaff / Licensed by VAGA,
New York, NY

Considered one of the pioneers of installation art, Judy Pfaff is celebrated for her multi-media site-specific work that synthesizes sculpture, architecture, painting, and found and natural materials to create complex dynamic environments. Born in England, Pfaff moved to the United States at the age of thirteen. She attended the Yale University School of Art and studied under the painter Al Held, who first encouraged her to break free of the canvas and spread her work out over the walls. When she moved to New York after her graduation in 1973, she was excited by work of the generation of post-minimalist artists such as Barry Le Va, Alan Saret, Lynda Benglis, Robert Morris, and Robert Smithson. These artists reacted against the "objecthood" of minimalism and used non-conventional art materials that brought the natural world into the gallery, and also broke through into the natural world. Although Pfaff's work often incorporates natural elements, such as tree roots and branches, her installations also explore the boundaries of painting by transforming traditional easel painting into sculptural and architectural environments.

During her stay as artist in residence at Dartmouth in the spring of 2000, Pfaff created an installation entitled *Notes on Light and Color* that occupied the entire Jaffe-Friede Gallery in the Hopkins Center. For this work, Pfaff filled the space with three large, white circular structures, one of which extended up to the ceiling. On the surrounding walls, Pfaff painted large discs of comparable scale in pale shades of pink, yellow, and black. The print included in this exhibition was created more than a decade earlier than her Dartmouth installation, but exhibits a similar interest in the possibilities of bold color and organic forms. The print, which measures over five feet wide and high, is actually a collage made up of silkscreen and woodcut elements. The print combines patterned and solid undulating shapes, some of which call to mind natural forms such as leaves, petals, vines, and branches. The various pieces interlock and balance the others, creating a vibrant, rotating composition that pushes at its own border. It is part of Pfaff's *Meloné* series of prints, which she produced with Crown Point Press, San Francisco, in 1987.

SGP

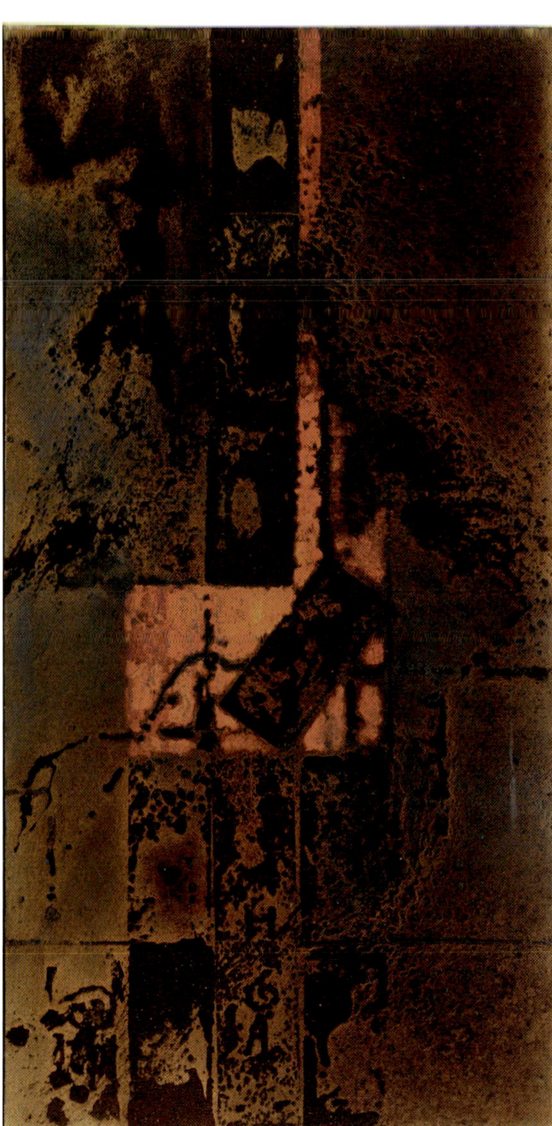

63

GYÖRGY KEPES
American, born in Hungary, 1906–2001
Tumbling Textures, 1977
Oil and sand on canvas, 58 x 30 in.
Collection of Varujan Boghosian, Hanover,
New Hampshire
With permission from Juliet K. Stone and
Imre P. Kepes

György Kepes was a Hungarian-born painter, photographer, filmmaker, designer, educator, and art theorist. He studied painting at the Royal Academy of Fine Arts in Budapest from 1924 to 1928, before moving to Berlin two years later to become the assistant to Lázló Moholy-Nagy, a Hungarian avant-garde photographer who had taught at the Dessau Bauhaus. In 1936 Kepes followed Moholy-Nagy to London, where they were forced to relocate due to the worsening political situation in Nazi Germany. While living in London, Kepes met his future wife, Juliet Appleby, a seventeen-year-old British woman who later became an accomplished artist and illustrator. In 1937 Moholy-Nagy agreed to become the director of a new art school in Chicago, which he dubbed the New Bauhaus (later Illinois Institute of Design). Kepes was also invited to join the faculty and taught design and design theory at the New Bauhaus from 1937 to 1943. In 1944 he published *Language of Vision*, an influential book about design, education, and visual perception that was informed by his teaching experiences in Chicago. Kepes subsequently taught at Brooklyn College, where the influential Russian-born architect Serge Chermayeff was chair of the Art Department, before accepting an invitation in 1947 from the School of Architecture and Planning at the Massachusetts Institute of Technology (MIT) to initiate a program there in visual design that would eventually become known as the Center for Advanced Visual Studies. While teaching at MIT, where he remained until his retirement in 1974, Kepes was part of a collaborative community of artists, designers, architects, and scientists, including Marcel Breuer, Charles Eames, Buckminster Fuller, and Walter Gropius.

Kepes devoted his early career to making experimental photographs that combined the eccentric angles and rigid geometry of Bauhaus photography with the transforming power of light. After World War II, the artist began making abstract paintings based on scientific imagery, which led him to publish, in 1956, *The New Landscape in Art and Science*, in which modern artworks were paired with "abstract" images made from x-ray machines, stroboscopic photography, electron microscopes, high-powered telescopes, and other mechanical devices. Kepes created *Tumbling Textures* during his stay at Dartmouth as artist-in-residence in the fall of 1977. As its title suggests, this vertiginous composition contains a series of glowing abstract shapes that appear to fall and tumble in a shallow pictorial space enlivened by the addition of sand to an otherwise pristine painted surface.

MRT

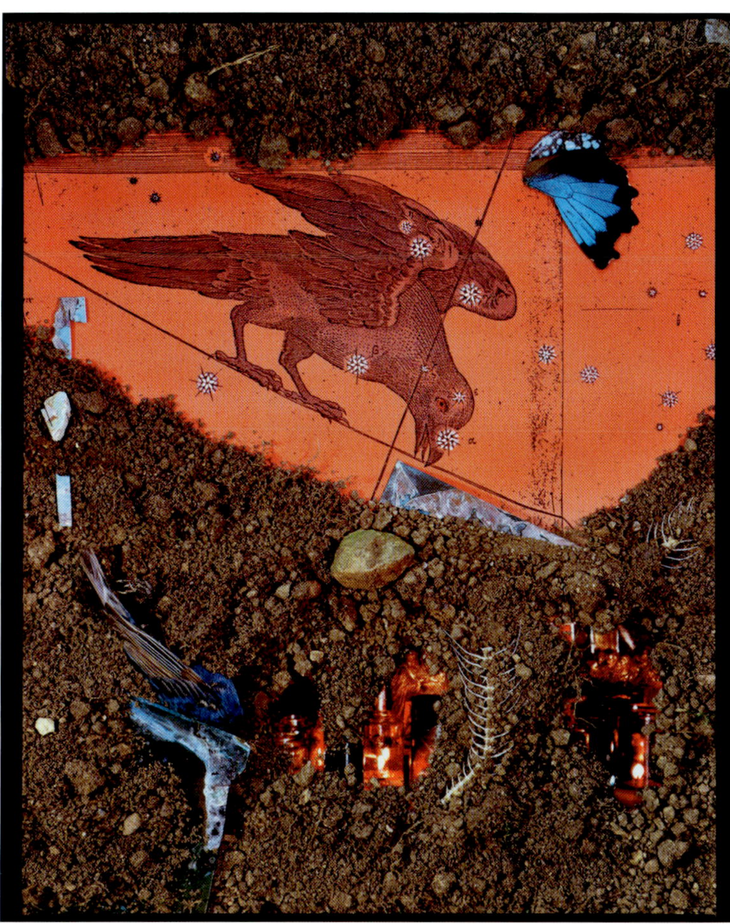

OLIVIA PARKER
American, born 1941
Raven with Stars in His House, 1988
Cibachrome print, image: 13⁷/₈ x 10¹/₂ in.;
sheet: 14 x 11 in.
Gift of the artist; PH.990.23.2
© Olivia Parker

Olivia Parker's primary preoccupation as a photographer has been with the genre of still life. She graduated from college with an art history degree and began her professional career as a painter. In 1970, however, she took up photography and has focused on this medium for more than forty years. In particular, she was attracted by the camera's ability to capture light and transform objects. She has said that she works intuitively and often arranges her subjects—among them books, flora, fauna, printed images, and shadows—to create photographs that invite, in her words, "speculation and invention." To this end, Parker collects objects in all sorts of places—junk shops, flea markets, or the forgotten corners of her own house. Although she does not cite the ideas of the surrealists as an influence, some of her work is closely linked to their practice of disassociating objects from their usual contexts to de-familiarize them, and also to bring them into a poetic framework. The most extreme of the surrealist objects were intended to provoke repugnance; however, they also evoke an associative state that unlocks the unconscious mind. Parker, by delving into the power of the relationship between materials—both natural and man-made—and light, both illuminating and obfuscating, creates dreamlike images that arouse imagination, reflection, and sensation.

Parker made *Raven with Stars in His House* in 1988, the year of her residency at Dartmouth. Varujan Boghosian, who was teaching in the Studio Art Department at that time, was a close friend, and they often went to flea markets and antique shops together, although he was away the term she was in residence. Boghosian creates through

assemblage—sculptures and collages that draw on found objects—and Parker's color photograph of arranged elements bears a clear relation to this practice. While in Hanover, she bought a seventeenth-century book of astronomy by Johann Bayer from a local dealer. She copied the image of the Raven (Corvus), a constellation in the southern sky, and used it as the focal piece for this photograph. The raven, a celestial object and creature of the air, is literally circumscribed in earth and bounded above by a butterfly wing and below by a partially covered Indigo Bunting (the bird had died after crashing into Parker's window, and was stored in her freezer), and a photograph of a shrine in New Mexico. The intense reds and earthy browns contrast with the cooler blues in the butterfly wing and a half-buried shell. In a newspaper interview at the time of her residency, Parker spoke of the difference between her work and sculptural assemblage. She arranges objects on a flat surface temporarily, to be photographed from above and presented as an image, whereas a sculptor adheres elements into a more permanent, three-dimensional object in itself. Parker's assemblages are made for and endure within the photographic medium, and the objects she transforms through this art exist in an imaginative, associative space outside their quotidian reality.

KWH

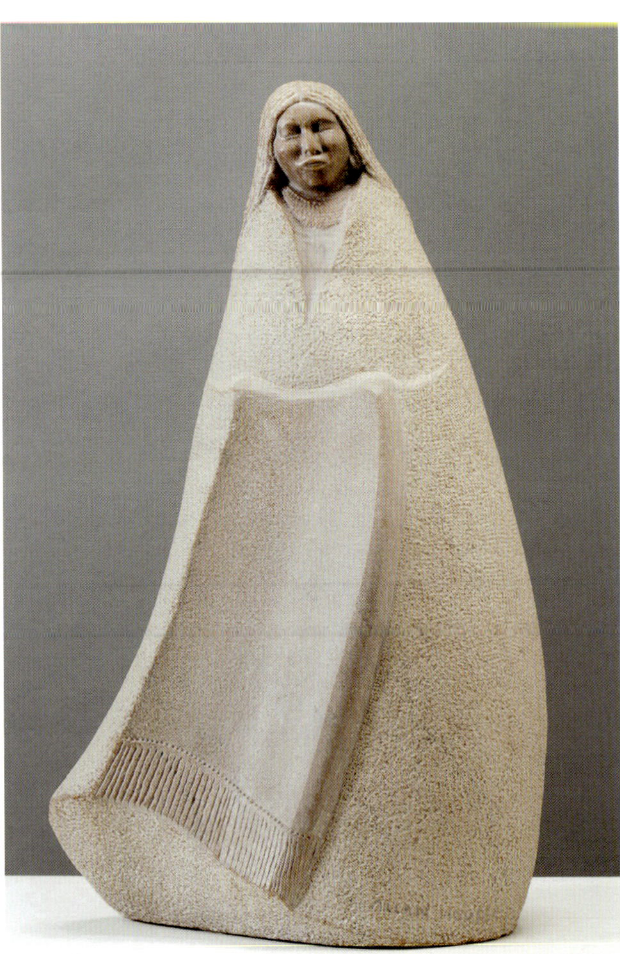

ALLAN C. HOUSER
American (Chiricahua Apache), 1914–1994
Young Apache Woman II, 1978
Pink Tennessee marble, 28 x 14 x 12 in.
Gift of Harry T. Lewis Jr., Class of 1955,
Tuck 1956, 1981P; 2013.28
© Chiinde LLC

Allan Houser is one of the best-known Native American artists of the twentieth century and has been an influential figure in the field of Southwestern sculpture in the United States. He is a member of the Chiricahua Fort Sill Apache, a group that was imprisoned for twenty-seven years after the surrender of Geronimo. Houser was the first child born out of captivity after they were released; his mother had been born while the group was still incarcerated. He enrolled in painting school at the Santa Fe Indian School as a young man and began his career as a mural painter at the end of the Depression. His first marble carving was a monument to the Native Americans from the Haskell School in Lawrence Kansas who died in World War II. In the early 1950s he began an eleven-year stint teaching art at the Inter-Mountain Indian School in Brigham City, Utah. In the early 1960s he became a professor at the Institute of American Indian Arts in Santa Fe, where he primarily taught sculpture, retiring in 1975 to pursue his artistic career. In sculpture, he worked in stone and bronze and, occasionally, wood. The Hood Museum of Art houses five sculptures by this important artist; this is the only work from the collection in stone.

Young Apache Woman II is typical of Houser's work in that it shows the figure enfolded in a long, encompassing cloak that gives an abstract form to the sculpture. The sense of stillness, meditative and inward looking, is a characteristic of many of his figures, particularly the women. The movement of the skirt of her robe as it sways to the left is in counterpoint to this calm; she stands upright despite the rush of wind against her body. Houser did many variations on this female type and it became one of his signature subjects. He admired the work of Henry Moore, whose influence is evident in Houser's stone sculpture in particular. His tendency to create nearly abstract, voluminous forms that gracefully define the mass of the figure reveals his engagement with European modernism. The outer surface of this sculpture is rough, making visible the basic qualities of the medium through the textured and incompletely worked surface. Houser used a number of types of stone for his sculpture, including Carrara, travertine, and Belgian marble, Tennessee black and pink marble, Indiana limestone, and alabaster.

KWH

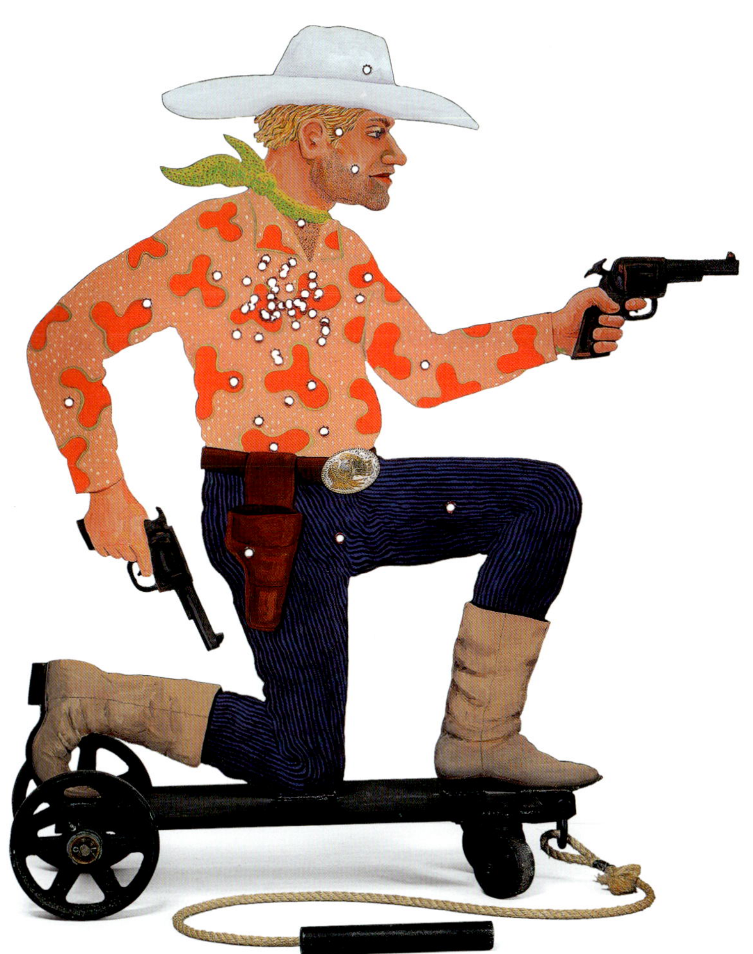

66

BOB HAOZOUS
American (Chiricahua Apache/Diné [Navajo]),
born 1943
Apache Pull-Toy, 1988
Painted steel, 54 x 48 x 16 in.
Purchased through the Joseph B. Obering '56
Fund; S.989.17
© Bob Haozous

Bob Haozous has devoted his career to addressing contemporary reali-ties and politics within the Native American community. The son of the celebrated Chiricahua Apache (Fort Still Apache) sculptor Allan C. Houser, Haozous was born in Los Angeles in 1943 and grew up in Cali-fornia, Oklahoma, and northern Utah. He attended Utah State Univer-sity before serving four years in the U.S. Navy. Haozous received a BFA from California College of Arts and Crafts in Oakland, California, in 1971. In 1999 and 2001 he helped organize the first Native American Pavilions at the Venice Biennale—a groundbreaking effort to inspire Indigenous artists to create a more meaningful contemporary statement of iden-tity. *Indigenous Dialogue*, a retrospective of Haozous's work, opened in 2004 at the Institute of American Indian Arts Museum in Santa Fe, New Mexico. This exhibition was followed two years later by *Relations: Indigenous Dialogue*, an exhibition that involved a dozen artists dis-cussing contemporary indigenous arts, artistic cultural responsibility, and the issue of relinquishing individual focus for community issues. The conversations that took place were transcribed and published with additional essays by scholars and critics to create the *Relations* catalogue. The resulting exhibition, which was a collaborative effort by all participants, challenged existing attitudes of artists, curators, and museums in their presentation of contemporary indigenous arts.

Haozous was artist-in-residence at Dartmouth in the summer of 1989, during which seventeen of his large-scale steel sculptures, includ-ing *Apache Pull Toy*, were exhibited in the Jaffe-Friede and Strauss Gal-leries from July 15 to September 17. A reverse cultural stereotype, this sculpture was fabricated from half-inch cut steel, creating a flat form like a paper doll on wheels, in which a cowboy target is shot full of bul-let holes. The heavy metal, welded-steel construction gives the work a sense of permanence. The work presents a rare opposing viewpoint to the Saturday morning matinees of the 1950s and 1960s that portrayed cowboys killing scores of Indians with Colt six-shooters. Haozous's artistic statement is satirical, humorous, and intellectually challenging, all in one shot. He brings into focus the idea that Native Americans did not disappear with the advent of colonial oppression, but still exist, with a heavy load of cultural trauma. This backward, simple, angry, and potentially violent toy is a reminder of the lingering stereotypes that persist in the Native experience in the twenty-first century.

JS

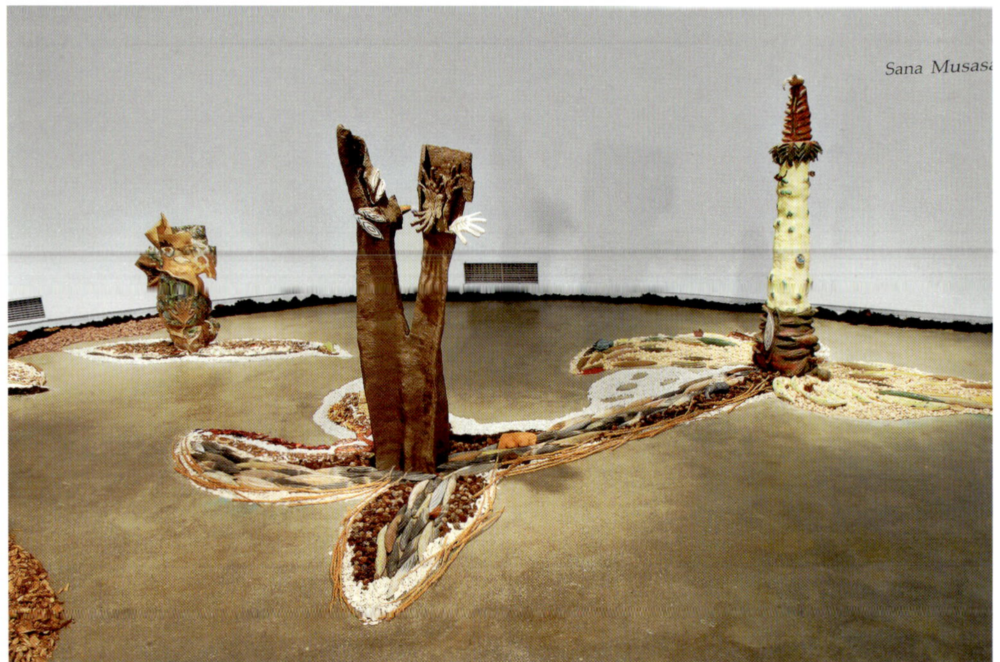

67

SANA MUSASAMA
American, born 1957
Yellowbird Bark, Slippery Rock, Pennsylvania,
1990
Ceramic (low-fire), mixed-media installation,
dimensions variable
Purchased through the Virginia and Preston T.
Kelsey 1958 Fund and the Kira Fournier and
Benjamin Schore Contemporary Sculpture
Fund; 2007.54.1
© Sana Musasama

68

SANA MUSASAMA
My Hand, My Heart, Den Bosch, Holland, 1992
Ceramic (low-fire), mixed-media installation,
dimensions variable
Purchased through the Virginia and Preston T.
Kelsey 1958 Fund and the Kira Fournier and
Benjamin Schore Contemporary Sculpture
Fund; 2007.54.2
© Sana Musasama

A ceramic artist who presents her work in large-scale mixed-media installations, Sana Musasama is also a human rights activist dedicated to challenging social and political systems around the world that deny women the right to free expression and full ownership of their bodies and their lives. She received a BA from the City University of New York in 1974 and an MFA from the College of Ceramics at Alfred University in Alfred, New York, in 1987. Her work has been informed by her travels to such countries as Cambodia, China, India, Japan, Sierra Leone, Thailand, and Vietnam. "I got on the road because clay exists all over the world," Musasama stated recently. "It's made by Mother Nature, so it doesn't matter where you go in the world, you'll find clay."[1] In addition to being exposed to different traditions of making pottery and ceramics, Musasama was also deeply disturbed by issues affecting women in these countries, including domestic violence, dowry burning, female genital mutilation, foot binding, and underage prostitution. Women's rights and experiences soon became central to Musasama's art, which seeks to give voice to those who are silenced or forgotten: "The artwork that I make is full of cries, it's full of tears, it's full of stories. But when I'm making it and putting it in this object and handing it to you, you are sharing my burden when you take it away and share that story with someone else."[2]

Yellowbird Bark, Slippery Rock, Pennsylvania and *My Hand, My Heart, Den Bosch, Holland* are part of an extended series of ceramic sculptures honoring the nineteenth-century Maple Tree Movement. When Europeans first arrived in North America, Native Americans showed the settlers how to harvest the sap of the maple tree. Cane sugar, maple sugar's competitor, was a commodity made possible because of the enslavement of thousands of Africans, who labored in the cane fields. Therefore, for early American abolitionists, domestically produced maple sugar could serve the goal of eliminating slavery. It is this notion of the maple tree as a symbol of liberation that has propelled Musasama to explore numerous variations on the tree form, creating colorful low-fired ceramic installations that pay tribute not only to the Maple Tree Movement, but to countless other histories that remain untold. These works were shown in an unforgettable installation in the Jaffe-Friede Gallery during Musasama's residency at Dartmouth in the winter of 2007.

MRT

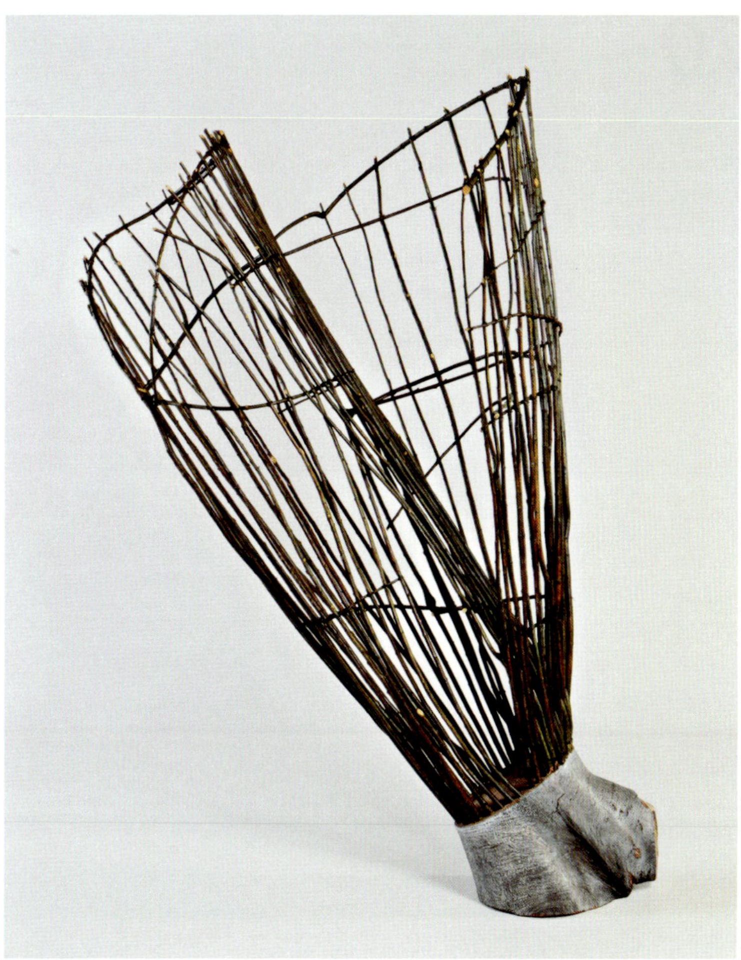

69

CAROL HEPPER
American, born 1953
Tropus, 1987
Copper beech, willow, wire, and pigment,
79 x 47 x 47 in.
Gift of Shelly Kolton; S.2002.5
© Carol Hepper

Now living and working in New York City and the Catskill Mountains in upstate New York, sculptor Carol Hepper was born in 1953 in McLaughlin, South Dakota, on the Standing Rock Sioux Reservation. Her personal history with the American West is often invoked in descriptions of her work, which, in both materials and subject matter, revolves around the natural world. Hepper is widely known for her use of nontraditional materials to produce sinuous sculptures; her earliest works were made from branches and stretched animal hides. Primarily a self-taught artist, Hepper received a BS from South Dakota State University in 1972. She has taught at colleges and universities across the country and was artist-in-residence at Dartmouth in the summer of 2000.

Tropus is constructed with copper beech trunk from which willow branches emanate into abstract, basket-like curvilinear shapes. The spiral silhouette of the work recalls the funnel clouds of a tornado, while the twisted branches seem to suggest an animal snare. Yet Hepper's works are not about anxiety or danger. Rather, the artist's sophisticated use of natural and non-traditional materials, her feeling for craft, and the transparency of her process create an exquisite object that evokes reverence. Although *Tropus* stands more than six feet tall, the multiple points of view it affords and the loops and circles of the woven branches make the sculpture seem delicate and finely formed. Meticulously gathered, cut, scraped, and bundled, the branches reveal the artist's process, and the acts of gathering, cutting, bending, and tying become part of the organic content of the final work.

ESB

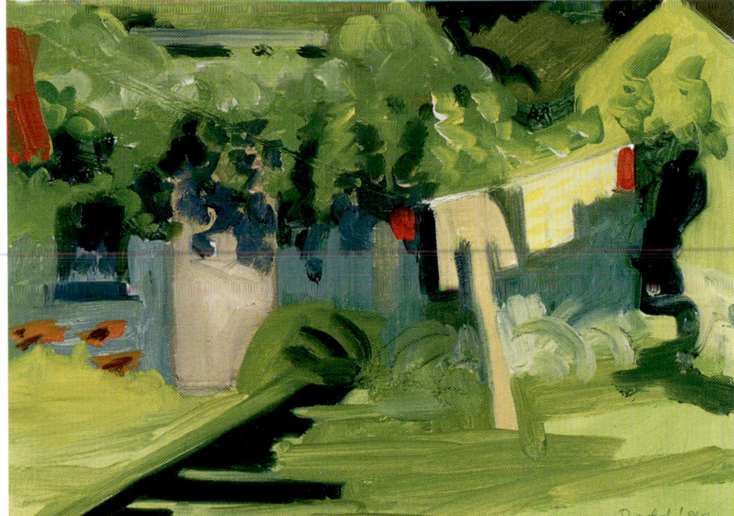

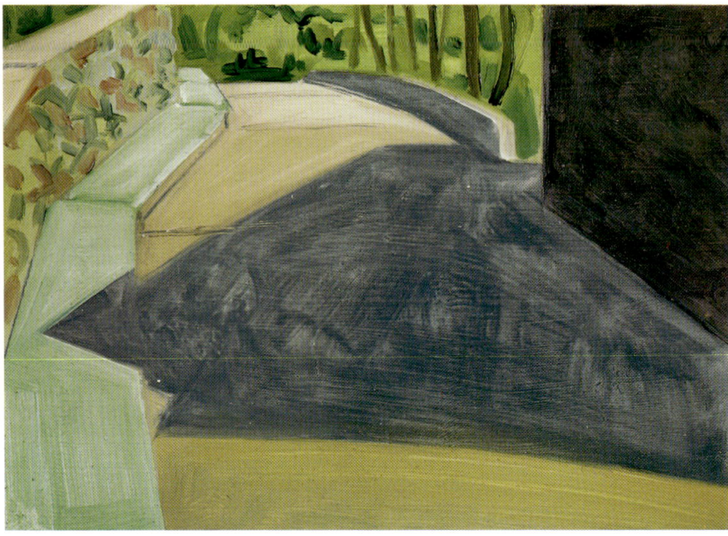

Born in Montclair, New Jersey, in 1927, Lois Dodd studied at Cooper Union in New York in the late 1940s. In 1954 Dodd had her first solo exhibition at the Tanager Gallery in New York, which at that time was the leading gallery for abstract expressionist painting. Dodd now lives and works in a loft apartment on the Lower East Side of New York; a house in Blairstown, New Jersey, which she acquired in 1976 to be near the Delaware Water Gap, a favorite subject of hers in wintertime; and a small house in Cushing, Maine, where she does much of her painting in the summer. In the summer of 2012, the Kemper Museum for Contemporary Art in Kansas City, Missouri, presented a major retrospective of her paintings that traveled to the Portland Museum of Art in Maine in the spring of 2013.

The two paintings seen here were completed during Dodd's tenure as artist-in-residence at Dartmouth in the fall of 1990. They are representative of the artist's plainspoken yet expressionistic landscapes. Evocative and poetic depictions of New England and New Jersey scenery, these paintings were part of a series that Dodd began that year, when a carpenter fixing the roof of her house left behind small rectangles of aluminum step flashing, which became a varying new surface on which the artist could work. Sometimes gessoing the flashing and sometimes painting directly on the bright aluminum, Dodd found a unique support for her oil paintings.

An atmosphere of intense solitude prevails in Dodd's paintings as she articulates a circumscribed world that resonates with absence. Though it includes some signs of domesticity, the scene in *Laundry, Sat. Aug. 4* is devoid of people. A riot of various greens dotted with red and yellow depicts the rich and moist foliage of New England on a warm, sunlit afternoon. While Dodd's paintings rarely feature any figures, through careful attention to composition and the picture plane she is able to shift the role of viewer from passive observer to active participant who can explore the image unchallenged. *Blairstown View* is such an image, as it pulls the viewer down a road winding into the distance between a wall and a house, while angular shadows play across its surface.

ESB

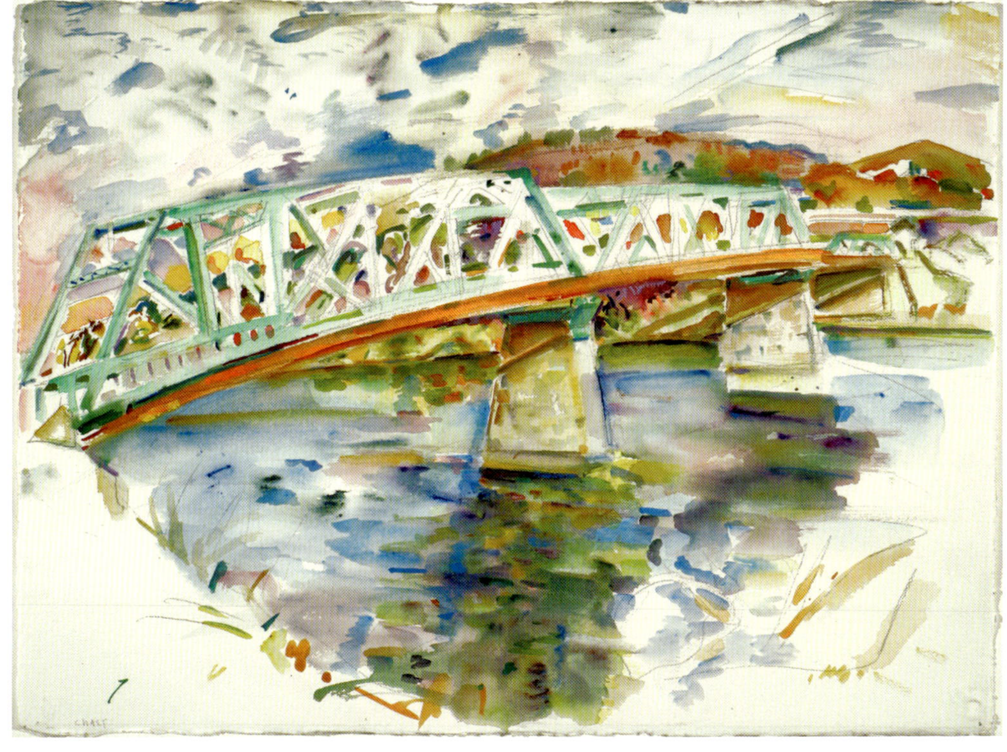

The late Bernard Chaet was a quintessential New England artist. Born in Boston, Chaet studied at the School of the Museum of Fine Arts, Boston, and Tufts University from 1942 to 1947. He went on to teach painting and drawing at Yale University, where he joined the faculty in 1951 and worked closely with Josef Albers to revamp Yale's art program. Between 1959 and 1962, he was the chair of what was then known as the Yale Department of Art in the School of Fine Arts, prior to becoming an independent professional school in 1973. In 1979 Chaet received the endowed position of the William Leffingwell Professor of Painting, which he held until his retirement in 1990, during which time the Yale University School of Art had become one of the leading art schools in the country. Chaet mentored several generations of emerging talents and many of his students, including Chuck Close, Janet Fish, and Richard Serra, went on to have notable art careers. In 1970 Chaet published *The Art of Drawing*, which was followed in 1979 by the publication of another important textbook, *An Artist's Notebook: Techniques and Materials*, both of which have been reprinted several times.

A "painter's painter," Chaet is best known for his vibrant, expressionistic landscapes, seascapes, and still-life paintings, many of which he painted around Cape Ann and Rockport, Massachusetts, where he had a home and summer studio. Chaet remained committed to traditional techniques and conventional subjects throughout his career, which overlapped with a series of competing and often contradictory art movements, including abstract expressionism, pop art, minimalism, and conceptual art. This does not mean, however, that Chaet was not interested in experimentation or innovation. Juxtaposing tradition with improvisation, the artist's paintings possess an extraordinary energy and formal daring, as seen in *The Bridge at White River Junction*, which was painted during Chaet's time as artist-in-residence at Dartmouth in the fall of 1986. In this work, the shimmering, translucent brushstrokes unify the composition, which, like all of Chaet's most successful paintings, consists of a carefully conceived balance of forms, colors, rhythms, and textures that evoke a myriad of sensations. The artist loved to work outdoors and later recalled that using watercolors transformed his work, as he sought to bring the immediacy and vitality of that medium to the oil paintings that he made at the end of his life.

MRT

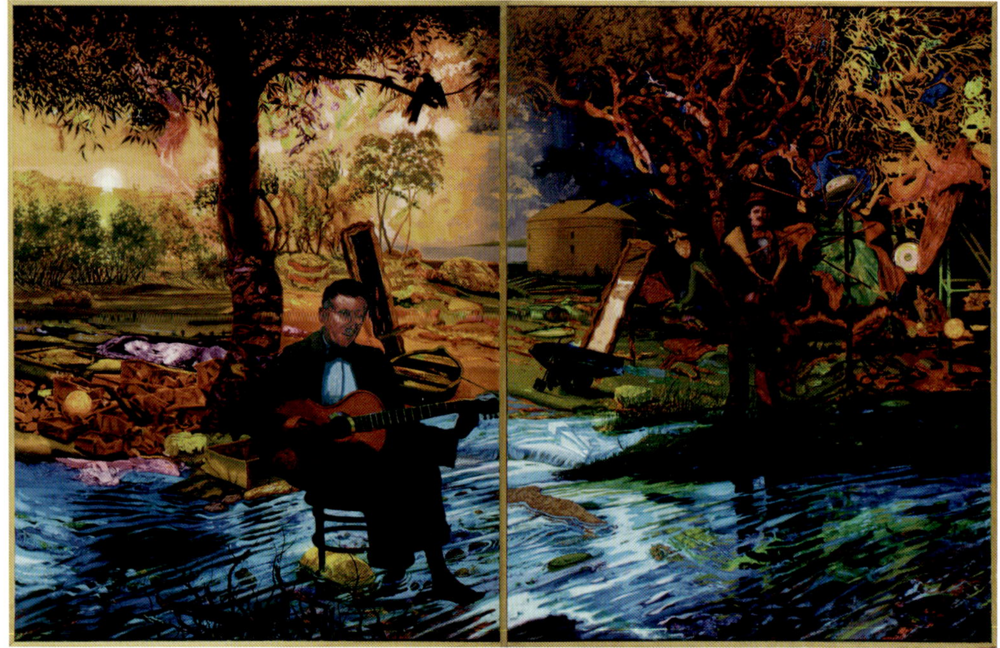

James McGarrell began painting at the age of twenty in the basement of his parents' house. He completed his BA at Indiana University in 1953, and spent a summer at the Skowhegan School of Painting and Sculpture in Maine before entering the graduate painting program at the University of California, Los Angeles, where he received an MA in 1955. That same year, McGarrell had his first solo exhibition at the Frank Perls Gallery in Los Angeles and received a Fulbright grant to study at the State Academy of Art and Design in Stuttgart (Staatliche Akademie der Bildenden Künste Stuttgart). After returning from Germany in 1956, McGarrell began teaching at Reed College in Portland, Oregon. Three years later, he returned to Indiana University to direct the graduate painting program. In 1981 he accepted a position in the School of Fine Arts at Washington University in St. Louis, where he taught until his retirement in 1993. While he was artist-in-residence at Dartmouth in the spring of 1993, McGarrell and his wife, the writer and translator Ann McGarrell, purchased an early-nineteenth-century house in Newbury, Vermont, which included a large mansard attic space that the artist transformed into a light-filled painting studio where he works to this day.

McGarrell is best known for his large-scale, complex figurative canvases, such as *The Grand Artificer, Young and Old (James Joyce)*, which was exhibited in the Jaffe-Friede Gallery during his residency. Reading Joyce's novel *Ulysses* in the 1950s had a profound effect on the artist and encouraged his commitment to the human figure and its narrative implications and possibilities. The Irish writer, McGarrell observed, "showed that no thing or idea was so trivial or personally anecdotal that it could not be transformed into the monumentally universal. In place of an imperative coherence of stylistic purity he posited the most raucous jumble of idiom, metaphor, and synthetic facture."[1] McGarrell's homage to Joyce takes the form of a richly colored diptych (a single painting composed of two canvases placed side-by-side) that is a work of fictive imagination rather than a record of perceived reality. Joyce is shown as a young man strumming a guitar in the left-hand panel and as an older man juggling canes on the right. The themes of memory and the passage of time are underscored by the shared iconography of trees in different seasons, as well as the flowing river that connects the two panels.

MRT

ROSEMARIE BECK
American, 1923–2003
House of Venus, 1994
Oil on linen, 58$^{7}/_{16}$ x 52$^{3}/_{16}$ in.
Partial gift from the Rosemarie Beck
Foundation and partial purchase through
the Claire and Richard P. Morse 1953 Fund;
P.2004.29
© Rosemarie Beck

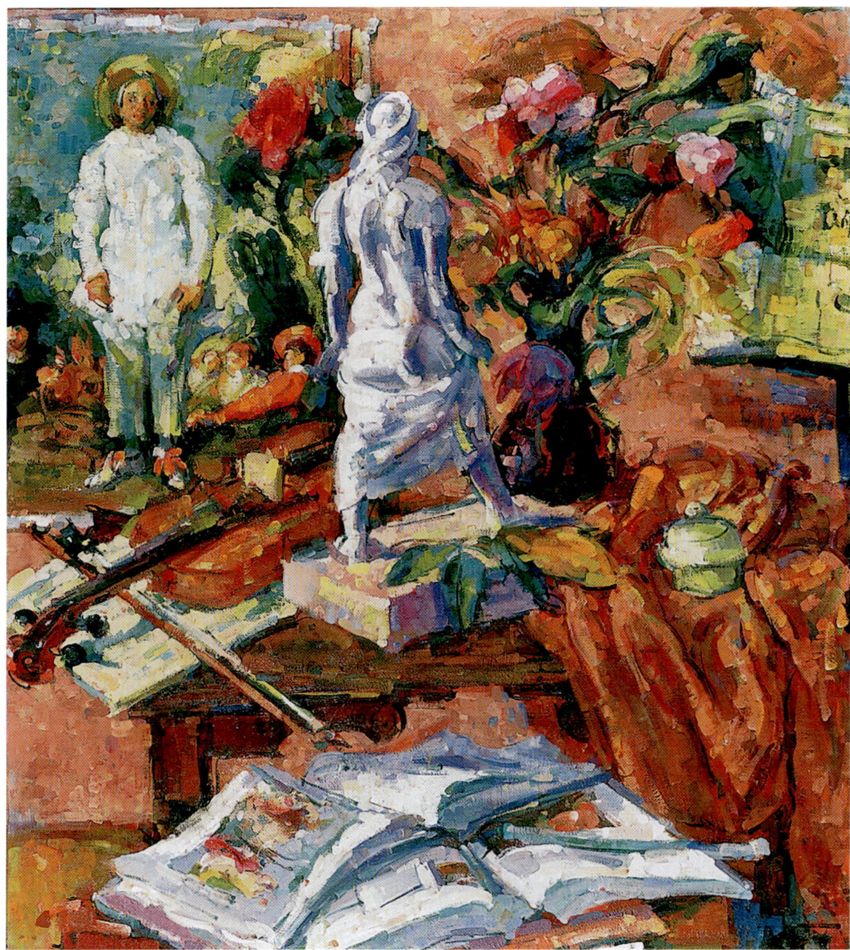

Rosemarie Beck was artist-in-residence at Dartmouth in the spring of 1992. Born in Westchester County, New York, in 1923 of Hungarian immigrants, she and her siblings were encouraged in the study of music, performing, and the visual arts by their parents. An art history major at Oberlin College, from which she graduated in 1944, she played violin professionally into the 1960s until a hand injury caused her to change course. Beck then focused on the art that she had begun making at the Institute of Fine Arts at New York University and had continued at the Art Students League and in painting classes in the studios of Kurt Seligmann and Robert Motherwell. She taught at Columbia University, Queens College, Vassar College, Middlebury College, and the University of Pennsylvania in the 1960s and 70s in one- and two-year appointments. She was a resident at New Hampshire's MacDowell Colony in 1967–70 and received honors including the Rockefeller Foundation Grant at Bellagio, National Endowment and ADEC grants to work in France, and—twice in the 1980s—the Altman Figure Prize at the National Academic of Design.

A reference to the artist's life's passions is evident in *House of Venus*. Antoine Watteau's famous early-eighteenth-century French painting of a commedia dell'arte player, *Pierrot (also known as Giles)*, complete with background figures and a hint of landscape, occupies the top left corner, hanging on the wall of a loosely defined interior space. A violin is laid aside, on a table crammed with such typical objects of still-life painting—a figurine, a vase of flowers, and a ceramic pot on a draped cloth—that we cannot help reading them as symbols, also of

a love for the subject matter of painting. The open books in the foreground reveal the continuously searching, curious mind of the artist, not as ready to give up on learning and making music as the resigned stance of Pierrot may imply. In her essay "Rosemarie Beck: Never Form but Forming" (the title itself drawn from the artist's comment on her own work), art historian Martica Sawin writes of *House of Venus*:

> The figure strides to the right, Giles pulls the eye to the upper left, the cloth cascades to lower right, the bow juts out of the lower left, the flowers almost sway, while two open volumes in the center foreground anchor the whole. The senses are addressed by the rich and resonant color, by the references to music, fragrance and art; but what really astounds is that these various focal points, pulling in different directions in a crowded and ambiguous space, ultimately all resonate together like the instruments in a quartet.[1]

In addition to this painting, a partial gift from the Rosemarie Beck Foundation a year after the artist's death, the Hood Museum of Art's collection includes a sketchbook from Beck's time as artist-in-residence in 1992 and six oil-on-canvas and oil-on-paper sketches for *House of Venus*.

JMB

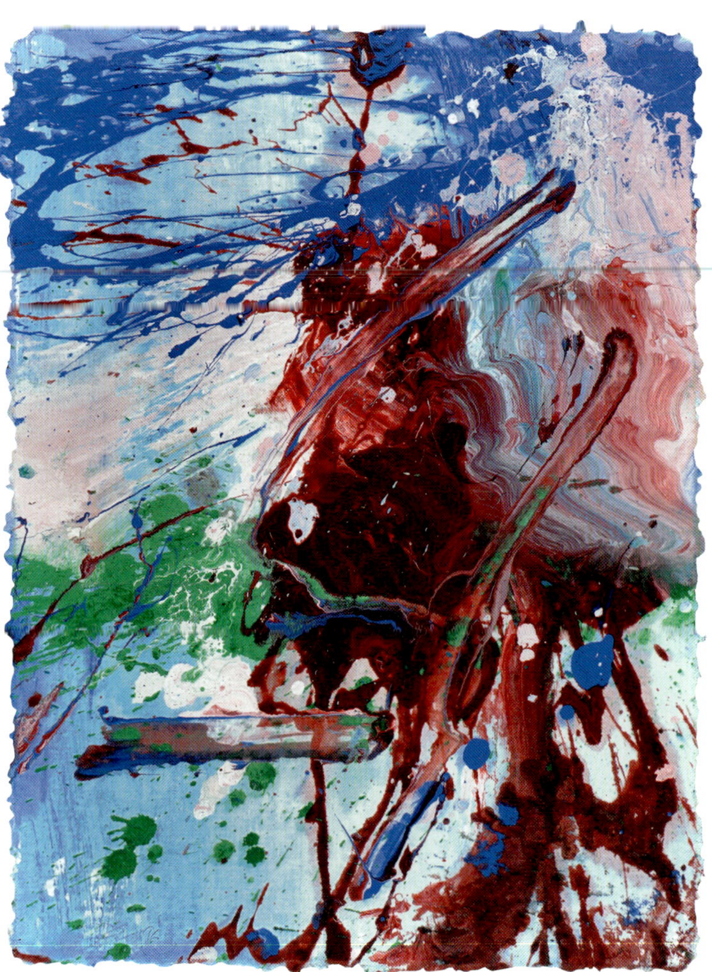

JAMES BOHARY
American, born 1940
Water System, 1996
Acrylic on paper, 17¹/₂ x 13 in.
Gift of Varujan Boghosian; 2008.79.2
© James Bohary

James Bohary is an abstract painter best known for his dynamic, thickly layered, and boldly colored work. His vigorous brushwork and lushly painted surfaces follow in the tradition of first-generation abstract expressionist painters, such as Willem de Kooning, Jackson Pollock, and Philip Guston. Born in Brooklyn to an English mother and an Indonesian father, Bohary received a BS in art education from New York University in 1968. He then studied painting at the New York Studio School with Philip Guston. Early in Bohary's career, he met the artist Elaine de Kooning, who would become a close friend and mentor, and would remain an artistic and personal influence until her death in 1989. Bohary was artist-in-residence at Dartmouth in the winter of 1998. His invitation was suggested by Dartmouth professor of painting Colleen Randall, whom he had met in New York in the mid-1980s.

Bohary's work is informed by the landscape and natural surroundings of the various places where he lives and works. Although based in New York City and Binghamton, New York, where he teaches, he moves fluidly between different environments, such as the Long Island shore, upstate New York, and the coasts of Newfoundland, where his wife, Sandy, was born. More recently, he spends much of the year in the mountains of Puerto Rico, where he owns a rustic piece of land, with a renovated house and a newly built studio.

Despite references to the natural world, Bohary's paintings are grounded in the materiality of paint and canvas. His work often takes years to make, during which the artist slowly builds up layer upon layer of wet paint, developing complex colors and textures on the surface of the canvas. He considers painting to be a universal form of communication that transcends language and allows understanding across cultures. *Water System*, with its vibrant blues, greens, and browns, clearly refers to natural elements, and encourages the viewer to recall familiar views of coasts or lakeshores. The subject, however, is elusive, and Bohary's painting remains anchored to the tactility of its materials—thickly applied layers of acrylic paint on paper.

SGP

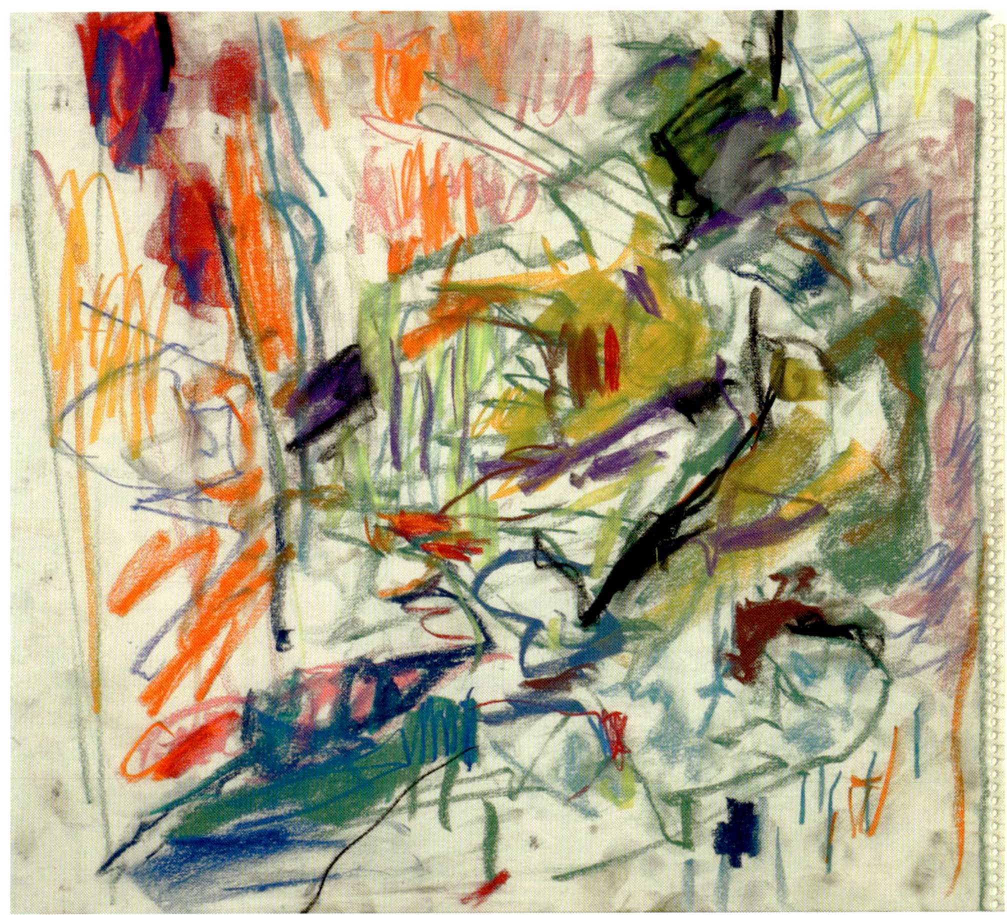

LOUIS FINKELSTEIN
American, 1923–2000
Landscape, 1994
Pastel on paper, 13³/₄ x 14 in.
Purchased through the Hood Museum of Art
Acquisitions Fund; D.995.18.2

Louis Finkelstein was a highly regarded painter, art critic, and professor who served as head of the Art Department at Queens College, City University of New York, for more than twenty-five years. Born in New York, Finkelstein studied painting at Cooper Union, the Art Students League, and the Brooklyn Museum School of Art. In 1957 Finkelstein studied in Italy on a Fulbright Scholarship and when he returned to New York the following year he joined the burgeoning abstract expressionist movement. Inspired by the work of Paul Cézanne and Henri Matisse, as well as his contemporary Willem de Kooning, Finkelstein developed an abstract mode of painting and continued to extend the basic stylistic premises of gestural painting long after the movement itself had waned.

Although a landscape artist throughout his professional career, Finkelstein altered the way he approached the natural environment in the early 1970s. Prior to that time, he generated ideas and subjects in his head and painted from memory. In 1971, while consciously following in the footsteps of Paul Cézanne, the artist embarked on a lengthy painting campaign in the sun-drenched Aix en Provence region in the south of France. During this trip, Finkelstein began painting directly from nature and thus entered one of the most productive phases of his entire career. This 1994 painting on paper, which was exhibited in the Jaffe-Friede Gallery during Finkelstein's residency at Dartmouth in the spring of 1995, belongs to this impressive body of work, in which he used bright, vivid colors and gestural mark-making to imbue his landscapes with a three-dimensional aspect. Rendered in pastel, a medium for which the artist developed an increasing affinity during the last decade of his life, *Landscape* shows the artist at the height of his powers, as he spontaneously responds to the natural landscape under changing light and weather conditions. The passages of orange, blue, green, yellow, and purple, which pile up in multiple directions as layers of color are applied, eventually coalesce into a dynamic vision of a lush landscape on a summer's day.

MRT

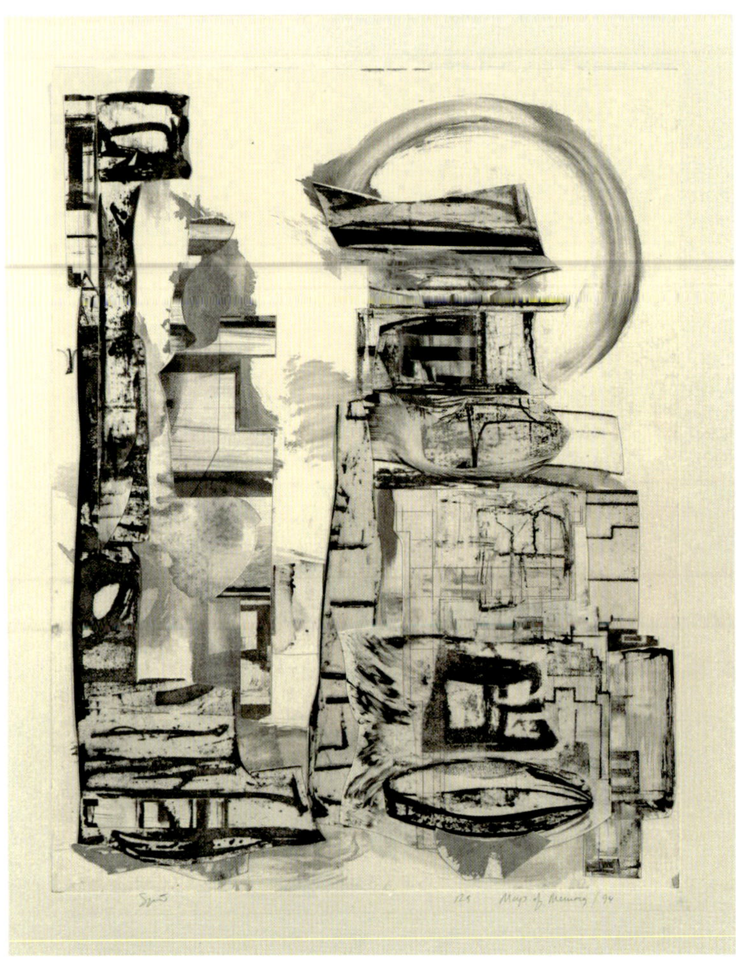

MICHAEL SINGER
American, born 1945
Map of Memory, from the *Ritual Series*, 1994
Etching and collage on wove paper,
23³/₄ x 17¹⁵/₁₀ in.
Purchased through the Phyllis and Bertram
Geller 1937 Memorial Fund; PR.995.33
© Michael Singer

Michael Singer, artist-in-residence at Dartmouth in the spring of 1996, has been internationally renowned since the early 1970s. He is the founder of Michael Singer Studio with locations in Wilmington, Vermont, (where he has lived for forty years) and Delray Beach, Florida. Conceived in tandem with the collaborative and interdisciplinary model that Singer has always used in approaching his work, the studios function to realize Singer's large-scale architectural, sculptural, and landscape projects. Singer's monumental outdoor sculptures and constructions respond to his deep respect for and symbiotic approach to nature—they change the landscape, but heighten our experience of it. Because of this, some have deemed him an environmental artist, but his body of work encompasses more of the human experience than this label suggests. To consider Michael Singer's oeuvre is to confront a continuum of engagement with human interactions with the world around us—from his many engravings, collages, and series of indoor and outdoor sculpture, to large-scale landscape projects such as the South Cove Regeneration Project in West Palm Beach, Florida, or the Troja Basin Revitalization Project in Prague, Czech Republic.

Singer's work in the collection of the Hood Museum of Art, the etching and collage *Map of Memory* from the *Ritual Series*, appears as if it might be a sketch or model for one of his sculptural or architectural projects. In his essay for the catalogue that accompanied Singer's artist-in-residence exhibition at Dartmouth, then-director of the Hood Timothy Rub wrote that in the artist's prints and drawings, "contrasting forms and pictorial elements are skillfully juxtaposed or placed in opposition to each other in order to create compositions that are balanced and harmonious and, at the same time, full of movement and life."[1] This life is evident in *Map of Memory*, and we can discern a variety of textures and materials in the imaginary constructed towers that fade into the distance, bringing to mind at once totem poles, watchtowers, a cistern, and even something futuristic in the mysterious arc in the top left. The collage's title reinforces this idea of imagination and things past but not forgotten: the structures suggest an imaginary archaeological site and therefore note the passage of time. Singer recently described his works on paper to Else Marie Bukdahl, the curator of a major 2011 exhibition of his work at the Utzon Center in Aalborg, Denmark, as "a compilation of marks that are often repeated and explored until they appear as 'powerful forms.' They then may be cut out or manipulated in various ways and after that rearranged in a composition on the paper. Work with the collages on paper is thus a very careful and time consuming process."[2]

JMB

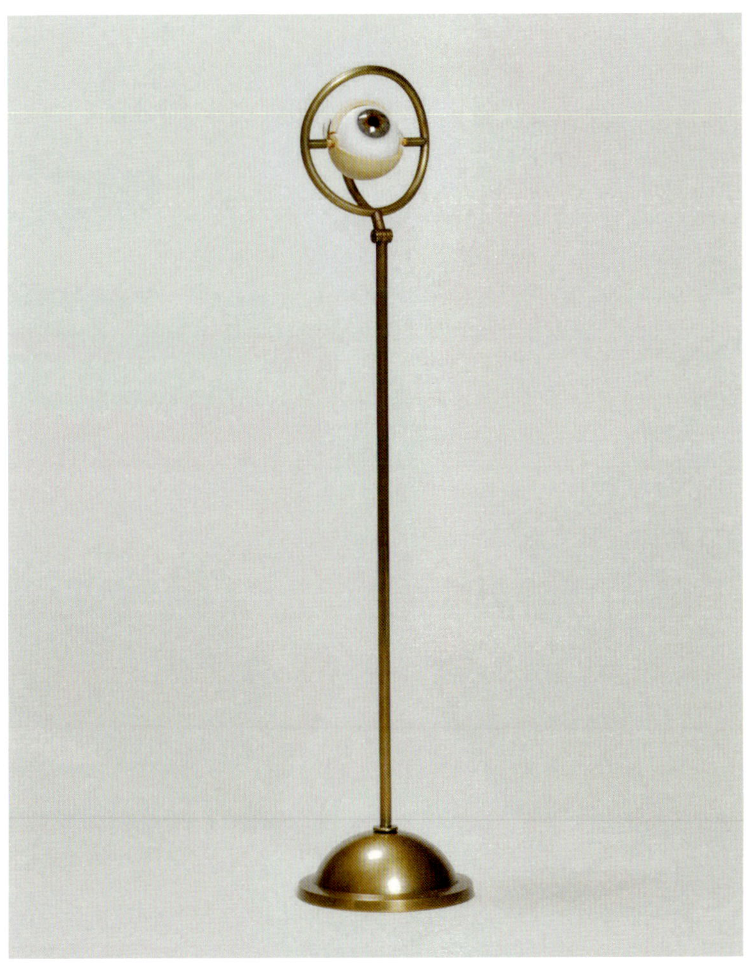

ELIZABETH KING
American, born 1950
Idea for a Mechanical Eye, 1988–90
Cast acrylic, wood, brass, 10^1/$_2$ x 2^1/$_4$ x 2^1/$_4$ in.;
diameter: ^{7}/$_8$ in.
Purchased through the Virginia and
Preston T. Kelsey '58 Fund; 2008.37
© Elizabeth King

In the early 1970s, Elizabeth King studied sculpture at the San Francisco Art Institute, where she became interested in creating a separate world of objects that involved animation and puppetry. In an early student work called *Theater*, the viewer is seated between two halves of a box attached on either side of a chair at eye level. When closed, they surround the viewer's head, and within this enveloping dollhouse one sees a type of miniature stage set. Along one wall is a closet with a posed figure. King soon began creating such figures exclusively (without surrounding environments), drawing on the age-old craft of mechanical puppetry. She became immersed in sculpting meticulously crafted figures or parts of figures with intricately jointed moving parts. In the early 1990s she also began to animate them for film. When speaking of her fascination with this type of sculpture, King describes growing up with a mother who suffered from the effects of polio. Her early life naturally included the prosthetics and crutches that aided her mother. King cites this as perhaps the reason for her focus on creating eerily lifelike articulated hands and arms that have the ability to mirror subtle human movements.

The life-sized eyeball of *Idea for a Mechanical Eye* is unusual in her work, as King typically plays with a discrepancy in scale between her sculptures and their human models. Her fascination with the creation of glass eyes as prosthetics led to an informal apprenticeship from 1981 to 1991 with ocularist Earle Schreiber in Newark, New Jersey, in the making of blown-glass artificial human eyes. She had also worked, while a student in San Francisco in the early 1970s, with makers of cast acrylic eyes, the medium used in this work. In *Idea for a Mechanical Eye*, a perfectly modeled eyeball is carefully held in a brass scaffold, highlighting its segregation from the rest of the body. Stripped of flesh and bone, the eye stares upward into space, as if it has been forever trapped in a scientific examination. For all of the meticulous care King takes to render the eye, she does not aspire to create a seamless illusion of life, but rather a reflection of it, a conjuring of its most basic questions: Where does the self reside? Is there a point at which substance defers to spirit? Here, the eye—often considered the portal to the soul, a true communicator of emotions, and a mediator for direct experience—becomes the site for exploring this sense of self.

KWH and ESB

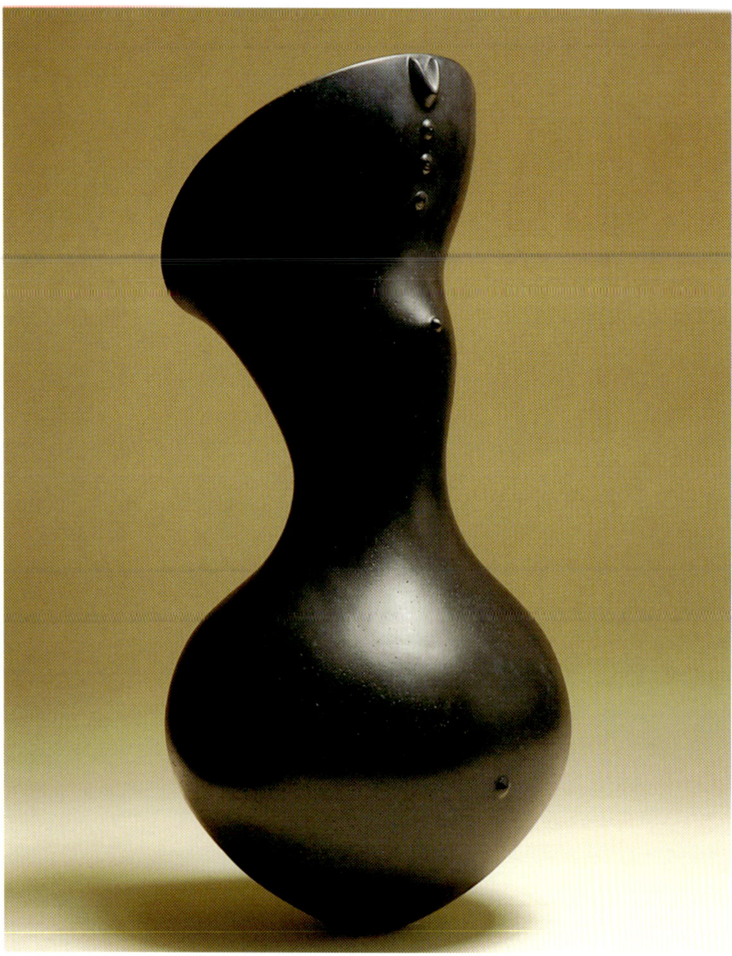

The celebrated British-based ceramicist Magdalene Odundo was artist-in-residence at Dartmouth in the fall of 2008. She began her career as a graphic artist in Kenya but turned to ceramics while completing her MA at the Royal College of Art in London, where she studied from 1979 to 1982. A keen observer of nature, culture, performance, and beauty, Odundo creates sculptural ceramics that capture the essence of form and motion as seen in the unfurling of a new plant, the silhouette of a pregnant woman, or period representations of female beauty.

The Hood Museum of Art's 2001 untitled work and *Tear Drop*, for example, pay tribute to "classic" beauties of the past with their ever-changing and culture-specific tenets of ideal womanhood. In the anthropomorphized and asymmetrical untitled vessel, Odundo reinterprets colonial-era depictions of Mangbetu women from central Africa in the early twentieth century. Celebrated for their regal splendor accentuated by an elongated head and haloed coiffure, Mangbetu women inspired both European and African artistic representations of idealized African beauty. *Tear Drop*, on the other hand, recalls European ideals of female beauty in the second half of the sixteenth century. The vessel's rotund body and long neck ending in a flaring lip evoke the opulence of Elizabethan gowns tailored with finely laced ruffs, generously pleated or puffed sleeves, and tightly corseted bodices and waistlines atop ballooning skirts, or kirtles.

Odundo first captures her chance encounters and observations on paper, pushing and pulling the naturalistic lines, volumes, and dimensions until she has reduced her initial impressions into sculptural abstractions. Through the malleable medium of clay, she then returns to three-dimensional representation by reinterpreting the sketched images into vessel forms—her primary visual language. She uses the coiling technique of handbuilding found in pottery traditions around the world to create extraordinarily thin-walled and lightweight vessels with delicate bases that often defy rational symmetry or tease out the limitations of gravity. The slipped and burnished surfaces of her vessels turn bright red-orange or glimmering jet black, depending on whether they are fired in a gas kiln with an oxygen-rich or oxygen-deprived atmosphere. The final result of her graceful vessels mimics a subtle dance filled with the tensions between motionlessness and action, positive and negative space, earth and fire, all the while maintaining the beauty and balance that Odundo sees around her in fleeting moments.

BT

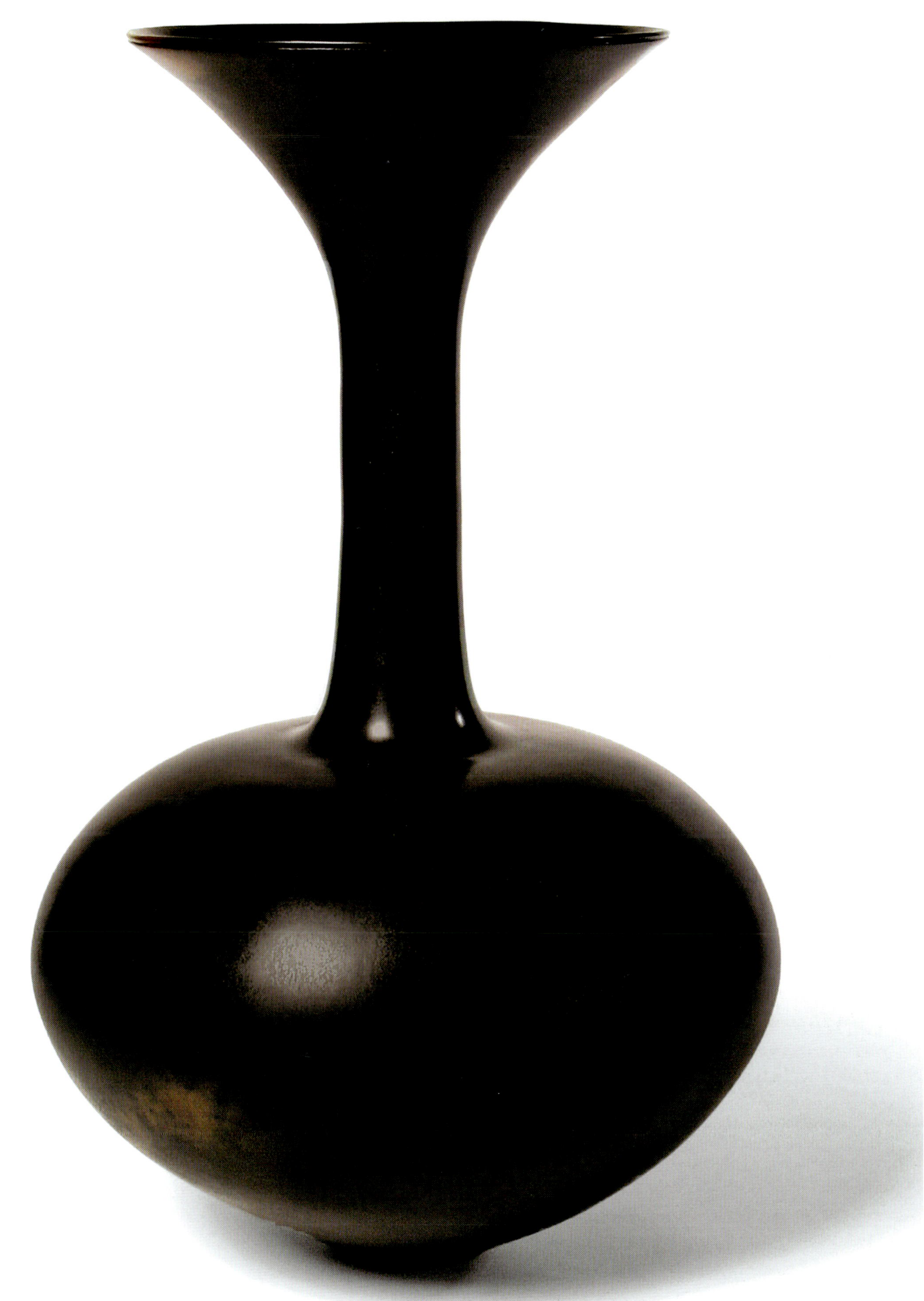

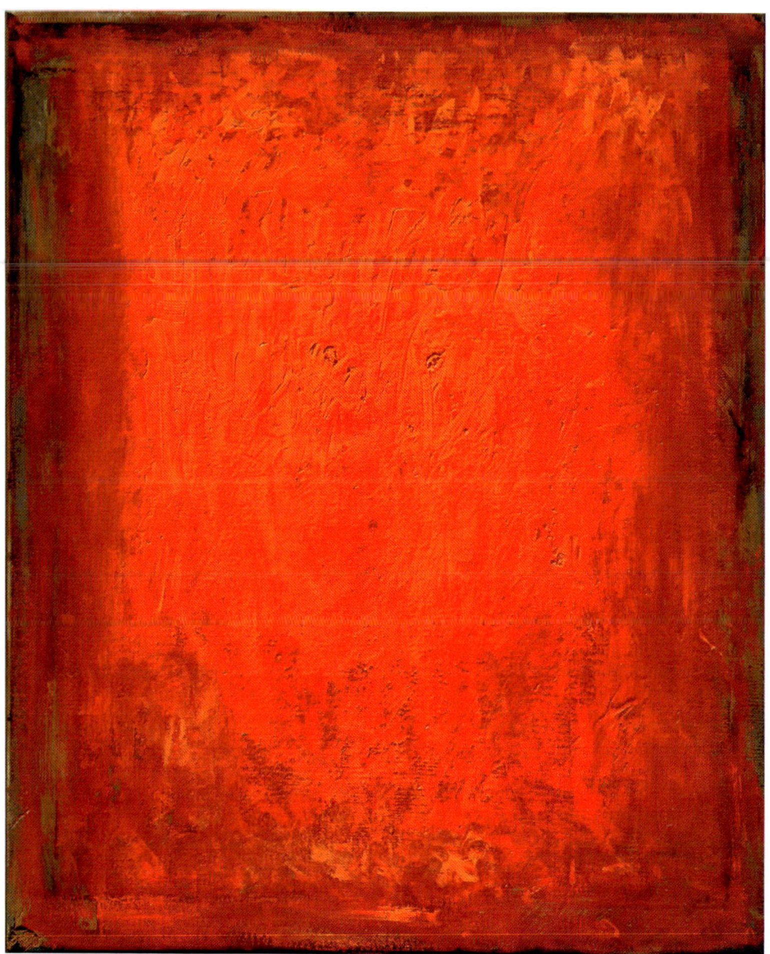

81

JAKE BERTHOT
American, born 1939
Beforehand, 1995
Oil on gessoed paper mounted on aluminum,
sheet: 21¹/₄ x 17 in.
Purchased through the William S. Rubin Fund,
the Claire and Richard P. Morse 1953 Fund,
and the Hood Museum of Art Acquisitions
Fund; P.996.7
© Jake Berthot

Born in Niagara Falls, New York, Jake Berthot spent his childhood in Pennsylvania before moving to New York City in 1959. Though he studied briefly at the Pratt Institute of Design and the New School for Social Research in New York from 1960 to 1962, Berthot is a largely self-taught artist who has been strongly influenced by the work of the abstract expressionist painters Mark Rothko and Milton Resnick, especially the rich color and subtle nuance of their paintings' surfaces. Berthot emerged as a mature artist in the late 1960s when there was much discussion about "pure" painting, a dialogue with which his work continues to engage.

Berthot made *Beforehand* during his residency at Dartmouth in the fall of 1995. Like many of his paintings, *Beforehand* focuses on basic formal problems such as the exploration of movement across canvas and the knitting together of surface and shape. Here, a red rectangle that is almost as large as the sheet of paper itself is centered on the surface and then worked in such a way as to complicate and call into question the relationship between the two. Berthot's work primarily reveals a dynamic interest in gesture and the transcendent and spiritual possibilities of purely abstract painting, much like his artistic hero, Rothko. Berthot's thickly layered abstractions evoke a spectrum of emotions. With a loaded monochromatic red that simultaneously suggests both a rich sensuality and the violence of spilled blood, Berthot employs the language of form, color, and texture to hint at an abstract narrative. And indeed, the artist identifies this narrative, saying that he is trying to "paint silence before it completely disappears."[1] What further stirs this silence are the scarred ridges on the painting's surface where the artist has scraped away pigment, leaving documentation of his process as well as a surface replete with shadowy meanings.

ESB

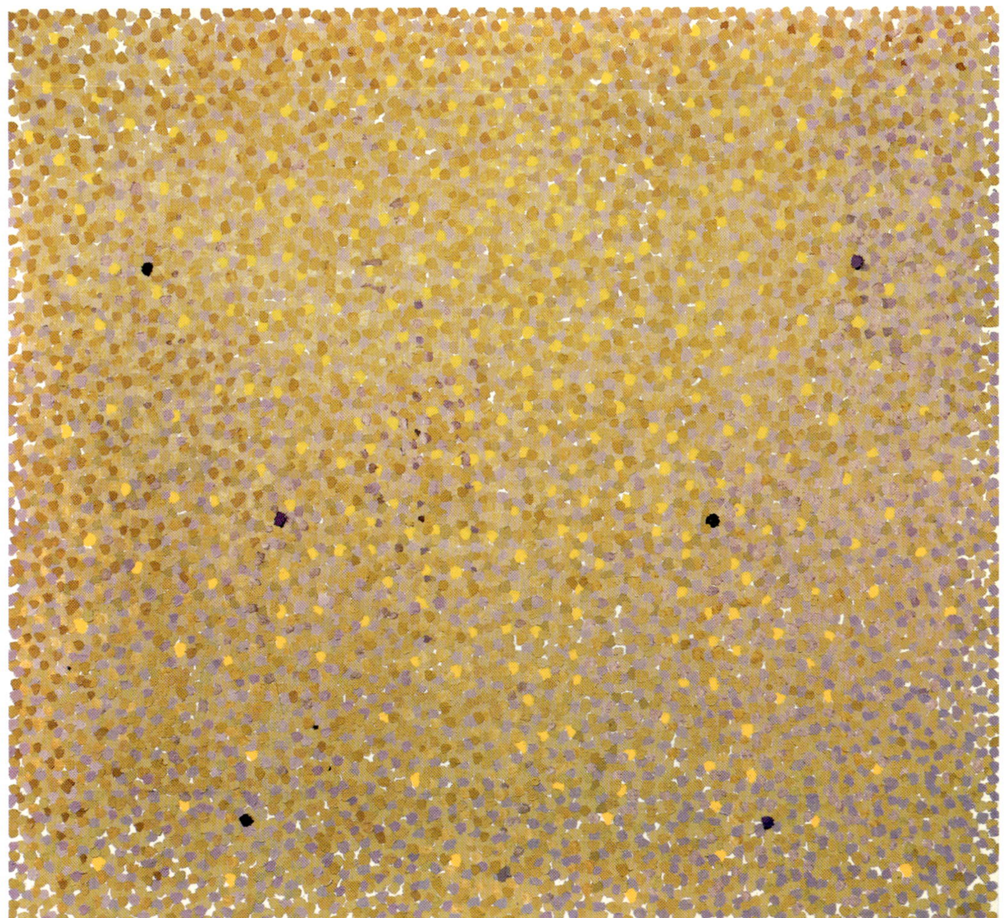

ANDREW MURRAY FORGE
English, 1923–2002
Forsythia, 1997
Oil on canvas, 30$^{1}/_{4}$ x 32$^{1}/_{8}$ in.
Gift of the artist; P.999.59
© Ruth Miller Forge

Born in Hastingleigh, England, in 1923, Andrew Forge moved in 1972 to the United States, where as a dean of painting at the Yale School of Art he became equally well known as an artist, critic, and teacher. He employed a subtle abstraction in his painting, creating luminous, slowly vibrating expanses of dots. Wholly absorbed by fundamental issues of seeing, Forge limited his formal vocabulary to two small, basic units: tiny dots and short, thin dashes of paint that he called "sticks." His works defy everyday vision as they examine the artist's perception of the world through paint on canvas, revealing, in particular, the sensory effects of color.

Forge continually plays with spatial complexity as he tests the line between legibility and abstraction. He explains:

Each painting starts with a single dot, and it grows as dots accrue over the field of the canvas. During the early stages, the formative principle is simply the vibration of the dots, whether in ordered constellations or randomly dispersed. As the white field of the canvas is covered dot by dot, color reveals itself; the light of the canvas must be rediscovered and reconstructed out of the interaction of the dots. Slowly, ways of reading the painting come up. Areas press forward or drop back. There are alternatives of substance and transparency.[1]

Forsythia was chosen from Forge's artist-in-residence exhibition at Dartmouth in the fall of 1999. A spatter of glimmering yellow hovers in front of a field of lilac dots, as light emanates from the depths of the painting. This is not a simple allusion to the real, but there can be no doubt that the work references the genus of flowering plants by the same name that produce bright yellow flowers in the early spring. Countless elusive internal rhythms, divisions, and startling structures, all created by unpredictable color shifts, gradually begin to declare themselves to the viewer.

ESB

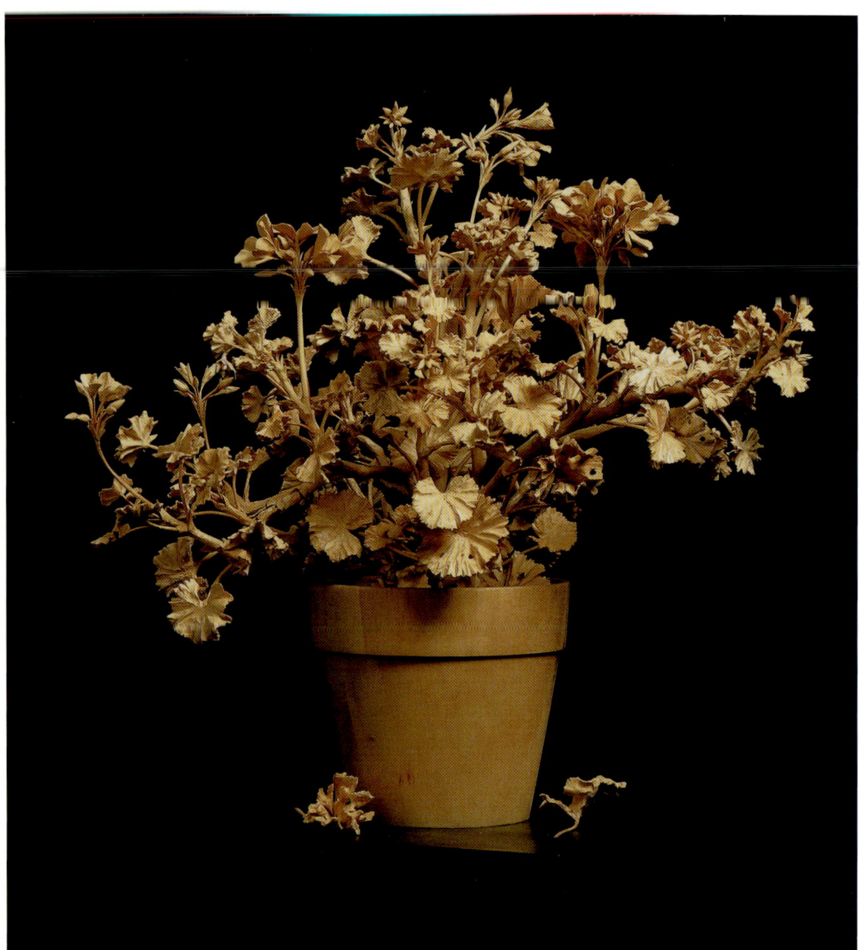

FUMIO YOSHIMURA
American, born in Japan, 1926–2002
Geraniums, 1997
Lindenwood, 32^1/$_2$ x 28^1/$_4$ x 28^3/$_4$ in.
Purchased through the Virginia and
Preston T. Kelsey 1958 Fund; the Guernsey
Center Moore 1904 Memorial Fund; the
Phyllis and Bertram Geller 1937 Memorial
Fund; the Katharine T. and Merrill G. Beede
1929 Fund; a gift from Adele Baron Marks
in memory of David N. Marks, Class of 1930,
with love; and a grant from the Richard
Florsheim Art Fund; S.999.12
© Fumio Yoshimura

The Japanese-born sculptor Fumio Yoshimura immigrated to the United States in 1962 after studying painting at the Tokyo University of Fine Arts and Music. Shortly after arriving in New York, Yoshimura taught himself to sculpt wood using a variety of tools and soon left painting behind. He came to Dartmouth as artist-in-residence in 1981 and stayed at the College until 1993, teaching sculpture as an adjunct professor in the Studio Art Department.

Geraniums is typical of Yoshimura's mature work in that it is a meticulously carved wooden reproduction of a seemingly mundane object. In the artist's hands, common items were transformed into elegant, intricate aesthetic and technical wonders. Yoshimura worked thousands of hours painstakingly carving these objects, creating wooden tomato plants, motorcycles, a hot dog stand, fish skeletons, and—most famously—bicycles. Yoshimura described his work as creating the "ghost" of an object, and the white, unfinished lindenwood he used imbued his sculptures with a decidedly ghostly pallor. Although Yoshimura has often been identified with the superrealist movement, he did not paint his sculptures to mirror their sources, nor did he use trompe l'oeil techniques common in the work of other artists who work in this style. Instead, the delicate and naturally wood-colored petals, stems, and leaves of his geranium seem to capture the soul of the particular plant that inspired them. Astounding technical virtuosity aside, the artist transcended both craft and process, creating sculptures driven entirely by the need to divine and preserve the essential spirit of everyday things.

ESB

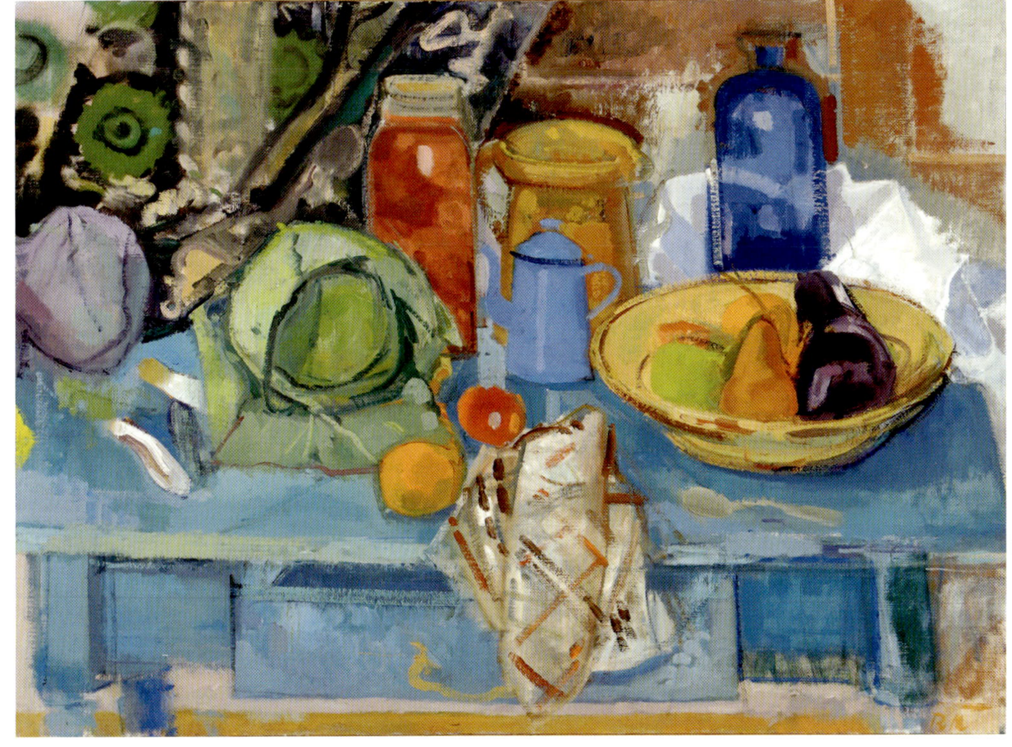

Ruth Miller was artist-in-residence at Dartmouth in the fall of 1999. Miller, known for her long career as a painter of still-lifes and landscapes, lives and works in Washington Depot, Connecticut. She was born in Columbia, Missouri, and received her bachelor's degree from the University of Missouri before moving to New York and studying at the Art Students League. She spent a decade in Pennsylvania with her first husband and taught at the Philadelphia School of Art and Design before moving back to New York in 1972, when she began teaching at the New York Studio School and continues to do so today. She also taught at Queens College and Parsons School of Design. In New York, she married former painter and critic Andrew Forge. Miller's work has been shown extensively over the past forty decades at galleries in New York, Pennsylvania, and Connecticut, and is featured in the collections of, among others, the Delaware Art Museum, the Corcoran Gallery, and the National Academy of Design, of which she is a member. As a result of Miller receiving the Henry Ward Ranger Purchase Award in 2000, *Blue Table Still Life* was sold to the National Academy of Design and placed on extended loan to the Hood Museum of Art.

Many artists and critics have noted the sense of vitality with which Miller imbues her still-life paintings. This seeming contradiction is reconciled when contemplating a work such as *Blue Table Still Life*. Each of the objects in the painting—her angular and expressive cabbages and blue teapot (signatures of this moment in her painting), the fruit in the bowl, and the cloth overhanging the edge of a table—vibrates with something that artist Rosemarie Beck likens to listening to the unfolding of a piece of classical music.[1] Miller presents her subject to the viewer close to the surface of the picture plane, with little to no foreground or background, which serves to heighten the liveliness of the assembled objects as much as the sketch-like quality of the painting itself situates it firmly in the realm of imagination. Commenting on an exhibition of Miller's work in New York just before her Dartmouth residency, critic Nancy Grimes of *Art in America* observed, "Although the brushiness and weight of the paint in the still lifes conveys a sense of the material heft of and blowsy ripeness of cabbages and eggplants . . . the real subject of these works is the conversation between Miller's hand, eye, and intellect."[2]

JMB

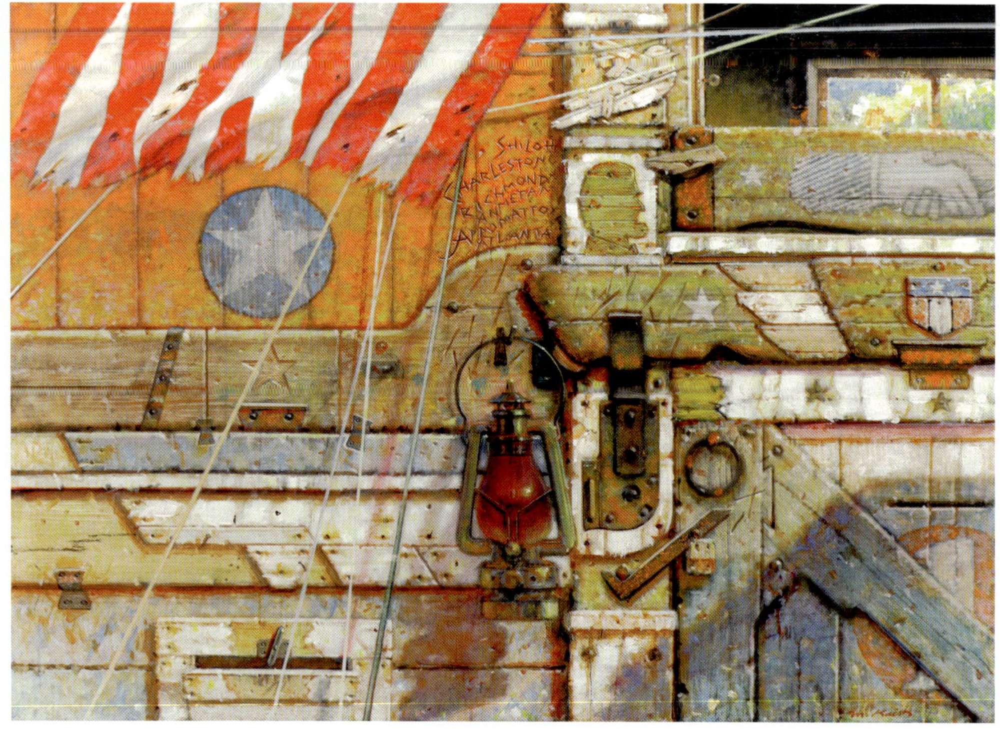

85

MORTON KAISH
American, born 1927
Freedom Door, from the *America Series*, 1998
Acrylic on linen, 44 x 60 in.
Gift of Melissa Kaish Dorfman, Class of 1983;
2009.91
© Morton Kaish

Morton Kaish, along with his wife Luise Kaish, was artist-in-residence at Dartmouth in 1974, sharing the post as painter and sculptor, respectively. Born in Newark, New Jersey, Kaish spent his undergraduate years at Syracuse University, graduating in 1949, and then studied at the Academie de la Grande Chaumière in Paris, the Instituto d'Arte in Florence, and the Accademia delle Belle Arti in Rome during the 1950s. He taught at the Art Students League and the New School in New York as well as the Fashion Institute of Technology, State University of New York, and was visiting artist at institutions including Boston University, Columbia University, Queens College, the Parsons School of Design, and the Philadelphia College of Art. He exhibited with Staempfli Gallery in New York until it closed in 1988, and also with Hollis Taggart Galleries.

Kaish painted the *America Series* after a tour of the United States in search of a visual representation of the American vernacular. He found it not in a particular place, but in the idea of the Civil War as a defining moment in the country's history. Consequently, the painted doors in this series, including *Freedom Door*, are not those that he encountered, but are purely constructions of his imagination. The marks of conflict and aspirations for reconciliation are hinted at in the flat geometry of Kaish's composition. The viewer's only glimpse of the world beyond the door is visible in the upper right of the canvas, through a window in the back of the house or barn, but that appears to be a roughly framed painting itself, and therefore more of an aspiration than reality. References to Civil War conflicts—Shiloh, Charleston, Richmond, Appomattox, and

Atlanta, battles lost and won through incalculable suffering on both sides—are carved into the wood. Kaish depicts wood worn over time and through repeated use, skillfully crafted hardware, a battle-weary but vibrant American flag, and the profile of Abraham Lincoln—the only human presence—with meticulous precision and bursts of bright color. Indeed, Kaish is known as a colorist, as Matthew Wysocki explained in 1974 when Kaish was at Dartmouth: "The success of Morton Kaish's paintings stems from his love of color. As a colorist, he has captured the luminosity and interaction of spatial relationships in a highly individual manner."[1] Kaish reflects on his work, "These structures . . . speak of time, loss, change, the seasons, of fragility and monumentality and the miracle by which America has survived." The door as metaphor represents entrances and exits, the past and the future, and the possibilities brought through change and transition.

JMB

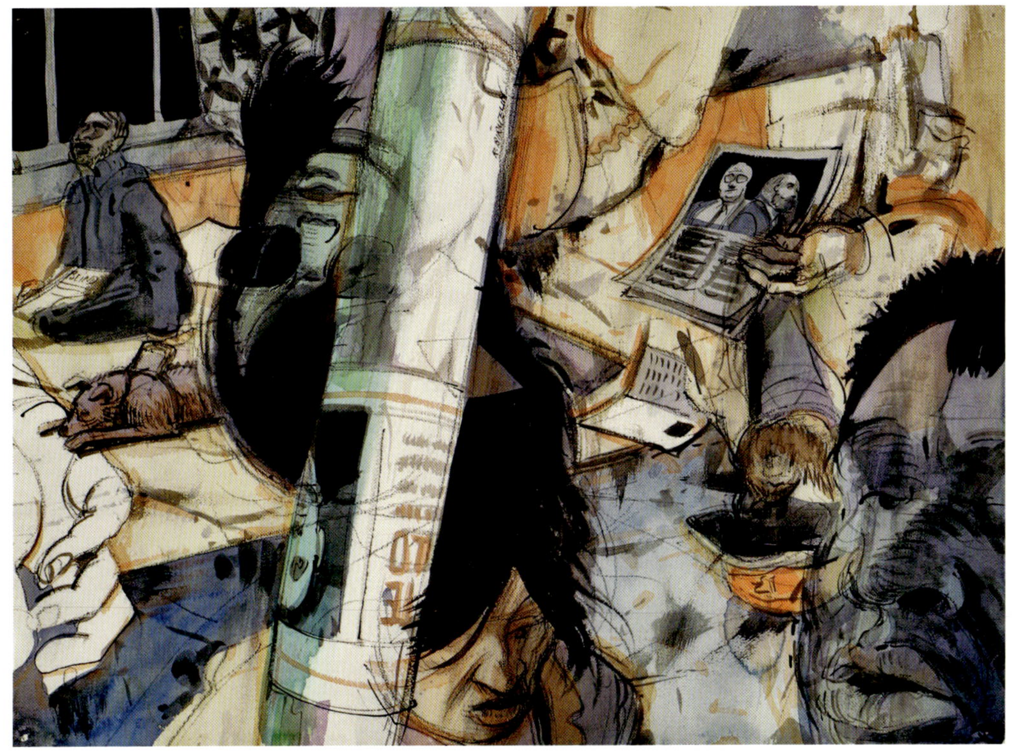

ROBERT BIRMELIN
American, born 1933
The Crowd/Others, 1999
Pen with India ink and watercolor with traces
of conte pencil on Fabriano watercolor paper,
$22^{5}/_{8}$ x $30^{1}/_{6}$ in.
Purchased through a gift from Robert A.
Levinson, Class of 1946; W.999.25.2
© Robert Birmelin

The experience of being in a crowd—the jostling, the press of people, the constant movement, the obstructed sight—was Robert Birmelin's primary subject from 1977 until 1992. Birmelin began drawing as a child. He attended Cooper Union, and then received a BFA and an MFA from Yale University in 1956 and 1960, respectively. He also attended the University of London's Slade School of Art the following year. From 1964 to 1998 he taught at Queens College, City University of New York, where he was appointed professor in 1974.

After 1992 his subject matter shifted away from crowded city scenes, but he returned to them in 1999 during his residency at Dartmouth College. Drawn during that period, *The Crowd/Others* captures the energy of the urban street. The strong pole in the center of the composition blocks the viewer's gaze, yet also prevents a collision with a dark-haired woman in the lower center of the composition. A seated blind man with a dog in the upper left—the only figure at a comfortable visual distance—offers some respite in the claustrophobic scene, while a large male face in the lower right presses into one's personal space. Above him an upside-down man in an orange baseball cap holds a newspaper printed with two more faces, and the central pole blocks a dark-haired woman in sunglasses shown in the same reversed orientation. These upside-down figures are intentional, as *The Crowd/Others* is one of Birmelin's reversible compositions, which can be displayed as illustrated here, or rotated 180 degrees. As Birmelin explained:

a configuration which "invites" a legible first glance and then subverts that first visual judgement [*sic*] by an equally plausible (or implausible) counter reading. The image remains "wrong" no matter how it is turned. This, I hope, provokes a state of visual permanent restlessness which is, in some sense, a metaphor, for our own fluctuating judgements [*sic*] regarding our own past actions and current motives.[1]

Indeed, looking at *The Crowd/Others* is a restless experience. Birmelin's marks are as frenetic and confusing as his subjects, his lines regularly escaping the contours of his color patches. While his figures have physical proximity, overlapping and even interpenetrating, they are psychologically distant from each other and the viewer. Here experience and perception meet representation as we enter the crowded, chaotic world of Birmelin's street.

ABK

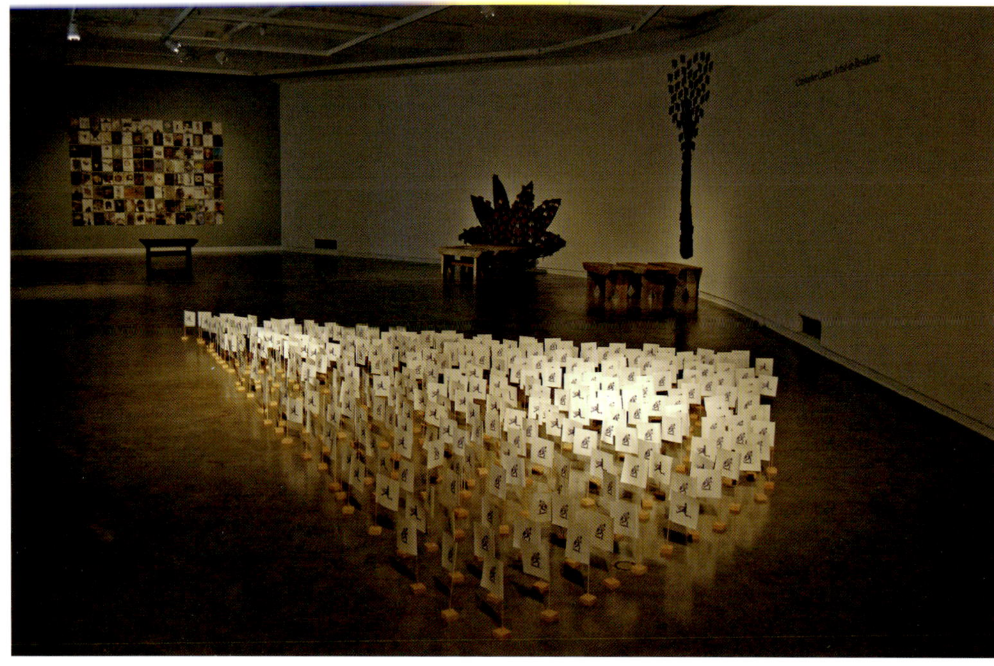

87

CHRISTOPHER COZIER
Trinidadian, born 1959
Cross Currents, 2001
Mixed-media installation (300 paper flags with rubberstamp prints mounted on individual blocks of wood), variable dimensions
Collection of the artist
© Christopher Cozier

Born in Port of Spain, Trinidad, where he lives and works to this day, Christopher Cozier is an artist, curator, and writer whose sketchbook drawings, prints, sound and video recordings, and multi-media installations address the history and legacy of the Caribbean's colonial past, as well as the present-day realities of what he calls "island identity." Cozier's work was exhibited in the fifth and seventh Havana Biennials, in 1994 and 2000 respectively. His work was also included in the 2009 exhibition *Contemporary West Indian Art* at Real Art Ways in Hartford, Connecticut, *Afro Modern: Journeys through the Black Atlantic* at Tate Liverpool in 2010, and *Into the Mix* at the Kentucky Museum of Art and Craft in 2012. In addition to his artistic practice, Cozier is a member of the editorial board of the distinguished journal *Small Axe: A Caribbean Platform for Criticism*, which is distributed by Duke University Press. As a curator, Cozier has organized numerous exhibitions, and in 2006 he co-founded Alice Yard, a non-profit art organization that produces regular exhibitions and performances in Trinidad. In 2010 he co-organized, with the independent curator Thomas Meijer zu Schlochtern, the exhibition *Paramaribo SPAN* in the Republic of Suriname in South America, followed by *Wrestling with the Image: Caribbean Interventions*, which he co-curated with art historian Tatiana Flores at the Art Museum of the Americas in Washington, D.C., in 2011.

Cross Currents, which the artist installed in the Jaffe-Friede Gallery during his residency at Dartmouth in the fall of 2007, consists of a triangular arrangement of three hundred printed flags in neat rows that the artist has connected with propaganda images of marching soldiers in North Korea. This 2001 work presents a dichotomy between the images of the sprinting black businessman holding a briefcase in front of him and the runaway slave with a bundle over his shoulder that Cozier printed on the flags using rubberstamps derived from nineteenth-century advertising stock images. "All the businessmen are running in one direction and all the runaways are going in another," Cozier explained in an interview in *The Dartmouth*. "It's kind of my reflection on globalization."[1] *Cross Currents* thus offers a profound meditation on money laundering and capital flight in an age of global capitalism, which, in turn, has had a negative impact on social, cultural, economic, and political conditions in Trinidad since the island's political independence from Great Britain in 1962.

MRT

PABLO DELANO
Puerto Rican, born 1954
*Sevilla House, Former Home of Manager of
Operations for Tate & Lyle Sugar Company,
Brechin Castle Sugar Estate, Trinidad, West
Indies*, 2012
Pigment print on Inkpress paper, 22 x 17 in.
Purchased through the Elizabeth and
David C. Lowenstein '67 Fund; 2013.40.1
© Pablo Delano

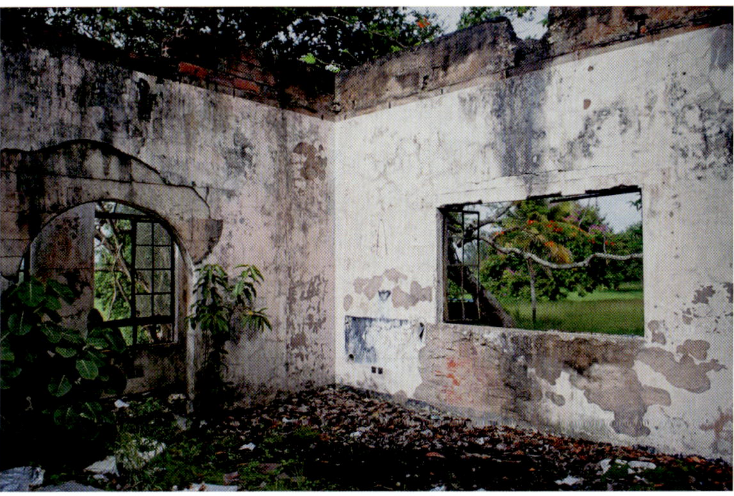

PABLO DELANO
*Interior, Brechin Castle Sugar Factory, Trinidad,
West Indies*, 2012
Pigment print on Inkpress paper, 22 x 17 in.
Collection of the artist
Purchased through the Elizabeth and
David C. Lowenstein '67 Fund; 2013.40.2
© Pablo Delano

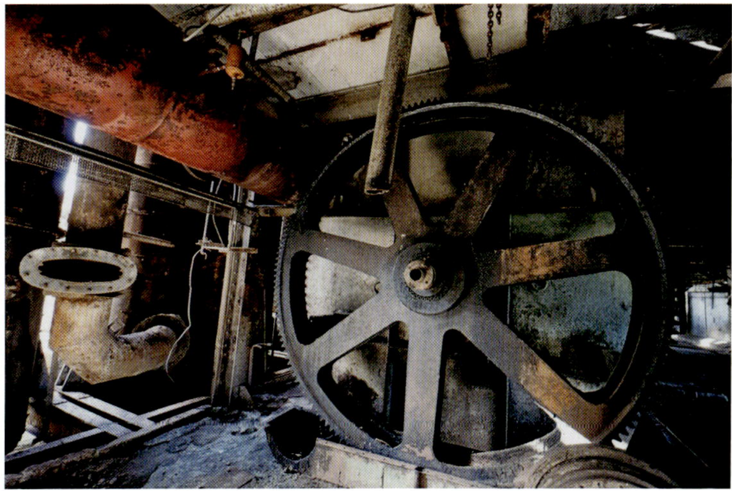

Born in San Juan, Puerto Rico, Pablo Delano was introduced to the art of photography at an early age by his father, the renowned photographer Jack Delano. He moved to the United States in 1972 at the age of eighteen to attend the Tyler School of Art in Philadelphia and later the Yale University School of Art, where he received an MFA in painting in 1979. Between 1979 and 1996 he lived and worked in New York, where he began his career as a freelance photographer carrying out several documentary projects relating to the history, aspirations, and cultural traditions of the Caribbean and Hispanic communities in the city. In 1992 Delano's celebrated book of photographs, *Faces of America*, was published by the Smithsonian Institution Press. His second book, *In Trinidad*, about public ritual, celebration, worship, and post-colonial identity in the Caribbean island of Trinidad, appeared in 2008. Subsequent projects have taken Delano to Honduras and Cambodia, as well as to the neighborhoods and landmarks of Hartford, Connecticut, where he teaches photography at Trinity College. He has also made photographs for several books on Puerto Rican folk art by the art historian Teodoro Vidal.

In 2013 Delano returned to Trinidad and embarked on a new series of photographs that document the abandoned sugar factories and crumbling mansions owned by their former managers. Like the photographs he made for *In Trinidad*, these works address the legacy of colonialism in post-independence Trinidad. However, while the earlier series depicted the diversity of Trinidad's multiethnic communities, works like *Sevilla House, Former Home of Manager of Operations for Tate & Lyle*

Sugar Company, Brechin Castle Sugar Estate, Trinidad, West Indies are eerily depopulated. The title of this photograph, which is deliberately factual and long-winded, evokes the captions assigned to photographs of similar buildings in colonial guidebooks. These decayed ruins are a visible reminder that the economy of this Caribbean island once depended on the exploitation of African slaves to feed the seemingly insatiable demand, in both Europe and the United States, for luxury food items like sugar, coffee, and cocoa. Following emancipation, British companies like Tate & Lyle arranged for indentured workers from India, another colony in the British Empire, to replace slave labor on the plantations of Trinidad by working under appalling conditions in these newly constructed factories, many of which were in operation until fairly recently.

MRT

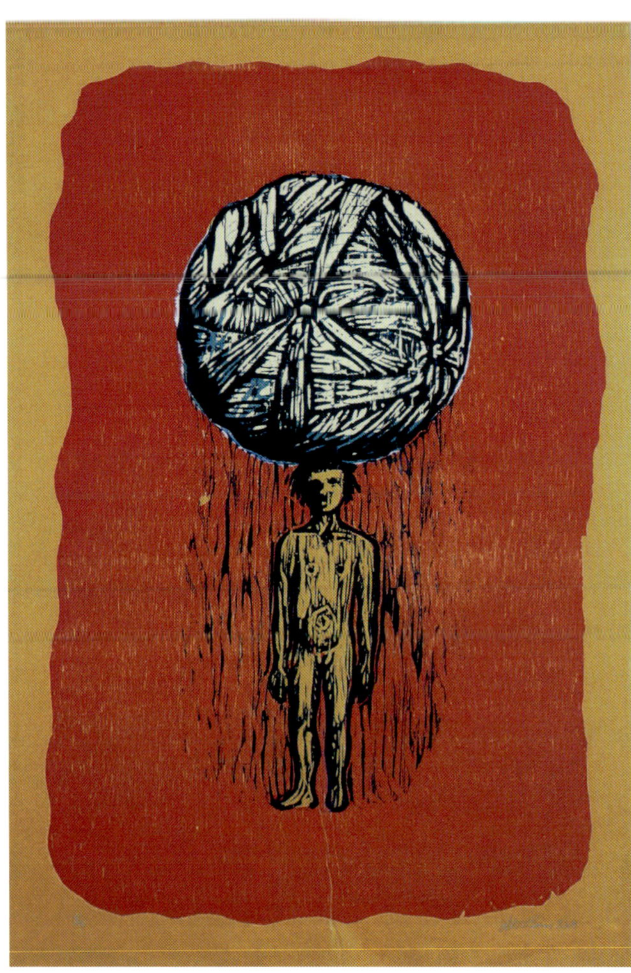

ALISON SAAR
American, born 1956
Inheritance, 2003
Woodblock print with chine collé, image:
28³/₄ x 18⁵/₁₆ in.; sheet: 31⁷/₈ x 21¹/₁₆ in.
Purchased through a gift from the
Lathrop Fellows; PR.2003.64.2
© Alison Saar

Combining woodcarving with found objects and industrial materials, Alison Saar constructs enigmatic large-scale figures whose origins seem rooted in folklore or legend. During her residency at Dartmouth in the spring of 2003, Saar created *Inheritance*, a woodblock print based on a six-foot-tall, tin-clad sculpture bearing the same name that was the centerpiece of her exhibition in the Jaffe-Friede Gallery. *Inheritance* was intended as both a tribute to her mother, the celebrated assemblage artist Betye Saar, and a bold evocation of the historical strength transmitted to the descendants of the African diaspora. The Hood Museum of Art later acquired *Caché*, Alison Saar's sculpture of a nude reclining woman whose mass of balled hair extends along the floor in front of her. Sheets of rusted and irregularly marked ceiling tin serve as the figure's exposed brown flesh; lined and imperfect, the tin suggests scars, wrinkles, and other signs of aging, while also evoking African scarification rituals. With both African and European ancestry, Saar often depicts figures of mixed heritage in order to express the complex social and historical connotations of racial identity. Her figure's thick accumulation of hair, represented by a sprawling ball of wire, has been straightened, a practice common to many African American women. The bundle of hair speaks not only to racial and cultural identity but also to the passage of time and the accumulated memories and experiences that this woman carries with her. Saar suggests that the woman's profound yet burdensome heritage, signified by this mass of hair, is not easily eluded.

The female nude often denotes vulnerability, ideal beauty, and sexual availability. Saar's figure, however, conveys decidedly different meanings. The woman's extended arm shields her body as she pushes down with her hand, poised to lift herself from the ground. This subtle gesture, along with her tough exterior of tin and nails, conveys strength and self-possession. Reclining on the ground in an active state of contemplation, her posture, aged skin, and mound of long hair suggest the profound knowledge that comes with lived experiences and maturation. The woman's nudity frees her from the specific cultural attributes conveyed by clothing, and thus represents a universal figure of womanhood. The title of the work refers to that which is hidden; the artist insinuates that this mysterious figure conceals a cache of heritage, thoughts, and desires.

PW

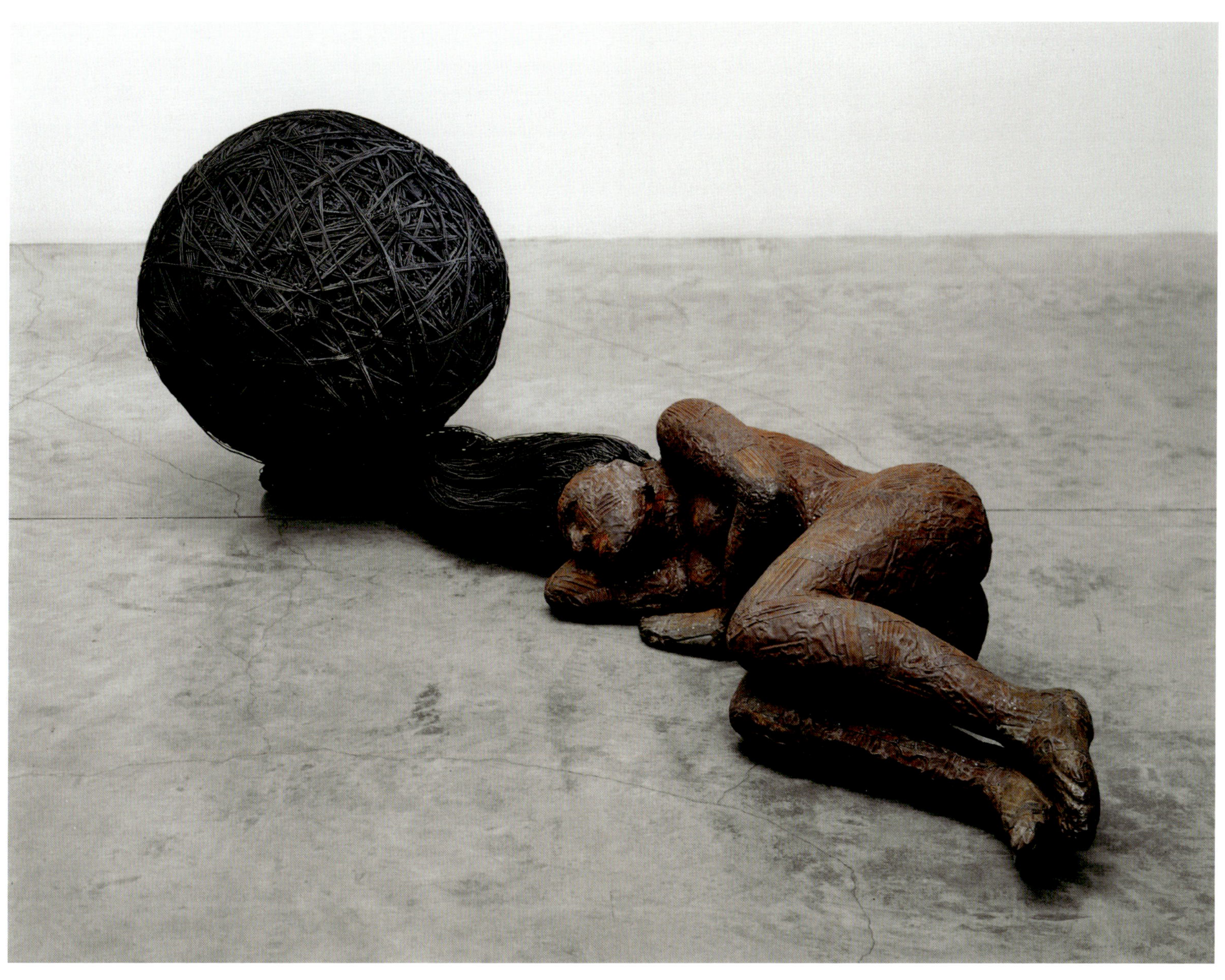

91

ALISON SAAR
Caché, 2006
Wood, ceiling tin, and wire, 28 x 26 x 90 in.
Purchased through the Virginia and
Preston T. Kelsey 1958 Fund; 2006.32
© Alison Saar

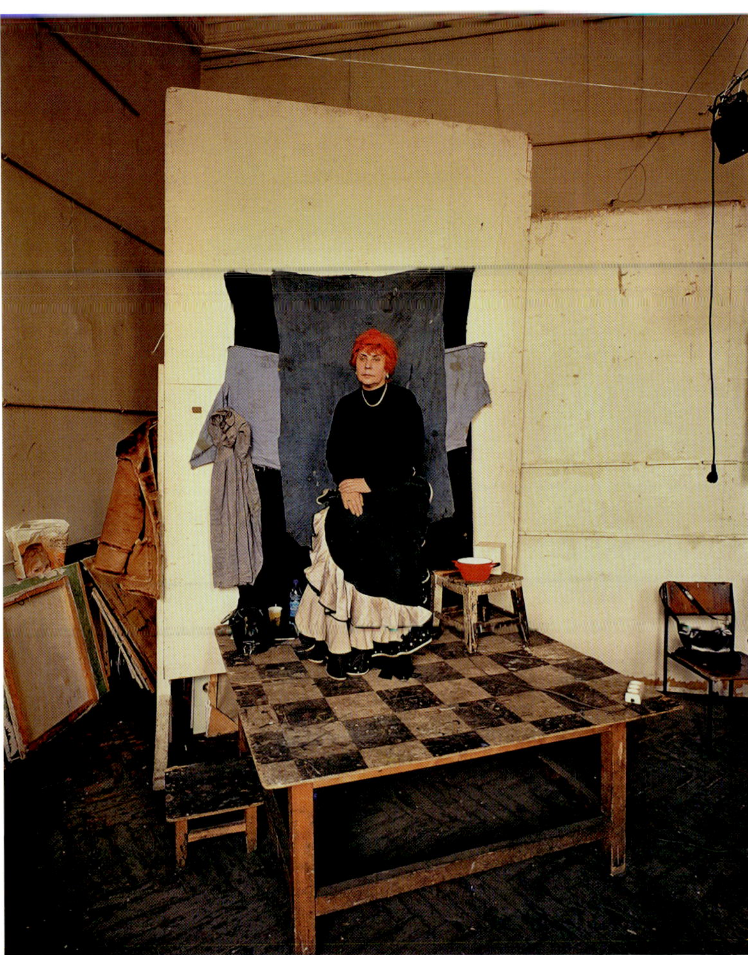

92

ANDREW MOORE
American, born 1957
Akademy Model, St. Petersburg, 2002
Chromogenic print, 56¹/₈ x 45 in.
Gift of Varujan Boghosian; 2007.74.1
© Andrew Moore

Andrew Moore uses a large-format camera to capture locations throughout the world, finding unexpected juxtapositions, vast differences in scale, and beauty in the most dilapidated of structures. Whether photographing an early-evening vista over the buildings of Vedado Azul in Havana, Cuba, or the pockmarked walls of abandoned structures in Sarajevo, Moore's eye is attuned to the nature and particularities of place. His photographs are often startlingly colorful, but not beautiful in the conventional sense. He uses long exposures as he works with available light, which gives his images a sense of stillness, of a moment frozen in time, but also timelessness. He returns repeatedly to countries, cities, or places that he has chosen to explore, and that investment is evident in the scope of his imagery. As noted by Nancy Princenthal in her essay for Moore's Dartmouth artist-in-residence exhibition catalogue, his influences are not the work of other photographers, but that of painters—the American luminists, such as Frederic Edwin Church, or the master of the nineteenth-century American scene, George Caleb Bingham. Like Bingham, Moore is interested in culture, its signs and accents. He also focuses on remnants of the past that exist indomitably in the present.

The Hood Museum of Art owns three photographs from Moore's fall 2006 artist-in-residence exhibition at Dartmouth, one from Cuba, another from Sarajevo, and *Akademy Model*, from the Russia series. Between 2000 and 2004, Moore made six trips to photograph cities and landscapes in Russia, where he found an unexpected visual world. He wrote of his first trip, "I was not prepared for . . . the strangeness and aesthetic oddity of this world apart. I had expected the drab and monumental, the dour and the suspicious, but I had not expected a visual world so independent of my previous experiences." His photographs for this series, as for many others, are about spatial relationships between structures and place, and when people inhabit these, he captures them as well. Moore published 120 of his Russian photographs in a book titled *Russia: Beyond Utopia* in 2005. This photograph, taken in the former Imperial Academy of Arts (founded in 1757 and now the St. Petersburg State Academic Institute of Fine Arts, Sculpture, and Architecture), shows an older model seated on a raised checkerboard platform next to a small table with a bright red pot and square white cube. She is silhouetted against a hanging gray cloth and stares patiently at a point beyond the viewer. The artificial red of her hair jars and aligns with the red pot; the rest of the picture is a symphony in shades of gray, black, and white, with accents of brown in the furniture, canvas stretchers, and the coat hanging to the side. The detail in the picture is endless, from the texture of the scuffed platform, the animal skin of the coat, and the canted purse on the chair in the background. Spatially it is off-kilter; the white false wall against which the figure sits is an unstable visual plane misaligned with the geometry of the room, pushing the model forward. Moore commented in his book on this project that he had to abandon his usual techniques for squaring up his images, as the structures he photographed in Russia were never quite plumb.

KWH

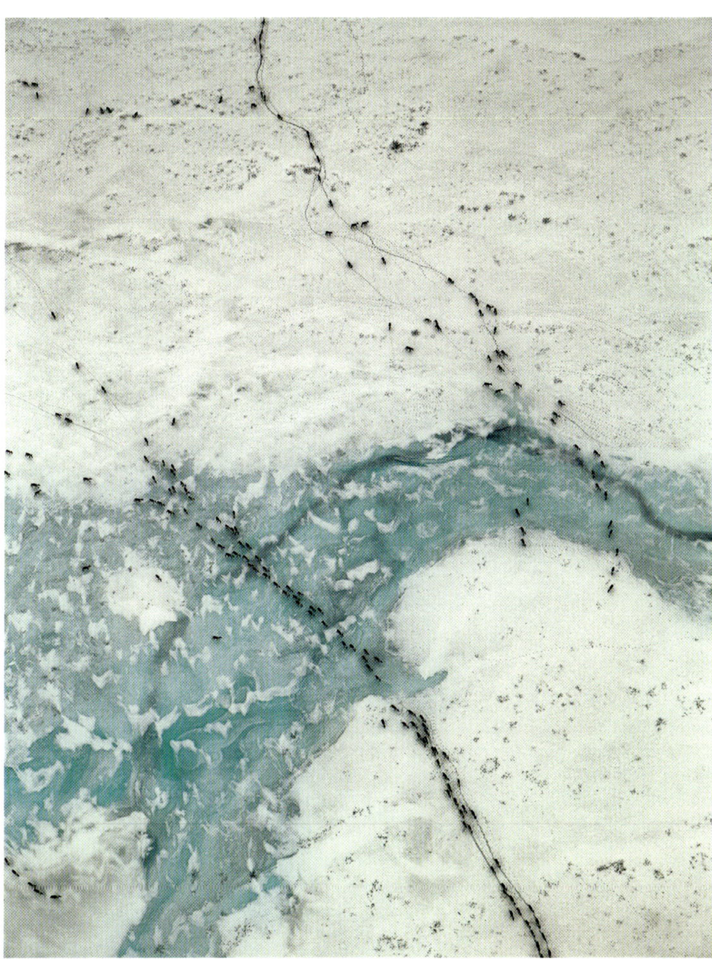

93

SUBHANKAR BANERJEE
American, born 1967 in India
Caribou Migration I, 2002
UltraChrome print, 39³/₄ x 29³/₄ in.
Purchased through the Charles F. Venrick
1936 Fund; 2006.61
© Subhankar Banerjee

An activist photographer, writer, and lecturer, Subhankar Banerjee first came to Dartmouth in 2007. The Hood Museum of Art had acquired *Caribou Migration I* the year before and had subsequently arranged for four of Banerjee's large-scale photographs to be exhibited in an installation titled *Resource Wars in the American Arctic*, which was on view in conjunction with two other Arctic-themed exhibitions that winter. During this visit, in addition to giving a public lecture on his photography of the Alaska National Wildlife Refuge and opposition to the Bush administration's push to drill for oil in this protected area, Banerjee spoke to classes taught by Ross Virginia in the Institute of Arctic Studies and Virginia Beahan in the Studio Art Department. His visit was so successful that he was invited back two years later to become an artist-in-residence. At that time Banerjee exhibited work from his new series, *Gwich'in and the Caribou*, along with work from other series such as *Coal and Caribou*, *Oil and the Geese*, and photographs on climate change as experienced by the Even and Yukaghir peoples of Siberia. During his term at the College, he invited Gwich'in elder Sarah James and Inupiat chief Robert Thompson to talk about "Land as Home" and the importance of conserving these protected areas that support the lifeways of the indigenous people of Alaska and Canada.

The herd of caribou seen in this photograph is named after the Porcupine River, which meanders through much of their range. Constantly on the move, this 169,000-strong herd's yearly migration pattern covers 250,000 square kilometers and traverses the Arctic National Wildlife Refuge and other parts of northern Alaska as well as the Canadian Northwest Territories and the Yukon. The herd spends winters in the southern part of their range, and then in April the females travel four hundred miles north to the coastal plain to give birth. Although the Porcupine herd's calving grounds and migration routes are largely protected, there have been precipitous declines in caribou populations in other regions over the last fifteen years. Changes in the Arctic tundra ecosystem due to global warming are projected to cause vegetative zones to shift upward, changing the type of plants that grow along the caribou range, negatively impacting the herd's ability to find food and raise their calves. Also, more extreme weather and ice storms are making it difficult to dig for food through the ice.

KWH

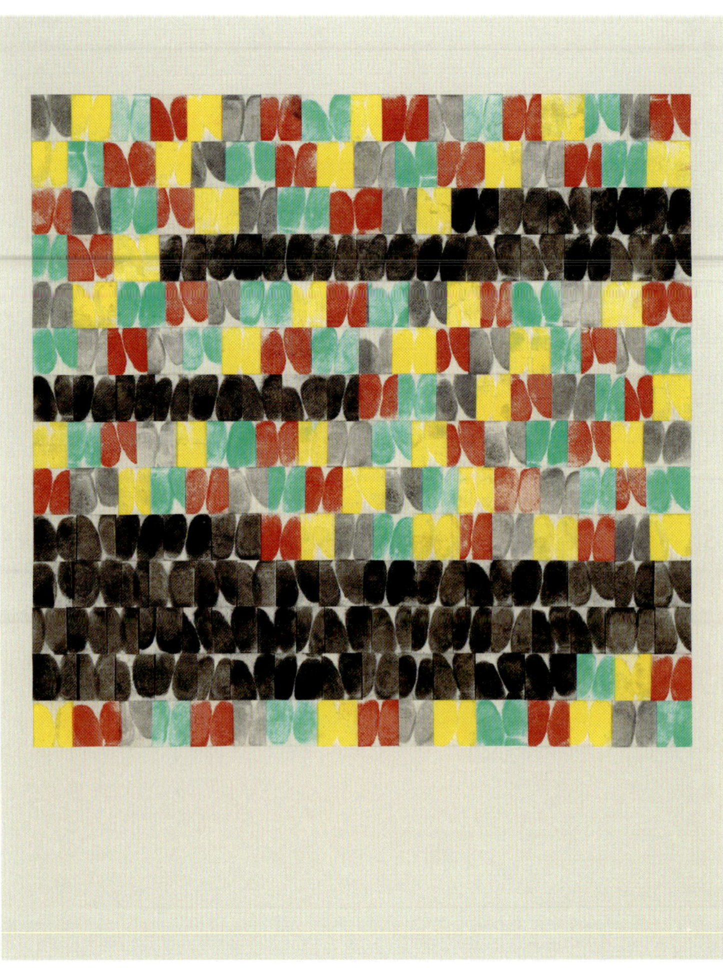

CHARLES SPURRIER
American, born 1958
Infinity Bond, 2002
Tape, pigment, and fingerprints
on paper, 26 x 20 in.
Collection of Como Thompson
© Charles Spurrier

The New York–based artist Charles Spurrier creates colorful abstract compositions through unexpected, everyday materials, such as bottle caps, chewing gum, light bulbs, milk crates, packing tape, Vaseline, and his own fingerprints. Spurrier received a BFA from the Cleveland Institute of Art in 1983 and an MFA in painting from the Yale University School of Art in 1985. Inspired by the work of Robert Rauschenberg and Kurt Schwitters, who also used seemingly banal, quirky, and inexpensive items in their assemblages, Spurrier began to create artworks with unconventional materials shortly after he graduated from Yale. He calls the use of such flagrantly anti-art items "spectacularizing the ordinary," which succinctly describes his vision and mission. The objects that Spurrier uses in his work often have a deeply personal meaning, including Scotch tape, which entered his artistic vocabulary as the adhesive ground for his paint-covered fingerprints and other forms of mark-making during his ailing mother's extended hospitalization, becoming a poignant metaphor for repairing and healing.

Spurrier was artist-in-residence at Dartmouth in the winter of 2002. During his time on campus, he made a series of fifty drawings entitled *We Are Connected*. Spurrier invited forty-nine people, including the president of Dartmouth College, members of the studio art faculty, every studio art major, and the staff of the Hood Museum of Art, to visit his studio to see all of the drawings together. Each person received a drawing through a lottery system of names and numbers. The previous person to receive a drawing picked the next person's name and then that person would draw the number for their drawing.

Once all forty-nine people had received a drawing, the remaining work belonged to Spurrier. As the artist later recalled, "With each person experiencing the whole by seeing all the drawings together and being a part of where the drawings went, then leaving and living with their part, I wanted an ongoing connection of our time together during the residency to take place through the drawings."[1] In addition to the *We Are Connected* series, Spurrier also made individual artworks, such as *Infinity Bond*, a grid-based abstraction that was created by placing the fingers of two individuals into wet paint and pressing them on Scotch tape. Their combined impressions formed an exuberant accumulation of colors and shapes and resulted in a unique work of art that again speaks to the artist's interest in friendship and connectedness.

MRT

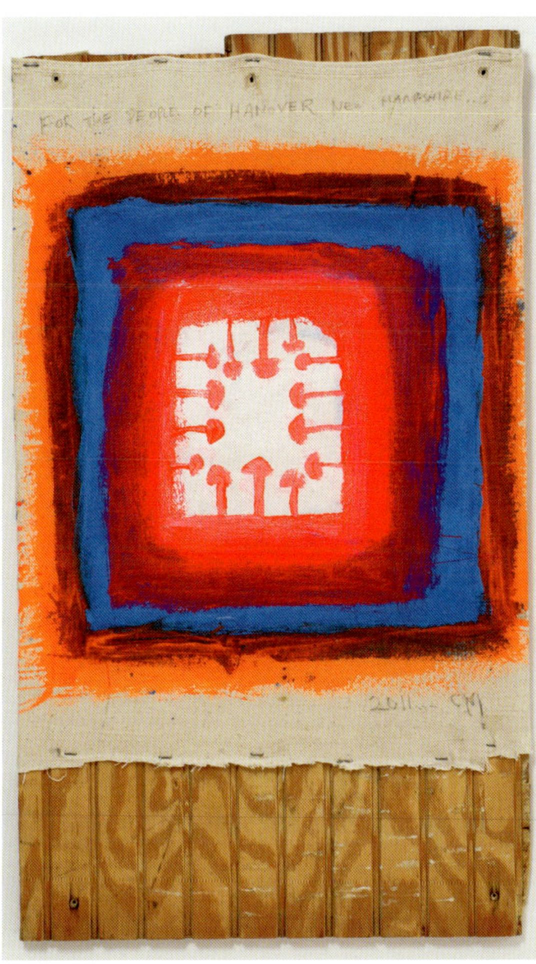

CHRIS MARTIN
American, born 1954
For the People of Hanover, New Hampshire,
2011
Oil on canvas mounted on plywood,
canvas: 24³/₄ x 17¹/₂ in.; mount: 31 x 17¹/₂ in.
Gift of the artist; 2012.79
© Chris Martin

This painting was left outside the Hopkins Center for the Arts during the artist's residency at Dartmouth in the winter of 2011. This gesture speaks to Chris Martin's maverick nature and ability to subvert artistic norms and museum conventions. Born in Washington, D.C., in 1954, Martin studied at Yale University from 1972 to 1975 and later received a BFA and Certificate of Art Therapy from the School of Visual Arts, New York, in 1992. Until 2004 Martin supported himself as an art therapist for AIDS patients and recovering drug addicts in New York, working in clinics in Chelsea, Harlem, the Lower East Side, and Brooklyn's Red Hook neighborhood, while also painting in the evenings and on the weekends. During the past decade, Martin's work has explored themes such as mysticism and psychedelia in colorful, often large-scale abstract canvases that frequently contain collage elements, such as glitter, feathers, old dog blankets, James Brown records, newspaper cuttings, and even bread. His deliberately naïve artistic vocabulary evokes American folk and outsider art, as well as such important forebears as Paul Feeley, Alfred Jensen, Yayoi Kusama, Purvis Young, and Al Held, who was Martin's teacher at Yale.

For the People of Hanover, New Hampshire depicts the back of a stretched canvas, including nails and wooden stretcher bars. Painted in glowing acrylic colors, the artist emphasized the abstract qualities of this motif, which is never seen in traditional gallery displays, but is always hidden, yet present, on the reverse side of the paintings that visitors enjoy at museums every day. This use of unconventional subject matter, coupled with the subversive act of installing the painting outside the Hopkins Center by mounting it on a wooden board and nailing it to the wall, is typical of Martin's uncompromising approach to art-making. As he stated in a 2003 essay, "The new abstract painting says 'Fuck you we will not stand guard at the tomb of Modernism but neither do we feel pressed to deliver the latest titillation.'" Above all, Martin would like viewers of his paintings to pay attention and has devoted his career to figuring out how to make paintings that function, in his words, as "a machine that wakes you up."[1]

MRT

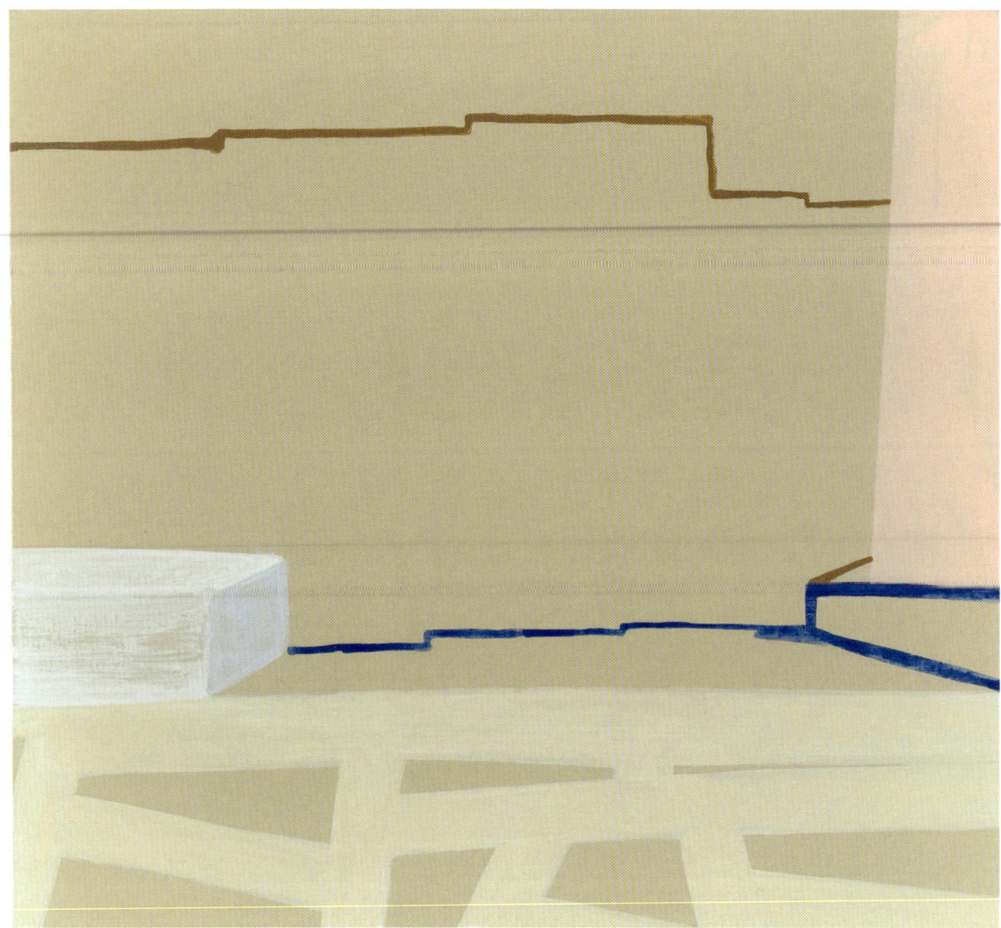

FRANCES BARTH
American, born 1946
Arizona pink, 2004
Acrylic on panel, 14 x 15 in.
Gift of the artist; 2013.56
© Frances Barth

Frances Barth's work combines abstraction, geology, and topography in intriguing ways. Barth was born in the Bronx, New York, and earned a BFA and an MA in painting from Hunter College. In 1972 her painting *Henning* was exhibited in the *Whitney Museum Painting Annual*. Initially she explored abstraction, creating complex space and using color as object and atmosphere. Barth had studied geology, and around 1980 she first included references to geologic time and mapping into her paintings. She also began thinking about how abstraction could hold meaning after visiting Hawaii and hearing a Maori chant that "read" the story of a voyage encoded in abstract patterns.

Arizona pink incorporates seemingly readable cartographic elements that introduce multiple ambiguities. While the perspective of the white box on the left and the blue outlined box on the right hint at recession into space, the flat pink rectangle and the solid plane of the background frustrate this sense of depth. The brown, stepped, horizontal line suggests a horizon, perhaps of a geologic formation, yet the color above is the same as the color below. The thick beige bands in the foreground seem simultaneously to recede slightly backward into space and to exist upright on the picture plane. Do they represent roads or a fence? This complex visual push-and-pull characterizes Barth's work. We think we might be looking at a schematic or a landscape, but identification is slippery and brings us back to abstract painting.

As Barth has explained, her paintings are highly thought out. In a conversation with curator Barbara O'Brien, she describes part of the process:

The weight of and association attached to every line is considered in exacting detail. The idea for the painting is based on the premise that something that was there is no longer there. I make a fault or make signs for sedimentation. I use a stencil so that a line feels more like an artificial line than a hard drawn line.

Her colors, often slightly strange hues, evoke the idea of a place, its light, rather than describe any specific object. Barth's paintings reveal a cohesive world of her own creation.

ABK

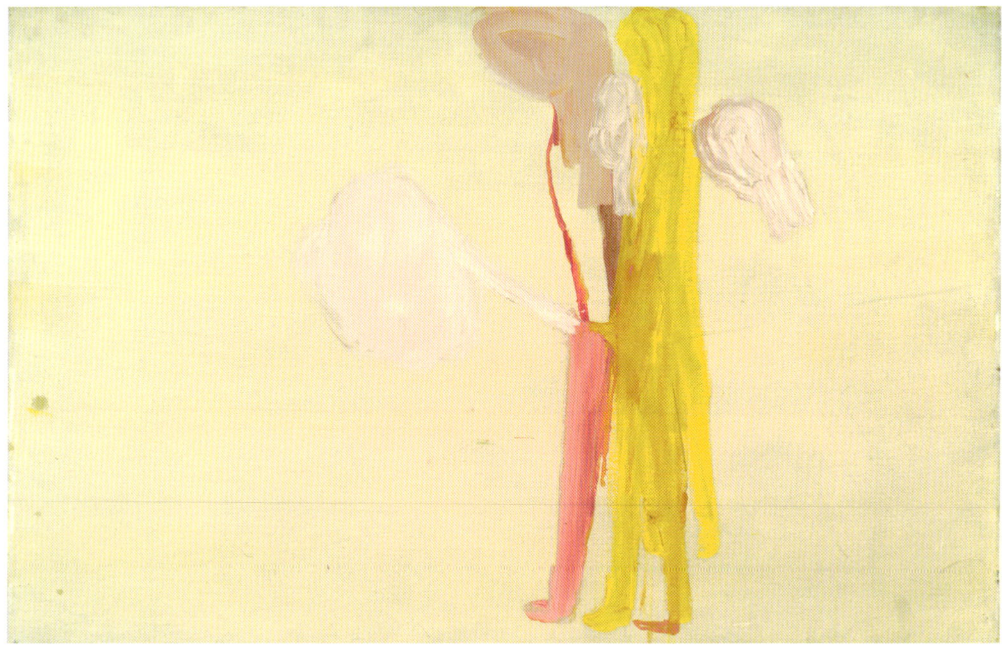

AMY SILLMAN
American, born 1945
Letters from Texas (19), 2003
Oil on canvas, 26 x 40 in.
Collection of the artist
© Amy Sillman

Amy Sillman, Dartmouth's artist-in-residence in the fall of 2002, lives and works in New York. She holds degrees from Beloit College, New York University, the School of Visual Art, and Bard College, where she is co-chair of painting at the Milton Avery Graduate School of the Arts. Her work has been exhibited in countless exhibitions and at galleries in the United States and Europe, and it was notably included in the Whitney Museum of American Art's important exhibition *Blues for Smoke* in 2013. Sillman's first solo museum survey exhibition, *Amy Sillman: One Lump or Two*, was organized by the Institute of Contemporary Art, Boston, and on view in the fall of 2013. Often compared to such artists as Philip Guston and Willem de Kooning, Sillman works in a style that evokes abstract expressionism while retaining a figurative impulse discernible in even her most abstract works.

Sillman's 2002 exhibition at Dartmouth College was titled *Letters from Texas* and presented the work of that title, which she had completed earlier in the year after a several-months' stay in Texas. It consists of multiple canvases, each twenty-six inches in height but of varying lengths, that are installed end-to-end, and in no particular order, in a long strip around the walls of a gallery. The work is not meant to have any coherent narrative continuity; rather, it conveys snippets of thoughts, ideas, and impressions from a particular time in the artist's life. Sillman's 2007 remarks on her approach to painting are instructive when looking at that series, of which this painting, *Letters from Texas (19)*, is part.

I have always been a feminist, since I was in high school. Meanwhile, I am trying to make paintings with a complex psychological presence. I am interested in spanning spaces from intuition to conception, from utterance to image to icon, from stillness to action, construction, or erasure and destruction. My process is interior, personal, often illogical, about folk tales, memories, fragments, daydreams . . . but also about observation from life and looking, and about straightforward formal concerns like color and shape.[1]

Indeed, *Letters from Texas (19)* appears as if it could be a fragment from a story that the viewer is left to interpret. It depicts two human-like blob figures with few apparent physical features floating in the unarticulated space of an unpainted canvas. The spare composition and exaggerated body proportions suggest that the humor for which the artist is often known is at play in this work as well. Is the yellow figure an angel with wings, and might its penis be ejaculating a cloud? Is the pink figure a separate being, or perhaps another side of the first as it rotates in space, and what is the nature of their relationship? The ambiguity inherent in this painting, as in much of Sillman's work, allows for multiple interpretations.

JMB

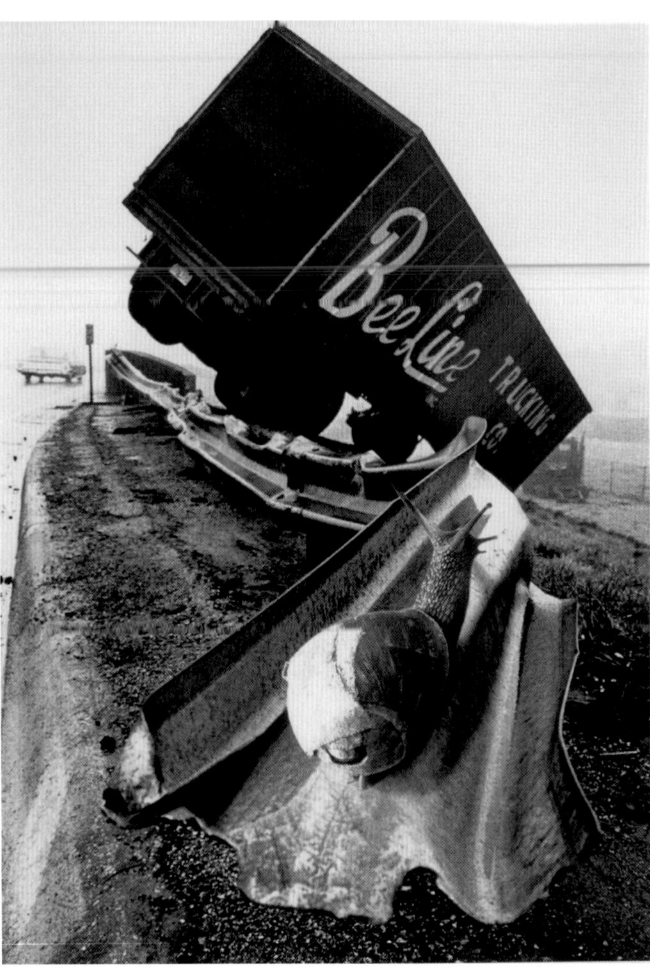

JANE HAMMOND
American, born 1950
Bee-Line Trucking, 2004–5
Selenium-toned gelatin silver print,
image: 12⅛ x 8⅜ in.; sheet: 13⅞ x 10⅞ in.
Purchased through the Sondra and Charles
Gilman Jr. Foundation Fund; 2006.33.1
© Jane Hammond

Conceptual artist Jane Hammond works in a variety of media, including painting, sculpture, collage, and photography. Often created from collections of things—images, ideas, words, poetry, and patterns—her work reveals her to be a deeply intellectual, engaged, and creative *bricoleur*, someone who recombines and assembles. Although intuition is an important part of her creative process, Hammond often begins with a preconceived idea. One aspect of her work is to explore the structures of visual and textual language. This led her to engage in a multi-year project in the 1990s for which she made paintings with 276 found images—many of them on paper—which she de- and re-contextualized. The titles that inspired the paintings came from the poet John Ashberry, who provided her with a list of forty-four quickly penned phrases. In a 2005 interview with Douglas Dreishspoon, she stated, "I am starting to brew up a theory about this that revolves around the fact that my work is fundamentally about information." Thus it is not surprising that while she was at Dartmouth as artist-in-residence in the spring of 2006, she became interested in the work of faculty members outside of the arts, such as a philosophy professor who works on the nature of pictorial representation.

This system of rethinking how we receive and perceive information (in this case the visual kind) underlies what she calls "making photography." She works with found images, vintage photographs that she collects from dealers, the Internet, tag sales, and flea markets. She forms ideas about these images (or goes looking for them if she has an idea) and has the elements scanned at high resolution. She then works with an expert in Photoshop to create an almost seamless digital interweaving of the parts. These digital images, such as the one that constitutes *Bee Line Trucking*, are then converted into LVT negatives and printed as gelatin silver prints. The results are in some cases startling, in others, more subtle. Some possess deep and satisfying humor; others create anxiety or dislocation. The Hood Museum of Art's photograph, one of two purchased from Hammond's artist-in-residence exhibition, is an image that plays with scale and language. The oversize snail on the guardrail seems to take advantage of the truck going off the road. The truck is making a beeline for disaster instead of its promised destination. A car leaves the scene of the crime, oblivious to the drama in its rearview mirror.

KWH

99

DAVID HILLIARD
American, born 1964
Rock Bottom, 2008
Chromogenic print on paper, each panel: 24 x
20 in.; overall: 24 x 60 in.
Purchased through the Sondra and Charles
Gilman Jr. Foundation Fund; 2010.70.1–3
© David Hilliard

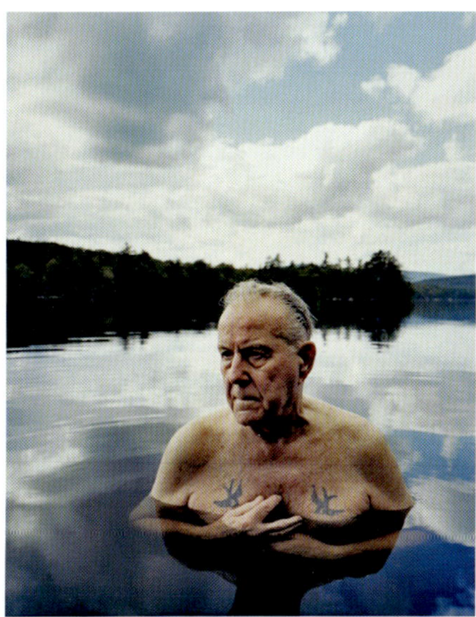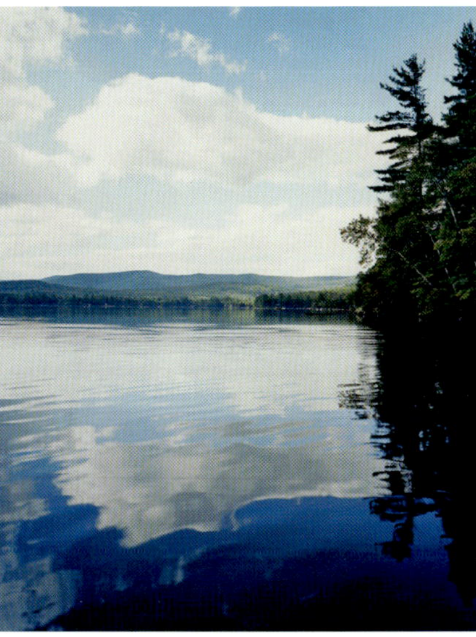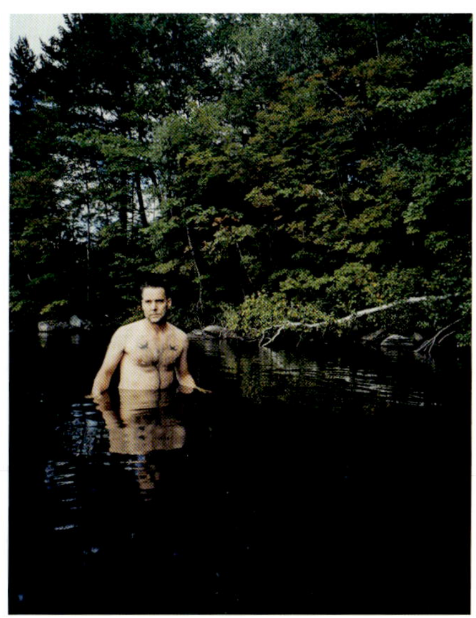

David Hilliard photographs people in their environments, his subjects often family, lovers, or friends and the relationships between them. He has worked for some time in the form of the triptych, which heightens the sense of narrative and time in his photographs. The sometimes imperceptible shift between panels in the triptychs alters the point of view so that the figures in them often have a strange spatial relationship to one another. Hilliard describes his work as a type of fiction and, in this respect, it relates to that of other photographers such as Gregory Crewdson and Tina Barney. Unlike Crewdson's work, however, Hilliard's has a believability and less constructed quality—no matter how he has arranged his subjects—that imparts a truth or truths about the people he photographs. They are revealed in a way that straightforward portraiture might not achieve. He collaborates with his subjects and they have an agency in their portrayals. The meaning in the work in part derives from the spaces between figures, the direction of their gazes, the posture of their bodies, the positioning of their limbs.

One of Hilliard's recurring subjects is his father; he has taken many pictures of him—standing outside his house in Massachusetts in his underwear, reading in bed, eating fast food and looking at pornography on the television with his brother—and of his father's hands as they frame the open pages of his journal. *Rock Bottom* shows Hilliard standing with his father in a lake in New England. The father is on the left panel of the triptych, the son on the right, with the vista of the lake in between, separating them from one another. The father gazes out into the distance to his right, the son gazes at the father. Both stand in water up to their chests, the father more submerged that the son. Both have blue swallows tattooed on each side of their chests. The metaphor of life's journey is an obvious one—with the father deeper in the waters of time than his son. But the way the son looks at the father, the emulation present in the tattoos, coupled with the knowledge that the father is straight and the son gay, and the father's unique place within Hilliard's work, are markers of the complex, close, and unconventional relationship between these two men.

KWH

Rebecca Purdum was born in Idaho Falls, Idaho. After studying for a year at Saint Martin's School of Art in London, she earned a BFA from Syracuse University in 1981. She moved to New York after graduation and in 1985 began showing at Jack Tilton Gallery, which still represents her today. Purdum now lives and paints in Ripton, Vermont, and her many honors include grants from the Joan Mitchell Foundation, the Louis Comfort Tiffany Foundation, the National Society of Arts and Letters, and the Ford Foundation. Her work was included in the 1991 Whitney Biennial and has also been exhibited at the San Francisco Museum of Modern Art, the Corcoran Gallery of Art, the Middlebury College Museum of Art, the MIT List Visual Arts Center, and most recently at Jack Tilton Gallery in 2011.

While she was artist-in-residence at Dartmouth in the fall of 2009, her exhibition in Jaffe-Friede Gallery included Purdum's luminous abstract painting *Ripton 76 (Yellow)*, named for the town in Vermont where she lives. At once a meditation on color and natural phenomena reminiscent of Monet's *Waterlilies*, Purdum's work is wholly a painter's painting. Her approach to the canvas is visceral, bodily, and immediate: she favors her two gloved hands as painting tools, although she also employs brushes, palette knives, and objects like newspaper. The meditative quality of her abstraction, achieved over months of work and layers of carefully applied paint, causes many to liken her work to that of Mark Rothko—an artist whose work she admires and from whom she has drawn inspiration. The space she creates in her work, however, draws the eye to every edge of the canvas and back again,

darting as if in playful rhythm like an imagined light on gently lapping waves. Indeed, talking about her relationship to painting, Purdum has stated,

> I think the experience of color is like being at the seashore, spending all your time watching the waves crash on the rocks. The feelings colors produce in us are like those pounding waves, never at rest, always crashing around. At some point, however, you look up from all that turmoil and you sense the depth of the ocean itself, and see the endless horizon marking the infinite sky above. That vast uneasy calm is the unchanging yet unspecific emotion that paint produces. Feelings change, colors change, but the emotion, the paint, is constant.[1]

Purdum's work was first exhibited at the Hood Museum of Art in 2003, when she was chosen by Emmie Donadio, curator at the Middlebury College Museum of Art, for inclusion in a group exhibition of New Hampshire and Vermont artists titled *Regional Selections 30*, marking the thirtieth anniversary of and last exhibition in that series, which began in the Hopkins Center Galleries in 1973, over a decade before the Hood was founded. In the exhibition catalogue, Donadio wrote, "Purdum thinks, therefore she paints."[2]

JMB

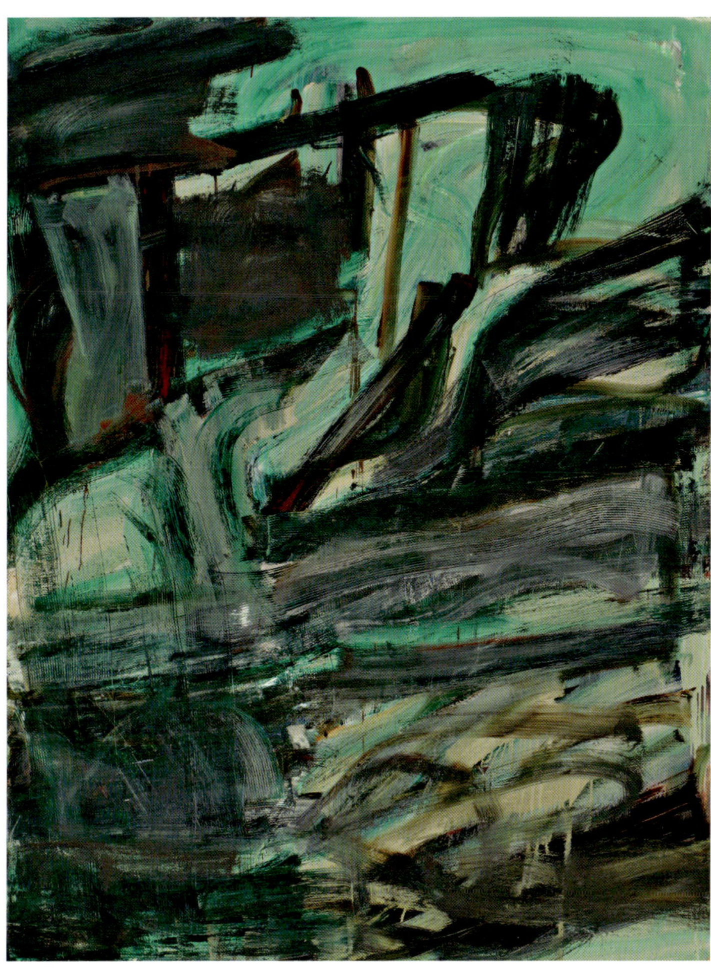

101

LOUISE FISHMAN
American, born 1939
Green's Apogee, 2005
Oil on canvas, 88 x 70 in.
Gift of Mr. and Mrs. Joseph H. Hazen,
by exchange; 2013.23
Courtesy Cheim & Read, New York

One of the most admired and influential abstract painters of her generation, Louise Fishman was born in Philadelphia on January 14, 1939. She attended the Philadelphia College of Art between 1956 and 1957 before completing her undergraduate education at the Pennsylvania Academy of the Fine Arts in Philadelphia. She later completed a BFA and BS at the Tyler School of Art in Elkins Park, Pennsylvania, and in 1965 received an MFA from the University of Illinois, Champaign. In 1965 she moved to New York, where she has lived and worked ever since. Her early work consisted of grid-based abstract paintings inspired by the work of Agnes Martin, who was a great friend and mentor to the artist. However, in the late 1960s her paintings began to be informed by the burgeoning feminist and lesbian and gay rights movements (Fishman came out as a lesbian in 1957, at the age of eighteen) and reflected her anger and frustration at the lack of critical attention given to women artists compared to their male counterparts. In 1973 she completed thirty text-based "portraits" of her women friends and heroes—including Agnes Martin, Joan Mitchell, and Gertrude Stein—which are known today as the *Angry Women* paintings. Fishman returned to abstract painting shortly thereafter and continues to make large-scale gestural paintings to this day.

Green's Apogee was completed shortly before Fishman's stay at Dartmouth as artist-in-residence in the spring of 2007. Rendered in powerful, sweeping green and black brushstrokes that reflect the pleasures and physical energies of action painting, the towering *Green's Apogee* is one of the artist's largest and most successful abstract canvases. The dense network of rugged, monumental forms, which Fishman constructed through an intuitive process of painting, scraping, sanding, and painting again, recalls the enormous scaffolded structures of Franz Kline's abstract expressionist paintings. Fishman has also connected *Green's Apogee* to the bravura paint handling found in the work of Chaïm Soutine, another artist hero. "Soutine taught me the possibility of the freedom of no restrictions in making paintings," Fishman recalled in March 2006, "and to still make paintings that were an expression of my deepest spirit, ambitions, failures, the despair of humiliation, and the possibility of grandeur."[1]

MRT

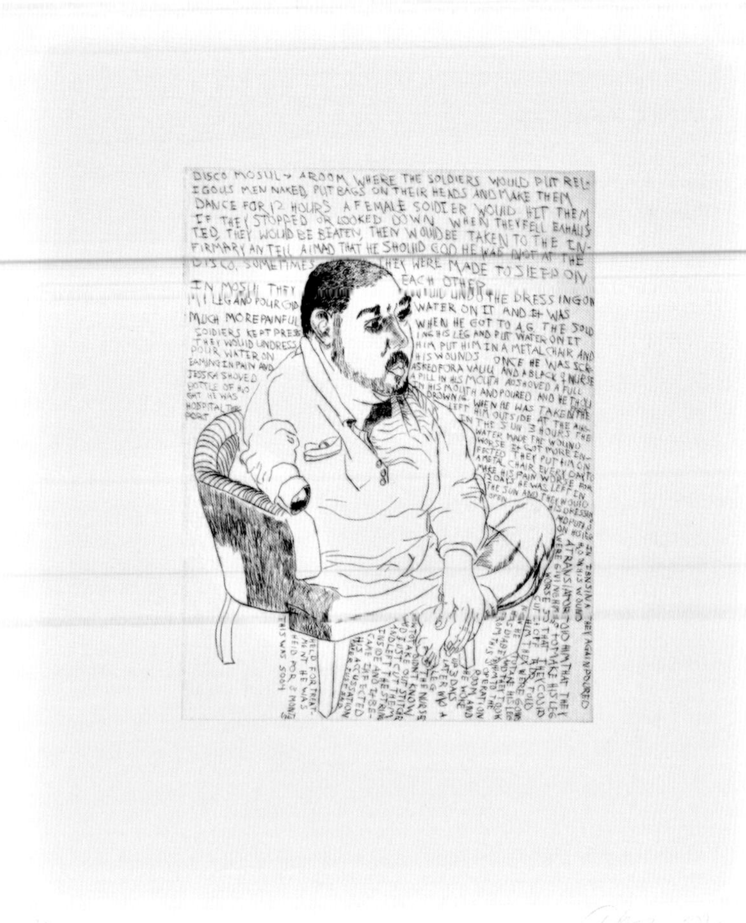

102

DANIEL A. HEYMAN
American, born 1963
Disco Mosul, from the Amman series of
The Abu Ghraib Project, March 2006
Drypoint on Rives BFK paper,
plate: 15¹¹/₁₆ x 11¹¹/₁₆ in.;
sheet (irreg.): 27¹/₂ x 22⁹/₁₆ in.
Purchased through the Anonymous
Fund #144; 2007.66.3
© Daniel Heyman

Daniel Heyman, Dartmouth Class of 1985, has returned several times to the College to lecture and also meet with students in the Studio Art Department, and was artist-in-residence in the fall of 2013. He is both a painter and printmaker and after Dartmouth earned his MFA at the University of Pennsylvania. His beliefs and instincts have led him toward the political dimension of art-making. The Hood Museum of Art's collection includes his 2002 portfolio series *Tattoo*, which shows male odalisques whose sinuous bodies question the usual tropes of male sexuality. In recent years, he has dedicated his art to issues of civil liberties and its abuses, as in the Amman series from his *Abu Ghraib Project*, which the Museum acquired in 2007. He writes:

> Too rarely, a work of visual art can break through the complacency of our lives and bring to us vital information that . . . reveals a larger and much more important role of the artist in society—one that . . . holds up a mirror to our collective face and asks "Is this who we want to be?" At that point, it is how we recognize ourselves and what we do about who we are that creates the art.

Not long after American soldiers' pictures of torture at Abu Ghraib prison in Iraq were released in 2004, Heyman met Susan Burke, who was the lead lawyer of a team that was preparing a reparations case against the interrogators and translators of prisoners there. In March 2006 she invited him to join the team on its trip to Amman, Jordan, where he listened to the depositions of former prisoners, twelve men and one woman. During those interviews, which took place over six days at a hotel, he drew directly on copper plates, first making the portrait of the person to be deposed, and then recording the prisoner's words as they were spoken in real time, writing backwards so that they would print legibly. Heyman did not do portraits of all those interviewed. The woman's story, for instance, was particularly difficult and she declined to be drawn. This print, one of eight that Heyman made on this trip to Jordan (he would eventually do a number of other series on Iraq including watercolor portraits), shows a man whose torture led to the amputation of his leg. Heyman wished to bring attention to these stories and literally make visible the individuals' suffering, giving them a voice within the context of his work. The title refers to a name the torturers gave to a form of abuse in which prisoners were coerced to dance for hours at a time and also beaten.

KWH

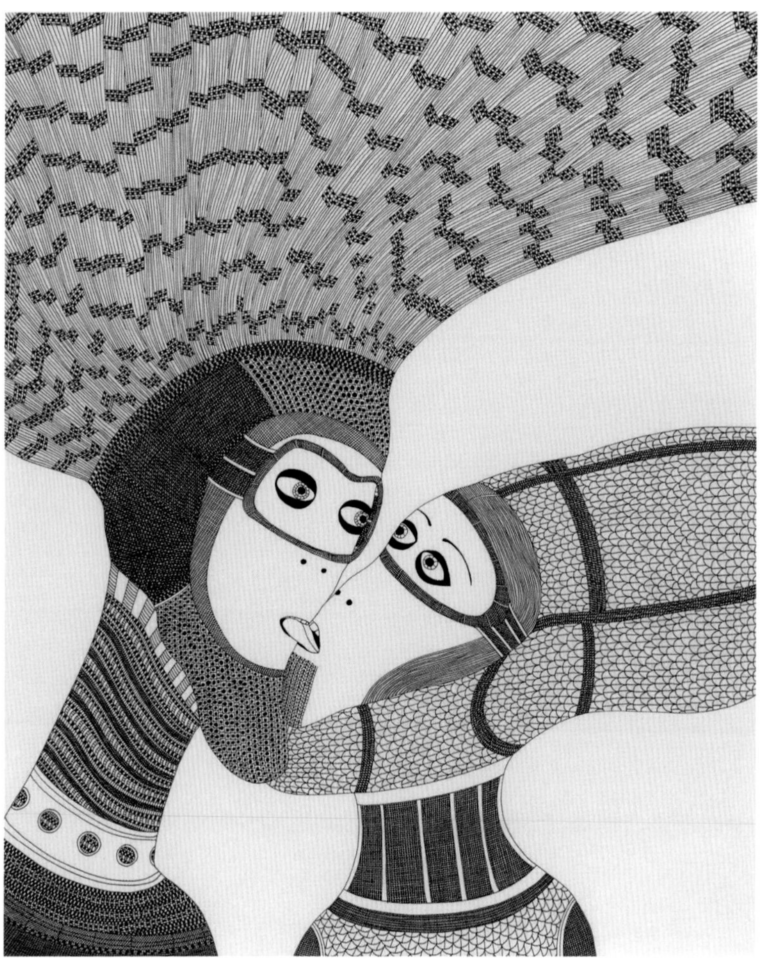

LAYLAH ALI
American, born 1968
Untitled, from the *Typology* series, 2006–7
Ink and pencil on paper, sheet: 24 x 19 in.;
frame: 33 x 28¹/₈ in.
Purchased through the Phyllis and Bertram
Geller 1937 Memorial Fund and the Claire and
Richard P. Morse 1953 Fund; 2012.15
© Laylah Ali

The work of the prominent African American artist Laylah Ali is intended to shock and perplex. Ali graduated from Williams College in Williamstown, Massachusetts, in 1991 with a BA in Studio Art and English and earned her MFA from Washington University in Saint Louis in 1994. Since 2001 Ali has taught in the Studio Art Department at Williams College as an associate professor and was promoted to the rank of full professor in 2011. Over the past two decades, Ali has worked on two prolonged series—the *Greenheads* and *Typology*. The *Greenheads* series, a collection of gouache paintings featuring costumed androgynous, green-headed forms rendered in a simple and whimsical manner but intended to provide complex social commentary, catapulted Ali to national and international renown in the late 1990s. Selections from the *Typology* series of black-and-white drawings in ink and pencil on paper were shown in the Jaffe-Friede Gallery during Ali's time on campus as artist-in-residence in the winter of 2012.

This untitled drawing epitomizes the *Typology* series, in which Ali renders characters that embrace ambiguity and refute inherited constructions of race and gender. She has endeavored to make each figure in the series utterly individualistic, while also exploring the ways that racial and gender identity are conveyed and perceived, whether by hairstyle, skin color, clothing, or other physical characteristics. By refusing to provide a recognizable setting or context, Ali allows viewers to create their own stories for the humanoid figures she depicts, based upon their own belief systems, cultural biases, familial histories, and political ideologies. The works in this series are thus a successful attempt to comment on the absurdity of the now-obsolete branch of anthropology, popular in the eighteenth and nineteenth centuries, known as typology. The figures in her drawings are outfitted in masks, exotic headdresses, and patterned clothing, and are intended to be understood as "primitive" or "non-Western." These intricately detailed drawings thus challenge the derogatory representation of non-Western people throughout history. Ali is also interested in depicting exchanges of power and violence between members of different groups of people. Her kissing figures exemplify this concern, rather than being simply romantic or erotic. Ali describes the interaction between the embracing couple as "tongue-probing," rather than kissing, and she seeks to capture the moment "when a touch becomes a threat rather than a caress."[1]

MRT

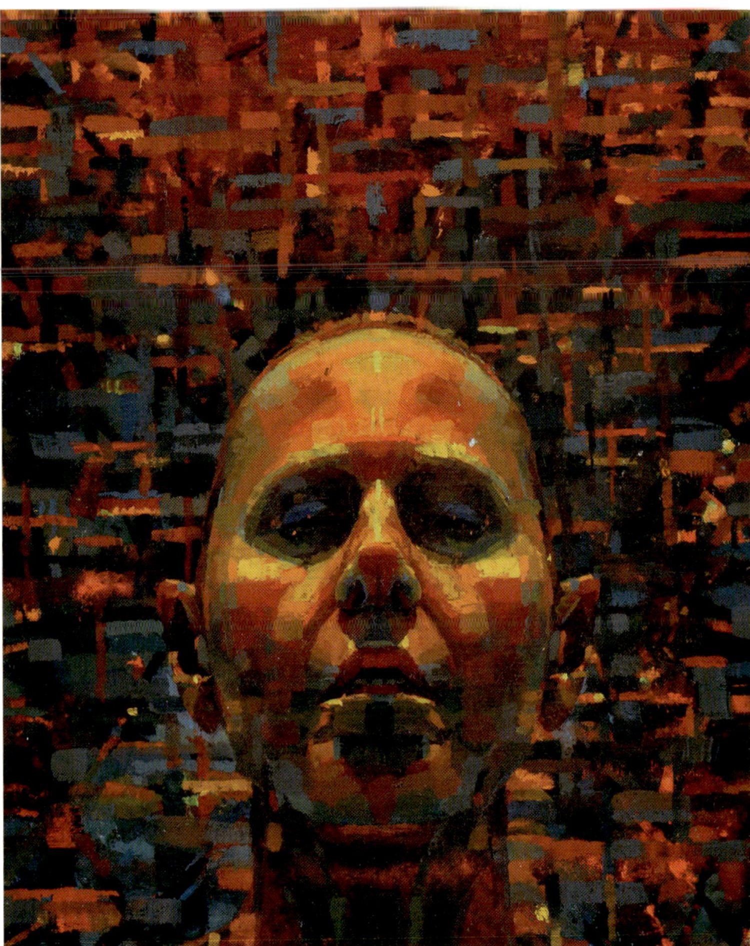

104

SUSANNA COFFEY
American, born 1949
Intake, 2008
Oil on panel, 15 x 12 in.
Purchased through the Contemporary
Art Fund; 2013.24
© Susanna Coffey

Susanna Coffey divides her time between her studio in New York's Clemente Soto Velez Cultural Center and the School of the Art Institute of Chicago, where she is the Frank Harold Sellers Professor of Painting. Born in New London, Connecticut, Coffey received her BFA at the University of Connecticut in 1977 and her MFA at the Yale University School of Art in 1982. Since the early 1990s, she has devoted herself almost exclusively to the genre of self-portraiture, which she has reinvented through paint in much the same way that Cindy Sherman reinvented self-portraiture in photography. Coffey always paints herself from the neck up and has used a variety of props, including makeup, headgear (hats, scarves, gloves, and earrings), lighting effects, background patterning, and surface textures, so that no one painting resembles another and her identity remains fluid and unfixed. Coffey began painting self-portraits as a studio exercise while a graduate student at Yale and soon became fascinated with the idea of challenging stereotypes and artificial categories of appearance, such as personality, age, class, and culturally prescribed gender roles.

While her early self-portraits, including the paintings that she made as artist-in-residence at Dartmouth in the fall of 1998, represent defiant responses to the social convention that women "make up" their faces in the mirror as a ritual of feminine beauty, Coffey's recent works, such as *Intake*, have begun to explore various facets of her inner self and the experience of a heightened level of consciousness. These paintings dramatize the relationship between the pure materiality of paint and its power of illusionistic description. In *Intake*, the artist's visage slowly emerges from the free, lush passages of pigment. The title references the intake of breath through the artist's open mouth, as well as her understanding of both inner and external worlds, which is nourished by the self-imposed isolation that Coffey experiences in the studio every day, as she seeks "to purify memories and reconstruct the universe under a new light . . . because of the measureless understanding of solitude."[1]

MRT

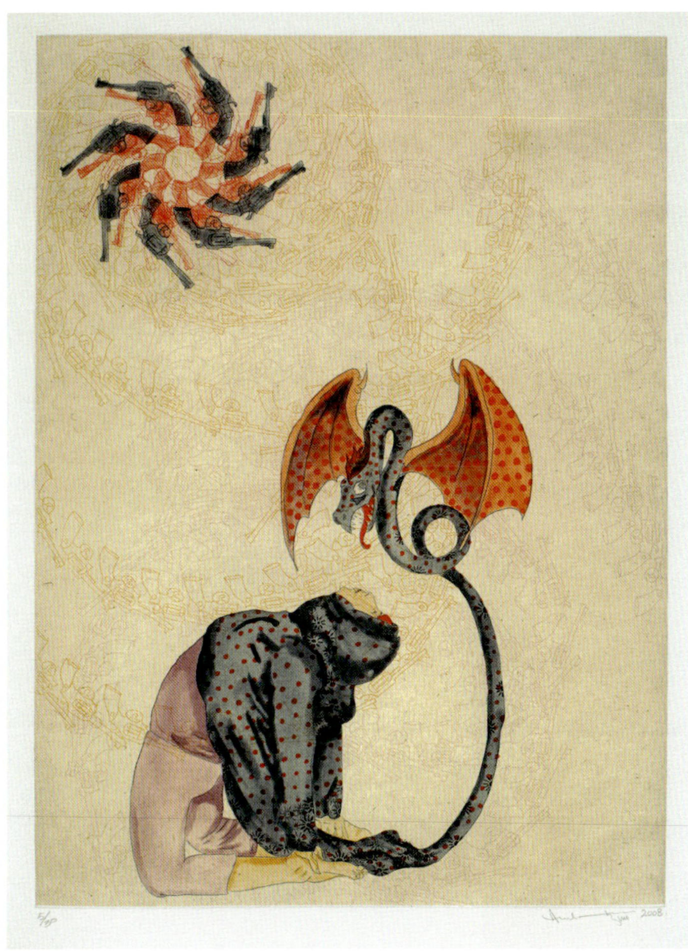

AMBREEN BUTT
Pakistani, born 1969
Untitled (Woman/Dragon), 2008
Softground etching, aquatint, spite bite
aquatint, lift ground aquatint, drypoint,
and chine collé etching on paper,
plate: 13 x 18 in.; sheet: 19 x 25 in.
Purchased through the Claire and Richard P.
Morse 1953 Fund; 2009.47.2
© Ambreen Butt

Ambreen Butt's work tackles the complexities of coming from one culture and living in another. Her stories are personal and universal, her subjects modern and mythological. Butt was born in Pakistan and studied at the National College of Arts in Lahore. After receiving her BFA in traditional Indian and Persian miniature painting, she moved to Boston in 1993. There she received her MFA from the Massachusetts College of Art and Design in 1997. She has exhibited widely and lives and works in Boston, Massachusetts.

Untitled (Woman/Dragon) is the second in the five-print series *Daughter of the East*. Each print presents a woman or group of women engaging with various animals and weapons. Female figures occur frequently in Butt's work. Often modeled after the artist, they are heroic despite finding themselves in complex and challenging situations. In this series Butt has also incorporated images from online world news sites, adding another layer of contemporary culture over her traditional style.

The woman in *Untitled (Woman/Dragon)* bends over backwards as her blue-gray robe falls open and becomes a flying dragon. The robe's red spots and sunburst pattern crawl up the creature's back. The dragon confronts the woman's calm expression, its protruding red tongue echoing the color of her headscarf. Above, like a sort of sun, is a spiral of guns. Echoed in black, red, yellow, and purple, they arc and swirl, creating a subtle background motif that repeats across the page. There is tension here and the threat of violence, both modern and bestial. The dragon seems to challenge the woman, and yet also to come

from her, perhaps as part of herself. Her backwards pose can be read as a calm and meditative yoga stretch—perhaps inviting an awakening—or as an awkward, uncomfortable position, a forced confrontation. Behind the pair, the specter of weaponry, of implied violence, is so pervasive it becomes part of the background. Butt invites us to confront our demons, personal and cultural, as the woman confronts hers.

ABK

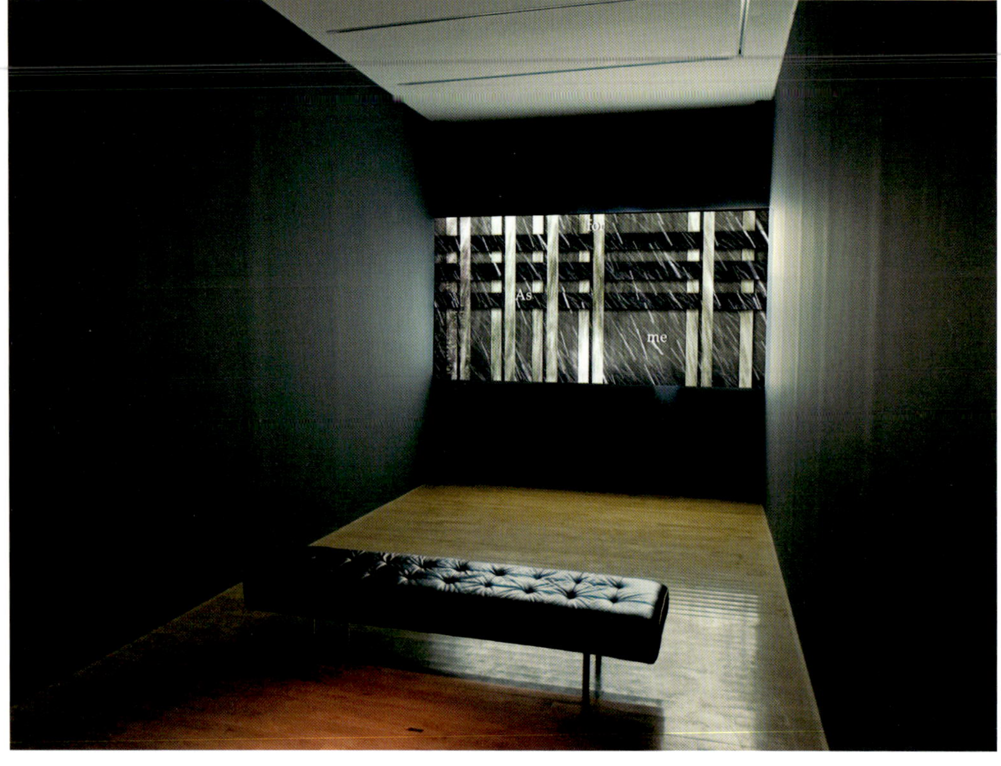

BERYL KOROT
American, born 1945
Florence, 2008
Single-channel video, stereo sound,
10^{1}/$_{2}$ min.
Purchased through the Mrs. Harvey P. Hood
W '18 Fund; 2013.18
© Beryl Korot
Photo by Chad Kleitsch

Beryl Korot is an internationally recognized pioneer in the field of video and installation art. The artist first became known for her early multiple-channel works, *Dachau* (1974) and *Text and Commentary* (1977), and her two collaborations with her husband, the avant-garde composer Steve Reich, *The Cave* (1989–93) and *Three Tales* (1998–2002), both of which brought video art into a theatrical context as video operas accompanied by contemporary classical music. Korot attended the University of Wisconsin for two years and then transferred to Queens College, New York, where she graduated in 1967 with a BA in English literature. During the late 1960s she joined a community of radical artists dedicated to bringing the world of video art and cultural cybernetic thinkers together. In 1970 Korot and Phyllis Gershuny edited *Radical Software*, the first magazine to be devoted to video art. Six years later, Korot and Ira Schneider published *Video Art: An Anthology*, one of the first readers on video art. During this period, Korot began to explore the structural relationship between computer programming and the ancient technology of the loom, which has become one of the hallmarks of her mature video works and text-based hand-woven canvases.

In her 2008 single-channel video *Florence*, Korot extracted phrases from the memoirs of Florence Nightingale, the founder of modern nursing who revolutionized the care of wounded and dying British soldiers during the Crimean War, to form a soliloquy or poem. The work began with the artist's signature digital background of woven lines.

As I viewed the weaving I'd made on the computer the name Florence Nightingale came to mind, and I realized that though her name had become a cliché, I had no idea who she really was. And so I sifted through hundreds of pages of her brilliant writings, which included an intense rejection of her upper-class English background. At thirty, she set off with a rag-tag group of women to save men outside of Istanbul during the brutal Crimean War, and transformed what had been complete neglect on the battlefield into a system of caring for the wounded.[1]

In the finished work, which was shown in the Jaffe-Friede Gallery during Korot's artist-in-residence exhibition in the fall of 2011, the weaving structure became a background for Nightingale's words, which float and fall rhythmically to the bottom of the screen much like the video clips of falling water and snow that also accompany them.

MRT

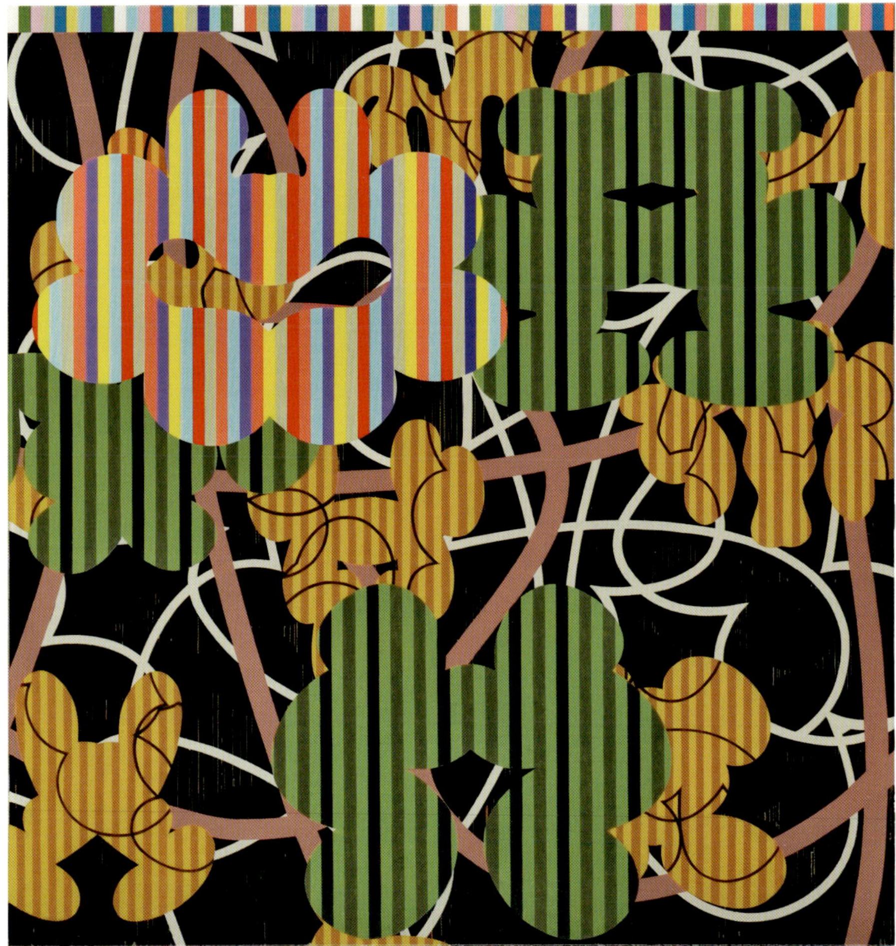

CHARLES BURWELL
American, born 1955
Reflection, 2012
Acrylic on canvas, 60 x 56 in.
Purchased through a gift from Dennis Alter
and the Hood Museum of Art Acquisitions
Fund; 2012.67
© Charles Burwell

Charles Burwell is one of the most respected and influential abstract painters working today. Born in Henderson, North Carolina, Burwell received his BFA from the Tyler School of Art at Temple University, Philadelphia, in 1977, and his MFA from the Yale University School of Art in 1979. Throughout his career, Burwell's dense, multi-layered paintings have made the process of their making an evident and integral part of the finished work. Inspired by the paintings of Mark Tobey and Cy Twombly, and loosely affiliated with the pattern and decoration movement, Burwell's early work juxtaposed networks of lines, organic shapes, and geometric patterns in dimly lit, amorphous environments that suggest surreal landscapes or dreamscapes, while also remaining resolutely abstract in their appearance. He built up the surfaces of these works with layers of oil stick rubbed between coats of paint in a method akin to traditional glazing. Then, using crayon and pencil, Burwell drew upon these burnished fields, and further scraped and scratched into them with a variety of tools to reveal the under-layers of color and tone. This laborious, multistage process was typical of the paintings that Burwell was making around the time that he was artist-in-residence at Dartmouth College in 1995.

While his early paintings have an intensely hand-worked appearance and are imbued with a dense, dark, labyrinth-like quality, Burwell's most recent work, especially following the death of his beloved mother in 2011, for whom he had been the primary caregiver for several years, are suffused with light and vibrant color. The warm atmospheric quality found in *Reflection*, for example, stands in stark contrast to the somber palette of his earlier work. The painting's title, *Reflection*, relates to both the death of the artist's mother and the use of repeated patterns, reflections, and mirror images in his work. The artist's complex visual language of primordial shapes, geometric motifs, and scientific imagery, in combination with the evolutionary process of mark-making that occurs in each painting, inevitably stirs associations with life's creative processes and the passage of time. The dense, overlapping veils of patterns and symbols, and the allover dispersal of forms, with their under-layers still visible, turn the viewer into a sort of visual archaeologist, as his eyes scan the topographic layers of a painting like *Reflection* before standing back to appreciate the fine balance that the artist has achieved between abstract form and referential systems.

MRT

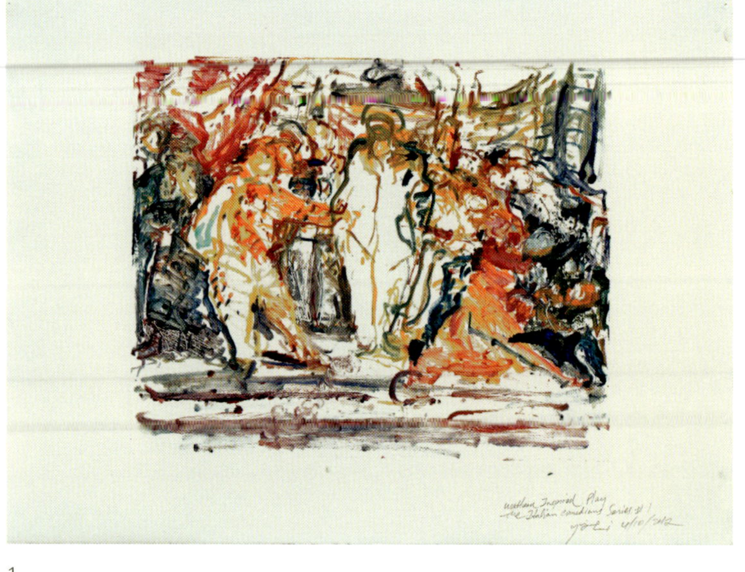

1

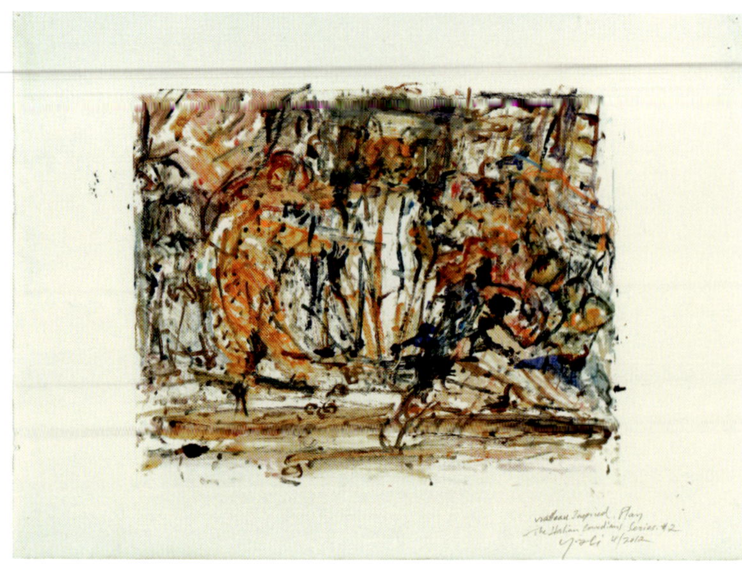

2

108

YING LI
American, born 1951 in China
Watteau Inspired: Play, from *The Italian
Comedian*, *Six Monotypes after Watteau*,
April 10, 2012
Monotype on paper, sheet: 22⅝ x 29⅞ in.;
plate: 16¼ x 19½ in.
Purchased through the Claire and
Richard P. Morse 1953 Fund; 2012.36.1–6
© Ying Li

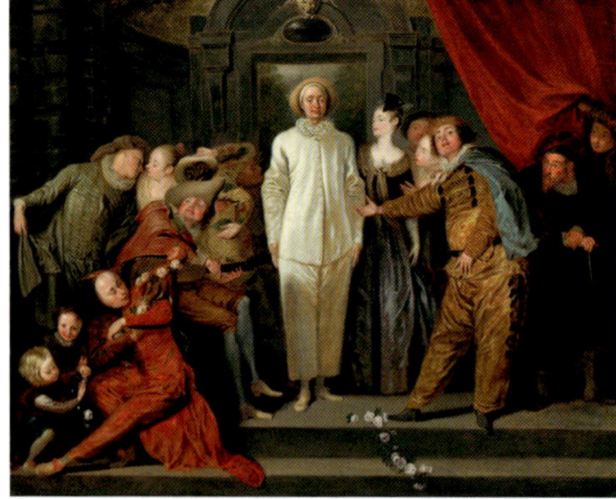

Fig. 26

Antoine Watteau, *The Italian Comedians*,
probably 1720, oil on canvas. National Gallery of
Art, Samuel H. Kress Collection; 1946.7.9.

Ying Li, who teaches painting at Haverford College, creates richly impastoed abstractions of landscapes, still lifes, interiors, and figure paintings. Born in Beijing to a father who taught Russian literature, she was first exposed to abstract art in a Russian magazine, where she saw an illustration of paintings by Matisse and Picasso. As a teenager, she was separated from her father during the Cultural Revolution and sent with her mother to an internment camp, where she did forced agricultural work for five years. According to the essay by William Corbett in her artist-in-residence catalogue, in that camp she was assigned to paint portraits of Chairman Mao, a rather unique beginning in the career of an abstract painter. After she was released from the camp, she dreamed of furthering her education and struggled to overcome a government prohibition against someone with her family's history attending university. Through the championing of an art professor who saw promise in her work, from 1974 to 1977 she was able to attend the art school at Anhui Teachers' University, located in the inland city of Hefei near Nanjing, where she also taught from 1977 through 1983. She immigrated to the United States in 1983 and earned her MFA from Parson's School of Design in New York in 1987. At this time, she began to paint abstractly, inspired by the work of Paul Cézanne and, later, Chaïm Soutine.

While she was at Dartmouth, Ying Li worked both on painting and monotypes. She had not worked in monotype before this residency, but through her new friendship with Louise Hamlin, who was teaching printmaking in Dartmouth's Studio Art Department, found that painting ink on copper plates was naturally sympathetic to her working methods. She experimented in particular with creating ghost prints that she could work and re-work to make varied impressions. In monotype, the artist uses inks directly on the plate, which is then covered with paper and run through the press. The paper does not absorb all the ink on the plate, so if printed again, the plate produces a ghost image of the

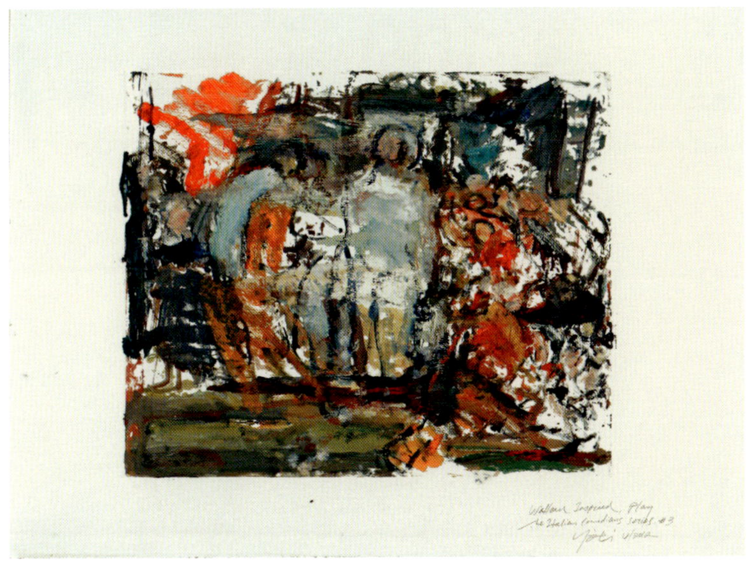

3

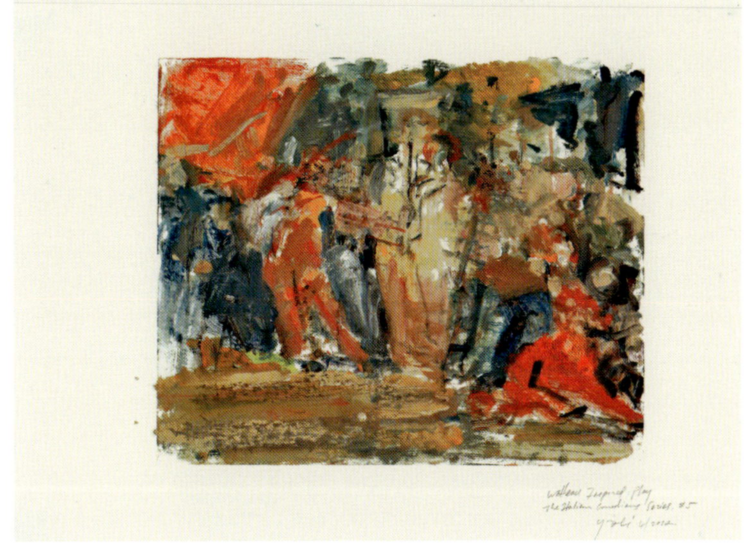

4

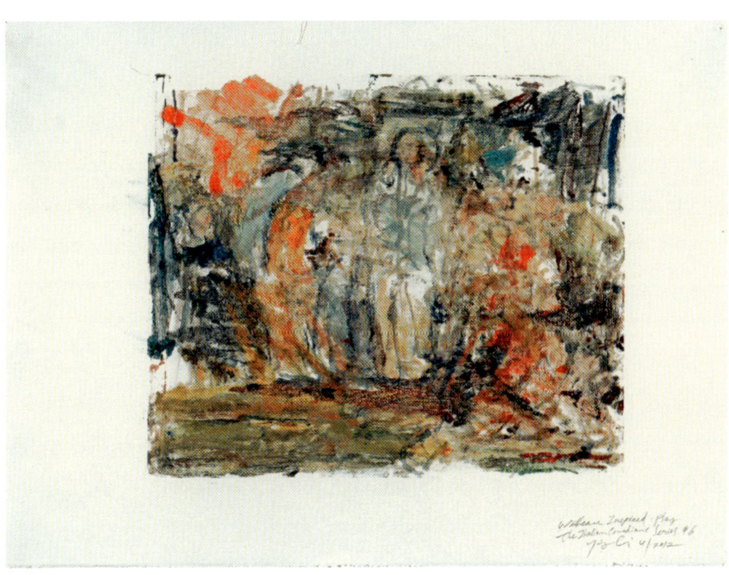

5

original print. Before reprinting, the artist can go back and re-work the plate, creating more variation from the original. In this homage to Watteau's *The Italian Comedians* (around 1720) from the National Gallery of Art's collection (fig. 26), she focuses on the central figure of Pierrot, who stands quietly during a curtain call amid other actors in his troupe. In number three of the series (above left), Li's vibrant color, a marker of her practice as a painter, is a wonderful arrangement of complementary blues and reddish-orange hues. She draws the scene with energetic stokes of line that delineate the figures, but breaks into unassociated gestural marks that emanate out from the central group. The ghost of the previous print provides a different kind of mark and a foil for her new additions, an amalgam of the past and present in one print.

KWH

6

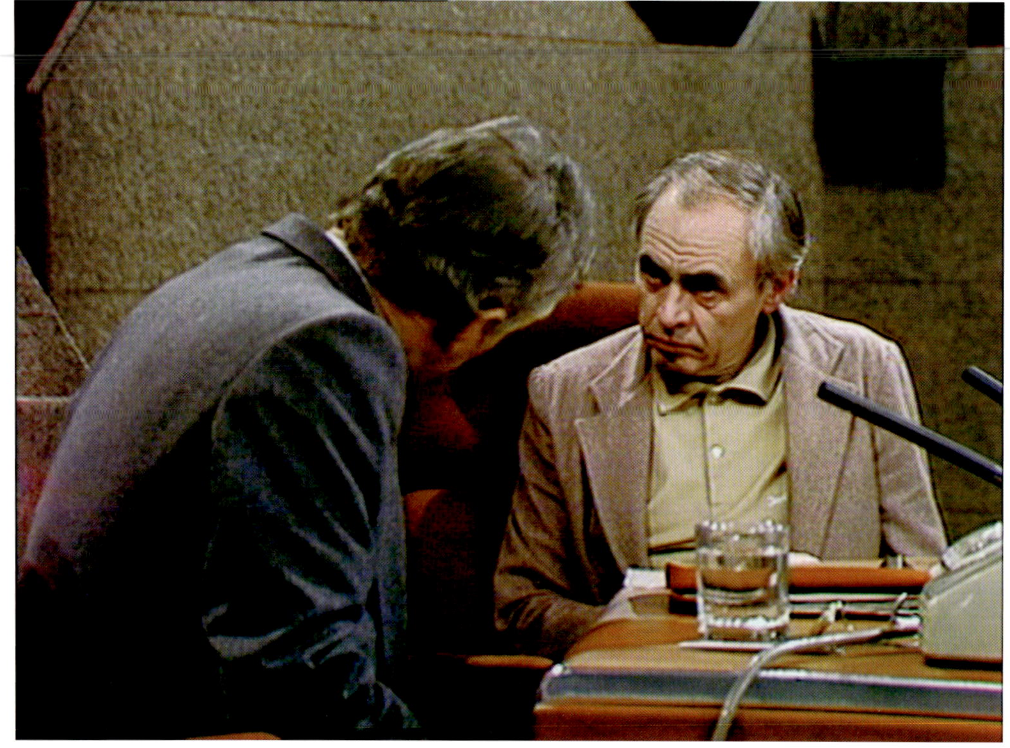

The Scottish documentary filmmaker, photographer, and musician Luke Fowler is best known for his film portraits of radical twentieth-century artists and thinkers, from the avant-garde composer–turned–political activist Cornelius Cardew (1936–1981) to the controversial Scottish psychiatrist R. D. Laing (1927–1989). Like Laing, Fowler was born in Glasgow. He studied printmaking at the Duncan of Jordanstone College of Art in Dundee, where he received a BA in Fine Art in 2000. In 2008 he was awarded the inaugural Derek Jarman Award, an annual prize inspired by one of Britain's most esteemed and controversial filmmakers. In the following year, Fowler had a retrospective exhibition at the Serpentine Gallery in London that cemented his reputation as one of the most innovative and exciting young filmmakers of his generation. In 2012 Fowler was short-listed for the prestigious Turner Prize, presented every year to a British artist under fifty for an outstanding exhibition in the previous twelve months. Fowler was nominated for his solo exhibition at Inverleith House in Edinburgh that showcased his new film *All Divided Selves*. In the spring of 2013, Fowler was artist-in-residence at Dartmouth, where he exhibited several recent composite photographs, whose random juxtapositions were determined by the laws of chance rather than by the artist, as well as his 2012 film, *The Poor Stockinger, the Luddite Cropper and the Deluded Followers of Joanna Southcott*, which reflects on the life and work of the British Marxist historian E. P. Thompson (1886–1946).

All Divided Selves is a haunting feature-length visual biography of R. D. Laing, a charismatic figure in the anti-psychiatry movement of the 1960s, which challenged conventional wisdom about the causes and treatment of mental illness. This wildly experimental documentary, commissioned by the Center for Curatorial Studies at Bard College, takes the form of a jagged, yet mesmerizing cinematic collage constructed from countless hours of historical, low-fidelity film and video footage, including Laing's numerous television appearances, interviews, and instructional documentation. Accompanied by a surround-sound score that features original music and field recordings by Eric La Casa, Jean-Luc Guionnet, and Alasdair Roberts, *All Divided Selves* details Laing's meteoric rise to fame as he transitions from a popular medical practitioner into a guru-like hero of the social and cultural revolutions of the 1960s. Named after Laing's 1960 study *The Divided Self*, which became an international bestseller, Fowler's film emotionally envelops and transports the viewer through a dazzling psycho-phenomenological viewing and listening experience.

MRT

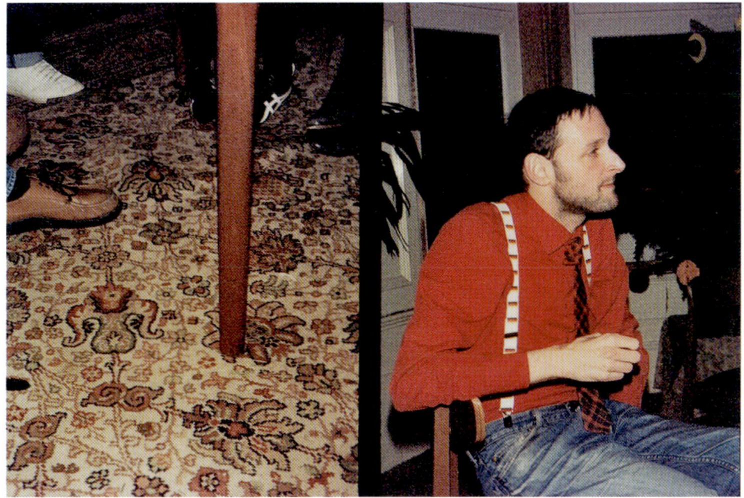

110

LUKE FOWLER
Alasdair, Hogmanay, Clouston Street, 2009
Chromogenic print, framed: 26^1/$_2$ x 26^1/$_2$ x
1^5/$_{16}$ in.; unframed: 25^7/$_{16}$ x 25^7/$_{16}$ in.
Purchased through the Virginia and
Preston T. Kelsey '58 Fund, the Anonymous
Fund #144, and the Mrs. Harvey P. Hood W'18
Fund; 2013.50.2
© Luke Fowler
Photo by Ruth Clark

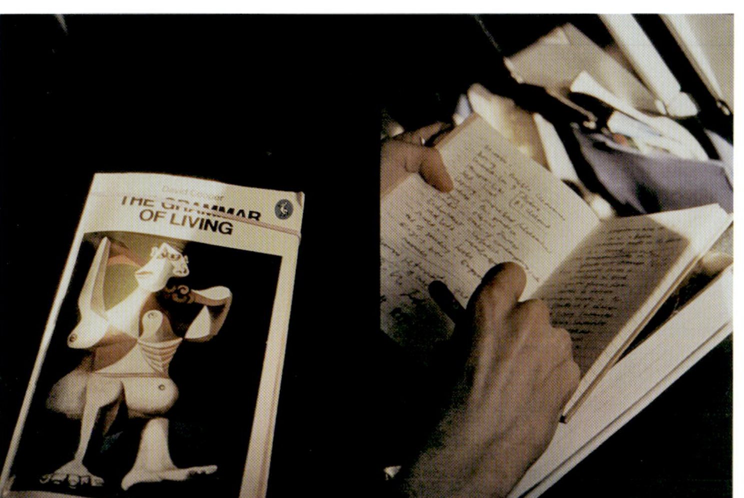

111

LUKE FOWLER
A Grammar of Moving, 2010
Chromogenic print, framed: 26^1/$_2$ x 26^1/$_2$ x
1^5/$_{16}$ in.; unframed: 25^7/$_{16}$ x 25^7/$_{16}$ in.
Purchased through the Virginia and
Preston T. Kelsey '58 Fund, the Anonymous
Fund #144, and the Mrs. Harvey P. Hood W'18
Fund; 2013.50.3
© Luke Fowler
Photo by Ruth Clark

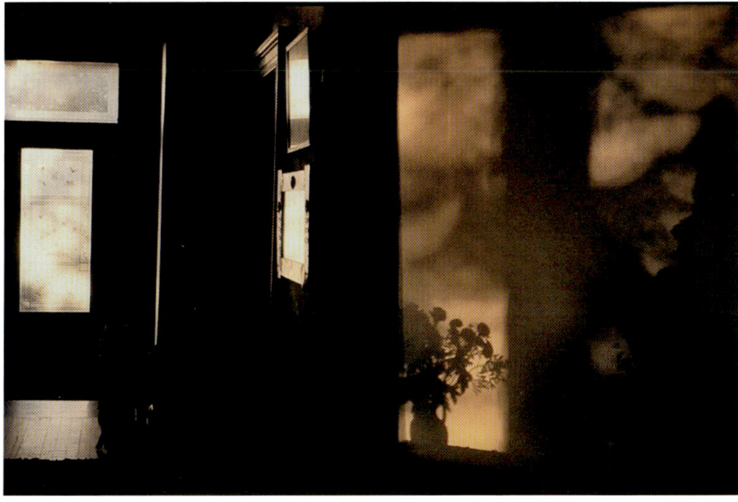

112

LUKE FOWLER
Just Leaving (Odd Harmonics), 2010
Chromogenic print, framed: 26^1/$_2$ x 26^1/$_2$ x
1^5/$_{16}$ in.; unframed: 25^7/$_{16}$ x 25^7/$_{16}$ in.
Gift of the artist; 2013.54
© Luke Fowler
Photo by Ruth Clark

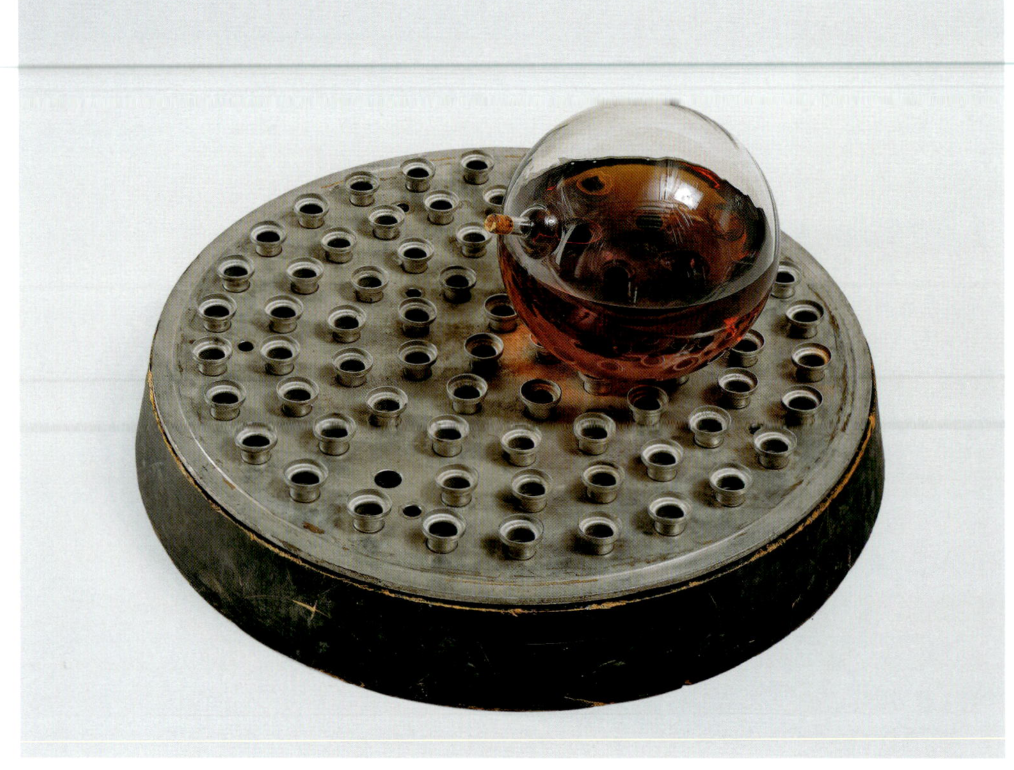

TERRY ADKINS
American, born 1953
Still, 2000
Steel, wood, glass, and whiskey,
height: 17 in.; diameter: 33 in.
Purchased through the Guernsey Center
Moore 1904 Fund; S.2003.39
© Terry Adkins

Born in Washington, D.C., in 1953, Terry Adkins received his BS from Fisk University in Nashville, Tennessee, in 1975 and his MFA from the University of Kentucky in 1979. He began his career as a musician and remains an active saxophonist and composer in the avant-garde music scene. Later inspired to become a visual artist, he began creating sculptures from discarded objects. Adkins explains, "My quest has been to find a way to make music as physical as sculpture might be, and sculpture as ethereal as music is . . . to make both of those pursuits do what they are normally not able to do."[1] In his work, Adkins brings to light underappreciated historical figures' contributions to society, frequently referencing the cultural traditions of the African American South, including crafts, folklore, and—most importantly—music. The artist continues, "My quest is to use abstract means, to educate the public about these figures through ways that are not image based or narrative based but to challenge them to think abstractly in relating to the stories of the lives of the people concerned."[2]

Still is composed of a circular wooden mold crowned by a perforated and cupped steel disc (which could be a nod to the shape of phonograph records, or a manhole cover). Upon it rests a nippled globe of blown glass half-filled with amber-colored whiskey. This work is a part of a series made during a residency in San Antonio, Texas, and exhibited during Adkins's artist-in-residence exhibition at Dartmouth in the summer of 2003. The artist was inspired by the remnants of Finesilver Manufacturing Company, a uniform-manufacturing operation across from the Gunter Hotel in San Antonio, where a number of blues artists

such as Blind Willie Johnson, Leadbelly, and Blind Lemon Jefferson first recorded their music. The multiple meanings of the title—its suggestions of time, a physical state of being, and the apparatus for distilling alcohol—combined with the resilience of the found objects and ethereal effect they produce, suggest the disorientation that alcohol induces as the real and imagined merge. Bridging the past and present in astonishing ways, a chorus of anonymous and timeless voices emanates from *Still*.

ESB

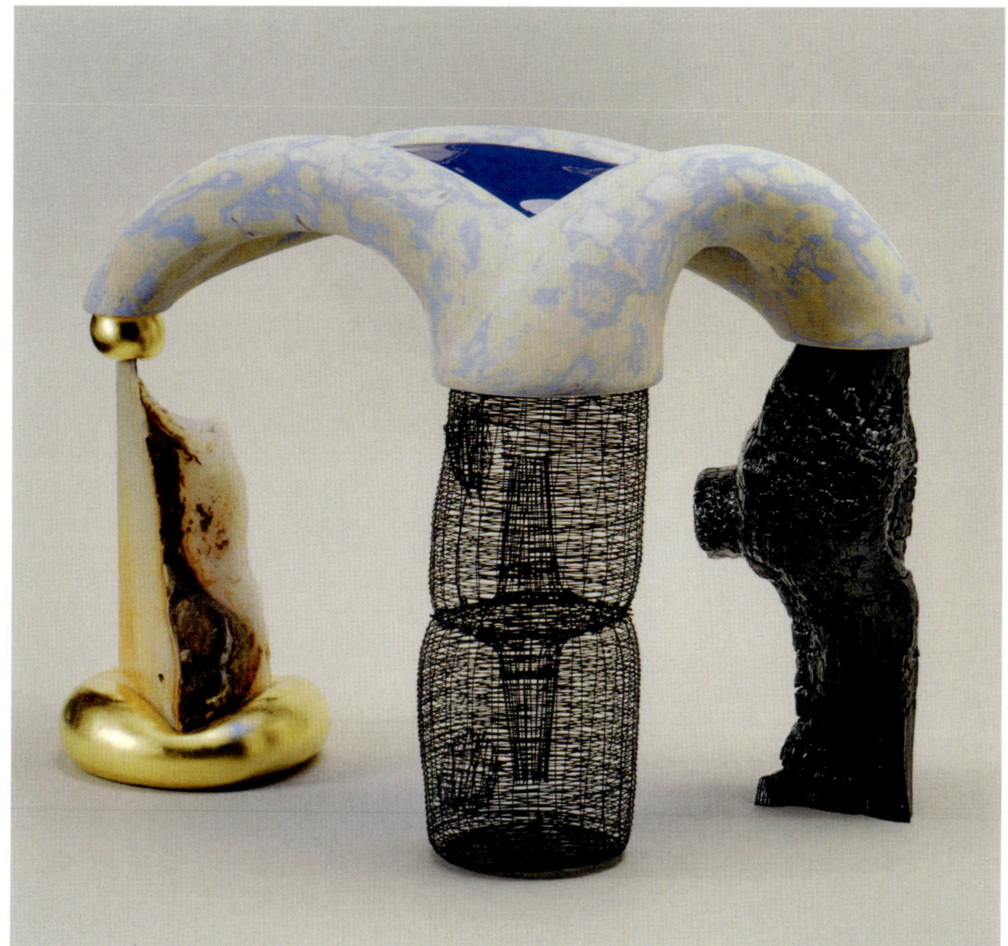

The celebrated sculptor John Newman was born in New York and continues to live and work in the Tribeca neighborhood of the city. He received his BA from Oberlin College in 1973 and his MFA from the Yale University School of Art in 1975. After graduating from Yale, Newman began to create minimalist sculptures in industrial materials, such as aluminum and steel, which were directly inspired by the "specific objects" of Donald Judd. Like Judd, Newman did not make these sculptures with his hands, choosing instead to have his works manufactured according to his precise specifications. Eventually, Newman tired of the restrictions that the legacy of minimalism placed on personal expression, form, and materials. Rejecting the reductive abstraction of Judd and other modernist sculptors, Newman's work, from the mid-1990s onward, began to embrace vibrant color and unexpected materials, such as papier-mâché, pumice stone, handmade paper, organza, tulle, two-way mirrored glass, and varnished nut husks from the Australian outback. These colorful, flamboyant, and often witty handmade works are intended to be viewed as table-top sculptures, as opposed to the monumental scale of his early work, so that their complex curving shapes and intricate details can be fully comprehended and enjoyed at eye level. This change in scale was partially informed by his travels to Australia, Africa, India, and Japan, where he encountered new materials and methods of construction, as well as cultures that placed special value on small-scale objects. The improvisation of jazz music is another important influence on Newman's recent assemblages, which play with textures and contrasts in much the same way that Charlie Parker's compositions do.

Blue Light Holds the Distance was created at Dartmouth during the artist's residency in the winter of 2013. The work contains an eclectic range of found objects, including a charred piece of wood that Newman connects with "a very troubling and difficult time in my personal life," steel-wire rat traps that he collected on a trip to Tanzania, and a piece of agate.[1] These disparate materials form the three legs of the sculpture and are held together by a computer-generated piece of vacuum-formed translucent Plexiglas that Newman created in collaboration with Max Fagin, a design fellow in the Thayer School of Engineering Machine Shop and a graduate of the Thayer Class of 2011. When light shines from above, this recessed Plexiglas casts a blue shadow that gives the work its title.

MRT

LINDA MATALON
American, born 1958
Untitled, Diptych (Touching), 2012
Graphite on wax-treated paper, 54 x 24 in.
Purchased through the Virginia and Preston T.
Kelsey '58 Fund, and the Contemporary Art
Fund, the Julia L. Whittier Fund, and the
Anonymous Fund #144; 2012.58
© Linda Matalon

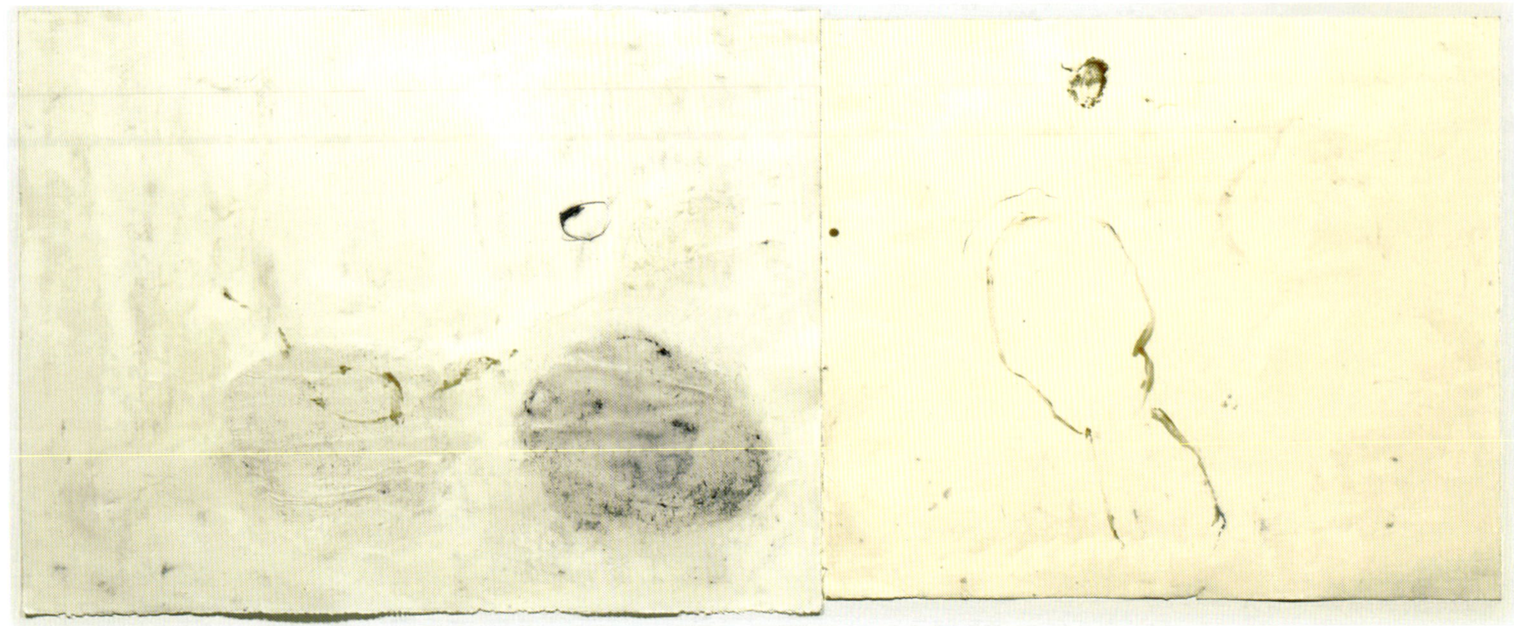

A self-taught artist who lives and works in Brooklyn, New York, Linda Matalon has been exhibiting her sculpture and works on paper in numerous solo and group exhibitions in the United States and Europe since 1991. Her work most recently was included in solo exhibitions at Bennington College, Vermont, in 2012, and the Blackston Gallery, New York, in 2013. Beginning her career as a sculptor, Matalon creates work that has been characterized as post-minimalist in its distillation of the natural world and lived experience into pure abstract forms bathed in a soft, translucent light. Although indebted to the codified formal language and abstract mark-making of Eva Hesse, Richard Serra, and Agnes Martin, Matalon's work is imbued with intense personal associations and feelings that were often banished from the reductive industrial aesthetics of minimalism. This can be seen in the drawing *Untitled, Diptych (Touching)*, where the touching forms of two pieces of handmade, wax-saturated paper become a metaphor for human contact and interpersonal relations. Matalon continued her more recent work in photography while in residence at Dartmouth in the fall of 2012, during which time she printed photographs that were later included in her exhibition at the Blackston Gallery.

Untitled, Diptych (Touching) is typical of Matalon's mature work and is considered by the artist to be one of her most "powerful, raw,

and difficult" drawings, in the sense that it contains a willful ambiguity that resists any one, fixed meaning. Matalon begins by making her paper by hand and then infuses it with wax in a hermetic heat process. Once the surface is ready she proceeds to animate it through a series of marks, brushstrokes, accidents, rubbings, and erasures that record the passage of time and possess a tough yet meditative beauty. The unevenness and physicality of the wax-treated paper and the drawn forms recall her origins as a sculptor. When selecting an exhibition of Matalon's work as one of the top ten best shows of 2010 for the December issue of *Artforum*, independent curator Victoria Noorthoorn wrote, "In Matalon's wax and graphite drawings . . . the slightest gesture becomes the basis for an intimate diary, a palimpsest of experience. . . . Each drawing challenges invisibility to speak not just of the sublime but of the coarse texture of the present."[1] This idea of Matalon's work as palimpsest is poignantly felt in this diptych, which hints at relationships past and present, changing and fading, but never forgotten.

MRT

NOTES

Cats. 1–2. Carlos Sánchez, *Self-Portrait* and *Young Man with Bird*
(pp. 24–25)
1. Annabelle Armstrong, "Father Sánchez: View from the 14th Floor,"
   The Baton Rouge Sunday Advocate, August 28, 1988.
2. Rod Dreher, "Father Sánchez: Retired Priest Found Calling
   Relatively Late," *The Baton Rouge Sunday Advocate*, June 16, 1991.
3. Armstrong, "Father Sánchez."
4. Ibid.

Cat. 12. Lawren Harris, *Mount Washington* (p. 30)
1. Bess Harris continued, "We worked—all drawings—every day
   from 10:30 a.m. to dark—so we have a winter's work ahead of us."
   Bess Harris to Doris Mills, December 1934, Speirs Papers, quoted
   by Dennis Reid in *Atma Buddhi Manas: The Later Work of Lawren
   S. Harris* (Toronto: Art Gallery of Ontario, 1985), 23. Harris also
   expressed his love of New Hampshire's "Northern" atmosphere
   and claimed that Hanover "is in the Boreal zone. I don't know how
   it got there, but it's colder and more northern in feeling than all of
   Southern Ontario." Harris to Yvonne McKague and Fred Housser,
   May 14, 1935, Public Archives of Canada, Ottawa. Quoted by Dennis
   Reid in ibid., 23.

Cat. 13. Lawren Harris, *Lake Superior* (p. 31)
1. In a letter dated April 13, 1988, Dennis Reid, then Curator of
   Canadian Historical Art at the Art Gallery of Ontario, wrote to the
   author: "Harris reclaimed the sketches and canvases about 1944,
   after he had re-settled in Canada, at Vancouver. We know of a small
   number of canvases that were subsequently painted based upon
   his earlier sketches. I believe that your canvas is one of these, and
   that it dates from c. 1948 or the year or so after." Strengthening
   the proposed date is the inscription on the painting's stretcher,
   "Reserved / Dr. Norman Mackenzie / 1948." The smaller *Lake
   Superior* surfaced in a May 17, 2012, sale at Heffel Fine Art Auction
   House, Vancouver (lot 120). In a January 12, 2012, email to Barbara
   MacAdam, Alison Meredith from the Heffel firm reported that,
   according to the consigner of the work, the consigner's mother
   believes she acquired the oil sketch before 1945 and that her friends
   Harris and Ira Dilworth selected it for her. If this recollection is
   correct and Harris accessed the study for reference before parting
   with the painting, one could make the case for a date of about
   1944–45 for the larger work.
2. On May 4, 1951, Churchill P. "Jerry" Lathrop, Chairman of
   Dartmouth's Art Department, wrote to Harris, expressing pleasure
   at the artist's proposed gift to Dartmouth of one of his paintings
   in memory of his uncle: "We would prefer to leave the choice of
   the picture to you, for we have full faith in your knowledge and
   judgment in the matter. My personal feeling leans toward one of
   your bold and patternized northern landscapes, which I believe,
   would make an impressive and widely appreciated memorial to
   the strength and friendly dignity of Will." On May 13, 1951, Harris
   replied: "I have only one painting left which I feel would be suitable
   as a memorial to Will Stewart. It is a Lake Superior canvas, 34
   [inches] x 40 [inches]. I want to do a little work on it and also order
   a decent frame." Hood Museum of Art object files.

Cat. 14. Paul Sample, *Between Classes* (p. 32)
1. Among them is a watercolor in the Hood Museum of Art's
   collection, Sample's large springtime scene *Dartmouth Row* (1963),
   gift of Frank L. Harrington Jr., Class of 1956, in memory of Frank L.
   Harrington Sr., Class of 1924; 2006.6.

Cat. 15. Paul Sample, *Beaver Meadow* (p. 33)

1. Alfred Frankenstein, "Paul Sample," *Magazine of Art* (July 1938): 387.
2. Justus Bier, "Paul Sample: A Native of Louisville Gets a One-Man Exhibition," *The Courier-Journal Magazine* (April 22, 1951): 23.
3. Local historians have polled older residents and former residents of Beaver Meadow and identified the seated "Mrs. Roberts" as Edith Roberts; the woman with her arm extended toward the cats as Ida Wallace; the tall man facing her as Aaron Edmonds; the stout man facing an unidentified woman as Henry Burnor; and the couple in the carriage as Raleigh and Hattie Crawford; phone conversation between author and Elsie Sniffen of Norwich, Vermont, September 26, 2000. See also Elsie Sniffen, *The Good Men Do: A Tribute to the Folks of Beaver Meadow Community* (privately printed, 2003). Beaver Meadow's Union Chapel, dating to 1915, still stands and is on the National Register of Historic Places. Sample took artistic license with its structure, giving its roof a double slope.

Cat. 16. Paul Sample, *The Return* (p. 34)

1. Sample's related drawing is *Wells River, Vermont* (compositional study for *The Return*), Hood Museum of Art, gift of the artist, Class of 1920; 2000.54.
2. About a year later Sample painted another winter landscape as an advertisement for Maxwell House titled *Coffee Time in America* (about 1947–48), Hood Museum of Art, promised gift of Judith and Charles Hood, Class of 1951; EL.2010.55.8.

Cat. 17. Paul Sample, *Old Ledyard Bridge* (p. 35)

1. Letter from Noble O. Bowlby, Class of 1906, W. Franklin, N.H., to Roger C. Wilde, Class of 1921, Chairman of the Alumni Fund Committee, Hanover, N.H., March 31, 1954. Dartmouth College Library, President's Records, DP-12, box 7122—alumni fund.

Cat. 18. Paul Sample, *Will Bond* (p. 36)

1. Sample's graphite drawing of Will Bond (about 1948) is illustrated and discussed in Barbara J. MacAdam, *Marks of Distinction: Two Hundred Years of American Watercolors and Drawings from the Hood Museum of Art* (Hanover, N.H.: Hood Museum of Art, Dartmouth College, 2005), 186–87. The multifigure genre painting referred to is *Remember Now the Days of Thy Youth* (1950), Hood Museum of Art, gift of Frank L. Harrington, Class of 1924; P.962.80.

Cats. 20–22. Ralph Steiner, *Billowing Sheets, Hanging Sheets,* and *Hanging Sheets* (pp. 38–39)

1. Ralph Steiner in "Ralph Steiner: A Prospectus for a Portfolio of Prints Mostly From the 1920s," July 1976.
2. Ralph Steiner, *Ralph Steiner: A Point of View* (Middletown, Conn.: Wesleyan University Press, 1978), 6.
3. For more on the relationship between Steiner and Evans, see Jeff L. Rosenheim and Douglas Eklund, *Unclassified: A Walker Evans Anthology: Selections from the Walker Evans Archive, Department of Photographs, The Metropolitan Museum of Art* (New York: Metropolitan Museum of Art, 2000), 154, and Belinda Rathbone, *Walker Evans: A Biography* (London: Thames and Hudson, 1995), 47.
4. Steiner in "Ralph Steiner, A Prospectus."

5. His description of the film continued: "At first the sheets plunge wildly in a high breeze, and this is juxtaposed to Greek horses rearing and dashing. Then a sequence of smoothly flowing, gently floating sheets is compared to the wavelike lines in the clothing of Greek women. At the end of the film, sheets moving slowly and majestically are related to noble, stately statues of Greek gods." Steiner, *Ralph Steiner: A Point of View,* 120.
6. Steiner in "Ralph Steiner, A Prospectus."

Cat. 23. Friedel Dzubas, *Aegian* (p. 40)

1. Charles W. Millard, "Interview with Friedal Dzubas," in *Friedel Dzubas* (Washington, D.C.: Hirshhorn Museum and Sculpture Garden, Smithsonian Institution Press), 28.
2. Ibid., 30.

Cat. 25. Jason Seley, *The Boys from Avignon* (p. 42)

1. Jason Seley, *Jason Seley: Artist-in-Residence, Jaffe-Friede Gallery, Hopkins Center, Dartmouth College, February 8–March 4, 1968* (Lunenburg, Vt.: Stinehour Press, 1968).

Cat. 27. Lyman Kipp, *Median II* (p. 44)

1. D. J., "Lyman Kipp," *Arts Magazine* (September 1962): 51.

Cat. 30. Frank Stella, *Chocorua IV* (p. 47)

1. Frank Stella in an interview with Brian Kennedy, New York, November 6, 2009. The quotations from Stella that follow are from the same interview.
2. William S. Rubin, *Frank Stella* (New York: Museum of Modern Art, 1970), 112.
3. See Robert L. McGrath, *Gods in Granite: The Art of the White Mountains in New Hampshire* (Syracuse: Syracuse University Press, 2001), 58–60.

Cat. 32. Julian Stanczak, *Consonance* (p. 49)

1. Neil Rector, ed., *Communicating in a Different Way: The Julian Stanczak Interview* (self-published, 2000; accessed Hood Museum of Art files), 112.

Cat. 37. Hannes Beckmann, *Blue Diamond* (p. 54)

1. Steve Sherman, "Interview with Hannes Beckmann," *New Hampshire Times*, 1977. Republished in 1978 in a Plymouth State College Art Gallery exhibition catalogue.
2. Jan van der Marck, untitled essay in the 1978 Plymouth State College Art Gallery exhibition catalogue.

Cat. 39. Jack Tworkov, *Untitled (R.A. on P. #9)* (p. 56)

1. For this quotation and the following one, see Andrew Forge, "The Knight and the Barrier," *Jack Tworkov: Fifteen Years of Painting* (New York: Solomon R. Guggenheim Museum, 1982), 10–16.

Cat. 40. Walker Evans, *Trinity Church, Cornish, New Hampshire* (p. 57)

1. Belinda Rathbone, *Walker Evans: A Biography* (London: Thames, 1995), 290.
2. Typed transcript of interview between Matthew Wysocki and Timothy Rub, Director of the Hood Museum of Art, February 2, 1988, 5–6. HMA object files. Evans's August trip to the Upper Valley

is recorded in Jerry L. Thompson, *The Last Years of Walker Evans: A First-Hand Account* (New York: Thames and Hudson, 1997), 125. As documented by his negatives in the Metropolitan Museum of Art, Evans had previously visited Cornish around 1933–34. He was good friends with Charles Fuller, son of Cornish artists Lucia and Henry B. Fuller. Evans photographed local scenery and Charles's children at play when apparently visiting Fuller's family in Cornish at that time. Metropolitan Museum of Art online collections database, and Rathbone, *Walker Evans*, 76–77.

3. Evans's erudite passion for literature enabled him to befriend members of the English department, and his recently awakened compulsion to "collect" (in fact, pilfer) signs and advertisements—long-favored motifs in his art—deepened his sense of kinship with another member of the visual studies faculty, Varujan Boghosian, known for his evocative assemblages and collages made from found objects. Evans loved to explore the mounds of tantalizing, emotive objects in Boghosian's studio. Boghosian went so far in his support of Evans that he reluctantly helped him steal an old sign from a Hanover barbershop in broad daylight. Rathbone, *Walker Evans*, 290–91.

4. Agee continued: "It lost nothing at all in stasis but even more powerfully strove in through the eyes its paralyzing classicism. . . . And this light upon it was strengthening still further its imposal and embrace, and in about a quarter of an hour would have trained itself ready, and there would be a triple convergence in the keen historic spasm of the shutter." James Agee, "Near a Church," in Agee and Walker Evans, *Let Us Now Praise Famous Men* (Boston: Houghton Mifflin Company, 1941, 1969 [ninth printing]), 38–39.

Cats. 41–44. Walker Evans, four interior views of Alfred Petersen's home, Enfield, New Hampshire (p. 58–59)

1. Evans's retrospective at Dartmouth, *Walker Evans: Artist-in-Residence,* was held October 27–November 26, 1972, and featured one-hundred works, including *Trinity Church, Cornish, New Hampshire* (cat. 40) and the bed- and living room views from this series.

2. Typed transcript of interview between Matthew Wysocki and Timothy Rub, Director of the Hood Museum of Art, February 2, 1988, 6. HMA object files. The interview is printed in full in the present volume, beginning on page 13. From negatives in the Evans archives at the Metropolitan Museum of Art, it appears that he may have only shot one 36-exposure roll of 2 x 2 negatives in the area in 1972 (including negatives for the images featured in this publication, which dated from his August pre-visit). Any work that he might have done during his actual residency has not been located. Wysocki suggests that Evans's declining health intervened: "I made a record of places that he wanted to go back to photograph. But unfortunately, he became very ill and had a major operation here."

Cats. 47–49. Ashley Bryan, *Nobody Knows the Trouble I See*, *I Knew the Lord*, and *Somebody's Knocking at Your Door* (pp. 62–63)

1. Ashley Bryan, "Walk Together Children," in *Walk Together Children: Black American Spirituals*, selected and illustrated by Ashley Bryan (New York: Atheneum, 1974), n.p.

Cat. 57. Gillian Pederson-Krag, *Landscape* (p. 70)

1. Gillian Pederson-Krag, *Paintings and Etchings, 1970–2011: Reflections on Painting* (Burdette, N.Y.: Larson Publications, 2011), 24.

2. Ibid.

Cat. 58. Don Nice, *White River Junction Study Two* (p. 71)

1. Dave Coburn, "Art Unappreciation: $15,000 Mural Causes A Stir At VA Hospital," *Valley News*, 1982.

Cat. 60. Paul Resika, *Provincetown Pier: Yellow Wall* (p. 73)

1. Steven Harvey, "Architecture and Painting: The Provincetown Paintings of Paul Resika," *Light, Air and Color: Provincetown Paintings* (Provincetown, Mass.: Provincetown Art Association and Museum, 1997).

Cats. 67–68. Sana Musasama, *Yellowbird Bark, Slippery Rock, Pennsylvania* and *My Hand, My Heart, Den Bosch, Holland* (p. 80)

1. Joanna Hamer, "Musasama Makes Art Talk about the Unspeakable," *The Chautauquan Daily*, July 12, 2012. Accessed online, http://chqdaily.com/2012/07/12/musasama-makes-art-talk-about-the-unspeakable/, June 3, 2013.

2. Ibid.

Cat. 73. James McGarrell, *The Grand Artificer, Young and Old (James Joyce)* (p. 84)

1. James McGarrell, "Some Notes by the Artist," in *James McGarrell: Ten Years of Big Paintings with Smaller Canvases and Works on Paper* (Springfield, Mo.: Springfield Art Museum, 1994), 6–7.

Cat. 74. Rosemarie Beck, *House of Venus* (p. 85)

1. Martica Sawin, "Rosemarie Beck: Never Form but Forming," New York Studio School, 2008. Accessed online, http://www.nyss.org/exhibitions/rosemarie-beck-essay-by-martica-sawin/, May 15, 2013.

Cat. 77. Michael Singer, *Map of Memory* (p. 88)

1. Timothy Rub in *Michael Singer* (Hanover, N.H.: Studio Art Exhibition Program, Dartmouth College, 1996), 4.

2. Else Marie Bukdahl, "Working in and with Nature," in *The Re-enchantment of Nature and Urban Space: Michael Singer Projects in Art, Design and Environmental Regeneration* (Aalborg, Denmark: Utzon Center, 2011), 19.

Cat. 81. Jake Berthot, *Beforehand* (p. 92)

1. Betty Cunningham Gallery, *Jake Berthot: Recent Paintings and Drawings* (New York: Betty Cunningham Gallery, 2006).

Cat. 82. Andrew Murray Forge, *Forsythia* (p. 93)

1. Karen Wilkin, *Adolph Gottlieb: Pictographs* (Edmonton, Alberta: Edmonton Art Gallery, 1977).

Cat. 84. Ruth Miller, *Blue Table Still Life* (p. 95)

1. *Ruth Miller: Paintings* (Hanover, N.H.: Studio Art Exhibition Program, Dartmouth College, 1999).

2. Nancy Grimes, "Ruth Miller at Bowery," *Art in America* 87, no. 6 (1999): 123.

Cat. 85. Morton Kaish, *Freedom Door* (p. 96)
1. Matthew Wysocki in *Luise Kaish, Morton Kaish: Artists in Residence* (Hanover, N.H.: Studio Art Exhibition Program, Dartmouth College, 1974).

Cat. 86. Robert Birmelin, *The Crowd/Others* (p. 97)
1. Robert Bermelin, Notes, May 24, 1999, Studio Art Department files, Dartmouth College.

Cat. 87. Christopher Cozier, *Cross Currents* (p. 98)
1. Anna Lotko, "Installations Examine History, Politics and Island Identity," *The Dartmouth*, October 15, 2007. Accessed online, http://www.thedartmouth.com/2007/10/15/arts/cozier, June 14, 2013.

Cat. 94. Charles Spurrier, *Infinity Bond* (p. 104)
1. Charles Spurrier, Letter to Kellen G. Haak, undated. Hood Museum of Art object files.

Cat. 95. Chris Martin, *For the People of Hanover, New Hampshire* (p. 105)
1. Nancy Princenthal, "Wake-up Call," *Art in America*, October 15, 2011. Accessed online, http://www.artinamericamagazine.com/features/wake-up-call, November 16, 2012.

Cat. 97. Amy Sillman, *Letters from Texas (19)* (p. 107)
1. *Amy Sillman, Letters from Texas* (Hanover, N. H. : Dartmouth College, 2002).

Cat. 100. Rebecca Purdum, *Ripton 76 (Yellow)* (p. 110)
1. Rebecca Purdum, "Making Paintings," *New England Review* 28, no. 4 (2007).
2. Emmie Donadio, "Rebecca Purdum," *Regional Selections 30* (Hanover, N.H.: Hood Museum of Art, Dartmouth College, 2003), 60.

Cat. 101. Louise Fishman, *Green's Apogee* (p. 111)
1. Louise Fishman, "Statement to the Curators, March, 2006," in Maurice Tuchman and Esti Dunow, *The New Landscape / The New Still Life: Soutine and Modern Art* (New York: Cheim & Read, 2006).

Cat. 103. Laylah Ali, Untitled (p. 113)
1. Laylah Ali, Conversation with Michael Taylor, January 26, 2012.

Cat. 104. Susanna Coffey, *Intake* (p. 114)
1. Gabriel García Márquez, *One Hundred Years of Solitude* (New York: Harper Collins Publishers, 1991), trans. by Gregory Rabassa, 285; as quoted in Michael Rooks, *Susanna Coffey: Paintings* (Hanover, N.H.: Dartmouth College, 1998).

Cat. 106. Beryl Korot, *Florence* (p. 116)
1. Evelin Stermitz, "Text/Weave/Line—Video: An Interview with Beryl Korot," *Rhizome*, June 20, 2010. Accessed online, http://rhizome.org/discuss/view/46468/, May 24, 2013.

Cat. 113. Terry Adkins, *Still* (p. 122)
1. Dana Roc, Interview with Terry Adkins, 2006. Accessed online, http://www.danaroc.com/inspiring_020606terryadkins.html.
2. Ibid.

Cat. 114. John Newman, *Blue Light Holds the Distance* (p. 123)
1. John Newman, Email to Michael Taylor, May 8, 2013.

Cat. 115. Linda Matalon, *Untitled, Diptych (Touching)* (p. 124)
1. Ballroom Marfa, "Linda Matalon named as *ArtForum*'s Best of 2010," December 7, 2010. Accessed online, http://ballroommarfa.org/archive/linda-matalon-named-in-artforums-best-of-2010/, June 10, 2013.

Deborah T. Haynes

CHRONOLOGY OF ARTISTS-IN-RESIDENCE AND THEIR EXHIBITIONS AT DARTMOUTH COLLEGE

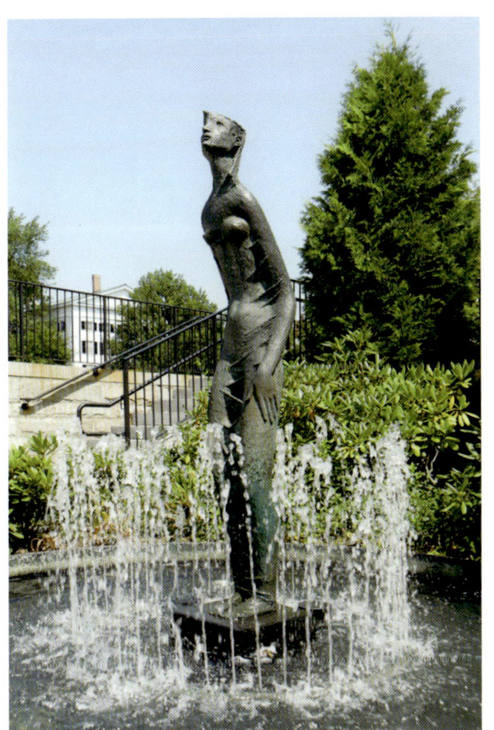

Fig. 27

Thomas Bayliss Huxley-Jones, *Fountain Figure*, 1963, bronze. Gift of the Class of 1943, in Memory of Our Classmates Who Gave Their Lives in Defense of Our Freedom, 1942–1945; S.964.204

1931–1962

Carlos Sánchez, Artist-in-Residence, 1931–32
(no exhibition documented)

José Clemente Orozco, Artist-in-Residence, 1932–34
(no exhibition documented)

Lawren Stewart Harris, informal artist-in-residence, 1934–38
(no exhibition documented)

Paul Sample, Artist-in-Residence, 1938–62
Paul Sample, Retrospective Exhibition, Carpenter Gallery, Carpenter Hall, June 3–July 6, 1941; annual exhibitions in Carpenter Hall through at least 1951; *Paul Sample Retrospective*, Jaffe-Friede Gallery, Hopkins Center, June 1963

1962

Friedel Dzubas, Artist-in-Residence, Fall 1962
Beaumont-May Gallery, Hopkins Center, December 1962

1963

Robert Rauschenberg, Artist-in-Residence, Winter 1963
Beaumont-May Gallery, Hopkins Center, February 3–28, 1963

James Rosati, Artist-in-Residence, Spring 1963
Beaumont-May Gallery, Hopkins Center, May 6–June 1, 1963

Frank Stella and Tal Streeter, Artists-in-Residence, Summer 1963
Beaumont-May Gallery, Hopkins Center, August 9–September 15, 1963

Thomas Bayliss Huxley-Jones, Artist-in-Residence, Fall 1963
Barrows Rotunda and Beaumont-May Gallery, Hopkins Center, December 2–30, 1963 (fig. 27)

1964

Paul Georges, Artist-in-Residence, Winter 1964
Beaumont-May Gallery, Hopkins Center, February 28–March 15, 1964

Max Bernd-Cohen, Artist-in-Residence, Spring 1964
Beaumont-May Gallery, Hopkins Center, May 22–June 7, 1964

David Porter, Artist-in-Residence, Fall 1964
Beaumont-May Gallery, Hopkins Center, November 14–December 16, 1964

1965

Lyman Kipp: Sculpture and Drawings, Artist-in-Residence, Winter 1965
Beaumont-May Gallery, Hopkins Center, February 9–28, 1965

Bizen Wares by Yu Fujiwara, Artist-in-Residence, Spring 1965
Beaumont-May Gallery, Hopkins Center, April 28–May 31, 1965

Xavier Esqueda, Artist-in-Residence, Fall 1965
Beaumont-May Gallery, Hopkins Center, November 8–December 5, 1965

1966

George Rickey: Lines and Planes, Artist-in-Residence, Winter 1966
Beaumont-May Gallery, Hopkins Center, February 11–28, 1966

Joseph Hirsch, Artist-in-Residence, Spring 1966
Beaumont-May Gallery, Hopkins Center, March 29–April 24, 1966

Donald Judd, Artist-in-Residence, Summer 1966
Beaumont-May Gallery, Hopkins Center, July 16–August 9, 1966

Walter Murch, Artist-in-Residence, Fall 1966
Beaumont-May Gallery, Hopkins Center, November 2–27, 1966

1967

Jacques Hurtubise, Artist-in-Residence, Winter 1967
Beaumont-May Gallery, Hopkins Center, January 6–29, 1967

Sorel Etrog, Artist-in-Residence, Spring 1967
Strauss Gallery, Hopkins Center, May 17–June 25, 1967

New Paintings by [Richard] Anuszkiewicz, Artist-in-Residence, Fall 1967
Jaffe-Friede Gallery, Hopkins Center, November 10–December 5, 1967

1968

Jason Seley, Artist-in-Residence, Winter 1968
Jaffe-Friede Gallery, Hopkins Center, February 8–March 4, 1968

Thomas Bayliss Huxley-Jones, Artist-in-Residence, Spring 1968
Barrows Rotunda and possibly Jaffe-Friede Gallery, Hopkins Center, April 10–May 1968

Varujan Boghosian, Artist-in-Residence, Summer 1968
Jaffe-Friede Gallery, Hopkins Center, July 4–29, 1968

Julian Stanczak, Artist-in-Residence, Fall 1968
Jaffe-Friede Gallery, Hopkins Center, October 18–November 15, 1968

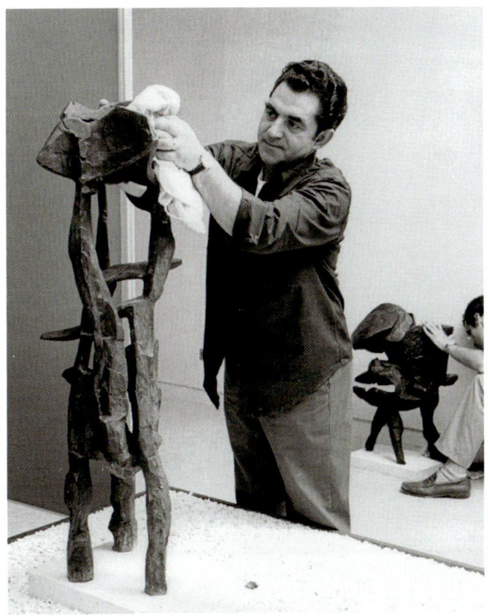

Fig. 28
Dimitri Hadzi installing his exhibition in the Jaffe-Friede Gallery, Hopkins Center, July 1969. Dartmouth College Library. Photo by Matthew Wysocki.

Larry Zox, Artist-in-Residence, Winter 1969
Jaffe-Friede Gallery, Hopkins Center, February 22–March 23, 1969

Will Carter, Artist-in-Residence, Spring 1969
Barrows Gallery, Hopkins Center, May 9–25, 1969

Dimitri Hadzi, Artist-in-Residence, Summer 1969
Jaffe-Friede Gallery, Hopkins Center, July 11–August 3, 1969 (fig. 28)

Nicholas Krushenick, Artist-in-Residence, Fall 1969
Jaffe-Friede Gallery, Hopkins Center, November 12, 1969–January 4, 1970

1970

Elbert Weinberg, Artist-in-Residence, Winter 1970
Jaffe-Friede Gallery, Hopkins Center, January 23–February 15, 1970

Hannes Beckmann: Paintings, Artist-in-Residence, Spring 1970
Beaumont-May Gallery, Hopkins Center, April 10–May 3, 1970

Jack Zajac, Artist-in-Residence, Summer 1970
Jaffe-Friede Gallery, Hopkins Center, July 10–August 30, 1970

Leroy Lamis: Sculpture, Artist-in-Residence, Fall 1970
Jaffe-Friede Gallery, Hopkins Center, October 22–November 22, 1970

1971

Dennis Kowal: Sculpture, Artist-in-Residence, Winter 1971
Jaffe-Friede Gallery, Hopkins Center, February 4–28, 1971

A. B. Jackson: Drawings and Paintings, Artist-in-Residence, Spring 1971
Jaffe-Friede Gallery, Hopkins Center, May 7–23, 1971

Richard Claude Ziemann, Artist-in-Residence, Summer 1971
Jaffe-Friede Gallery, Hopkins Center, July 9–August 8, 1971

Robert Sowers, Artist-in-Residence, Fall 1971
Beaumont-May Gallery, Hopkins Center, October 1–24, 1971

1972

Philip Grausman: Sculpture and Drawings, Artist-in-Residence, Winter 1972
Jaffe-Friede Gallery, Hopkins Center, February 4–27, 1972

Paul Resika, Artist-in-Residence, Spring 1972
Jaffe-Friede Gallery, Hopkins Center, May 5–28, 1972

Edward Giobbi, Artist-in-Residence, Summer 1972
Jaffe-Friede Gallery, Hopkins Center, July 14–August 27, 1972

Walker Evans, Artist-in-Residence, Fall 1972
Jaffe-Friede Gallery, Hopkins Center, October 27–November 26, 1972

1973

Jack Tworkov, Artist-in-Residence, Winter 1973
Jaffe-Friede Gallery, Hopkins Center, February 9–March 4, 1973

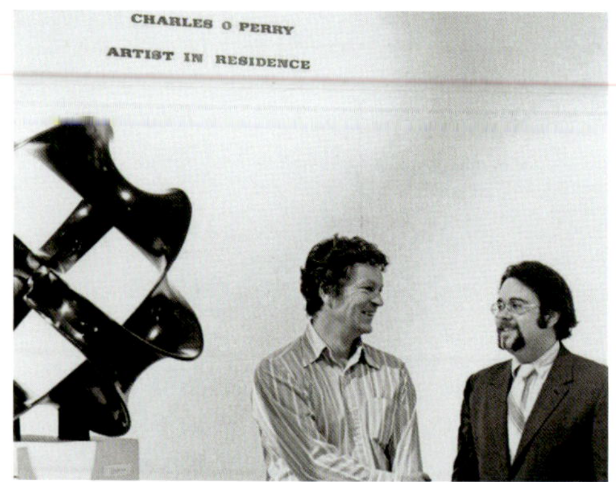

Fig. 29

Charles O. Perry and *Boston Globe* journalist and art critic William A. Henry III in the artist's exhibition in the Jaffe-Friede Gallery, Hopkins Center, summer 1973. Dartmouth College Library. Photo by Matthew Wysocki.

Paul Suttman, Artist-in-Residence, Spring 1973
Jaffe-Friede Gallery, Hopkins Center, May 4–20, 1973

Charles O. Perry, Artist-in-Residence, Summer 1973
Jaffe-Friede Gallery, Hopkins Center, August 3–September 3, 1973 (fig. 29)

Fritz Scholder, Artist-in-Residence, Fall 1973
Jaffe-Friede Gallery, Hopkins Center, September 28–October 21, 1973

1974

Ashley Bryan, Artist-in-Residence, Winter 1974
Jaffe-Friede and Strauss Galleries, Hopkins Center, February 1–March 3, 1974

Laura Ziegler, Artist-in-Residence, Spring 1974
Jaffe-Friede Gallery, Hopkins Center, May 3–26, 1974

Luise Kaish, Morton Kaish, Artists-in-Residence, Summer 1974
Jaffe-Friede and Strauss Galleries, Hopkins Center, August 2–September 3, 1974

Jim Dine: Recent Graphics, Artist-in-Residence, Fall 1974
Jaffe-Friede Gallery, Hopkins Center, November 8–December 8, 1974

1975

Donald Aquilino: Recent Work, Artist-in-Residence, Winter 1975
Beaumont-May Gallery, Hopkins Center, January 31–March 9, 1975

Gilbert Franklin: Sculpture—Drawings, 1955–1975, Artist-in-Residence, Spring 1975
Jaffe-Friede Gallery and Barrows Rotunda, Hopkins Center, April 18–May 18, 1975

T. C. Cannon, Artist-in-Residence, Summer 1975
Beaumont-May Gallery, Hopkins Center, July 18–August 31, 1975

Jack Youngerman, Artist-in-Residence, Fall 1975
Beaumont-May Gallery and Top of the Hop, Hopkins Center, October 17–November 23, 1975

1976

Erwin Hauer, Artist-in-Residence, Winter 1976
Beaumont-May Gallery, Hopkins Center, February 13–March 14, 1976

Robert Reed, Artist-in-Residence, Spring 1976
Beaumont-May Gallery, Hopkins Center, April 30–May 30, 1976

James Wines, Artist-in-Residence, Summer 1976
Beaumont-May Gallery, Hopkins Center, Summer 1976

Marie Cosindas: Polaroid Photographs, Artist-in-Residence, Fall 1976
Beaumont-May Gallery and Top of the Hop, Hopkins Center, November 5–December 5, 1976

1977

William Majors: Graphics, Artist-in-Residence, Winter 1977
Beaumont-May Gallery, Hopkins Center, January 28–March 6, 1977

John Willenbecher, Artist-in-Residence, Spring 1977
Jaffe-Friede Gallery, Hopkins Center, April 15–May 15, 1977

György Kepes, Artist-in-Residence, Fall 1977
Jaffe-Friede, Strauss, and Barrows Galleries and Barrows Windows, Hopkins Center, October 21–November 27, 1977

Walter Feldman: Hangings and Collages, Artist-in-Residence, Winter 1978
Jaffe-Friede Gallery, Hopkins Center, February 3–March 5, 1978

R. B. Kitaj, Artist-in-Residence, Spring 1978
Beaumont-May Gallery, Hopkins Center, April 7–May 21, 1978

Costantino Nivola: Works for Private Places, Artist-in-Residence, Fall 1978
Jaffe-Friede Gallery, Hopkins Center, October 20–December 3, 1978

1979

Ralph Steiner: A Retrospective Exhibition, Artist-in-Residence, Winter 1979
Jaffe-Friede, Strauss, and Barrows Galleries, Hopkins Center, January 26–February 25, 1979

Allan Houser, Artist-in-Residence, Spring 1979
Beaumont-May Gallery, Hopkins Center, April 20–May 20, 1979

Richard Stankiewicz, Artist-in-Residence, Summer 1979
Jaffe-Friede Gallery, Hopkins Center, August 3–September 3, 1979

Thomas George: Paintings and Pastels, 1973–1979, Artist-in-Residence, Fall 1979
Jaffe-Friede and Strauss Galleries, Hopkins Center, October 19–December 2, 1979

1980

Charles Simonds, Artist-in-Residence, Spring 1980
Beaumont-May Gallery, Hopkins Center, April 25–May 25, 1980

Tom Blackwell, Artist-in-Residence: Selected Works, 1970–1980, Artist-in-Residence, Fall 1980
Jaffe-Friede and Strauss Galleries, Hopkins Center, November 7–December 28, 1980

1981

Katherine Porter: Drawings 1980, Artist-in-Residence, Winter 1981
Beaumont-May Gallery, Hopkins Center, December 12, 1980–March 8, 1981

Fumio Yoshimura: Wood Sculpture, Artist-in-Residence, Spring 1981
Beaumont-May Gallery, Hopkins Center, May 1–July 5, 1981

John Alcorn, Artist-in-Residence, Fall 1981
Beaumont-May Gallery and Upper Jewett Exhibition Corridor, Hopkins Center, September 11–November 15, 1981

1982

Don Nice, Artist-in-Residence, Winter 1982
Beaumont-May Gallery, Hopkins Center, January 29–March 22, 1982

Leonardo Lasansky, Artist-in-Residence, Spring 1982
Beaumont-May Gallery, Hopkins Center, April 2–June 20, 1982

John Udvardy, The Dartmouth Portfolio: The Ocean Park Series, Artist-in-Residence, Fall 1982
Upper Jewett Exhibition Corridor, Hopkins Center, through November 11, 1982

1983

Peter Milton: Prints and Drawings, Artist-in-Residence, Winter 1983
Jaffe-Friede, Strauss, and Barrows Galleries, Hopkins Center, January 15–March 13, 1983

Philip Morsberger, Artist-in-Residence, Spring 1983
Strauss and Barrows Galleries, Hopkins Center, March 28–May 31, 1983

Irving Petlin: Drawings from the Studio, 1973–1983, Artist-in-Residence, Fall 1983
Upper Jewett Exhibition Corridor, Hopkins Center, through November 30, 1983

1984

"Pastel Light": An Exhibition by Wolf Kahn, Artist-in-Residence, Winter 1984
Upper Jewett Corridor, Hopkins Center, January 18–February 15, 1984

Woodcuts and Illustrated Books by Antonio Frasconi, Artist-in-Residence, Spring 1984
Treasure Room Corridor and Main Corridor, Baker Library, April 16–May 14, 1984

1985

Leo Manso, Artist-in-Residence, Winter 1985
Jaffe-Friede, Strauss, and Barrows Galleries, Hopkins Center, January 19–March 3, 1985

Frederick Brosen: Recent Watercolors, Artist-in-Residence, Spring 1985
Upper Jewett Exhibition Corridor, Hopkins Center, April 10–May 25, 1985

Richard Britell: Frescoes, Oil Paintings and Wash Drawings, Artist-in-Residence, Summer 1985
Jaffe-Friede Gallery, Hopkins Center, July 1–August 20, 1985

Joel Sternfeld: Recent Photographs, Artist-in-Residence, Fall 1985
Jaffe-Friede Gallery, Hopkins Center, September 23–December 4, 1985

1986

Richard Lytle: Recent Paintings, Artist-in-Residence, Spring 1986
Jaffe-Friede and Strauss Galleries, Hopkins Center, April 4–May 9, 1986

Bernard Chaet, Artist-in-Residence, Fall 1986
Jaffe-Friede and Strauss Galleries, Hopkins Center, October 10–November 30, 1986

1987

Robert Vickrey, Artist-in-Residence, Spring 1987
Jaffe-Friede and Strauss Galleries, Hopkins Center, April 4–12, 1987

Selected Works: Paintings and Etchings by Gabor Peterdi, Artist-in-Residence, Fall 1987
Jaffe-Friede and Strauss Galleries, Hopkins Center, September 26–December 2, 1987

1988

Anima Motrix, Photographs by Olivia Parker, Artist-in-Residence, Winter 1988
Jaffe-Friede and Strauss Galleries, Hopkins Center, December 12, 1987–February 28, 1988

Swietlan N. Kraczyna: Multi-plate Color Etchings, Artist-in-Residence, Fall 1988
Jaffe-Friede and Strauss Galleries, September 17–25, 1988

1989

Photographs by John Lueders-Booth, Artist-in-Residence, Spring 1989
Jaffe-Friede and Strauss Galleries, Hopkins Center, March 21–May 14, 1989

Bob Haozous: The Dartmouth Exhibition, Artist-in-Residence, Summer 1989
Jaffe-Friede and Strauss Galleries, Hopkins Center, July 15–September 17, 1989

Dean Chamberlain, Artist-in-Residence, Fall 1989
Jaffe-Friede and Strauss Galleries, Hopkins Center, September 24–December 11, 1989

1990

Sebastián, Artist-in-Residence, Spring 1990
Jaffe-Friede and Strauss Galleries, Hopkins Center, March 27–May 11, 1990

Lois Dodd, Artist-in-Residence, Fall 1990
Jaffe-Friede and Strauss Galleries, Hopkins Center, September 18–October 25, 1990

1991

Lynn Curtis: Recent Works, Artist-in-Residence, Winter 1991
Jaffe-Friede and Strauss Galleries, Hopkins Center, January 8–February 15, 1991

Jane Wilson, Artist-in-Residence, Spring 1991
Jaffe-Friede and Strauss Galleries, Hopkins Center, early April–May 15, 1991

James Lechay, Artist-in-Residence, Fall 1991
Jaffe-Friede and Strauss Galleries, Hopkins Center, mid-September–October 20, 1991

Hugh Townley, Artist-in-Residence, Fall 1991
Jaffe-Friede and Strauss Galleries, Hopkins Center, October 29–December 8, 1991

1992

Peter Feldstein, Artist-in-Residence, Winter 1992
Jaffe-Friede and Strauss Galleries, Hopkins Center, December 17, 1991–February 9, 1992

Rosemarie Beck, Artist-in-Residence, Spring 1992
Jaffe-Friede and Strauss Galleries, Hopkins Center, March 31–May 3, 1992

Byron Burford, Artist-in-Residence, Fall 1992
Jaffe-Friede and Strauss Galleries, Hopkins Center, early October–November 1, 1992

1993

David Bumbeck, Artist-in-Residence, Winter 1993
Jaffe-Friede and Strauss Galleries, Hopkins Center, mid-January–February 14, 1993

James McGarrell, Artist-in-Residence, Spring 1993
Jaffe-Friede and Strauss Galleries, Hopkins Center, March 16–April 25, 1993

Ben L. Summerford / Donald Weygandt, Artists-in-Residence, Fall 1993
Jaffe-Friede and Strauss Galleries, Hopkins Center, September 14–October 31, 1993

1994

Pat Adams, Artist-in-Residence, Winter 1994
Jaffe-Friede and Strauss Galleries, Hopkins Center, January 11–February 13, 1994

Steven Trefonides, Photographs, Artist-in-Residence, Fall 1994
Jaffe-Friede and Strauss Galleries, Hopkins Center, September 20–October 23, 1994

1995

Abstract Complexities: The Works of Charles Burwell, Artist-in-Residence, Winter 1995
Jaffe-Friede and Strauss Galleries, Hopkins Center, January 10–March 5, 1995

1996

Michael Singer: Recent Projects, Artist-in-Residence, Spring 1996
Jaffe-Friede and Strauss Galleries, Hopkins Center, April 9–May 5, 1996

Charles Cajori, Artist-in-Residence, Fall 1996
Jaffe-Friede and Strauss Galleries, Hopkins Center, October 10–November 10, 1996

1997

Pablo Delano: Photographs: Public and Private, Artist-in-Residence, Winter 1997
Jaffe-Friede and Strauss Galleries, Hopkins Center, January 7–February 16, 1997

Reeva Potoff: Zero Gravity: Photomurals, Artist-in-Residence, Spring 1997
Jaffe-Friede and Strauss Galleries, Hopkins Center, April 1–May 4, 1997

Ed Smith: Recent Work, Artist-in-Residence, Fall 1997
Jaffe-Friede and Strauss Galleries, Hopkins Center, October 14–November 7, 1997

1998

James Bohary, Artist-in-Residence, Winter 1998
Jaffe-Friede and Strauss Galleries, Hopkins Center, January 13–February 12, 1998

Wlodzimierz Ksiazek: Paintings, Artist-in-Residence, Spring 1998
Jaffe-Friede and Strauss Galleries, Hopkins Center, April 14–May 10, 1998

Susanna Coffey: Paintings, Artist-in-Residence, Fall 1998
Jaffe-Friede and Strauss Galleries, Hopkins Center, September 22–October 29, 1998

1999

Jin Soo Kim: Tracks, Artist-in-Residence, Winter 1999
Jaffe-Friede and Strauss Galleries, Hopkins Center, January 12–February 8, 1999

Robert Birmelin: The Difficulty of Getting It Right: Paintings of the 1990s, Artist-in-Residence, Spring 1999
Jaffe-Friede and Strauss Galleries, Hopkins Center, April 6–May 9, 1999

Ruth Miller: Paintings, Artist-in-Residence, Fall 1999
Jaffe-Friede and Strauss Galleries, Hopkins Center, September 28–October 31, 1999

Andrew Forge: Paintings, Artist-in-Residence, Fall 1999
Jaffe-Friede and Strauss Galleries, Hopkins Center, November 9–December 5, 1999

2000

Don Hanlon: Recent Work, Artist-in-Residence, Winter 2000
Jaffe-Friede and Strauss Galleries, Hopkins Center, January 11–February 6, 2000

Judy Pfaff: Notes on Light and Color, Artist-in-Residence, Spring 2000
Jaffe-Friede and Strauss Galleries, Hopkins Center, April 4–May 14, 2000

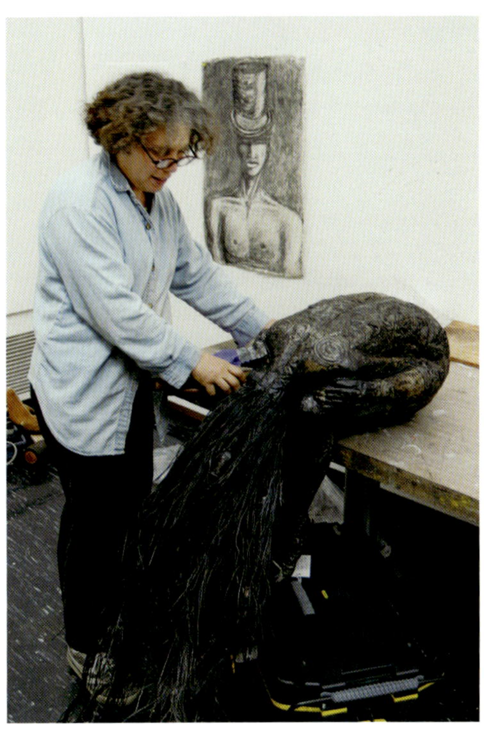

Fig. 30

Alison Saar working in the artist-in-residence studio at the Hopkins Center, May 28, 2003. Photo by Gerald Auten.

Carol Hepper: Wet Paint, Artist-in-Residence, Summer 2000
Jaffe-Friede and Strauss Galleries, Hopkins Center, June 27–July 30, 2000

2001

Gillian Pederson-Krag: Landscape, Artist-in-Residence, Winter 2001
Jaffe-Friede and Strauss Galleries, Hopkins Center, January 9–February 4, 2001

Stanley Lewis: Paintings and Drawings, Artist-in-Residence, Spring 2001
Jaffe-Friede and Strauss Galleries, Hopkins Center, April 3–May 6, 2001

Thomas Butter: Sculpture and Monotypes, Artist-in-Residence, Fall 2001
Jaffe-Friede and Strauss Galleries, Hopkins Center, October 2–28, 2001

2002

Charles Spurrier, Artist-in-Residence, Winter 2002
Jaffe-Friede and Strauss Galleries, Hopkins Center, February 19–March 17, 2002

Barbara Grossman: Paintings and Works on Paper, Artist-in-Residence, Spring 2002
Jaffe-Friede and Strauss Galleries, Hopkins Center, April 2–May 5, 2002

Amy Sillman: Letters from Texas, Artist-in-Residence, Fall 2002
Jaffe-Friede and Strauss Galleries, Hopkins Center, October 1–November 3, 2002

2003

William Christenberry, Artist-in-Residence, Winter 2003
Jaffe-Friede and Strauss Galleries, Hopkins Center, January 14–February 16, 2003

Alison Saar, Artist-in-Residence, Spring 2003
Jaffe-Friede and Strauss Galleries, Hopkins Center, April 1–May 4, 2003 (fig. 30)

Terry Adkins: Towering Steep, Artist-in-Residence, Summer 2003
Jaffe-Friede and Strauss Galleries, Hopkins Center, June 24–July 27, 2003

Peter Garfield: Objects with Potential, Artist-in-Residence, Fall 2003
Jaffe-Friede and Strauss Galleries, Hopkins Center, September 30–October 26, 2003

2004

James Cutler: Making Things Fit: The Work of Cutler Anderson Architects, Artist-in-Residence, Spring 2004
Jaffe-Friede and Strauss Galleries, Hopkins Center, April 6–May 2, 2004

Toon Verhoef: Paintings 2002–2004, Artist-in-Residence, Fall 2004
Jaffe-Friede and Strauss Galleries, Hopkins Center, September 28–October 31, 2004

2005

Paul Bowen: Sculpture: 1974–2004, Artist-in-Residence, Winter 2005
Jaffe-Friede and Strauss Galleries, Hopkins Center, January 11–March 13, 2005

Frances Barth: Paintings, Artist-in-Residence, Summer 2005
Jaffe-Friede and Strauss Galleries, Hopkins Center, June 28–July 24, 2005

Michael Spafford, Artist-in-Residence, Fall 2005
Jaffe-Friede and Strauss Galleries, Hopkins Center, September 27–December 4, 2005

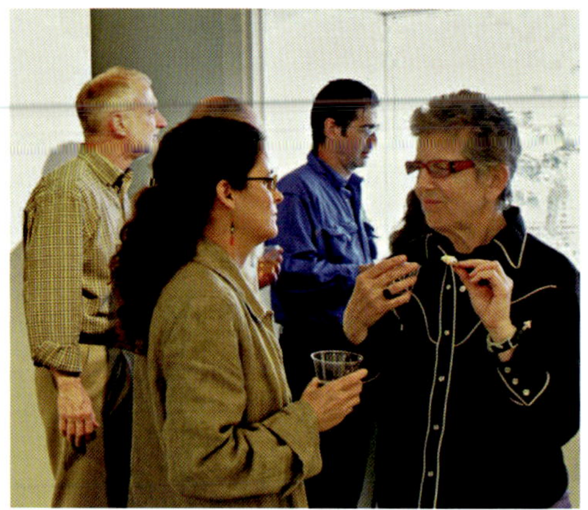

Fig. 31

Professor Brenda Garand in conversation with Louise Fishman, May 7, 2007. Photo by Gerald Auten.

2006

Jane Hammond: Recent Photographs, Artist-in-Residence, Spring 2006
Jaffe-Friede and Strauss Galleries, Hopkins Center, April 4–May 7, 2006

Andrew Moore, Artist-in-Residence, Fall 2006
Jaffe-Friede and Strauss Galleries, Hopkins Center, September 26–December 3, 2006

2007

Sana Musasama: Ambivalent Beauty, Artist-in-Residence, Winter 2007
Jaffe-Friede and Strauss Galleries, Hopkins Center, February 13–March 11, 2007

Louise Fishman: The Tenacity of Painting, Paintings from 1970 to 2005, Artist-in-Residence, Spring 2007
Jaffe-Friede and Strauss Galleries, Hopkins Center, April 3–May 6, 2007 (fig. 31)

Christopher Cozier: Little Gestures: From the Tropical Night Series, Artist-in-Residence, Fall 2007
Jaffe-Friede Gallery, Hopkins Center, October 2–November 4, 2007

2008

Vincent Desiderio, Artist-in-Residence, Winter 2008
Jaffe-Friede Gallery, Hopkins Center, January 15–March 16, 2008

Elizabeth King: The Size of Things in the Mind's Eye, Artist-in-Residence, Spring 2008
Jaffe-Friede Gallery, Hopkins Center, April 1–May 4, 2008

Magdalene Odundo: Ceramic Work and Drawings, Artist-in-Residence, Fall 2008
Jaffe-Friede Gallery, Hopkins Center, September 30–December 7, 2008

2009

Subhankar Banerjee, Artist-in-Residence, Winter 2009
Jaffe-Friede Gallery, Hopkins Center, January 13–February 8, 2009

Marjetica Potrč: Florestania, Artist-in-Residence, Spring 2009
Jaffe-Friede Gallery, Hopkins Center, April 9–May 3, 2009

Rebecca Purdum, Artist-in-Residence, Fall 2009
Jaffe-Friede Gallery, Hopkins Center, September 29–October 25, 2009

2010

David Hilliard: Highway of Thought, Artist-in-Residence, Spring 2010
Jaffe-Friede Gallery, Hopkins Center, April 6–May 2, 2010

Ambreen Butt: Dirty Pretty and Other Stories, Artist-in-Residence, Fall 2010
Jaffe-Friede Gallery, Hopkins Center, September 28–October 24, 2010

2011

Chris Martin, Artist-in-Residence, Winter 2011
Jaffe-Friede Gallery, Hopkins Center, January 11–March 6, 2011

Won Ju Lim: Untitled Silence, Artist-in-Residence, Spring 2011
Jaffe-Friede Gallery, Hopkins Center, April 5–May 1, 2011

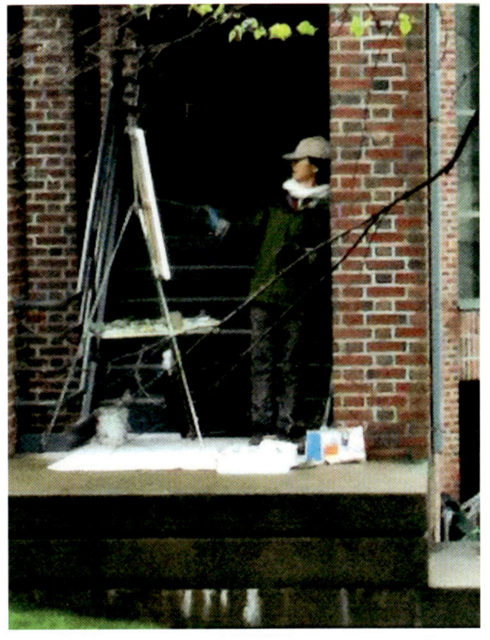

Fig. 32

Ying Li painting on the stairs leading to the Hood Museum of Art, May 2012. Photo by Gerald Auten.

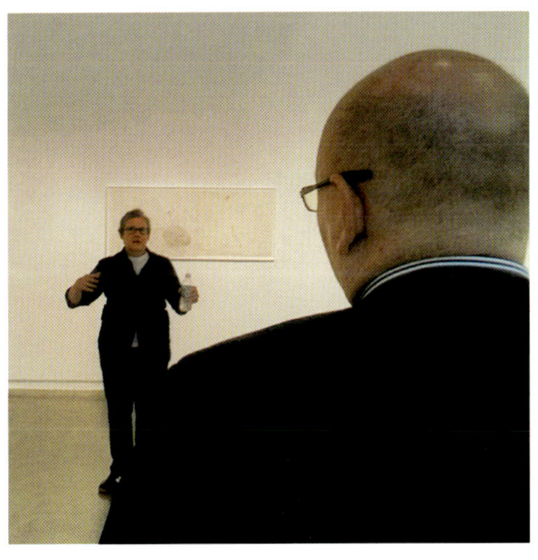

Fig. 33

Linda Matalon in conversation with Michael Taylor in her exhibition in the Jaffe-Friede Gallery, Hopkins Center, September 27, 2012. Photo by Gerald Auten.

Beryl Korot: Video — Text/Weave/Line, Artist-in-Residence, Fall 2011
Jaffe-Friede Gallery, Hopkins Center, September 27–December 4, 2011

2012

Laylah Ali: Drawings, Artist-in Residence, Winter 2012
Jaffe-Friede Gallery, Hopkins Center, January 10–March 4, 2012

Ying Li: Paintings and Drawings, Artist-in-Residence, Spring 2012
Jaffe-Friede Gallery, Hopkins Center, April 3–May 6, 2012 (fig. 32)

Linda Matalon: Work: 1977–2012, Artist-in-Residence, Fall 2012
Jaffe-Friede Gallery, Hopkins Center, September 18–October 14, 2012 (fig. 33)

2013

John Newman: Everything Is on the Table, Artist-in-Residence, Winter 2013
Jaffe-Friede Gallery, Hopkins Center, January 15–March 10, 2013

Luke Fowler, Artist-in-Residence, Spring 2013
Jaffe-Friede Gallery, Hopkins Center, April 2–May 5, 2013

Daniel Heyman, Artist-in-Residence, Fall 2013
Jaffe-Friede Gallery, Hopkins Center, September 24–November 24, 2013